LANGUAGE!®

4TH EDITION

TEACHER
RESOURCE
GUIDE

Sopris West®
EDUCATIONAL SERVICES

A Cambium Learning® Company

BOSTON, MA • LONGMONT, CO

6   7   8   9   HPS   15   14   13   12

Authors:
Jane Fell Greene, Ed.D.
Nancy Chapel Eberhardt

ISBN 13: 978-1-60218-677-4
ISBN: 1-60218-677-4
169210/2-12

Printed in the United States of America

Published and distributed by

Sopris West®
EDUCATIONAL SERVICES

A Cambium Learning® Company

4093 Specialty Place • Longmont, CO 80504 • (303) 651-2829
www.voyagerlearning.com

TABLE OF CONTENTS

TABLE OF CONTENTS

TABLE OF CONTENTS

K

L

WELCOME TO
LANGUAGE! 4TH EDITION

Welcome to *LANGUAGE!*, The Comprehensive Literacy Curriculum. As all educators know, there are few shortcuts for teaching our students to read and write. Literacy instruction is a challenging and complex task that can only be mastered through practice, experience, and quality professional development. The purpose of this resource guide is to support you during training, as well as serve as a ready reference to help you implement *LANGUAGE!* with confidence and fidelity.

This *Teacher Resource Guide* spans the entire curriculum, from Books A through F. As part of its mission, this guide contributes to the professional development needs of literacy intervention teachers by providing:

- Reference material for face-to-face and/or on-line training

- Implementation recommendations

- Evidence-based instructional practices

- Methods for differentiating lessons to match student needs

- Strong assessment-to-instruction linkage

- Strategies for explicit instruction

- Scientific research base and efficacy data

In the past decade, knowledge about reading research, effective instructional practices, and the challenges faced by struggling readers has greatly increased. Still, as Dr. Louisa Moats writes, "the fruits of these scientific labors cannot be realized unless teachers understand and are prepared to implement them."

LANGUAGE! is carefully crafted to help bring the latest research, best practices, and accessible instruction and assessment into your classroom. Working together, our common goal is to join students in striving to make the most of our abilities—proceeding, as Jane Fell Greene, Ed.D, encourages, "as quickly as we can, and as slowly as we must."

LANGUAGE!
PROGRAM OVERVIEW

Table of Contents

A

REACHING OUR STRUGGLING READERS

At the lunch table in the teacher's lounge, Mrs. Brinkman sighs. "I just don't understand Felippe. He is so pleasant in class and seems to be paying attention, but he hasn't turned in an assignment this quarter. Then he just handed in a blank sheet of paper for his essay on *Romeo and Juliet.*"

Mr. Jackson smiles as Julia enters the resource room. "How did your science test go?" She hands it to him, but her down-turned face tells the story. He looks over the exam. "Oh, you must be so disappointed," he says. "You really seemed to know the material when we worked on the review together." "Mr. Jackson," Julia says softly, "Ms. Ferris changed the words in the definitions. She didn't ask the questions the same way she did on the study guide."

Ms. Welch watches Jason wander into her English class, still joking with some of his friends in the hall. As she asks students to get out their textbooks and homework assignments, she knows he will not have either one. And before she can begin the lesson, Jason is called to the office. *What is it this time?* she wonders. His discipline problems keep him in the office and out of class. Whatever the reason, once again his desk is empty.

Chances are that you and your colleagues have had a Felippe, Julia, or Jason in your classroom. These students are struggling and frustrated, and their difficulties do not just show up in D's and F's on their report cards, but also in their attitudes, behaviors, and lives beyond the school walls. For each of them, the roots of their academic troubles lie in literacy deficiencies. Traditional reading instruction has left them behind. Although their barriers to educational success differ, their needs are similar: knowledge of the structure and functions of the English language and carefully guided practice at unlocking its gifts.

LANGUAGE! provides the research-based strategies, tools, and training to address the needs of struggling readers. Often our schools adopt three different curricula for these three groups of students—English Learners, those with learning disabilities, and Curriculum Casualties—each requiring a significant investment in materials and training. *LANGUAGE!*, in contrast, allows schools to consolidate resources and personnel, meet these students at their varying skill levels, and significantly improve their literacy skills.

English Language Learners

Curriculum Casualties

Need to Acquire Knowledge of Academic Language

Language-Based Learning Disabilities

Reading Instruction: A National Priority

The pervasive literacy crisis in this country speaks to the need to re-examine the traditional approach to teaching reading. The literacy crisis among American students is well-documented (e.g. Biancarosa & Snow, 2004). Federal and state initiatives for the early intervention and prevention of reading difficulty among primary grade students have received wide support. Today, educators are equally concerned about older students who cannot read well enough to perform at grade level. The 2007 National Assessment of Educational Progress (NAEP) shows that 27 percent of eighth grade students are reading below basic levels—the lowest possible rank, less than even partial mastery.

In eighth grade, ethnic minority and English Learners (EL) are failing to learn to read at alarming rates: 46 percent of black, 43 percent of Hispanic, 42 percent of American Indian, and 71 percent of EL students score below basic reading levels (Lee, Grigg, & Donahue, 2007). According to recent statistics, the national graduation rate is between 68 and 71 percent. When looking at African-American, Hispanic, and Native American students, the graduation rate drops to 50 percent. Nearly one-third of all public school students fail to graduate with their class. Reading disability is also overrepresented among youths in the juvenile justice system (Shelly-Tremblay, O'Brien, & Langhinrichsen-Rohling, 2007). The National Institute of Child Health and Human Development (NICHD) views reading difficulty as a public health concern because of its correlation to these high dropout rates, as well as delinquency, unwanted pregnancy, and chronic underemployment.

High school dropouts...

- are 3 times more likely to be arrested than high school graduates

- make up 75% of state prison and 50% of federal prison inmates

- earn about $260,000 less over a lifetime than high school graduates

- have significantly higher rates of unemployment than high school graduates

NEA, 2005

Now the Good News

In spite of these grim statistics, indicators show that significant improvement is within the grasp of educators and their students. Schools across the country are focusing more attention on reading and dedicating more time and effort to improving students' literacy skills. At the elementary level, 2007 NAEP scores showed that 18 states had made significant growth in reading scores compared to 2005 results. These scores also reflect a closing of the achievement gap between White, Black, Hispanic, and Asian-Pacific Islander students.

Summaries of reading research (Adams, 1990; Snow, Burns & Griffin, 1998; Fletcher & Lyon, 1998; Pressley, 2006; National Institute of Child Health and Human Development, 2000) show that all but 2 to 5 percent of children can learn to read, even in populations where the incidence of poor reading is often far higher than the average. For these students to succeed, however, their teachers must use research-based practices and programs. These teachers require sufficient training, skill, and administrative support to implement these programs and practices with fidelity and intensity.

> *Summaries of reading research show that all but 2 to 5 percent of children can learn to read, even in populations where the incidence of poor reading is often far higher than the average. For these students to succeed, however, their teachers must use research-based practices and programs. These teachers require sufficient training, skill, and administrative support to implement these programs and practices with fidelity and intensity.*

The challenge, then, is putting the necessary resources in the hands of educators while providing ample professional development to set these changes in motion. In the most expert and closely supervised settings, where small groups were taught for two hours daily, poor readers who scored in the lowest 20th percentile improved to the middle of the average range and maintained average scores over the following two years (Torgesen et al., 2001, 1997). Done with dedication and resolve, a commitment to literacy will deliver the positive results our students, schools, and communities need.

LANGUAGE! at Work

Now in its 4th Edition, *LANGUAGE!* is a complete literacy curriculum deeply rooted in research. The program's Six Step lesson plans integrate the range of literacy skills, with frequent assessments and detailed differentiation guides to gauge mastery, allow timely adjustments in instruction, and promote student achievement.

As you'll see, the *LANGUAGE!* program leaves no aspect of literacy development to chance. Starting with phonemic awareness, students practice the alphabetic principle and begin reading and spelling words. The next layer tackles meaning and morphological aspects of word knowledge. Usage and mechanics reinforce proper application of words in written and oral contexts. Equipped with these skills, students work with connected text that builds fluency and comprehension. Early on, students also respond to text using oral and written expression. The scope and sequence of *LANGUAGE!* explicitly weaves among the steps, incorporating research that has revealed how these different literacy skills reinforce and build on each other. Explicit instruction embraces best practice to link these developing skills across a unit as well as from unit to unit.

In conception and structure, *LANGUAGE!* is a research-based curriculum that refuses to leave struggling readers behind. It turns classrooms into places where Felippe and other English learners, Julia and other students with Learning Disabilities, and Jason and other Curriculum Casualties, can enter with hope and anticipation—and leave with the ability to read and write.

A COMPREHENSIVE CURRICULUM

The *LANGUAGE!* curriculum weaves together all elements of literacy to create a comprehensive curriculum. Students with reading delays usually exhibit deficits in all aspects of reading and writing—from phonemic awareness to comprehension to spoken and written rhetoric. Overall improvement depends upon corresponding growth across the spectrum of these skills.

English learners, students with language-based learning disabilities, and "Curriculum Casualties"—students in these target populations confront similar challenges. For them, literacy development has been interrupted or never had the chance to take root. A quick fix through decoding, or an attempt at intervention by means of isolated comprehension strategies, cannot provide the breadth and depth of recovery that they need. And the central role of literacy in our students' overall academic and life-long achievement is impossible to overstate.

That is the research-based thinking behind *LANGUAGE!*'s comprehensive curriculum; and the program's integrated structure provides the means to achieve literacy objectives. The core concept, "Six Steps From Sound to Text," guides students to mastery of these individual skills, while teaching the skills in dynamic, reinforcing partnerships. Every lesson explicitly incorporates material from each of these content areas, circling back to previously taught material with regular reviews, assessments, and differentiated instruction. In every lesson, students weave between the steps that link sound to text.

> *LANGUAGE!* gains instructional power by integrating concepts and skills among its six steps.

From Sound

STEP 1 Phonemic Awareness and Phonics

STEP 2 Word Recognition and Spelling

STEP 3 Vocabulary and Morphology

STEP 4 Grammar and Usage

STEP 5 Listening and Reading Comprehension

STEP 6 Speaking and Writing

To Text

in every lesson

LANGUAGE! is for struggling readers in grades 3 through 12 who are scoring below the 40th percentile on standardized tests. The curriculum is designed to accelerate literacy development for intermediate, middle, and high school students reading two or more years below their grade level. These students need to upgrade their understanding of academic language, as well as improve their overall facility with the structure and function of English.

LANGUAGE! places special emphasis on serving three groups of students:

- English Learners—students who are not proficient with English as their primary language

- Curriculum Casualties—struggling readers who qualified or have not been tested for special education but are at risk for reading failure

- Students With Special Needs—students with language-based learning disabilities, such as dyslexia, whose difficulties are in basic reading, reading comprehension, basic writing, and/or written expression.

For further discussion on these groups, please see the section on Differentiated Instruction.

How Can *LANGUAGE!* Serve All Struggling Readers?

LANGUAGE! positions students according to instructional need, based on assessment measures rather than by grade level. An accurate and insightful initial assessment is the first step in helping poor readers move toward reading proficiency.

Students who demonstrate a deficiency in basic decoding and fluency will begin in Book A. Students who show proficiency with basic sound-symbol correspondences, but shortcomings in higher levels of word and text analysis, will start in Book C or Book E, depending on placement results.

LANGUAGE! helps all students learn the skills and concepts necessary to progress from a below grade level reading ability to a 10th-grade reading level. This progression allows students to read and comprehend expository and literary selections equal to those required in a general education high school classroom. In addition, *LANGUAGE!* includes specific instruction regarding the academic language necessary to effectively interpret and utilize English across the school curriculum.

LANGUAGE! FITS TIERED INTERVENTION

Crafting appropriate and effective interventions is vital to aiding struggling readers, and is a central tenet of *LANGUAGE!* The curriculum structures its Responsiveness to Intervention (RTI) to follow the evidence-based tiered approach, with increasing intensity at each tier (Cortiella, 2005).

In Tier 1, all students are provided with quality instruction and progress monitoring. Students that continue to struggle in Tier 1 are reassigned to more strategic intervention in Tier 2, featuring more small-group work. If that intervention proves successful, the student returns to Tier 1. But if a Tier 2 student still requires more intensive intervention, that student may be shifted to Tier 3 for more individualized attention. When Tier 3 students make significant progress, they can transition to Tier 2. Accurate diagnostic information is crucial, of course, when moving students from one stage of support to the next (Duffy, 2007).

Students identified for *LANGUAGE!* typically fit into Tier 2 or Tier 3. Initial placement tests ensure proper entry into the curriculum as well as provide baseline data to measure growth at the end of each student text. Ongoing formative assessments allow educators to adjust instruction at the unit level and track progress as the students progress through the curriculum.

Response to Intervention Model

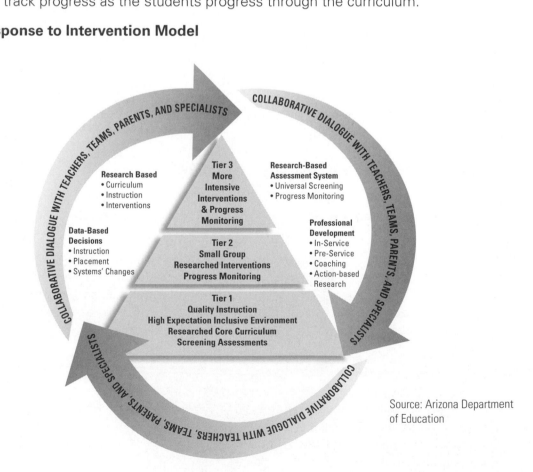

Source: Arizona Department of Education

THREE ENTRY POINTS FOR *LANGUAGE!*

A

Data from the *LANGUAGE!* Reading Scale Placement Test indicates which curriculum entry point is appropriate for students. The placement test is a reading comprehension tool based on the Lexile readability scale. (For a more complete explanation of the Lexile scale and its uses, please see Step 5: Listening and Reading Comprehension.)

LANGUAGE! prescribes three entry points into the curriculum based on the Reading Scale Placement Test:

- **Book A:** This initial entry point allows students who demonstrate deficiencies in basic decoding and reading at a pre-primer to 2.5-grade level to experience early progress and success.

- **Book C:** This second entry point is for students who show proficiency with beginning sound-symbol correspondences, but struggle with higher word-analysis skills. Most students in this group read at the 3rd to 5th grade levels.

- **Book E:** The third entry point meets the needs of students in grades 7 to 12 who are proficient with sound-symbol correspondences and higher levels of word analysis, but who are reading two or more years below grade level.

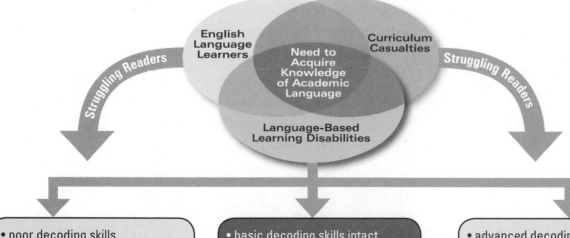

• poor decoding skills • glued to print • reading comprehension at the pre-primer -2.5 G.E.	• basic decoding skills intact • lack of advanced word-analysis skills • reading comprehension at the 3.0-5.0 G.E.	• advanced decoding skills • reading comprehension two or more years below current grade level

Teacher Edition Book A   *Teacher Edition Book C*   *Teacher Edition Book E*

KEY COMPONENTS OF *LANGUAGE!*

LANGUAGE! components—from texts to assessments to technology tools—interlock and reinforce one another at every step in the program. Each book, from Book A to Book F, utilizes a set of teacher and student materials proven to develop critical literacy skills. Each Teacher Edition (TE) orchestrates the curriculum by coordinating what to teach, and when and how to teach it. TE units and lesson plans integrate the *Student Text, Interactive Text,* Assessment booklets, and Differentiation and Multisensory tools.

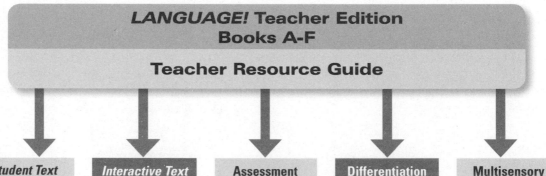

LANGUAGE! Teacher Edition Books A–F
Teacher Resource Guide

Student Text Books A–F	*Interactive Text* Books A–F	Assessment Tools	Differentiation Tools	Multisensory Tools
• Handbook	• Interactive text pages	• Placement test	• EL Picture Cards	• Timer
• Lexiled reading selections	• Charts	• Baseline tests	• *eReader* CD	• Pocket Chart
• Visual Vocabulary	• Checklists	• Formative tests	• *Sortegories* CD	• Letter Cards
	• Fluencies	• Summative tests	• *Words for Teachers* CD	• Morpheme Cards
		• Online Assessment System	• *Instructional Planning Tools* CD	• Overhead Tiles
				• Transparencies

LANGUAGE! TRAINING: MATERIALS CHECKLIST

✔ Please take a moment to check your *LANGUAGE!* training kit for the following materials.

Books for Teachers
- ☐ Teacher Edition, Book A, C, or E, Volume 1
- ☐ Teacher Edition, Book A, C, or E, Volume 2
- ☐ Teacher Resource Guide
- ☐ Placement: Teacher Edition
- ☐ Assessment: Teacher Edition
- ☐ Teacher Edition, Bridge, Book C or E

Books for Students
- ☐ Student Text, Book A, C, or E
- ☐ Interactive Text, Book A, C, or E
- ☐ Placement: Student Edition
- ☐ Assessment: Content Mastery
- ☐ Summative Assessments
- ☐ Bridge Interactive Text

Technology for Teachers
- ☐ Instructional Planning Tools for Teachers CD
- ☐ Words for Teachers CD

Technology for Students
- ☐ Sortegories CD
- ☐ eReader CD: Book A

Supplemental Material
- ☐ Letter Cards
- ☐ Morphemes for Meaning Cards
- ☐ Transparencies and Templates
- ☐ Pocket Chart
- ☐ Plastic Overhead Tiles
- ☐ TeachTimer®
- ☐ Large-Format Picture Cards

LANGUAGE!
TEACHER EDITION

The Teacher Editions for Books A–F provide a clear and organized path through 36 units of instruction. *LANGUAGE!* lessons are designed for daily 90-minute instructional blocks with each unit scheduled over a 15-day time frame. At the same time, the modular nature of *LANGUAGE!* builds in flexibility to fit different schedules.

Each Teacher Edition has two volumes of three units for a total of six units per book. Each unit has 10 lessons. This translates to a full school year of guided yet flexible instruction:

- 10 lessons X 6 units = 60 lessons per book

- 60 lessons X 15 days = approximately 90 days per book

- 2 books or 12 units = approximately 180 school days.

Teacher Edition Features

Each *LANGUAGE!* Teacher Edition is structured for effective and convenient access in the classroom. Each TE includes:

- Instructional objectives at point of use

- Icons highlighting ways to differentiate instruction

- Lesson planners that provide 10 lessons at a glance

- Answer keys for *Student* and *Interactive Text* exercises at the end of each lesson

- The complete *Student Text* in the Appendix

- Contrastive Analyses for 10 languages in the Appendix.

From Objectives to Lesson Planning

LANGUAGE! Teacher Editions are constructed to move smoothly from content to unit objectives to lesson planning—while keeping the curriculum on task and on schedule. To view these materials in more detail, see pages F30–F35 in the front of your Teacher Edition.

Content Map

The Content Map provides specific content addressed throughout the unit. This map identifies the content focus in each lesson.

At a Glance for Teachers

The At a Glance for Teachers provides the unit objectives that identify content and skills covered in the unit. The objectives are closely aligned with areas monitored by assessment and fluency tasks. The grid shows the lesson-by-lesson designation of instruction for each objective.

Lesson Planner

The Lesson Planner maps out "How to Teach" instruction, activities, and assessment necessary to develop the concepts and skills within and across The Six Steps from Sound to Text.

THE *STUDENT TEXT*

Each *Student Text* contains high-interest stories included in six units of instruction. Each unit features three levels of text of increasing complexity and sophistication. Genres range from fiction to expository, poetry to adventure, essays to screenplays.

Decodable Text from Book B

Text Selections

The reading selections in the *Student Texts* follow carefully ramped readability levels that increase in difficulty as students progress through the unit as well as through *LANGUAGE!* overall. These text levels are:

- **Decodable Text** for Independent Reading: Incorporating 75% decodable words, these selections are the easiest stories in each unit. They help students apply decoding skills and develop fluency.

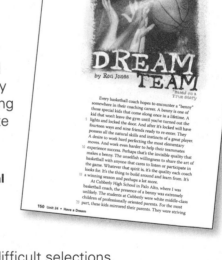

Instructional Text from Book D

- **Instructional Text** for Shared and Supported Reading: These mid-range selections explicitly teach targeted text structures while developing vocabulary and content knowledge to promote comprehension.

- **Challenge Text:** The most difficult selections, Challenge Texts further develop vocabulary, background knowledge, and offer more exposure to a variety of genres. Comprehension questions here are geared toward higher order thinking skills.

Challenge Text from Book F

Student Text Reference Tools

Two built-in reference tools can help students study independently while practicing useful reference skills.

- **Visual Vocabulary:** Located in Books A and B, this student-friendly vocabulary reference offers English learners a tool for building on vocabulary knowledge from their first language.

- **Student Handbook:** This reference tool uses straightforward examples and illustrations to make abstract concepts concrete.

Visual Vocabulary

Interactive Text and Homework

LANGUAGE!'s *Interactive Text* and printable homework pages present manageable activities and exercises that let students practice, drill, and refine their skills.

- ***Interactive Text:*** Organized by unit and lesson, the exercises and activities in each *Interactive Text* reinforce material in the *Student Text*. The *Interactive Text* also includes exercises in phonemic and syllable awareness, and other vital listening skills.

- **Homework Options:** For further unit reinforcement, lesson-by-lesson options for printable homework are available on the *Instructional Planning Tools* and *Words for Teachers* CDs and described in detail in the Teacher Edition.

Student Handbook

Interactive Text

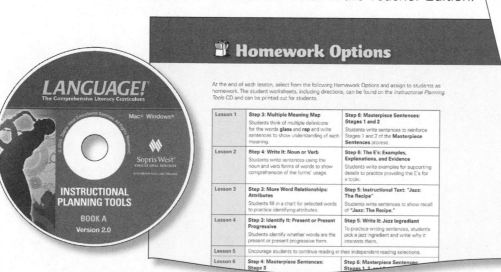

Homework Options

At the end of each lesson, select from the following Homework Options and assign to students as homework. The student worksheets, including directions, can be found on the *Instructional Planning Tools* CD and can be printed out for students.

Lesson 1	Step 3: Multiple Meaning Map	Step 6: Masterpiece Sentences: Stages 1 and 2
	Students think of multiple definitions for the words **glass** and **rap** and write sentences to show understanding of each meaning.	Students write sentences to reinforce Stages 1 and 2 of the **Masterpiece Sentences** process.
Lesson 2	Step 4: Write It: Noun or Verb	Step 6: The E's: Examples, Explanations, and Evidence
	Students write sentences using the noun and verb forms of words to show comprehension of the forms' usage.	Students write examples for supporting details to practice providing the E's for a topic.
Lesson 3	Step 3: More Word Relationships: Attributes	Step 5: Instructional Text: "Jazz: The Recipe"
	Students fill in a chart for selected words to practice identifying attributes.	Students write sentences to show recall of "Jazz: The Recipe."
Lesson 4	Step 3: Identify It: Present or Present Progressive	Step 5: Write It: Jazz Ingredient
	Students identify whether words are the present or present progressive form.	To practice writing sentences, students pick a jazz ingredient and write why it interests them.
Lesson 5	Encourage students to continue reading in their independent reading selections.	
Lesson 6	Step 4: Masterpiece Sentences: Stage 3	Step 6: Masterpiece Sentences: Stages 1, 2, and 3

Homework Options

BASIC LESSON STRUCTURE

Every step in every lesson in every unit of *LANGUAGE!* explicitly addresses the five questions below to drive the program's basic lesson structure.

Why Do?		Each step of *LANGUAGE!* is based on current literacy research related to both the content and the methodology of instruction.
Content emphasis— What to teach?		Each step focuses on a specific building block of the English language, with relevant sections of the scope and sequence appearing before each unit. Lessons teach content systematically and cumulatively.
Instructional focus— How to teach it?		The exercises and activities in *LANGUAGE!* incorporate these characteristics: • **Multisensory:** Activities often call on students to work with manipulatives. • **Cumulative:** New learning is explicitly connected to prior knowledge. • **Scaffolded instruction:** New concepts are introduced using the "I do," "We do," "You do" approach to develop students' confidence and skills. • **Conceptually based:** In contrast to rote memorization, conceptually based activities emphasize higher-order thinking skills. • **Explicit instruction:** Teachers model explicit strategies for decoding, encoding, reading comprehension, prewriting plans, and other skills. • **Mastery focused:** Activities build toward mastery and acknowledge the importance of providing sufficient practice so that discrete skills become reflexive.
Assessment— What have students learned?		Assessment is part of each book and each unit, but testing in *LANGUAGE!* is not an end unto itself. Results of Baseline Tests, Content Mastery tasks, Progress Indicators, and Summative Tests are explicitly linked to differentiated instruction. Throughout the program, responses to student performance are guided by prescriptive "If ... Then ..." boxes. These guidelines provide concrete suggestions about how teachers can help students shore up deficiencies through review and reteaching, or accelerate instruction for students that demonstrate significant improvement.
Differentiation— How to adjust instruction to meet student needs?		In response to assessments, *LANGUAGE!* provides multiple ways to differentiate instruction to meet the spectrum of student needs. These methods range from technology tools capable of creating individualized assignments, to suggestions for grouping formats for class discussion, to extra practice Why Do/How To activities.

PROGRESS MONITORING

The *LANGUAGE!* assessment system begins with accurate placement into the curriculum followed by ongoing and summative assessments that drive instruction.

A

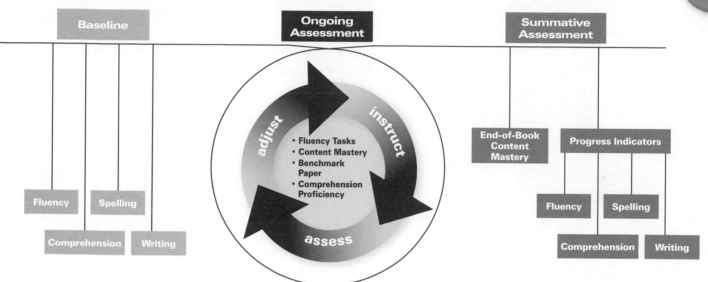

Baseline

The baseline tests are administered prior to entering Books A, C, or E. These tests give teachers a baseline indicator of students' skills that can be used to measure growth as students progress through the curriculum.

Ongoing assessment

Regular testing of student mastery of the content, concepts, and skills taught in the curriculum ensures that teachers have current information about each student in order to adjust pacing or provide instructional support activities for individual students.

Summative assessment

Given at the end of each book, Content Mastery tests provide teachers with a view of each student's overall mastery of curriculum content. The interpretation of these results guides teachers' decisions regarding whether to move students to the next book or to reteach particular concepts and provide additional practice for specific skills.

Progress Indicators monitor growth in the critical skills of literacy. These tests are the same ones used for baseline and are designed to provide valid and reliable measures of speed and accuracy of word reading, reading comprehension, spelling of regular and irregular words, and writing.

THE *LANGUAGE!* ASSESSMENT AND INSTRUCTIONAL SYSTEM

Designed to provide data to drive instructional decision-making and ways to differentiate instruction according to student needs.

LEVELS OF ENGAGEMENT

Multisensory techniques: *LANGUAGE!* uses multisensory techniques to increase student involvement. Interactive instruction allows teachers to monitor the level of student learning.

Scaffolded instruction: The lessons in *LANGUAGE!* follow the gradual-release model of instruction. Lessons are designed to transfer responsibility from the teacher to the students. As their skill increases, students work more independently. A system of icons cues teachers for the level of scaffolding.

Model	Teacher demonstrates or explains while students watch and listen.
Guide	Students work along with the teacher.
Pair/Share	Students work with other students in pairs or small groups while the teacher monitors for understanding.
On Their Own	Students apply the skill or strategy independently.

PERFORMANCE MONITORING

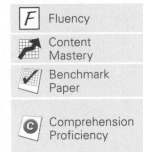 **F** Fluency	
Content Mastery	Ongoing assessment tools allow teachers to monitor content and skill acquisition within a unit every 2 to 3 weeks.
Benchmark Paper	
C Comprehension Proficiency	
End-of-Book Content Mastery	Summative assessment tools monitor student performance at the end of each book, or approximately every 12 to 18 weeks.
Progress Indicator	

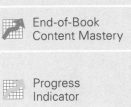

The *Online Assessment System* streamlines the recording and interpreting of test results.

DIFFERENTIATION OF INSTRUCTION

Performance data drives differentiation.

Prescriptive teaching boxes guide teachers to reinforce or reteach based on student performance.

If . . .	Then . . .
Students score below 80%	Reinforce: • Use **More About Adverbs** in Lesson 4, Step 4. • Use **Choose It and Use It** in Lesson 7, Step 4. • Use **Tense Timeline** in Lesson 9, Step 4.
Students score at or below 60%	Reteach: • Verbs: Use **Code It: Verbs** in Lesson 1, Step 4. • Use: **Review: Predicate Expansion** in Lesson 3, Step 4. • Use: **Masterpiece Sentences: Stage 3** in Lesson 5, Step 4.

Content Mastery retests allow teachers to check that mastery is achieved after reinforcing or reteaching content and skills.

Planning and Pacing Guides use icons—☆, ☀, and ✓—to identify activities that accommodate specific learner needs.

Technology tools help teachers develop materials to meet specific student instructional needs.

Interactive technology allows students to practice skills and content.

Homework Options provide practice beyond the *LANGUAGE!* classroom.

SIX STEPS
FROM SOUND TO TEXT

Central to the *LANGUAGE!* curriculum are the Six Steps from Sound to Text, built on the foundation of the National Reading Panel Report, and expanding beyond its prescriptions. The Six Steps provides the scope and sequence structure for *LANGUAGE!*, forming the backbone of lesson design and linkage between curriculum components.

Lesson by lesson, the Steps from Sound to Text feature:

- Simple to complex content and skill development

- Content that builds from known concepts to new content

- Scaffolded instructional activities that promote student achievement, progressing from "I Do," "We Do," to "You Do"

- Repetition and integration of key content within steps and across the lessons

- Practice of the critical skills for automaticity, reinforcement, and application

- Assessment that provides data for measuring student progress and mastery

- Differentiation of instruction linked to assessment.

From Sound

STEP **1** Phonemic Awareness and Phonics

STEP **2** Word Recognition and Spelling

STEP **3** Vocabulary and Morphology

STEP **4** Grammar and Usage

STEP **5** Listening and Reading Comprehension

STEP **6** Speaking and Writing

To Text

in every lesson

STEP 1 **Phonemic Awareness and Phonics**

In Step 1, students recognize that words are composed of phonemes or sounds that are represented by letters. Students learn phoneme and syllable awareness, sound-spelling correspondences, syllable types, multiple spellings for the same sound, and silent letters. Repeated practice featuring various approaches enhances automaticity.

STEP 2 **Word Recognition and Spelling**

In Step 2, students use the sound to letter correspondences from Step 1 as the basis for developing accurate and fluent reading and spelling. Encoding and decoding of high frequency and phonetically regular words are taught to mastery. Syllable types and syllable division provide strategies to decode multisyllabic words. Spelling rules are taught in Step 2 and are applied during writing in Step 6: Speaking and Writing.

STEP 3 **Vocabulary and Morphology**

In Step 3, students link meaning to the unit's target word and additional unit words they have learned to read and spell. Instructional activities include writing authentic definitions, exploring multiple meanings and word relationships, as well as idioms and common expressions. Latin and Greek roots, prefixes, and suffixes open the window to the meanings of more than 60% of English words. Knowledge of the unit words is applied to reading comprehension in Step 5.

STEP 4 **Grammar and Usage**

In Step 4, students learn that word function and arrangement in a sentence creates meaning, and contributes to comprehension. Unit words are combined to increase understanding of sentence parts and patterns. Grammatical forms, functions, and sentence patterns are taught stressing proper mechanics such as capitalization and punctuation. These skills receive further application in Step 6: Speaking and Writing.

STEP 5 **Listening and Reading Comprehension**

In Step 5, students read multiple text selections from different genres to develop fluency, build background, learn vocabulary, and understand text structure. Comprehension, context-based vocabulary, question interpretation at all levels of Bloom's Taxonomy, and text structure are taught using three different levels of text. Students listen to or read more complex Challenge Text selections and answer critical thinking questions through group discussions.

STEP 6 **Speaking and Writing**

In Step 6, students engage in higher order thinking while generating oral and written responses using Bloom's Taxonomy. They also alternate between writing sentences, paragraphs, and compositions based on the text they have read and prompts that elicit their imagination and personal experiences.

The Steps from Sound to Text in *LANGUAGE!*

STEP 1 Phonemic Awareness and Phonics

STEP 2 Word Recognition and Spelling

STEP 3 Vocabulary and Morphology

Helps students learn the building blocks of the English language

Teaches students how to use the sound-spelling correspondences to fluently read and spell words

Develops the meanings of words that students can read and spell

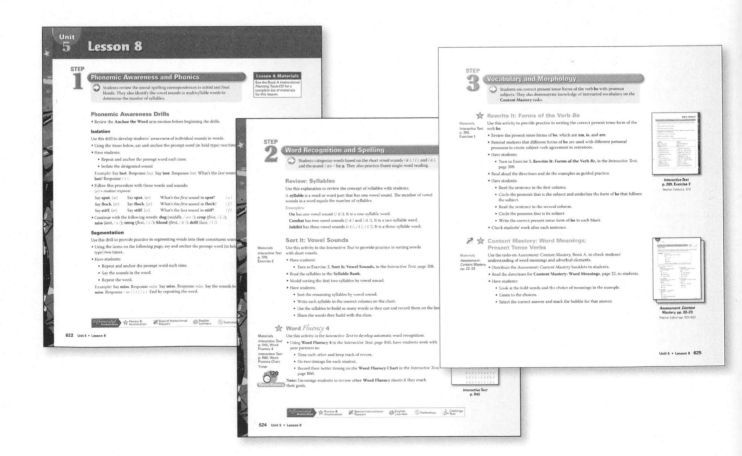

A

STEP 4 Grammar and Usage

STEP 5 Listening and Reading Comprehension

STEP 6 Speaking and Writing

Increases understanding of sentence parts and patterns

Teaches comprehension using three different levels of text, each with an increasing level of difficulty

Develops communication skills through speaking and writing

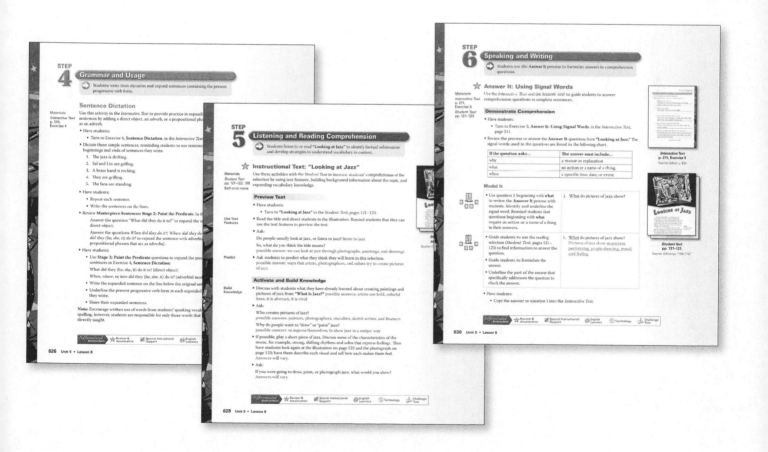

THE SCOPE AND SEQUENCE FOR *LANGUAGE!*

Step	Book A (Units 1–6)	Book B (Units 7–12)	Book C (Units 13–18)

STEP 1 Phonemic Awareness and Phonics	• Phoneme and syllable awareness
	• Sound-spelling conventions for common phoneme/grapheme relationships:
	  • Short vowels / ă /, / ĭ /, / ŏ /
	  • Stable consonants
	• Closed syllables
	• Fluency: Letter-sound; letter-name
		• Phoneme and syllable awareness
		• Sound-spelling conventions for common phoneme/grapheme relationships:
		  • Short vowels / ĕ /, / ŭ /
		  • Long vowels—final silent **e** pattern
		  • Consonant digraphs, blends, clusters
		• Syllable types: closed; final silent **e**
			• Phonemes for **y**, (/ ĕ /, / ĭ /, / ī /, based on position in word
			• Syllable awareness in multisyllable words
			• Schwa (con' vict vs. con vict')
			• Syllable types: closed; **r**-controlled; open; final silent **e**

STEP 2 Word Recognition and Spelling	• Read/spell: new sound-spelling correspondences • Read/spell: 36 new high frequency words • Fluency: word recognition • Spelling: **Doubling Rule** • Syllabication patterns	• Read/spell: words based on new sound-spelling correspondences • Read/spell 36 new high frequency words • Fluency: word recognition • Contractions with **not**, **would**, and **will** • Spelling: **Drop "e" Rule** • Syllabication patterns • Common abbreviations	• Read/spell: words based on new sound-spelling correspondences • Read/spell 36 new high frequency words • Fluency: word recognition • Syllabication process for multisyllable words • Contractions with **be** and **have** • Spelling: **Change "y" Rule**
STEP 3 Vocabulary and Morphology	• Antonyms, synonyms, and attributes • Multiple meanings, multiple uses • Definition development using categories and attributes • Compound words • Inflectional forms: noun endings: number (**-s**), singular possessions (**'s**); verb endings: present tense (**-s**), progressive form (**-ing**) • Idiomatic expressions	• Antonyms, synonyms, attributes, and homophones • Definition development using categories and attributes • Inflectional forms: noun endings: plural (**-es**); plural possession (**s'**); verb endings: present (**-es**); past (**-ed**) • Idiomatic and common expressions	• Antonyms, synonyms, attributes, homophones, and analogies • Number: plural nouns • Prefixes: most common for meaning expansion of base words • Adjective endings: comparative (**-er**) and superlative (**-est**) • Idiomatic and common expressions
STEP 4 Grammar and Usage	• Grammatical forms: nouns, pronouns (subject (nominative, object), verbs (action, tense, be, present progressive form), adverbs, adjectives, prepositions • Grammatical functions: subject; predicate; direct object; object of preposition • Noun/verb agreement • Sentence pattern: simple • Mechanics: capitals and end punctuation; apostrophe	• Grammatical forms: pronouns (possessive), conjunctions, verbs (irregular) • Verb tense: present; past; future; progressive forms • Grammatical functions: complete subject; complete predicate; direct object; compound sentence parts: subject, verb, direct object • Sentence patterns: simple, compound (**and, but**) • Subject/verb agreement • Mechanics: commas	• Grammatical forms: verbs (helping, main), adjectives (comparative/superlative, present and past participles), adverbs (**-ly**) • Grammatical functions: complete subject; direct object, object of preposition, indirect object, appositive; complete predicate • Sentence patterns: compound sentences (**or**); compound sentence parts: subject, adjectives, adverbs, prepositional phrases, predicates • Text-based analysis and application of grammatical forms and functions • Mechanics: commas with appositives, in dates, in addresses
STEP 5 Listening and Reading Comprehension	• Fluency: sentences • Vocabulary: context-based strategies • Text features for content preview • Fluency: sentences • Activate and build knowledge • Text structure: main ideas and supporting details in informational text • Read (and listen to) varied genre selections • Comprehension: interpretation and response questions to open-ended questions: *who, what, when, where, why, how*; multiple choice questions	• Fluency: passages • Vocabulary: context-based strategies • Text features for content preview • Activate and build knowledge • Text structure: informational • Read (and listen to) varied genre selections • Higher-order thinking: retrieve and recall (remember); construct meaning (understand) • Summarization of main ideas from text selection	• Fluency: passages • Vocabulary: context-based strategies • Text features for content preview • Activate and build knowledge • Higher-order thinking: use information (apply); break down information (analyze) • Read (and listen to) varied genre selections • Literary terms and devices in text • Text structure: informational • Summarization of main ideas from text selection
STEP 6 Speaking and Writing	• Oral and written responses to *who, what, when, where, why,* and *how* questions • Fluency: sentence development • Pre-write: set purpose, content selection; organization using graphic organizers • Write: summary paragraph; expository paragraph including topic sentence, supporting details, elaborations • Edit and revise skills for coherence and content • Oral presentation	• Written responses based on higher-order thinking skills: remember; understand • Fluency: sentence development • Pre-write: set purpose, content selection; graphic organizers for reports, personal narratives, compare/contrast report • Write multi-paragraph expository report; personal narrative; compare/contrast report • Edit and revise skills for coherence and content • Oral presentation	• Written responses based on higher-order thinking skills: apply; analyze • Pre-write: set purpose, content selection; organization using informal outlines • Write: multi-paragraph report; expository (opinion) essay; expository (explanatory) essay; business letter • Edit and revise skills for coherence and content • Oral presentation

Book D (Units 19–24)	Book E (Units 25–30)	Book F (Units 31–36)
• Syllable types: closed, **r**-controlled, final silent **e**; vowel digraph (long and short); consonant + **le**; diphthong • Conditions for schwa • Syllabication process in multisyllable words • Multiple spellings for long vowels • Expansion of conditions governing schwa	• Sentence patterns for **c** and **g** • Alternate spellings for consonant sounds: / j / = **j**, **g**, **dge**; / f / = **ph**, **gh**; / s / = **sc**; / k / = **ch** • Common phonograms • English loan words, Romance languages: **i** = / ĕ /, **a** = / ŏ /, **e** = / ā /; African; Asian; Native American	• Common phonograms • r-controlled vowel sounds • Spelling patterns for / air /, / zh /, / sh ...r /, / sh / • Silent letters: **mb**, **kn**, **wr**, **mn**, **gn**, **lm**, **rh**, **ps**
• Read/spell: words based on new syllable patterns • Read/spell new high frequency words • Fluency: word recognition • Spelling: **Advanced Doubling Rule**	• Suffixation: pronunciation; spelling; word function impact • Read/spell: words based on new sound-spellings and phonograms • Read/spell new high frequency words • Fluency: word recognition • Spelling: review and apply all rules	• Read/spell: words based on new sound-spellings and phonograms • Read/spell new high frequency words • Fluency: word recognition • Spelling: review and apply all rules • Latin and Greek number prefixes
• Antonyms, synonyms, attributes, homophones, and analogies • Vocabulary expansion through Latin roots, prefixes, and suffixes • Prefix assimilation • Suffix impact on part of speech • Use of dictionary and thesaurus • Degrees of word meaning • Idiomatic and common expressions	• Antonyms, synonyms, attributes, homophones, and analogies • Vocabulary expansion through Latin roots, prefixes, and suffixes • Suffix impact on part of speech; spelling rules • Multiple meanings: using context • Use of dictionary and thesaurus • Degrees of word meaning • Idiomatic and common expressions	• Antonyms, synonyms, attributes, homophones, and analogies • Vocabulary expansion through Latin roots, prefixes, and suffixes; Greek combining forms • Suffix impact on part of speech; spelling rules • Multiple meanings: using context • Use of dictionary and thesaurus • Degrees of word meaning • Idiomatic and common expressions
• Grammatical forms: verbs (helping, linking, irregular); phrasal verbs; participles (present, past); indefinite pronouns • Grammatical functions: subject/verb agreement; indirect object; compound indirect objects • Sentence patterns: predicate nominative, predicate adjective • Text-based analysis and application of grammatical forms and functions • Mechanics: commas in series, in dates, in addresses; quotation marks; colons; semicolons	• Grammatical forms: relative pronouns; subordinating conjunctions; irregular verbs; past participles; perfect tense • Grammatical functions: subject/verb agreement • Clauses: independent; adjectival clauses (relative pronouns) and adverbial clauses (subordinating conjunctions) • Sentence pattern: complex • Sentence types: declarative, interrogative, imperative, exclamatory • Usage: confusing word pairs • Mechanics: colon	• Grammatical forms: irregular verbs; participial phrases • Grammatical functions: order of adjectives; pronoun antecedents • Sentence patterns: simple; compound; complex; compound/complex • Text coherence with transitional words and phrases • Usage: confusing word pairs
• Fluency: passages • Vocabulary: content-based strategies • Interpet text features (charts, graphics) for information and comprehension • Activate and build knowledge • Read (and listen to) varied genre selections • Higher-order thinking: judge information against criteria (evaluate); put information together in a new way (create) • Literary terms and devices in context • Text structure: plot • Summarization of main ideas from text selection	• Fluency passages • Vocabulary: context-based strategies • Interpet text features (charts, graphics) for information and comprehension • Activate and build knowledge • Read (and listen to) varied genre selections • Higher-order thinking: application of all levels • Literary terms and devices in context • Text structure: informational, fiction, persuasive essay • Elements of poetry	• Fluency: passages • Vocabulary: context-based strategies • Interpet text features (charts, graphics) for information and comprehension • Activate and build knowledge • Read (and listen to) varied genre selections • Higher-order thinking: application of all levels • Literary terms and devices in context • Text structure: narrative, report, play • Elements of poetry • Metacognition and comprehension: sampling, predicting; confirming in challenging text
• Written responses based on higher-order thinking skills: evaluate; create • Pre-write: set purpose, content selection (note-taking) organization using graphic organizers for reasons; persuasion; personal narrative; and outlining • Write: expository (explanatory) paragraph, essay: expository (descriptive) paragraph: literary analysis essay, narrative (short story) • Edit and revise skills for coherence and content • Debates, speeches, interviews	• Written responses based on higher-order thinking skills: all levels • Pre-write: set purpose, content selection (note-taking) organization using graphic organizers (comparison-contrast, narrative) and outlining • Write: personal narrative; descriptive essay; persuasive essay; autobiographical essay • Edit and revise skills for coherence and content • Multimedia presentation • Poetry recitations, debates	• Written responses based on higher-order thinking skills: all levels • Pre-write: set purpose, content selection (note-taking), organization using graphic organizers (narrative) and outlining (report); organize information across sources • Write: literary analysis essay; informational report; persuasive essay; personal essay • Edit and revise skills for coherence and content • Multimedia presentation

What are the unit objectives?

The **At a Glance for Teachers** provides the **Unit Objectives** that identify the content and skills covered in the unit.

The objectives are closely aligned with areas monitored by assessment and fluency tasks. The grid shows the lesson-by-lesson designation of instruction for each objective.

Timed fluency tasks are designated with an "F."

Instruction related to an objective is designated with a "•." This includes introductory, reinforcement, and assessment activities.

The icon designates lessons in which **Content Mastery** assessments occur.

Unit 1 — At a Glance for Teachers

Unit Objectives		1	2	3	4	5	6	7	8	9	10
STEP 1 Phonemic Awareness and Phonics	Write the letters for the consonant sounds / b /, / k /, / f /, / m /, / s /, and / t / and the short vowel **a** (/ ă /).	•	•	•	•	▨					•
	Say the sounds for consonants **b, c, f, m, s, t** and short vowel **a** (/ ă /).	•	•	F	F	F	•	•	•	•	
	Say the names for consonants **b, c, f, m, s, t** and short vowel **a** (/ ă /).								F	F	
STEP 2 Word Recognition and Spelling	Spell words with sound-spelling correspondences for this unit.	Pretest	•	•	•	▨	Pretest	•	•	•	▨
	Spell the **Essential Words**: a, I, is, that, this, the, are.		•	•	•						
	Read fluently words composed of sound-spelling correspondences for this unit.	•	F	F	F		F	•	•	•	
	Read fluently the **Essential Words**: a, I, is, that, this, the, are.	•	•	•	•				F		
STEP 3 Vocabulary and Morphology	Identify categories to build word meanings.	•	•	•					▨	•	
	Distinguish between singular and plural nouns.				•			•	▨		
STEP 4 Grammar and Usage	Identify nouns and verbs.	•	•	•	•				•	•	▨
STEP 5 Listening and Reading Comprehension	Read fluently phrases and sentences.	F	F	•			F	F	•		
	Preview reading selection using text features.			•					•		
	Make predictions about a reading selection.			•					•		
	Define vocabulary using a reference source or context-based strategies.			•					•		
	Identify factual information by listening to and reading informational text.			•					•		
	Identify topic, main ideas, and supporting details in informational text.				•	•				•	
	Write an IVF topic sentence.										•
STEP 6 Speaking and Writing	Answer comprehension questions beginning with **is** and **are** in complete sentences based on text.				•				•		
	Record information on a graphic organizer.					•			•		
	Write base sentences using a six-step process.	•	•					•	•		
	Write a summary of a nonfiction selection.										

Legend:
- • Instruction
- Ⓒ Comprehension Proficiency
- F Fluency
- ▨ Benchmark Paper
- ▨ Content Mastery
- ▨ Progress Indicator
- ▨ End-of-Book Content Mastery

2   Unit 1 • At a Glance for Teachers

Ⓒ **Comprehension Proficiency** indicates when comprehension is assessed during the unit.

The **Unit Concepts** column provides teachers with a **brief overview of content** covered in the unit.

Unit Concepts

Languages have two kinds of sounds: **consonants** and **vowels**.
▫ Consonants are closed sounds. They restrict or close the airflow using the lips, teeth, or tongue.
▫ Vowels are open sounds. They keep the airflow open.
Unit 1 has six consonants and one vowel sound. Letters represent the sounds. Consonants: **b**, **c** **f**, **m**, **s**, **t**; vowels: short **a**. The letter **s** has two sounds: / s / and / z /.

We put vowels and consonants together to make words. Every English word has at least one vowel.

Adding **-s** to nouns changes the word to mean **plural**, or "more than one." Word definitions are often composed of a category plus attributes that distinguish the thing from others in its category.

In English, words have different functions (jobs). Sometimes the same word can have multiple functions.
▫ **Nouns** name people, places, or things.
▫ **Verbs** describe actions.
Sentences convey a complete thought by answering two questions: Who (what) did it? and What did they (he, she, it) do? In English, we put nouns and verbs together to make sentences.

When we listen to and read informational text, we pay attention to the topic, **main ideas**, and **supporting details** in the text. Highlighting the main ideas and supporting details helps us recall important information and understand how the ideas work together.

We use different types of sentences when we speak and write.
▫ Some sentences tell something. These are called statements.
▫ Some sentences ask for information. These are called questions.
Questions begin with words that signal the kind of information required in the answer. Formulating oral or written answers to questions involves recognizing and understanding the **signal words** and using the text for information.
A **summary** of an informational selection includes the main ideas and important details of the text. Recording the topic, main ideas, and supporting details in a graphic organizer can help writers plan a summary.

Unit Word List

Essential Words

a, are, I, is, that, the, this

Unit Words

m, **s**, **t**, **c**, **f**, **b**, **a** for short / *a* /

act	bat	fast
am	cat	fat
at	fact	sat

Spelling Lists

Lessons 1–5		Lessons 6–10	
a	sat	act	cab
are	tab	am	cat
fat	*that*	as	fact
I	*the*	at	fast
is	*this*	bat	tact

Bonus Words can be found in the *Student Text*, page H74. These are additional words based on the same sound-spelling correspondences from this unit. Use these words for expanded reading, spelling, and vocabulary development.

Essential Words are **high- frequency words** needed to read and spell approximately 85 percent of words found in print.

Unit Words are **composed of the sound-spelling correspondences** from the current and previous units.

Two **Spelling Lists** per unit assess students' knowledge of the unit's sound-spelling correspondences, **Essential Words**, and spelling rules.

Bonus Words provide additional words based on cumulative sound-spelling correspondences. These words are used for additional practice.

Unit 1 • At a Glance for Teachers 3

Unit 2 At a Glance for Teachers

Unit Objectives

STEP 1 Phonemic Awareness and Phonics	• Write the letters for the consonant sounds / h /, / j /, / l /, / n /, / p /, and / r /.
	• Say the sounds for consonants **h**, **j**, **l**, **n**, **p**, and **r**.
	• Say the names for consonants **h**, **j**, **l**, **n**, **p**, and **r**.
STEP 2 Word Recognition and Spelling	• Spell words with sound-spelling correspondences from this and previous unit.
	• Spell the **Essential Words**: *do, said, to, who, you, your*.
	• Read fluently words composed of sound-spelling correspondences from this and previous unit.
	• Read fluently the **Essential Words**: *do, said, to, who, you, your*.
STEP 3 Vocabulary and Morphology	• Identify categories to build word meanings.
	• Distinguish between singular possessive and plural nouns.
STEP 4 Grammar and Usage	• Identify subjects and predicates.
STEP 5 Listening and Reading Comprehension	• Read fluently phrases and sentences.
	• Preview reading selection using text features.
	• Make predictions about reading selection.
	• Define vocabulary using a reference source or context-based strategies.
	• Identify factual information by listening to and reading informational text.
	• Identify topic, main ideas, and supporting details in informational text.
	• Write an IVF topic sentence.
STEP 6 Speaking and Writing	• Answer comprehension questions beginning with **do** and **who** in complete sentences based on text.
	• Record information on a graphic organizer.
	• Write base sentences using a six-step process.
	• Write a summary of a nonfiction selection.

Unit 3 At a Glance for Teachers

Unit Objectives

STEP 1 Phonemic Awareness and Phonics	• Write the letters for the consonant sounds / g /, / d /, / v /, and short vowel **i** (/ ĭ /).
	• Say the sounds for consonants **g**, **d**, **v**, and short vowel **i** (/ ĭ /).
	• Say the names for consonants **g**, **d**, **v**, and short vowel **i** (/ ĭ /).
STEP 2 Word Recognition and Spelling	• Spell words with sound-spelling correspondences from this and previous units.
	• Spell the **Essential Words**: *from, of, they, was, were, what*.
	• Read fluently words composed of sound-spelling correspondences from this and previous units.
	• Read fluently the **Essential Words**: *from, of, they, was, were, what*.
STEP 3 Vocabulary and Morphology	• Identify categories to build word meanings.
	• Distinguish between synonyms and antonyms.
STEP 4 Grammar and Usage	• Identify subjects and direct objects.
STEP 5 Listening and Reading Comprehension	• Read fluently phrases and sentences.
	• Preview reading selection using text features.
	• Make predictions about a reading selection.
	• Define vocabulary using a reference source or context-based strategies.
	• Identify factual information by listening to and reading informational text.
	• Answer multiple choice comprehension questions.
STEP 6 Speaking and Writing	• Answer comprehension questions beginning with **what** and **who** in complete sentences based on text.
	• Record information on a graphic organizer.
	• Write base sentences using a six-step process.
	• Identify parts of a paragraph.
	• Write a topic sentence.
	• Write an expository (explanatory) paragraph on a nonfiction selection.

Unit 4 — At a Glance for Teachers

Unit Objectives

STEP 1 Phonemic Awareness and Phonics	• Write the letters for the consonant sounds / w /, / y /, / z /, / k /, and the short vowel **i** (/ ĭ /).
	• Say the sounds for consonants **w**, **y**, **z**, **k**, and short vowel **i** (/ ĭ /).
	• Say the names for consonants **w**, **y**, **z**, **k**, and short vowel **i** (/ ĭ /).
STEP 2 Word Recognition and Spelling	• Spell words with sound-spelling correspondences from this and previous units.
	• Spell the **Essential Words**: *be, does, he, she, we, when*.
	• Read fluently words composed of sound-spelling correspondences from this and previous units.
	• Read fluently the **Essential Words**: *be, does, he, she, we, when*.
STEP 3 Vocabulary and Morphology	• Identify categories to build word meanings.
	• Distinguish between plural nouns or singular present tense verbs.
STEP 4 Grammar and Usage	• Identify pronouns (including nominative), prepositions, and adverbs.
STEP 5 Listening and Reading Comprehension	• Read fluently phrases and sentences.
	• Preview reading selection using text features.
	• Make predictions about a reading selection.
	• Define vocabulary using a reference source or context-based strategies.
	• Identify factual information by listening to and reading informational text.
	• Prepare to write an expository (explanatory) paragraph.
STEP 6 Speaking and Writing	• Answer comprehension questions beginning with **when**, **what**, and **who** in complete sentences based on text.
	• Summarize information from a nonfiction selection.
	• Record information on a graphic organizer to write a paragraph.
	• Write sentences using a six-step process.
	• Write topic sentences.
	• Write supporting detail sentences.
	• Use transition words.
	• Write an expository (explanatory) paragraph on a nonfiction selection.

Unit 5 — At a Glance for Teachers

Unit Objectives

STEP 1 Phonemic Awareness and Phonics	• Write the letters for the consonant sounds / l /, / f /, / z /, / s /, and the short vowel **o** (/ ŏ /) or / aw /).
	• Say the sounds for consonants **l**, **f**, **z**, **s**, and short vowel **o** (/ ŏ /) or / aw /).
	• Say the names for consonants **l**, **f**, **z**, **s**, and short vowel **o** (/ ŏ / or / aw /).
STEP 2 Word Recognition and Spelling	• Read and spell words with double final consonants from this unit (-**ff**, -**ll**, -**ss**, -**zz**).
	• Spell words with sound-spelling correspondences from this and previous units.
	• Spell the **Essential Words**: *here, there, these, those, where, why*.
	• Read fluently words composed of sound-spelling correspondences from this and previous units.
	• Read fluently the **Essential Words**: *here, there, these, those, where, why*.
STEP 3 Vocabulary and Morphology	• Identify categories to build word meanings.
	• Use verb endings -**s** and -**ing** to identify present/present progressive verb forms.
STEP 4 Grammar and Usage	• Identify adverbs and prepositional phrases that act as adverbs.
	• Identify present tense verb forms.
STEP 5 Listening and Reading Comprehension	• Read fluently phrases and sentences.
	• Preview reading selection using text features.
	• Make predictions about a reading selection.
	• Define vocabulary using a reference source or context-based strategies.
	• Identify factual information by listening to and reading informational text.
	• Summarize key points from a nonfiction selection.
	• Prepare to write an expository (explanatory) paragraph.
	• Answer multiple-choice comprehension questions.
STEP 6 Speaking and Writing	• Answer comprehension questions beginning with **where**, **why**, **what**, and **when** in complete sentences based on text.
	• Write sentences using a six-stage process.
	• Record information in an informal (two-column) outline.
	• Choose E's (examples, evidence, and explanations) to develop supporting detail sentences.
	• Write a concluding sentence by restating the topic sentence of the paragraph.
	• Write an expository (explanatory) paragraph on a nonfiction selection.

Unit 6 — At a Glance for Teachers
Unit Objectives

STEP 1 — Phonemic Awareness and Phonics
- Write the letters for the consonant sounds / ks / and / kw /.
- Say the sounds for consonants **x** and **qu**.
- Say the names for consonants **x** and **qu**.
- **End-of-Book Content Mastery: Phonemic Awareness and Phonics**

STEP 2 — Word Recognition and Spelling
- Spell words with sound-spelling correspondences from this and previous units.
- Spell the **Essential Words**: *how, now, down, her, me, for.*
- Read fluently words composed of sound-spelling correspondences from this and previous units.
- Read fluently the **Essential Words**: *how, now, down, her, me, for.*
- **Progress Indicator: Spelling**
- **Progress Indicator: Reading Fluency**

STEP 3 — Vocabulary and Morphology
- Identify categories to build word meanings.
- Use verb endings **-s** and **-ing** to identify present and present progressive verb forms.
- Classify words by attributes.
- **End-of-Book Content Mastery: Vocabulary and Morphology**

STEP 4 — Grammar and Usage
- Replace nouns with pronouns (subject and object forms).
- Identify prepositions and prepositional phrases.
- Identify adjectives that tell *which one, how many,* or *what kind.*
- **End-of-Book Content Mastery: Grammar and Usage**

STEP 5 — Listening and Reading Comprehension
- Read fluently phrases and sentences.
- Preview reading selection using text features.
- Define vocabulary using a reference source or context-based strategies.
- Identify factual information by listening to and reading informational text.
- Prepare to write an expository (explanatory) paragraph.
- **Progress Indicator: Reading Comprehension**

STEP 6 — Speaking and Writing
- Answer comprehension questions beginning with **how, what, why,** and **where** in complete sentences based on text.
- Use the **Six Traits of Effective Writing** to revise a paragraph.
- Record information in an informal (two-column) outline.
- Write an expository (explanatory) paragraph on a nonfiction text including all components of a paragraph (topic sentence, supporting detail sentences, elaborations (E's), and concluding sentence).
- **Progress Indicator: Writing**

Unit 7 — At a Glance for Teachers
Unit Objectives

STEP 1 — Phonemic Awareness and Phonics
- Write the letters for the consonant sound **x** (/ gz /).
- Say the sounds for consonant **x** and short vowel sound for the vowel **e** (/ ĕ /).
- Say the names for the consonant **x** and the vowel **e**.
- Write the letter for the short vowel sound / ĕ /.

STEP 2 — Word Recognition and Spelling
- Read and spell contractions with **not**.
- Read fluently and spell words with sound-spelling correspondences for this and previous units.
- Read fluently and spell the **Essential Words**: *all, call, into, our, small, their.*

STEP 3 — Vocabulary and Morphology
- Recognize synonyms and antonyms.
- Identiy the meaning of words with **-s, -es,** and **'s**.

STEP 4 — Grammar and Usage
- Identify and write regular past tense verbs.
- Identify verb forms.
- Combine subjects to form a compound subject with correct subject-verb agreement.

STEP 5 — Listening and Reading Comprehension
- Read phrases and passages fluently.
- Preview reading selection using text features.
- Define vocabulary using a reference source or context-based strategies.
- Identify factual information by listening to and reading informational text.

STEP 6 — Speaking and Writing
- Answer comprehension questions beginning with **state, recognize, name, locate, list,** and **choose** in complete sentences based on text.
- Distinguish fact and opinion statements.
- Generate sentences using a six-stage process.
- Write an expository paragraph.
- Identify and write parts of an expository report including introductory paragraph, transition topic sentence, E's, and concluding paragraph.
- Record information in a two-column outline.
- Write a multi-paragraph expository report.

Unit 8 — At a Glance for Teachers

Unit Objectives

STEP 1 Phonemic Awareness and Phonics	• Write the letters for the consonant digraphs **sh**, **th**, **ch**, **wh**, and **-ng** and the trigraph **-tch**. • Say the sounds for consonant digraphs **sh**, **th**, **ch**, **wh**, and **-ng** and the trigraph **-tch**. • Say the names for the consonant digraphs **sh**, **th**, **ch**, **wh** and **-ng** and trigraph **-tch**.
STEP 2 Word Recognition and Spelling	• Spell words with sound-spelling correspondences for this and previous units. • Spell the **Essential Words**: *about, any, many, out, word, write*. • Read fluently words composed of sound-spelling correspondences for this and previous units. • Read fluently the **Essential Words**: *about, any, many, out, word, write*.
STEP 3 Vocabulary and Morphology	• Recognize synonyms, antonyms, and homophones. • Identify present tense, past tense, and present progressive verbs using verb endings (**-s**, **-ed**, **-ing**).
STEP 4 Grammar and Usage	• Identify simple subject(s). • Identify regular and irregular verbs. • Identify simple predicate(s).
STEP 5 Listening and Reading Comprehension	• Read phrases and passages fluently. • Preview reading selection using text features. • Define vocabulary using a reference source or context-based strategies. • Identify factual information by listening to and reading informational text.
STEP 6 Speaking and Writing	• Generate sentences using a six-stage process. • Answer comprehension questions beginning with **state, describe, recognize,** and **name** in complete sentences based on text. • Record information in an informal (two-column) outline. • Write a multi-paragraph expository report including an introductory paragraph, body paragraphs with transition sentences, E's, and a concluding paragraph. • Edit and revise an expository report.

Unit 9 — At a Glance for Teachers

Unit Objectives

STEP 1 Phonemic Awareness and Phonics	• Say the name for the letters inculding **u**. • Write the letter for the vowel sounds / ŭ / (**u** or **o**) and / ŏŏ / (**u**). • Say the sounds for vowel **u** (/ ŭ / and / ŏŏ /).
STEP 2 Word Recognition and Spelling	• Spell words with sound-spelling correspondences for this and previous units. • Spell the **Essential Words**: *been, could, should, too, two, would*. • Read fluently words composed of sound-spelling correspondences for this and previous units. • Read fluently the **Essential Words**: *been, could, should, too, two, would*. • Read and spell contractions with **would**.
STEP 3 Vocabulary and Morphology	• Recognize synonyms, antonyms, and homophones. • Identify plural nouns and third person singular, present tense verbs using the suffix -es.
STEP 4 Grammar and Usage	• Identify irregular past tense and past progressive verb forms. • Identify compound direct objects.
STEP 5 Listening and Reading Comprehension	• Read phrases and passages fluently. • Preview reading selection using text features. • Define vocabulary using a reference source or context-based strategies. • Identify factual information by listening to and reading informational text. • Answer multiple choice comprehension questions.
STEP 6 Speaking and Writing	• Generate sentences using a six stage process. • Answer comprehension questions beginning with **tell, define, predict, conclude, illustrate,** and **locate** in complete sentences based on text. • Distinguish fact and opinion statements. • Write a personal narrative including an introduction, story and conclusion. • Edit and revise a personal narrative.

Unit 10 — At a Glance for Teachers

Unit Objectives

STEP 1 Phonemic Awareness and Phonics	• Say the names for the letters including all vowels.
	• Write the final silent **e** pattern to represent long vowel sounds: a_e, e_e, i_e, o_e.
	• Say the long vowel sound for the vowels **a**, **e**, **i**, **o**, **u**.
STEP 2 Word Recognition and Spelling	• Spell words with sound-spelling correspondences from this and previous units.
	• Spell the **Essential Words**: *almost, alone, already, also, although, always*.
	• Read fluently words composed of sound-spelling correspondences from this and previous units.
	• Read fluently the **Essential Words**: *almost, alone, already, also, although, always*.
	• Read and spell contractions with **will**.
STEP 3 Vocabulary and Morphology	• Recognize synonyms, antonyms, and homophones.
	• Identify present tense, past tense, present progressive, and past progressive verb forms using endings -s, -ed, -ing.
STEP 4 Grammar and Usage	• Identify and write past, present, and future tense verb phrases.
	• Identify compound subjects, compound predicates, compound direct objects, and compound sentences.
STEP 5 Listening and Reading Comprehension	• Read phrases and passages fluently.
	• Preview reading selection using text features.
	• Define vocabulary using a reference source or context-based strategies.
	• Identify factual information by listening to and reading informational text.
STEP 6 Speaking and Writing	• Generate sentences, including compound parts, using a six stage process.
	• Answer comprehension questions beginning with **identify**, **explain**, **discuss**, **paraphrase**, and **tell** when in complete sentences based on text.
	• Write a personal narrative including an introduction, story, and conclusion.

Unit 11 — At a Glance for Teachers

Unit Objectives

STEP 1 Phonemic Awareness and Phonics	• Say the names for the letters.
	• Write the letters for the sounds in consonant blends and clusters.
	• Say the sounds for **l**, **r**, **s**, and **w** consonant blends and **s**-consonant clusters.
STEP 2 Word Recognition and Spelling	• Read fluently and spell words with sound-spelling correspondences for this and previous units.
	• Read fluently and spell the **Essential Words**: *body, each, every, know, thought, very*.
STEP 3 Vocabulary and Morphology	• Identify the meanings for **Unit Words**.
	• Identify meanings using noun endings for singular, plural, and possessive -s and 's.
STEP 4 Grammar and Usage	• Identify and write future and future progressive verb forms.
	• Form compound sentences using **but**.
STEP 5 Listening and Reading Comprehension	• Read phrases and passages fluently.
	• Preview nonfiction reading selection using text features.
	• Define vocabulary using a reference source and/or context-based strategies.
	• Read and understand informational text.
	• Answer multiple choice comprehension questions.
STEP 6 Speaking and Writing	• Generate sentences using a six stage process.
	• Answer comprehension questions beginning with **categorize**, **compare**, **contrast**, **sort**, **conclude**, **describe** and **list** in complete sentences based on text.
	• Distinguish fact and opinion statements.
	• Write a compare and contrast report.
	• Edit and revise a compare and contrast report.

A

Unit 12 At a Glance for Teachers

Unit Objectives

STEP 1 Phonemic Awareness and Phonics	• Say the sounds and names for the consonants and consonant combinations: digraphs, trigraphs, blends, and clusters.
	• Write the letters for the sounds in consonant digraphs, trigraphs, blends, and clusters; long, short vowels.
	• Say the short and long vowel sound for each vowel.
	• **Summative Test: Phonemic Awareness and Phonics**
STEP 2 Word Recognition and Spelling	• Read fluently and spell words with sound-spelling correspondences for this and previous units.
	• Read fluently and spell the **Essential Words**: *Dr., Mr., Mrs., Ms., find, only.*
	• **Progress Indicator: Spelling**
	• **Progress Indicator: Reading Fluency**
STEP 3 Vocabulary and Morphology	• Identify and generate synonyms, antonyms, and homophones for **Unit Words**.
	• Use suffixes to form plurals, possessives, and verb tenses.
	• **Summative Test: Vocabulary and Morphology**
STEP 4 Grammar and Usage	• Identify nouns as subjects, direct objects, or objects of a preposition in sentences.
	• Identify verb tenses: past, present, and future.
	• Identify compound sentences joined with **and** or **but**.
	• **Summative Test: Grammar and Usage**
STEP 5 Listening and Reading Comprehension	• Read phrases and passages fluently.
	• Preview nonfiction reading selection using text features.
	• Define vocabulary using a reference source or context-based strategies.
	• Identify factual information in an informational text.
	• Prepare to write a compare and contrast report and a personal narrative essay.
	• **Progress Indicator: Reading Comprehension**
STEP 6 Speaking and Writing	• Answer comprehension questions beginning with **match, classify, compare, contrast, describe,** and **conclude**.
	• Use graphic organizers to plan a compare and contrast report and a personal narrative essay.
	• Write a compare and contrast report and personal narrative.
	• Edit and revise writing using checklists based on the Six Traits of Effective Writing.
	• **Progress Indicator: Writing**

Unit 13 At a Glance for Teachers

Unit Objectives

STEP 1 Phonemic Awareness and Phonics	• Identify closed syllables.
	• Identify stressed and unstressed syllables in multisyllable words.
	• Recognize the schwa in multisyllable words.
STEP 2 Word Recognition and Spelling	• Spell words composed of closed syllables.
	• Spell the **Essential Words**: *gone, look, most, people, see, water.*
	• Read fluently words composed of closed syllables and words with prefixes **dis-, in-, non-, un-**.
	• Read fluently the **Essential Words**: *gone, look, most, people, see, water.*
	• Read and spell contractions with **am** and **is**.
STEP 3 Vocabulary and Morphology	• Identify synonyms, antonyms, homophones, and attributes for **Unit Words**.
	• Identify the meaning of prefixes in words.
STEP 4 Grammar and Usage	• Identify and use **be** as a helping verb.
	• Identify the noun or pronoun as subject.
	• Identify direct objects.
STEP 5 Listening and Reading Comprehension	• Read phrases and passages fluently.
	• Define vocabulary using context-based strategies or a reference source.
	• Preview reading selection using text features.
	• Identify factual information in informational text.
STEP 6 Speaking and Writing	• Generate sentences using a six-stage process.
	• Write responses to questions with the signal words: **use, generalize, infer, illustrate, explain**.
	• Write an expository paragraph.
	• Record information in an informal (two-column) outline.
	• Identify and write parts of an expository report including introductory paragraph, transition topic sentence, E's, and concluding paragraph.
	• Write an expository report.

Unit 14 At a Glance for Teachers

Unit Objectives

STEP 1 — Phonemic Awareness and Phonics
- Say the sounds for **ar, or, er, ir, ur**.
- Write the letters for the sounds / âr /, / ôr /, / êr /.
- Identify syllables in words including **r**-controlled.
- Identify stressed syllables.

STEP 2 — Word Recognition and Spelling
- Spell words with sound-spelling correspondences for this and previous units.
- Spell the **Essential Words**: *day, little, may, new, say, way*.
- Read fluently words composed of sound-spelling correspondences for this and previous units.
- Read fluently the **Essential Words**: *day, little, may, new, say, way*.
- Read and spell contractions with **are**.

STEP 3 — Vocabulary and Morphology
- Identify synonyms, antonyms, and attributes for **Unit Words**.
- Use comparative and superlative adjectives **-er, -est**.

STEP 4 — Grammar and Usage
- Identify and use nouns, verbs, adjectives, and prepositions.
- Identify complete subjects and complete predicates.
- Form sentences with compound parts using **or**.

STEP 5 — Listening and Reading Comprehension
- Read phrases and passages fluently.
- Preview nonfiction reading selection using text features.
- Define vocabulary using context-based strategies.
- Read and understand informational text.

STEP 6 — Speaking and Writing
- Generate sentences using a six stage process.
- Distinguish fact and opinion statements.
- Answer comprehension questions using **infer, define, predict, generalize, use, explain, show**, and **classify**.
- Organize ideas and information in a two-column outline for an expository (opinion) essay.
- Write an expository (opinion) essay including an introduction and concluding paragraph.
- Edit and revise an expository (opinion) essay.

Unit 15 At a Glance for Teachers

Unit Objectives

STEP 1 — Phonemic Awareness and Phonics
- Say the long vowel sounds for: **a**, **e**, **i**, **o**, and **u**.
- Identify open syllables in words.
- Identify stressed syllables.

STEP 2 — Word Recognition and Spelling
- Spell words with sound-spelling correspondences, syllable types, and prefixes from this and previous units.
- Read fluently and spell the **Essential Words**: *good, great, right, though, through, year*.
- Read fluently words composed of sound-spelling correspondences, syllable types, and prefixes from this and previous units.
- Read and spell contractions with **have**.

STEP 3 — Vocabulary and Morphology
- Identify synonyms, antonyms, and attributes for **Unit Words**.
- Identify verbs with **-ing** endings (present participles) that act as adjectives.

STEP 4 — Grammar and Usage
- Identify prepositions and the meaning of prepositional phrases.
- Identify and use **have** as a main or helping verb.
- Identify and write sentences with compound direct objects.

STEP 5 — Listening and Reading Comprehension
- Read phrases and passages fluently.
- Preview nonfiction reading selection using text features.
- Define vocabulary using context-based strategies.
- Read and understand informational text.
- Answer multiple-choice and open-ended comprehension questions.
- Set a purpose, use a two-column outline, and write a concluding paragraph for an opinion essay.

STEP 6 — Speaking and Writing
- Generate sentences using a six-stage process.
- Distinguish fact and opinion statements.
- Answer comprehension questions using **infer, identify, list, state, use, name, discuss, explain**, and **describe**.
- Write an expository (opinion) essay.
- Edit and revise an expository (opinion) essay.

Unit 16 — At a Glance for Teachers

Unit Objectives

STEP 1 — Phonemic Awareness and Phonics	• Practice syllable segmentation and identify stressed syllables in multisyllable words.
	• Identify final silent <u>e</u> syllables in words.
	• Identify vowel phonemes.

STEP 2 — Word Recognition and Spelling	• Spell words with sound-spelling correspondences, syllable types, and prefixes from this and previous units.
	• Spell the **Essential Words**: *again, sound, today, tomorrow, want, work.*
	• Read fluently words composed of sound-spelling correspondences, syllable types, and prefixes.
	• Read fluently the **Essential Words**: *again, sound, today, tomorrow, want, work.*
	• Read and spell contractions with **had** and **has**.

STEP 3 — Vocabulary and Morphology	• Use antonyms, synonyms, and attribute relationships to define **Unit Words**.
	• Identify past and present participles used as adjectives.

STEP 4 — Grammar and Usage	• Identify plural and possessive noun forms.
	• Identify prepositions and prepositional phrases.
	• Identify and use the verbs **be** and **have**.
	• Identify adjectives of the same kind in sentences.

STEP 5 — Listening and Reading Comprehension	• Read phrases and passages fluently.
	• Preview nonfiction reading selection using text features.
	• Define vocabulary using context-based strategies.
	• Read and understand informational text.
	• Review the components and label the parts of a business letter.

STEP 6 — Speaking and Writing	• Generate sentences using a six-stage process.
	• Distinguish fact and opinion statements.
	• Answer comprehension questions using **describe, use, infer, explain, select, distinguish, tell.**
	• Write a business letter.
	• Write an expository essay using a two-column outline, and including an introductory paragraph, body paragraphs, and concluding paragraph.
	• Edit and revise an expository essay.

Unit 17 — At a Glance for Teachers

Unit Objectives

STEP 1 — Phonemic Awareness and Phonics	• Segment syllables in multisyllable words.
	• Say the vowel sounds represented by **y** / ĭ /, / ī /, / ē /.
	• Identify the stress pattern and conditions for each vowel sound represented by **y**.

STEP 2 — Word Recognition and Spelling	• Spell words with sound-spelling correspondences, syllable types, and prefixes for this and previous units.
	• Spell the **Essential Words**: *answer, certain, engine, laugh, oil, poor.*
	• Read fluently words composed of sound-spelling correspondences, syllable types, and prefixes for this and previous units.
	• Read fluently the **Essential Words**: *answer, certain, engine, laugh, oil, poor.*
	• Spell words following the Change **y** rule.

STEP 3 — Vocabulary and Morphology	• Use antonyms, synonyms, word attributes, and relationships to define **Unit Words**.
	• Use suffixes -**er**, -**est**, and -**ly** to change the meaning of words.

STEP 4 — Grammar and Usage	• Write phrases using a possessive noun.
	• Identify and use adverbs and prepositional phrases that act as adverbs.
	• Identify **do** as a main verb or helping verb.
	• Identify and analyze sentences with indirect objects.

STEP 5 — Listening and Reading Comprehension	• Read phrases and passages fluently.
	• Preview nonfiction reading selection using text features.
	• Define vocabulary using context-based strategies.
	• Read and understand informational text.
	• Answer multiple choice comprehension questions.

STEP 6 — Speaking and Writing	• Generate sentences using a six-stage process.
	• Distinguish fact and opinion statements.
	• Answer comprehension questions using **list, organize, select, explain, describe, infer, tell, outline,** and **distinguish.**
	• Write an expository (explanatory) essay including a two-sentence introductory paragraph, body paragraphs, and a concluding paragraph.
	• Edit and revise an expository (explanatory) essay.

Unit 18 — At a Glance for Teachers

Unit Objectives

STEP 1 Phonemic Awareness and Phonics	• Segment syllables in multisyllable words. • Identify stressed syllables in multisyllable words. • Identify closed, open, <u>r</u>-controlled, and final silent <u>e</u> syllables • **End-of-Book Content Mastery: Phonemic Awareness and Phonics**
STEP 2 Word Recognition and Spelling	• Read fluently and spell words with sound-spelling correspondences, syllable types, and prefixes from this and previous units. • Read fluently and spell the **Essential Words**: *to, there, answer, their, people, what, too, want, who, two.* • **Progress Indicator: Test of Silent Contextual Reading Fluently** • **Progress Indicator: Test of Written Spelling = 4**
STEP 3 Vocabulary and Morphology	• Use antonyms, synonyms, homophones, and attributes to define **Unit Words**. • Use suffixes to form singular, plurals, and possessives with nouns. • Review prefixes. • **End-of-Book Content Mastery: Vocabulary and Morphology**
STEP 4 Grammar and Usage	• Use **and, but,** and **or** in compound sentences. • Review noun categories and functions. • Review helping verbs **be, have,** and **do.** • **End-of-Book Content Mastery: Grammar and Usage**
STEP 5 Listening and Reading Comprehension	• Read phrases and passages fluently. • Preview nonfiction reading selection using text features. • Define vocabulary using context-based strategies. • Read and understand informational text. • **Progress Indicator: *Language!* Reading Scale**
STEP 6 Speaking and Writing	• Generate sentences using a six-stage process • Distinguish fact and opinion statements. • Answer comprehension questions using **explain, distinguish, infer, use, describe, contrast.** • Write an informal outline, introductory, body paragraph, and conclusion for an expository (explanatory) essay. • Revise an expository (explanatory) essay. • **Progress Indicator: Writing**

Unit 19 — At a Glance for Teachers

Unit Objectives

STEP 1 Phonemic Awareness and Phonics	• Say the sounds for vowel digraphs <u>ai</u>, <u>ee</u>, <u>oa</u>. • Write the letters for the sounds /ā/, /ē/, /ō/ using vowel digraphs. • Identify vowel digraph syllables
STEP 2 Word Recognition and Spelling	• Read and spell words composed with the vowel digraphs <u>ai</u>, <u>ee</u>, <u>oa</u>. • Read and spell the **Essential Words**: *abroad, against, captain, curtain, language, nuisance.* • Read and spell words with prefixes and suffixes from this and previous units.
STEP 3 Vocabulary and Morphology	• Identify and use homophones. • Use the meanings of prefixes and suffixes to understand the meaning of words.
STEP 4 Grammar and Usage	• Identify and use **be** as a linking verb. • Identify irregular verbs. • Identify and write sentences with a predicate nominative. • Use suffixes to identify words as nouns or adjectives.
STEP 5 Listening and Reading Comprehension	• Use charts to gain information. • Use context-based strategies to define words. • Read phrases and passages fluently. • Identify reasons and supporting evidence in informational text. • Identify character traits as part of plot analysis.
STEP 6 Speaking and Writing	• Answer comprehension questions beginning with **assess, justify, summarize, predict.** • Organize information from reading text in a graphic organizer to prepare to write. • Write an expository (explanatory) paragraph. • Write a literary analysis (character trait) paragraph.

A

Unit 20 At a Glance for Teachers

Unit Objectives

STEP 1 Phonemic Awareness and Phonics	• Say the sounds for vowel digraphs **ay**, **ea**, **ie**, **ey**, **ow** and **oe**. • Write the letters for the sounds / ā /, / ē /, / ī /, / ō / using vowel digraphs. • Identify vowel digraph syllables.
STEP 2 Word Recognition and Spelling	• Read and spell words composed of syllables with the vowel digraphs **ay**, **ea**, **ie**, **ey**, **ow**, and **oe**. • Read and spell the **Essential Words**: *course, friend, guard, guess, guest, guarantee.* • Read and spell words with prefixes, suffixes, and roots from this and previous units.
STEP 3 Vocabulary and Morphology	• Identify and use homophones. • Use the meanings of prefixes, suffixes, and roots to understand the meaning of words.
STEP 4 Grammar and Usage	• Identify adjectives. • Identify and use **be** as a linking verb. • Use commas in series, dates, and addresses. • Identify irregular verbs. • Identify predicate adjectives in sentences.
STEP 5 Listening and Reading Comprehension	• Use context-based strategies to define words. • Read passages fluently. • Identify parts of a story. • Identify character traits as part of plot analysis. • Orally summarize a story.
STEP 6 Speaking and Writing	• Answer questions beginning with the signal words: **critique, judge, explain, identify, compare**. • Organize supporting evidence from text in a graphic organizer. • Write literary analysis (character trait) essays using evidence from the text. • Edit and revise literary analysis (character trait) essays using writer's checklist.

Unit 21 At a Glance for Teachers

Unit Objectives

STEP 1 Phonemic Awareness and Phonics	• Identify stressed and unstressed syllables in multisyllable words. • Recognize the schwa sound in multisyllable words. • Identify conditions when vowels are reduced to schwa.
STEP 2 Word Recognition and Spelling	• Read and spell words containing syllables reduced to schwa. • Read and spell the **Essential Words**: *beautiful, beauty, business, busy, leopard, women.* • Read and spell words with prefixes, suffixes, and roots from this and previous units.
STEP 3 Vocabulary and Morphology	• Identify antonyms. • Use the meanings of prefixes, suffixes, and roots to understand the meaning of the words.
STEP 4 Grammar and Usage	• Identify nouns and adjectives. • Identify and use the forms of the verb **be**. • Identify predicate nominatives or predicate adjectives in sentences. • Use commas in a series.
STEP 5 Listening and Reading Comprehension	• Use context-based strategies to define words. • Read passages fluently. • Identify character traits as part of plot analysis. • Answer multiple choice questions.
STEP 6 Speaking and Writing	• Answer questions using the signal words: **assess, critique, judge, justify**. • Organize supporting evidence from text in a graphic organizer. • Write an expository (explanatory) paragraph using information from the text selection. • Write a literary analysis paragraph using evidence of character traits from the text.

Unit 22 At a Glance for Teachers

Unit Objectives

STEP 1 Phonemic Awareness and Phonics	• Identify conditions for the final consonant + **le** syllable type and spelling pattern. • Say short sounds for vowel digraphs **ou**, **ui**, and **ea**. • Write the letters for the sounds / ŭ /, / ĭ /, and / ĕ / using vowel digraphs.
STEP 2 Word Recognition and Spelling	• Read and spell words with final consonant + **le** syllables. • Read and spell words containing vowel digraphs representing short vowel sounds. • Read and spell the **Essential Words**: *colleague, extraordinary, iron, journal, journey, peculiar.* • Read and spell words with prefixes, suffixes, and roots from this and previous units.
STEP 3 Vocabulary and Morphology	• Identify and use attributes. • Identify and define adjective suffixes. • Use meanings of prefixes, suffixes, and roots to identify the definition for words. • Use assimilation to identify words with the prefix **dis-** and assimilated forms.
STEP 4 Grammar and Usage	• Identify adjectives. • Identify phrasal verbs and their meaning. • Identify compound predicate nominatives and compound predicate adjectives in sentences. • Identify prepositions and prepositional phrases. • Use commas in a series, in a date, and in an address.
STEP 5 Listening and Reading Comprehension	• Read passages fluently. • Use context-based strategies to define words. • Identify and map the parts of a plot in a story.
STEP 6 Speaking and Writing	• Answer questions beginning with the signal words: **plan, design, compose.** • Organize information from a story into a graphic organizer. • Present an oral plot summary based on a story. • Write a short story with characters, setting, initiating event, rising action, and solution. • Edit and revise a short story using writer's checklist.

Unit 23 At a Glance for Teachers

Unit Objectives

STEP 1 Phonemic Awareness and Phonics	• Say sounds for vowel diphthongs **oi**, **oy**, **ou**, and **ow**. • Write the letters for the sounds / oi / and / ou /. • Identify the position-spelling patterns of the diphthongs **oi** and **oy** for / oi / and **ou** and **ow** for / ou /.
STEP 2 Word Recognition and Spelling	• Read and spell words containing diphthong syllables. • Read and spell the **Essential Words**: *courage, debt, herb, honest, honor, hour.* • Read and spell words with prefixes, suffixes, and roots from this and previous units.
STEP 3 Vocabulary and Morphology	• Identify synonyms. • Use meanings of prefixes, suffixes, and roots to understand the meaning of words. • Use assimilation to identify words with the prefix **ex-** and assimilated forms.
STEP 4 Grammar and Usage	• Identify prepositions and prepositional phrases. • Identify phrasal verbs and their meaning. • Identify and write sentences with compound predicate nominatives, compound predicate adjectives, and compound predicate direct objects. • Identify the use of quotation marks in dialog.
STEP 5 Listening and Reading Comprehension	• Use context-based strategies to define words. • Read passages fluently. • Identify descriptive (sensory) information in stories. • Identify parts of the plot in a story. • Answer multiple choice questions.
STEP 6 Speaking and Writing	• Answer questions beginning with the signal words: **hypothesize, summarize, assess, paraphrase, generalize, explain, compose.** • Organize descriptive information to write a paragraph. • Write a literary analysis (setting) paragraph using evidence from the text. • Edit and revise a paragraph using writer's checklist. • Tell a short story incorporating descriptive information.

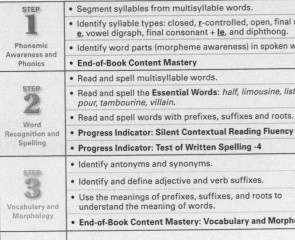

Unit 24 — At a Glance for Teachers

Unit Objectives

STEP 1 Phonemic Awareness and Phonics	• Segment syllables from multisyllable words.
	• Identify syllable types: closed, **r**-controlled, open, final silent **e**, vowel digraph, final consonant + **le**, and diphthong.
	• Identify word parts (morpheme awareness) in spoken words.
	• **End-of-Book Content Mastery**
STEP 2 Word Recognition and Spelling	• Read and spell multisyllable words.
	• Read and spell the **Essential Words:** *half, limousine, listen, pour, tambourine, villain.*
	• Read and spell words with prefixes, suffixes and roots.
	• **Progress Indicator: Silent Contextual Reading Fluency**
	• **Progress Indicator: Test of Written Spelling -4**
STEP 3 Vocabulary and Morphology	• Identify antonyms and synonyms.
	• Identify and define adjective and verb suffixes.
	• Use the meanings of prefixes, suffixes, and roots to understand the meaning of words.
	• **End-of-Book Content Mastery: Vocabulary and Morphology**
STEP 4 Grammar and Usage	• Identify adjectives and nouns.
	• Identify irregular verbs.
	• Identify predicate adjectives, predicate nominatives, and direct objects.
	• **End-of-Book Content Mastery: Grammar and Usage**
STEP 5 Listening and Reading Comprehension	• Use context-based strategies to define words.
	• Read passages fluently.
	• Organize main ideas and supporting evidence.
	• Identify character traits as part of plot analysis.
	• **Progress Indicator: *LANGUAGE!* Reading Scale**
STEP 6 Speaking and Writing	• Answer questions beginning with the signal words: **explain, justify, hypothesize.**
	• Organize main ideas and supporting evidence from text in a graphic organizer.
	• Write an expository (explanatory) paragraph.
	• Organize character traits in a graphic organizer.
	• Write a literary analysis (character trait) essay.
	• Edit and revise writing using a checklist based on the **Six Traits of Effective Writing**.
	• **Progress Indicator: Writing**

Unit 25 — At a Glance for Teachers

Unit Objectives

STEP 1 Phonemic Awareness and Phonics	• Identify conditions for the soft **c** (/ s /) and soft **g** (/ j /).
	• Say the sound for -**dge**.
	• Write the sound-spelling correspondence for -**dge** for / j /.
	• Identify the conditions for the multiple spellings of / j /: **j, g,** or -**dge**.
STEP 2 Word Recognition and Spelling	• Read and spell multisyllable words.
	• Read and spell the **Essential Words:** *carriage, machine, marriage, pigeon, shoes, surgeon.*
	• Read and spell words with prefixes, suffixes, and roots from this and previous units.
STEP 3 Vocabulary and Morphology	• Identify attributes.
	• Identify and define adjective suffixes.
	• Use meanings of prefixes, suffixes, and roots to understand the meaning of words.
STEP 4 Grammar and Usage	• Identify adjectives and nouns.
	• Identify past participles of regular and irregular verbs.
	• Identify phrases.
	• Identify clauses.
	• Use semicolons to write compound sentences.
	• Identify the four basic sentence types.
STEP 5 Listening and Reading Comprehension	• Interpret visual information.
	• Use context-based strategies to define words.
	• Identify thought in poetry.
	• Identify form in poetry.
STEP 6 Speaking and Writing	• Use visual and text information to answer questions.
	• Write resonses to questions using the signal words.
	• Organize information in a graphic organizer to prepare to write compare and contrast compositions.
	• Write a compare and contrast paragraph.
	• Write a compare and contrast essay.
	• Edit and revise written compositions using the appropriate writer's checklist for the type of writing

Unit 26 At a Glance for Teachers

Unit Objectives

STEP 1 — Phonemic Awareness and Phonics
- Say the sounds for <u>oo</u> (/ ŏŏ / as in *took* and / ōō / as in *moo*).
- Say the sounds for <u>ue</u> as in *blue*, <u>ui</u> as in *suit*, and <u>ou</u> as in *soup* (/ ōō /).
- Write the sound-spelling correspondences for / ŏŏ / and / ōō /.

STEP 2 — Word Recognition and Spelling
- Read and spell multisyllable words.
- Read and spell the **Essential Words**: *four, lose, move, movement, movie, prove.*
- Read and spell words with prefixes, suffixes, and roots from this and previous units.

STEP 3 — Vocabulary and Morphology
- Identify antonyms and synonyms.
- Identify and define noun and adjective suffixes.
- Use the meanings of prefixes, suffixes, and roots to understand the meaning of words.

STEP 4 — Grammar and Usage
- Identify subordinating conjunctions.
- Identify participial phrases.
- Identify adverbial clauses.
- Identify past participles of regular and irregular verbs.
- Identify the four basic sentence types.
- Use a colon to introduce a list.

STEP 5 — Listening and Reading Comprehension
- Interpret visual information.
- Use context-based strategies to define words.
- Identify aspects of plot and character development.

STEP 6 — Speaking and Writing
- Use visual and text information to answer questions.
- Write resonses to questions using the signal words.
- Use a graphic organizer to prepare to write.
- Write a compare and contrast (literary analysis) paragraph.
- Write a compare and contrast (character analysis) essay.
- Edit and revise compositions using writer's checklist.

Unit 27 At a Glance for Teachers

Unit Objectives

STEP 1 — Phonemic Awareness and Phonics
- Say the sounds for the vowel digraphs: <u>ui</u> (/ ī / as in *guide*), <u>ou</u> (/ ō / as in *soul*), <u>ey</u> (/ ā / as in *they*), <u>ei</u> (/ ē / as in *either* and / ā / as in *vein*).
- Write the letters for the sounds / ā /, / ē /, / ī /, and / ō / using vowel digraphs.

STEP 2 — Word Recognition and Spelling
- Read and spell multisyllable words.
- Read and spell the **Essential Words**: *billion, million, opinion, region, religion, union.*
- Read and spell words with prefixes, suffixes, and roots from this and previous units.

STEP 3 — Vocabulary and Morphology
- Identify synonyms.
- Identify and define noun suffixes.
- Use the meanings of prefixes, suffixes, and roots to understand the meaning of words.

STEP 4 — Grammar and Usage
- Identify subordinating conjunctions.
- Identify participial phrases.
- Identify adverbial clauses.
- Identify past participles of regular and irregular verbs.
- Use a colon to introduce a list.

STEP 5 — Listening and Reading Comprehension
- Interpret visual information.
- Use context-based strategies to define words.
- Identify setting and rising action.
- Answer multiple-choice and open-ended comprehension questions.

STEP 6 — Speaking and Writing
- Use visual and text information to answer questions.
- Write resonses to questions using the signal words.
- Organize information in a plot analysis graphic organizer to prepare for an oral plot summary.
- Orally summarize the plot of a story.
- Organize information for a problem-solution composition.
- Write a problem-solution composition.
- Edit and revise written compositions using the appropriate writer's checklist for the type of writing.

Unit 28 At a Glance for Teachers

Unit Objectives

STEP 1 Phonemic Awareness and Phonics	• Say the sounds for vowel phonograms: **aw** (/ ô / as in *saw*), **au** (/ ô / as in *pause*), **ew** (/ ōō / as in *chew* and / yōō / as in *few*), **eu** (/ ōō / as in *sleuth*, / yōō / as in *eulogy*, and / ŏō / as in *neuron*).
	• Write the letters for the sounds / ô /, / yōō /, / ōō /, and / ŏō / using vowel phonemes.
STEP 2 Word Recognition and Spelling	• Read and spell multisyllable words.
	• Read and spell the **Essential Words**: *aunt, bought, brought, caught, source, view.*
	• Read and spell words with prefixes, suffixes, and roots from this and previous units.
STEP 3 Vocabulary and Morphology	• Identify synonyms.
	• Identify and define noun suffixes.
	• Use the meanings of prefixes, suffixes, and roots to understand the meaning of words.
STEP 4 Grammar and Usage	• Identify relative pronouns.
	• Identify participial phrases.
	• Identify adjectival clauses.
	• Identify the present perfect tense.
	• Identify past participles of regular and irregular verbs.
STEP 5 Listening and Reading Comprehension	• Interpret visual information.
	• Use context-based strategies to define words.
	• Identify setting and rising action.
	• Identify different ways to end a story.
STEP 6 Speaking and Writing	• Use visual and text information to answer questions.
	• Write responses to questions using the signal words.
	• Organize descriptive information to write a paragraph.
	• Write a descriptive paragrpah.
	• Identify point of view (1st, 2nd, 3rd person) when writing.
	• Use dialog in writing a personal narrative.
	• Organize information for a personal narrative.
	• Write a personal narrative.
	• Edit and revise compositions using writer's checklist.

Unit 29 At a Glance for Teachers

Unit Objectives

STEP 1 Phonemic Awareness and Phonics	• Say the sounds for the phonograms: **al** (/ ô / as in *call*), **alk** (/ ôk / as in *talk*), **wa** (/ wŏ / as in *swap*), **qua** (/ kwŏ / as in *quad*), **war** (/ wôr / as in *ward*), **wor** (/ wûr / as in *word*), and **war** (/ wər / as in *backward*).
	• Write the letters for the sounds (/ ôl /, / ôk /, / wŏ /, / kwŏ /, / wôr /, / wûr /, and / wər /) using phonograms.
STEP 2 Word Recognition and Spelling	• Read and spell multisyllable words.
	• Read and spell the **Essential Words**: *oh, straight, whole, whom, whose, wolf.*
	• Read and spell words with prefixes, suffixes, and roots from this and previous units.
STEP 3 Vocabulary and Morphology	• Identify multiple meanings for words.
	• Identify and define noun suffixes.
	• Use the meanings of prefixes, suffixes, and roots to understand the meaning of words.
STEP 4 Grammar and Usage	• Identify relative pronouns.
	• Identify participial phrases.
	• Identify adjectival clauses.
	• Identify the past perfect tense.
STEP 5 Listening and Reading Comprehension	• Interpret visual information
	• Use context-based strategies to define words.
	• Identify images in poetry.
	• Identify features of persuasive writing.
	• Answer different types of comprehension questions
STEP 6 Speaking and Writing	• Use visual and text information to answer questions.
	• Write responses to questions using the signal words.
	• Organize information for a persuasive composition.
	• Write a persuasive composition.
	• Organize information for a descriptive paragraph
	• Write a descriptive paragraph including figurative language
	• Write a response to literature
	• Edit and revise written compositions using the appropriate writer's checklist for the type of writing.

Unit 30 — At a Glance for Teachers

Unit Objectives

STEP 1 — Phonemic Awareness and Phonics	• Say the sounds for the letter combinations: **ch** (/ k / as in *chord*), **que** (/ k / as in *oblique*), **ph** (/ f / as in *phone*), **gh** (/ f / as in *enough*), and **sc** (/ s / as in *science*).
	• Write the various letters or letter combinations for the sounds / k /, / f /, and / s /.
	• **End-of-Book Content Mastery**
STEP 2 — Word Recognition and Spelling	• Read and spell multisyllable words.
	• Read and spell the **Essential Words:** *behalf, bouquet, broad, mountain, sew, shepherd.*
	• Read and spell words with prefixes, suffixes, and roots from this and previous units.
	• **Progress Indicator: Test of Silent Contextual Reading Fluency**
	• **Progress Indicator: Test of Written Spelling - 4**
STEP 3 — Vocabulary and Morphology	• Identify and define noun and adjective suffixes.
	• Use the meaning of prefixes, suffixes, and roots to understand the meaning of words.
	• **End-of-Book Content Mastery: Vocabulary and Morphology**
STEP 4 — Grammar and Usage	• Identify relative pronouns.
	• Identify adjectival clauses.
	• Identify subordinating conjunctions.
	• Identify adverbial clauses.
	• Identify the perfect tenses.
	• Identify the basic sentence patterns.
	• **End-of-Book Content Mastery: Grammar and Usage**
STEP 5 — Listening and Reading Comprehension	• Use visual and text information to answer questions.
	• Use context-based strategies to define words.
	• Identify elements of plot.
	• Identify, understand, and answer questions with signal words.
	• **Progress Indicator: *LANGUAGE!* Reading Scale**
STEP 6 — Speaking and Writing	• Use visual and text information to answer questions.
	• Write responses to questions using the signal words.
	• Use cause and effect to understand develop plot
	• Organize information in a graphic organizer for a plot summary.
	• Write a plot summary
	• Write an alternative ending to a story
	• Edit and revise writing using the Six Traits of Effective Writing
	• **Progress Indicator: Writing**

Unit 31 — At a Glance for Teachers

Unit Objectives

STEP 1 — Phonemic Awareness and Phonics	• Say the vowel sounds for the letter combinations: **ear/air/ar** for / âr / as in *bear, air, care*; **ar/arr** for / ăr / as in *parody, arrow*; **ear** for / är / as in *heart*; **ar/er/err** for / ĕr / as in *primary, very, berry*; **oar** for / ôr /, **ear** for / ûr / as in *earth*; **ear/eir/ier/er/eer** for / îr / as in *ear, weird, pier, series, deer.*
	• Say the variant sounds for the consonants **s** (/ s /, / z /, / sh /, and / zh /) and **g** (/ g /, / j /, and / zh /).
	• Write the various letter combinations representing **r-**controlled vowel sounds and the consonants **g** and **s**.
STEP 2 — Word Recognition and Spelling	• Read and spell words based on unit sound-spelling combinations.
	• Read and spell the **Essential Words:** *bury, buy, cough, penguin, soldier, toward.*
	• Read and spell words with Latin and Greek number prefixes.
	• Spell confusing words correctly.
STEP 3 — Vocabulary and Morphology	• Identify and define Latin and Greek number prefixes.
	• Use knowledge of word relationships to build word meanings.
STEP 4 — Grammar and Usage	• Identify correct adjective order.
	• Identify dangling participles.
	• Identify basic sentence patterns: simple, compound, and complex.
	• Use capital letters correctly in titles and letters.
STEP 5 — Listening and Reading Comprehension	• Use text features to understand informational text.
	• Use context-based strategies to define words.
	• Identify elements of plot.
	• Identify, understand, and answer questions that use different types of signal words.
	• Identify the strategies in SQ3R.
STEP 6 — Speaking and Writing	• Use text features to develop study questions.
	• Write responses to questions using the signal words.
	• Organize information in a plot anlaysis graphic organizer.
	• Write an e-mail message.
	• Write a literary analysis essay.
	• Use a genre-specific Writer's Checklist to revise and edit a literary analysis essay.

Unit 32 At a Glance for Teachers

Unit Objectives

STEP 1 Phonemic Awareness and Phonics	• Say the vowel sounds for phonograms **-old, -oll, -ost** for / ō / as in *cold, toll, most*; **-ind, -ild** for / ī / as in *find, wild*.
	• Write the letter combinations for the phonograms representing / ō / and / ī /.
STEP 2 Word Recognition and Spelling	• Read and spell words based on unit sound-spelling combinations.
	• Read and spell the **Essential Words**: *blood, both, door, flood, floor, pint.*
	• Read and spell words composed of Greek combining forms.
	• Spell confusing words correctly.
STEP 3 Vocabulary and Morphology	• Identify and define Greek combining forms.
	• Use knowledge of word relationships to build word meanings.
STEP 4 Grammar and Usage	• Identify linking verbs.
	• Identify correct subject-verb agreement.
	• Identify correctly formed negative statements.
STEP 5 Listening and Reading Comprehension	• Use text features to understand informational text.
	• Apply SQ3R to read informational text.
	• Use context-based strategies to define words.
	• Identify mood, meter, and melody in poetry.
	• Identify features of a screenplay.
	• Identify, understand, and answer questions that use different types of signal words.
STEP 6 Speaking and Writing	• Use text features to develop study questions.
	• Write responses to questions using the signal words.
	• Develop an informal outline to prepare to write.
	• Write literary analysis compositions.
	• Present a literary analysis orally.
	• Apply a genre-specific Writer's Checklist to revise and edit literary analysis compositions.

Unit 33 At a Glance for Teachers

Unit Objectives

STEP 1 Phonemic Awareness and Phonics	• Say the vowel sounds for the phonograms: **-eigh** for / ā / as in *eight*; **-igh** for / ī / as in *light*; **-ough** for / ō / as in *although*.
	• Write the letter combinations for the phonograms representing / ā /, / ī /, and / ō /.
STEP 2 Word Recognition and Spelling	• Read and spell words based on unit sound-spelling combinations.
	• Read and spell the **Essential Words**: *auxiliary, daughter, dinosaur, mortgage, ocean, tongue.*
	• Read and spell words composed of Greek combining forms.
	• Spell confusing words correctly.
STEP 3 Vocabulary and Morphology	• Identify and define Greek combining forms.
	• Identify multiple meanings for words.
STEP 4 Grammar and Usage	• Identify gerunds and gerund phrases.
	• Identify the function of gerunds and gerund phrases.
	• Identify passive voice verbs.
	• Review sentences to change passive to active voice verbs.
STEP 5 Listening and Reading Comprehension	• Use text features to understand informational text.
	• Apply SQ3R to read informational text.
	• Use context-based strategies to define words.
	• Identify features of a report.
	• Identify features of a journal.
	• Use a notetaking system to research content for a report.
	• Identify, understand, and answer questions that use different types of signal words.
	• Answer open-ended questions under timed conditions.
STEP 6 Speaking and Writing	• Use text features to develop study questions.
	• Prepare to write a research report including selecting and shaping a topic.
	• Organize information into an outline to write a research report.
	• Use **A Guide to Writing a Research Report** as a reference tool for writing a research report.

Unit 34 At a Glance for Teachers

Unit Objectives

STEP 1 Phonemic Awareness and Phonics	• Say the sounds for graphemes: **mb**, **mn**, and **lm** for / m / as in *comb, hymn, calm*; **kn** and **gn** for / n / as in *knock, sign*; **wr** and **rh** for / r / as in *wrong, rhyme*; **ps** for / s / as in *psychology*.
	• Write the letter combinations containing silent letters representing / m /, / n /, / r /, and / s /.
STEP 2 Word Recognition and Spelling	• Read and spell words based on unit sound-spelling combinations.
	• Read and spell the **Essential Words**: *bargain, clothes, island, ninth, often, sword*.
	• Read and spell words composed of Greek combining forms.
	• Spell confusing words correctly.
STEP 3 Vocabulary and Morphology	• Identify and define Greek combining forms.
	• Identify multiple meanings for words.
STEP 4 Grammar and Usage	• Identify appositives and appositive phrases.
	• Identify the function of noun clauses.
	• Identify sentence fragments.
	• Rewrite sentences to change sentence fragments to complete sentences.
STEP 5 Listening and Reading Comprehension	• Use text features, such as tables and graphs, to understand informational text.
	• Use context-based strategies to define words.
	• Identify, understand, and answer questions that use different types of signal words.
STEP 6 Speaking and Writing	• Use text features to develop study questions.
	• Write responses to questions using the signal words.
	• Write a research report including a thesis, footnotes and bibliography.
	• Present an oral summary of a research report.
	• Apply genre-specific Writer's Checklist to revise and edit a draft for a research report.
	• Use **A Guide to Writing a Research Report** as a reference tool for writing a research report.

Unit 35 At a Glance for Teachers

Unit Objectives

STEP 1 Phonemic Awareness and Phonics	• Identify syllable types: closed, <u>r</u>-controlled, open, final silent <u>e</u>, vowel digraph, final consonant + <u>le</u>, and diphthong.
	• Identify stress patterns.
STEP 2 Word Recognition and Spelling	• Read and spell multisyllable words.
	• Read and spell words composed of Greek combining forms.
STEP 3 Vocabulary and Morphology	• Identify and define Greek combining forms.
	• Identify multiple meanings for words.
STEP 4 Grammar and Usage	• Identify nominative, object, possessive, and demonstrative pronouns.
	• Identify correct pronoun usage in compounds.
	• Use transitional words and phrases for text coherence.
	• Identify sentences with complete comparative structure.
	• Identify and correct run-on sentences.
STEP 5 Listening and Reading Comprehension	• Use text features to understand informational text.
	• Use context-based strategies to define words.
	• Identify, understand, and answer questions that use different types of signal words.
	• Identify features of a personal essay.
	• Identify the elements of poetry in a poem.
STEP 6 Speaking and Writing	• Write responses to questions using the signal words.
	• Write an essay using a quick outline under timed conditions
	• Write a compare and contrast literary anlaysis essay.
	• Write a persuasive essay incorporating key features.
	• Apply genre-specific Writer's Checklist to revise and edit a draft and final copy for a persuasive essay and a literary analysis essay.

Unit 36 At a Glance for Teachers

Unit Objectives

STEP 1 Phonemic Awareness and Phonics	• Identify syllable types: closed, r-controlled, open, final silent e, vowel digraph, final consonant + le, and diphthong. • **End-of-Book Content Mastery: Phonemic Awarenss and Phonics**
STEP 2 Word Recognition and Spelling	• Read and spell multisyllable words. • **Progress Indicator: Test of Silent Contextual Reading Fluency** • **Progress Indicator: Test of Written Spelling - 4**
STEP 3 Vocabulary and Morphology	• Identify and define Greek combining forms. • Identify multiple meanings for words. • **End-of-Book Content Mastery: Vocabulary and Morphology**
STEP 4 Grammar and Usage	• Identify nominative and object pronouns. • Identify correct pronoun usage in compounds. • Identify adverbial, adjectival, and noun clauses. • Identify transitional words and phrases used for text cohesion. • Identify and correct run-on sentences. • Identify correct punctuation use. • **End-of-Book Content Mastery: Grammar and Usage**
STEP 5 Listening and Reading Comprehension	• Use text features to understand informational text. • Use context-based strategies to define words. • Identify, understand, and answer questions that use different types of signal words. • Identify the elements of drama. • **Progress Indicator: *LANGUAGE!* Reading Scale**
STEP 6 Speaking and Writing	• Write responses to questions using the signal words. • Edit and revise writing using a checklist based on the Six Traits of Effective Writing. • Develop an informal outline to prepare to write a personal essay. • Write a personal essay. • Apply a genre-specific Writer's Checklist to revise and edit a personal essay. • **Progress Indicator: Writing**

LANGUAGE! TRG
SCAVENGER HUNT

1. Find the brain research that will help your students understand the importance and power of the phonemic awareness drills.

   _____

2. Locate the fluency goals for all of the books in *LANGUAGE!*

   _____

3. Find the page that contains the rationale and directions for the Code It Why Do/How To activity.

   _____

4. Find the listing of the instructional activities used to teach Step 2.

   _____

5. Locate the diagrams showing desk arrangements in the classroom and how they relate to behavior management.

   _____

6. Find ideas for small group/independent work stations to serve as reinforcement.

   _____

7. Locate information about how *LANGUAGE!* can serve the deaf/hard of hearing population.

   _____

8. Find materials that relate to the value of sentence diagramming and its progression in the curriculum.

   _____

9. Locate research that supports the importance of teaching spelling.

   _____

10. Find independent reading suggestions for a 6th grader who is reading at a Lexile of 500.

    _____

11. Locate information about the order in which phonemes are introduced in *LANGUAGE!*

    _____

12. Find information about writing checklists that help students learn to edit and revise their writing.

    _____

RESEARCH AND BACKGROUND

Table of Contents

READING
AND THE BRAIN

Rigorous academic research offers exciting insights into what does and doesn't work in the classroom. This section presents various findings on reading instruction and outlines how LANGUAGE! aligns with evidence-based pedagogy.

Proficient Reading Depends on Many Skills
by Louisa C. Moats, Ed.D., and Carol Tolman, Ph.D.

The following is excerpted from *Language Essentials of Reading and Spelling (LETRS), Module 1: The Challenge of Learning to Read (2nd Edition);* Sopris West, 2009. Reprinted with permission.

The mechanics of fluent, accurate reading are quite remarkable. A proficient reader appears to scan the print effortlessly, extracting meaning and sifting through it, making connections between new ideas in the text and existing knowledge, and interpreting according to his or her purposes. The proficient reader figures out new words and names very quickly and with minimal effort, consciously sounding out new words if necessary. New words are decoded with minimal effort because the sounds, syllables, and meaningful parts of words are recognized automatically. If the good reader happens to misread a word or phrase or does not comprehend a word or phrase, he or she quickly adapts by rereading to make sense of the information and clarify what was unclear. As she reads along, the reader forms a mental model, or schema, for the meanings just extracted, linking new information to background knowledge. That schema, or mental construction, has a logical framework into which she files the information to remember. Reading is a complex mental activity!

The attainment of reading skill has fascinated psychologists and invited more study than any other aspect of human cognition because of its social importance and its complexity. The study of proficient reading and reading problems earned more funding increases from Congress in the 1990s than any other public health issue studied by the National Institute of Child Health and Human Development (Lyon & Chhabra, 2004). As a consequence of programmatic research efforts over many years, scientific consensus on some important issues in reading development and reading instruction has been reached (McCardle & Chhabra, 2004; Rayner et al., 2001).

Two Domains and Five Essential Components of Reading

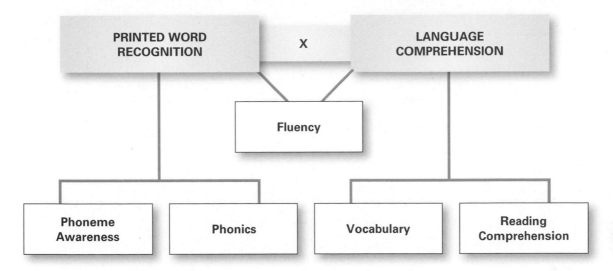

One important result of research is the finding that fluent reading for comprehension depends on the ability to recognize and attach meaning to individual words. Reading is the product of two major sets of subskills: printed word recognition and language comprehension. Printed words cannot be interpreted unless they are accurately pronounced or named (e.g., abroad is not aboard; scarred is not scared; etymology is not entomology). Pronouncing or decoding a word requires knowledge of the sounds in words (phoneme awareness) and the alphabetic system by which we represent those sounds (phonics). The meanings of those sounds must be recognized at the word level (vocabulary) and at the level of connected language (text comprehension).

A fluent reader carries out the process of word-naming with deceptive ease. A fluent reader recognizes or names words so rapidly and effortlessly that he or she is not aware of those mental processes. Automatic word recognition frees up cognitive resources (i.e., attention, self-monitoring, working memory) that can then be applied to comprehension. A short list of some major subskills of reading, then, is as follows:

- Phoneme awareness
- Use of phonics to decode words accurately
- Automatic recognition of words previously deciphered
- Knowledge of what most words mean
- Understanding sentences and language of books
- Constructing meaning (connecting ideas in the text and with each other and with prior knowledge)
- Monitoring comprehension and rereading or rethinking if miscomprehension occurs.

Four Processing Systems
That Support Word Recognition

Areas of the Brain Involved in Reading

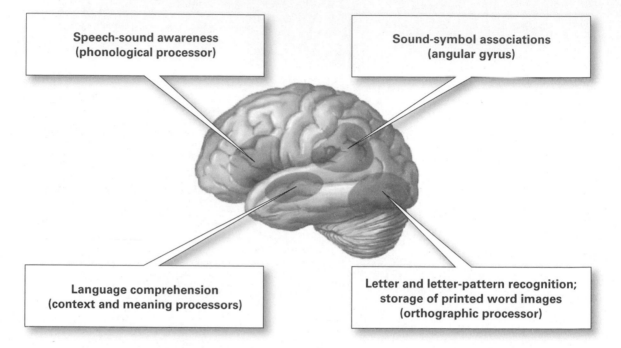

Speech-sound awareness
(phonological processor)

Sound-symbol associations
(angular gyrus)

Language comprehension
(context and meaning processors)

Letter and letter-pattern recognition;
storage of printed word images
(orthographic processor)

In order for reading to occur, several major regions of the left half of the brain must perform specific jobs in concert with the others. In most people, language functions are subsumed by the left cerebral hemisphere, and the processing of written language depends on networks that are located primarily in the language centers. The networks that are highlighted in [the figure above] include the **phonological processor** (in the back part of the *frontal lobe* of the brain); the **orthographic processor** (in the *lower back [occipital]* part of the brain); and the middle area (*temporal-parietal-occipital junction*, or **angular gyrus**), where these two processing systems communicate to support word recognition. In addition, pathways link the back and middle areas to the *temporal* areas, where **word meanings** and **connected language** are processed. Notice that the orthographic processor is on the side of the brain that serves language (left side) and that it is wired into the language centers. Learning to recognize words depends heavily on accurate matching of written symbols with sounds and the connection of those sound patterns with meaning.

Jobs of the Four Processing Systems

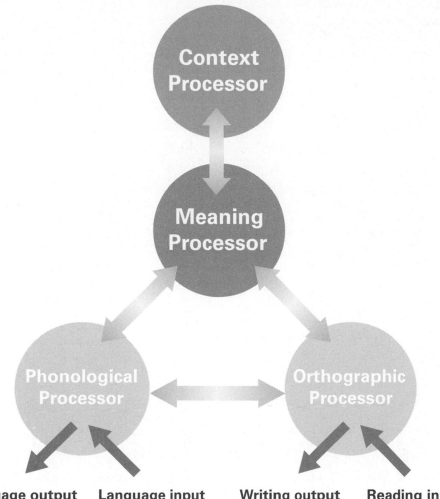

The schematic representation of the four brain-processing systems involved in word recognition [above] is based on cognitive psychological experimentation. It was originally proposed by Seidenberg and McClelland (1989) as a summation and synthesis of many experiments on the nature of skilled and unskilled reading. This model was developed before functional brain studies showed where and when these mental activities take place during reading (Berninger & Richards, 2002; Eden & Moats, 2002; Shaywitz, 2003). The model is discussed at length in Adams' (1990) landmark book, *Beginning to Read: Thinking and Learning About Print,* and two recent summary articles in *Psychological Science in the Public Interest* and *Scientific American* (Rayner, et al., 2001, 2002). The schematic representation of the systems simplifies the nature of skilled reading because several subcomponents within each processing system have also been identified (Vellutino et al., 2007).

The four-part processor concept, although a simplification, is useful because it suggests: (a) the various ways in which reading problems might develop; and (b) why reading instruction should target several kinds of skills. The model reminds us that instruction should aim to educate all of the processing systems and enable them to work together. It shows why recognition and fast processing of sounds, letter patterns, and morphemes—as well as word meanings, language comprehension, and background knowledge—are all important components of skilled reading. The model also helps researchers decide what questions or hypotheses to test in scientific studies. For example:

- Is one processing system more important to educate than the others at a given stage of reading development?

- How do these systems interact?

- What kinds of experiences are necessary for each processing system to learn its job in the reading brain?

- Is it possible to be a good reader if one system is not functioning well?

Next, we will explore in more detail what each of the four processors is responsible for and how each one contributes to proficient reading and writing.

The Job of the Phonological Processor

This processing system enables us to perceive, remember, interpret, and produce the speech-sound system of our own language and learn the sounds of other languages. The phonological processor enables us to imitate and produce *prosody*, or the stress patterns, in speech, including the rise and fall of the voice during phrasing. It is responsible for such functions as:

- Mentally categorizing and identifying the phonemes in a language system;

- Producing the speech sounds and syllable sequences in words;

- Comparing and distinguishing words that sound similar (e.g., **reintegrate** vs. **reiterate**);

- Remembering and repeating the words in a phrase or the sounds in a word;

- Retrieving specific words from the mental dictionary (lexicon) and pronouncing them;

- Holding the sounds of a word in memory so that a word can be written down; and

- Taking apart the sounds in a word so that they can be matched with alphabetic symbols.

The phonological processor has many jobs, all of them related to the perception, memory, and production of speech. *Phoneme awareness* is one job of the phonological processor. Children who have trouble with phonological processing show a variety of symptoms, such as difficulty remembering sounds for letters or blending them together, difficulty recognizing the subtle differences between similar words, and trouble spelling all the speech sounds in a word....

The Job of the Orthographic Processor

The orthographic processing system receives visual input from printed words. It perceives and recognizes letters, punctuation marks, spaces, and the letter patterns in words. The orthographic processor enables us to copy lines of print, recognize words as whole units, or remember letter sequences for spelling. When we look at print, its features are filtered, identified, and matched to images of letters or letter sequences already in our orthographic memory. If the letters or letter sequences are familiar, we associate them with sounds and meanings.

Most people have no trouble interpreting widely varying print forms, including individual handwriting styles, type fonts, or uppercase and lowercase letters. The size, style, and case of print are not major factors in word recognition once a reader knows letters and letter-sound relationships. Letters are recognized by their distinguishing features, including curves, straight lines and angles.

The orthographic processing system stores information about print that is necessary for word recognition and spelling. The speed with which letters are recognized and recalled is very important for proficient reading. Obviously, print images must be associated with meaning for reading comprehension to occur. Children with orthographic processing weaknesses will have trouble forming "sight word" habits, will be poor spellers, and will often read slowly because they are sounding everything out long after they should be doing that....

The Job of the Meaning Processor

According to the four-part processing model, recognizing words as meaningful entities requires communication among the phonological processor, orthographic processor, and meaning processor. The meaning processor is also called the semantic processor because it interprets the meanings of words in and out of context. If we associate speech sounds with print symbols but do not access the meaning processor, we may read a foreign language (or our own!) without knowing what it means, read nonsense words, or read a new name by sounding it out but with no possibility of comprehension. The meaning processor stores the inventory of known words, organizes the mental dictionary or lexicon, and constructs the meanings of any new words that are named during reading. The context of the passage supports the construction of those meanings.

A word filed in your mental dictionary is a linguistic entity with many facets. When words are known in depth, their sounds, spellings, meaningful parts, typical uses, alternative meanings, and customary uses are known. The meaning processor is structured according to a number of semantic organization features such as synonym relationships, roots and other morphemes, spelling patterns, common meaning associations, and connotations. It expands and reorganizes itself as new vocabulary is learned.

In the lexicon, or mental dictionary, words are "filed" in meaning networks. Words are typically learned in relation to one another, not in isolation. We learn words best if we can connect them to something we already know. We learn words more readily if they are connected to images of their sounds and their spellings, as well as the contexts in which they are usually used. Children with weak vocabularies, limited knowledge of English, and/or weaknesses in verbal reasoning ability may have trouble reading. In these cases, children's decoding skills may or may not be better than their skills in meaning-making....

The Job of the Context Processor

[The context processor's] primary job is to interact with and provide support for the meaning processor. The term "context" refers to the sentence and sentence sequence in which a word is embedded, and the concepts or events that are being discussed or reported in the text. Context provides the referent for a word's meaning. Many same-sounding words have multiple meanings, but only one is correct when used within a specific sentence. For example, the spelling of a word such as **passed** or **past** is determined by its meaning in the context of a sentence:

- The quarterback **passed** the ball to the receiver for the touchdown.
- Champions of the **past** were guests at the start of the game.

Context may help us find or figure out a word's intended meaning if we do not already know the word. Context also enriches our knowledge of how each word is typically used in our language system. Context will resolve ambiguities associated with multiple meanings of many words. Context may also help us catch decoding errors and cause us to reread for clarification. Well-developed background knowledge and verbal abilities as well as adequate reading fluency enable readers to use context productively.

A major point about the function of context in word recognition is that it plays only a limited role in facilitating word-naming itself. Word recognition and pronunciation are primarily the job of the phonological and orthographic processors. Students cannot comprehend text if they cannot read it accurately and fluently!...

Moving Beyond Cueing Systems

In the early 1980s, an alternative conception about the nature of reading was promoted in the non-scientific literature on reading instruction, although the origin of this model is unclear (Adams, 1998). Known as the "Three Cueing Systems" model, it proposed that word recognition depends on three systems of linguistic cues that reside in a text. The model proposed that these three systems are used during reading as needed to decode words: (1) a *graphophonic* ("visual") system; (2) a *semantic* (meaning) system; and (3) a *syntactic* system that provides linguistic context to process words in sentences. The cueing systems model was embedded in the miscue analysis procedure in "running records" or oral reading assessments and also was used as a rationale for whole-language approaches to reading instruction.

The Seidenberg and McClelland (1989) Four-Part Processing model departs from the Three Cueing Systems model in several critical ways. In the Four-Part Processing model, which converges with modern brain science, the phonological processor is separate and distinct from the orthographic processor. Each is only indirectly influenced by or driven by context. To educate the phonological processor and the orthographic processor, we teach children about speech sounds and print patterns, and then teach them how the two are linked. Accurately read words are then associated with meaning and placed in context.

In the Three Cueing Systems model, the phonological and orthographic processing systems are unified and characterized as "visual" instead of linguistic. The role of phonological processing in word recognition is minimized and obscured because it does not exist in the diagram. Teachers are not helped to understand or teach phonology directly, and teachers are encouraged to use meaning and context as a *replacement for* systematic instruction in the alphabetic code.

The Three Cueing Systems model overemphasizes the usefulness of context and meaning in word recognition. It encourages teachers to say to students who are stuck on a word, "What would make sense here?" before they expect the student to decode the word or blend the sounds together. It encourages teachers to believe that phonics strategies are a last resort and that systematic phonics instruction is unnecessary because children can rely on meaning to figure out words. The cueing model fosters dependence on pictures, prereading rehearsal, and context for identifying words. Unfortunately, these are the strategies that poor readers rely on when they are having difficulty deciphering the alphabetic code.

The Four-Part Processing model explains why a systematic, organized approach to teaching sounds and spellings is necessary and productive for many children. Until decoding skills are known, the most productive prompt to a student who is stumbling on a word is, "Look carefully at all the letters. Sound it out. Does that make sense?" Guessing at words on the basis of context, even with reference to an initial consonant sound, is not a good habit to encourage when children are first learning to read. Later reading fluency depends on early mastery of associations between letters, letter patterns, and speech sounds. Moreover, context use is an accurate way to identify unknown words only about one out of four to one out of ten times!

You Try It!

The Four Processors at Work in the Classroom

Read the following sentences, then use the *LANGUAGE!* **Sort It** exercise to explore the role of the four processors in reading instruction.

Instructions: Sort the task number in the box(es) of the processor(s) that is/are probably activated by the described task.

1. Decode and pronounce the unfamiliar printed word **chimera**.
2. Repeat the spoken phrase "Riki-tik tembo no serembo."
3. Orally give a synonym for the word **anthology**.
4. Read a passage to determine which meaning of the word **affirmative** is intended.
5. Determine whether the spoken words **does** and **rose** end with the same speech sound.
6. Underline all the words on a page in which the letter **c** is followed by **e**, **i**, or **y**.
7. Write this sentence: *My mental lexicon craves enrichment.*
8. Read and comprehend the next paragraph of this book.

Sort It

phonological processor	orthographic processor
meaning processor	**context processor**

The Four Processing Systems and *LANGUAGE!*

The chart shows the alignment of *LANGUAGE!* instruction with the major processing requirements of reading.

Key Processing System	Instructional Implication	*LANGUAGE!* Alignment	Step of Instruction
The Phonological Processor processes the speech sound system. This includes: • Identification, comparison, and manipulation of sounds • Pronunciation and production of sounds and words • Memory for sounds, words, and phrases • Linkage between sounds, spellings, and meanings	Teach phoneme identification, pronunciation, and awareness.	*LANGUAGE!* teaches: • Speech sounds • Phoneme manipulation • Production and replication of sounds • Phoneme awareness (isolation, segmentation, blending, rhyming, deletion, substitution, and reversal)	Step 1: Phonemic Awareness and Phonics
The Orthographic Processor processes letters, letter patterns, and whole words. This includes: • Recognition and formation of letters • Association of letters with speech sounds • Recognition of letter sequences, patterns, and whole words • Recall of letters for spelling	Call attention to the internal details and patterns of printed words. Link phonemes and graphemes. Build automatic word recognition for fluent reading of words, phrases, sentences, and passages.	*LANGUAGE!* teaches: • Word patterns • Word families • Latin and Greek roots • Sound-spelling correspondences • Syllables and syllable types • Sight words • Words based on phonemic concepts and high-frequency words • Letter-naming, word, and passage fluency	Step 1: Phonemic Awareness and Phonics Step 2: Word Recognition and Spelling
The Meaning Processor stores word meanings in relation to: • Other words in the same semantic field • Categories and concepts • Example of words in phrase context • The sounds, spelling, and syllables in the word • Meaningful parts (morphemes)	Teach vocabulary with attention to all these dimensions of meaning.	*LANGUAGE!* teaches: • Word meanings and multiple meanings • Morphemes (inflectional and derivational) • Latin and Greek roots, prefixes, and suffixes • Word relationships, including antonyms, synonyms, homophones, and analogies • Word categorization • Words in context • Syllable types	Step 3: Vocabulary and Morphology Step 5: Listening and Reading Comprehension
The Context Processor interprets words we have heard, named, or partially identified with reference to: • Language • Experience • Knowledge of the concepts	Teach the background that children need to interpret what they read. Teach awareness of academic language syntax; genre conventions; and discourse structure (paragraphs, story grammar, etc.). Teach the use of context to derive word meanings.	*LANGUAGE!* teaches: • Knowledge needed for understanding text through vocabulary preview and review, group discussion, and question strategies • Language syntax, genre conventions, and discourse structure systematically and cumulatively • Targeted strategies to enable students to derive word meaning from context	Step 4: Grammar and Usage Step 5: Listening and Reading Comprehension Step 6: Speaking and Writing

HOW CHILDREN LEARN TO READ

The Continuum of Reading and Spelling Development

by Louisa C. Moats, Ed.D., and Carol Tolman, Ph.D.

The following is excerpted from *Language Essentials for Teachers of Reading and Spelling (LETRS), Module 1: The Challenge of Learning to Read (Second Edition)*; Sopris West, 2009. Reprinted with permission.

The Developing Reading Brain

Models of proficient reading and an understanding of the many **cognitive** systems that support it do not tell us how people learn to read. Researchers have, however, investigated how the nature of skilled reading changes over time. At the end point, the proficient reader has learned to recognize words and interpret text rapidly, accurately, and often effortlessly. All processors are functioning and support reading. However, the role that each processor plays in reading development and the functional relationships among the processing systems change as reading skill develops.

Reading Levels and Reliance on Different Regions of the Brain

Proficient readers rely more on back regions of the brain after word images are learned and can be automatically recognized.

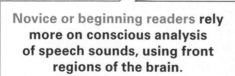

Novice or beginning readers rely more on conscious analysis of speech sounds, using front regions of the brain.

Good readers' brain activation patterns change with experience in reading. When children first learn to read, they are novices who must learn each component skill. During this time (refer to [figure above]), novice readers show greater activation in the parieto-temporal (front to mid-back, left side) region than skilled readers do because they must dismantle words for step-by-step, sound-symbol analysis. Novice good readers are aware of the sound-symbol connections in words and can use those to sound out words.

With practice and reading experience, however, good readers' brain patterns change slightly. More experienced good readers become more reliant on the occipito-temporal (farther back, left side) region to recognize words. They are more fluent because word recognition is automatic. At this stage of experienced good reading, readers often think that they are reading "by sight." While experienced good readers still activate the sounds in words and use phonics to decode words, they are unaware of this happening. Word recognition becomes a subconscious process, freeing up attention so that the reader can focus on the ultimate goal of reading, which is to understand what is being read.

Scarborough's "Rope" Model of Reading Development

The Four-Part Processing model represents a simplified version of what really takes place during word reading. In actuality, reading is much more complex. Scarborough (2001) conceptualized the various complexities in both decoding and language comprehension with a rope image. Note that there are many more "threads" to add when language comprehension must be considered in addition to word recognition.

The Many Strands That Are Woven Into Skilled Reading

(Scarborough, 2001)

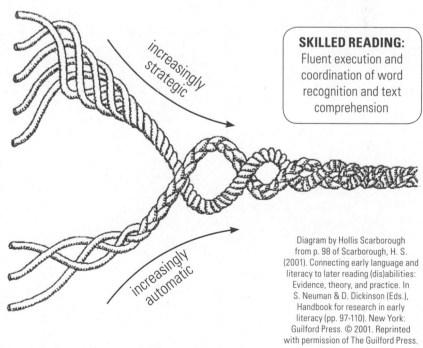

LANGUAGE COMPREHENSION

BACKGROUND KNOWLEDGE
(facts, concepts, etc.)

VOCABULARY
(breadth, precision, links, etc.)

LANGUAGE STRUCTURES
(syntax, semantics, etc.)

VERBAL REASONING
(inference, metaphor, etc.)

LITERACY KNOWLEDGE
(print concepts, genres, etc.)

WORD RECOGNITION

PHONOLOGICAL AWARENESS
(syllables, phonemes, etc.)

DECODING (alphabetic principle,
spelling-sound correspondences)

SIGHT RECOGNITION
(of familiar words)

increasingly strategic

increasingly automatic

SKILLED READING:
Fluent execution and coordination of word recognition and text comprehension

Diagram by Hollis Scarborough from p. 98 of Scarborough, H. S. (2001). Connecting early language and literacy to later reading (dis)abilities: Evidence, theory, and practice. In S. Neuman & D. Dickinson (Eds.), Handbook for research in early literacy (pp. 97-110). New York: Guilford Press. © 2001. Reprinted with permission of The Guilford Press.

Scarborough conceptualizes skilled reading as a combination of strands, or subskills, that interact with one another and that combine into an increasingly tighter woven "rope" as reading skill is acquired. [The figure above] shows clearly that fluent reading depends on automatic execution of both word recognition and comprehension subskills.

The Connecticut Longitudinal Study

The two major subcomponents of reading—word recognition and text comprehension—change in relationship to each other between grades 1 and 8 (Foorman et al.,1997; Tannenbaum, Torgesen, & Wagner, 2006; Torgesen, 2005). Started in 1983 at the Yale University School of Medicine, the Connecticut Longitudinal Study (Foorman et al., 1997; Shankweiler, et al., 1999; Shaywitz, 2003) randomly selected a sample of 445 kindergarten children in various Connecticut public schools and tracked their progress for more than 20 years. Each child was tested yearly with the Woodcock-Johnson Achievement Test reading subtests (Woodcock & Johnson, 1989), which include tests of word reading (real and nonsense words) and a test of passage comprehension. [The table below] shows how the relative importance of word reading skill to passage reading comprehension changed over time.

How the Relationship Between Decoding and Comprehension Changes Over Time

(based on data from the Connecticut Longitudinal Study, Foorman et al., 1997)

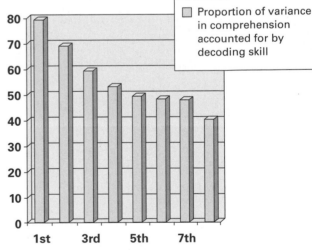

The correlations between these two components of reading changed as students learned to read. The correlations reflect the strength of association between decoding and comprehension. Initially, the ability to decode—the ability to read the words accurately—accounted for about 80 percent of passage reading comprehension ability. (The proportion of variance accounted for in one variable by another variable is obtained by squaring a correlation between the two.) Phonic decoding and fast word recognition were the most important tasks for first-grade students to master if they were going to be able to read a simple text passage and understand it. Passage comprehension at that level depended almost entirely on the ability to read single words accurately.[1]

---

[1] An analogy to math learning and teaching may be helpful here. To teach division, we first teach underlying skills, including number sense, addition, subtraction, multiplication, and place value. Reading comprehension depends on children recognizing words accurately.

B

By fourth grade, about 50 percent of the ability to comprehend passages was accounted for by the ability to read the words and apply phonics in word reading. As students progressed, comprehension of text depended more and more on other skills such as verbal reasoning, background knowledge, and knowledge of academic language. The Connecticut Longitudinal Study did not assess reading fluency. Torgesen (2005), at the Florida Center for Reading Research, has shown that verbal reasoning, topic knowledge, and language ability become even more important than fluency as students progress beyond the fifth grade.

These findings and others (Connor, Morrison, & Underwood, 2007) make it clear that the teaching of reading is not simply an equal "balance" of all subskills at each grade level. Rather, expert teachers know what subskills and processing capabilities to emphasize for which grade levels in order to get to the end goal of reading, which is comprehension. Many instructional approaches acknowledge the importance of all reading subskills, but an equal balance is not necessarily what gets the best results. Rather, the subskills of word recognition (i.e., phonology, letter naming, phonics, and word attack) should receive more emphasis early in reading development rather than later and will be more important for poor readers than good readers as students get older. Vocabulary and comprehension are important targets for reading instruction no matter what the student's age.

Chall's Pioneering Description of Reading "Stages"

Jeanne Chall, a professor of reading at Harvard for many years, developed the first-stage theory of reading development (Chall, 1996). Dr. Chall argued that "reading" was a word with very different meanings for children and adults of different ages and skill levels. In brief, her conceptual outline of reading stages differentiated the characteristics and demands of reading in six major periods of reading development. Her stages described well what children typically had to master as they progressed through a school curriculum. Chall's stage framework is still useful in understanding how the challenges of learning and teaching reading change over time. Her stages were defined as follows:

- **0 Prereading**; also called *Prealphabetic, Logographic*, and *Preconventional* (typical of preschool through late kindergarten)

- **1 Initial Reading or Alphabetic Decoding**; also called *Alphabetic Decoding Stage for Learning to Read Words* (typical of late kindergarten through early grade 2)

- **2 Confirmation and Fluency** (typical of grades 2 and 3)

- **3 Reading to Learn** (typical of grades 4 to 8)

- **4 Multiple Points of View** (typical of high school)

- **5 Construction and Reconstruction** (typical of college and adulthood)

Subsequent reading research has modified Chall's framework, especially in the areas of early word recognition and spelling. Current theories of early word-reading development emphasize the simultaneous and reciprocal growth of skill in all major processing systems (Ehri, 1996; Ehri & Snowling, 2004; Rayner et al., 2001; Stanovich, 2001) and the "amalgamation" of sound, spelling, and meaning in word learning. Phonological processing, orthographic processing, and meaning-making develop on a continuum, in tandem. Fluency is an essential component of skill development at each stage of learning. Verbal comprehension and vocabulary develop from the time children are infants. Exposure to text and reading practice are critical in moving the growth process along.

Ehri's Model of Reading Progression

Ehri's phases of word-reading development (Ehri, 1996; Ehri & Snowling, 2004), summarized in [the figure below] are widely referenced because their description rests on multiple experiments conducted over many years that have been replicated by other researchers. In Ehri's model, the ability to recognize many words "by sight" during fluent reading rests on the ability to map phonemes to graphemes or to master the alphabetic principle.

At first, children may recognize a few words as wholes by their configuration or the context in which they are found, such as on labels, boxes, or lists. However, progress in reading an alphabetic system occurs only if children learn how letters and sounds are connected. It is impossible for children to memorize more than a few dozen words without insight into the purpose of alphabetic symbols. Alphabetic learning is acquired through progressive differentiation of both the sounds in words and the letter sequences in print. Phoneme awareness is the foundation upon which letter-sound association can be constructed.

Ehri's Phases of Word-Reading Development

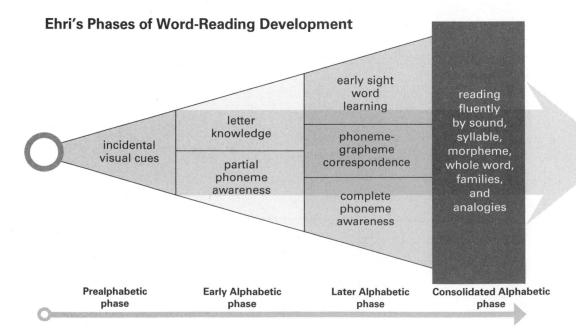

incidental visual cues

letter knowledge

partial phoneme awareness

early sight word learning

phoneme-grapheme correspondence

complete phoneme awareness

reading fluently by sound, syllable, morpheme, whole word, families, and analogies

| Prealphabetic phase | Early Alphabetic phase | Later Alphabetic phase | Consolidated Alphabetic phase |

As students learn phoneme-grapheme mapping, their orthographic processors begin to store memories for recurring letter patterns in the form of "chunks"— syllable spellings, common endings and word parts, and high-frequency words. Accurate and fluent perception of chunks, however, rests on phoneme-grapheme mapping.

[The table below] documents the phases of gradual integration of information from the four processing systems that underlie word recognition. To illustrate, children at the beginning decoding stage, who have been exposed often to print in books, often show surprising awareness of the letter sequences and orthographic patterns that characterize English spelling. They may not associate familiar letters and letter sequences with speech sounds, but they know something about the sequences of letters in print just from looking at so many examples (Treiman & Bourassa, 2000). For example, they may know that -**ck** is used at the ends, not at the beginnings, of words; that letters can be doubled at the ends, not at the beginnings, of words; that only certain letters are doubled; and that syllables typically contain a vowel letter. Orthographic knowledge, or knowledge of the spelling system itself, develops when children have internalized an awareness of the sounds in words to which the letters correspond.

Phases of Reading and Spelling Development

Phase ⟶	Prealphabetic phase	Early Alphabetic phase	Later Alphabetic phase	Consolidated Alphabetic phase
How Child Reads Familiar Words	Rote learning of incidental visual features of a word; no letter-sound awareness	Partial use of letter-sound correspondence; initial sound and salient consonants	Pronunciation of whole word on basis of complete phoneme grapheme mapping	Variously by phonemes, syllabic units, morpheme units, and whole words
How Child Reads Unfamiliar Words	Guessing constrained by context or memory of text	Constrained by context; gets first sound and guesses	Full use of phoneme-grapheme correspondence; blends all sounds left to right; begins to use **analogy** to known patterns	Sequential and hierarchical decoding; notices familiar parts first, reads by analogy to similar known words
Other Indicators	Dependent on context; few words; errors and confusions; cannot read text	Similar-appearing words are confused	Rapid, unitized reading of whole familiar words is increasing	Remembers multisyllabic words; analogizes easily, associates word structure with meaning
Spelling	Strings letters together, assigns meaning without representing sounds in words	Represents a few salient sounds, such as beginning and ending consonants; fills in other letters randomly; some letter names for sounds	Phonetically accurate; beginning to incorporate conventional letter sequences and patterns; sight word knowledge increasing	Word knowledge includes language of origin, morphemes, syntactic role, ending rules, prefix, suffix, and root forms

analogy
comparison

How *LANGUAGE!* Incorporates Reading Development Research

Chall's Stages of Reading Development	Typical of ...	How *LANGUAGE!* responds and incorporates this research to meet the needs of struggling readers:
0 Prereading	preschool through kindergarten children	Starting in Book A, students receive focused instruction on phonemic awareness and knowledge of the alphabetic code at the level of the word. This is complemented by an emphasis on deciphering and building meaning by focusing on the alphabetic code. *LANGUAGE!* builds in Ehri's contributions to this research through instruction that draws on the four language processing systems "in tandem."
1 Initial Reading or Alphabetic Decoding	students in late kindergarten through early grade two	
2 Confirmation and Fluency	students in grades two and three	Starting in Book C, *LANGUAGE!* students at this stage of reading development focus on integrating knowledge of the code with a focus on multisyllabic words and connected text to promote automaticity in reading. The emphasis on building meaning and understanding text structure continues. In accordance with Ehri's model, these students have mastered phoneme/grapheme mapping that empowers their orthographic processors to perceive syllables or "chunks."
3 Reading to Learn	students in grades four to eight	Starting in Book E, students at these stages of reading development broaden their focus to fictional text as well as expository text incorporating metacognitive strategies to deepen comprehension. Instruction expands the integration of scaffolded vocabulary, grammar, and written expression to interpret and create meaning, as we well as deepening the understanding of ways that writing shapes its voice through word choice and platform. Literacy skills, although more sophisticated, continue to be developed "in tandem."
4 Multiple Points of View	high school students	
5 Construction and Reconstruction	college students and adults	Through explicit instruction, *LANGUAGE!* helps students transition into self-motivated, life-long readers.

> **metacognitive**
> self-aware or self-monitoring

VOCABULARY DEVELOPMENT

"Brick and Mortar Words"

by Susana Dutro and Carrol Moran

The following is an excerpt from Dutro, S., & Moran, C. (2003). Rethinking English language instruction: An architectural approach. In G.C. Garcia (Ed.), *English Learners: Reaching the Highest Level of English Literacy* (pp. 239–241). Copyright 2003 by the International Reading Association. Reprinted with permission.

Through innumerable interactions in classroom, playground, home, and community settings, students are exposed to a range of language forms and may recognize and use an advanced form while lacking competence in more basic ones...

We define *forms* to include not only grammatical forms but vocabulary. Knowledge of word usage along with a rich and varied vocabulary are critically important aspects of language proficiency and essential to academic success (Beimiller, 1999; Kam'enui & Simmons, 1998; Moats, 2000; Stahl, 1999). An intervention study showed that the vocabulary knowledge and reading comprehension gap between English language learners and native English speakers can be significantly reduced through enriched vocabulary instruction (McLaughlin et al., 2000).

One way to think of vocabulary is as comprising "general-utility" and "content-specific" words. Continuing our architectural metaphor, we refer to these, respectively, as "brick" and "mortar" words. "Brick" words are the vocabulary specific to the content and concepts being taught in a given lesson and might include words (to pick a random sample) such as *government, revolt, revolution, polarized, habitat, climate, arid, predator, adaptations, germinate,* and *mitosis*. Traditionally, this is the vocabulary teachers preteach at the beginning of a content area lesson or unit. In the earlier grades, many of these words are nouns—*giraffe, hoof, stem, leaf*—and can be illustrated or labeled. In later grades these words tend to be conceptual.

"Mortar" words and phrases are the general-utility vocabulary required for constructing sentences—the words that determine the relation between and among words. They are the words that hold our language together, and understanding them is essential to comprehension. Some examples of mortar words are

- connecting words required to construct complex sentences: *because, then, but, sometimes, before, therefore, however, whereas*
- prepositions and prepositional phrases: *on, in, under, behind, next to, in front of, between*
- basic regular and irregular verbs: *leave, live, eat, use, saw, go*

- pronouns and pronominal phrases: *she, his, their, it, us, each other, themselves*
- general academic vocabulary: *notice, think, analyze, direct, plan, compare, proof, survive, characteristics.*

Many mortar words and phrases are basic vocabulary that may be unfamiliar to students who are learning English. Such vocabulary is best taught explicitly in the context of language use, as these words do not generally stand alone, but function within the context of a sentence or phrase along with brick, or content, words. Without deliberate instruction in the use of these words, students may not discern the time/place relationships among the rest of the words in a sentence or passage...

To illustrate the importance of addressing both brick and mortar vocabulary in language teaching that links function and form, let us consider ... the language function of *comparison.* Students are called on to compare across content areas. Teachers might expect students, for example, to describe the similarities and differences among geometric shapes or between the values of numbers *(larger/smaller, less/more)*, the relative nutritional value of different foods, the characteristics of bats and owls, or the personality traits of two characters in a novel.

Some possible brick vocabulary useful in discussing the similarities and differences between marine mammals and ocean fish, for example, is shown on the Venn Diagram... This vocabulary is essential to expressing the idea that there are physical and behavioral similarities and differences between these two types of animals. However, the brick (content-specific) words of the Venn diagram do not by themselves equip students to demonstrate their comprehension of that idea. They also need mortar words and phrases in order to generate the sentences that make it possible to make the comparison.

By removing the brick words that are specific to content, the mortar words and phrases used in sentences are revealed. For example,

> Marine mammals are warm-blooded, but fish are cold-blooded.
>
> _____ are _____ , but ___ are _____ .

The basic subject/verb/predicate adjective structure of this comparison sentence can be adapted by varying the verbs (e.g., *have, are, can, do, use*) or conjunctions *(however, whereas)*. The ability to manipulate these basic sentence structures using a variety of content is necessary for demonstrating conceptual understanding in a lesson calling for comparison.

B

Marine Mammals

- Born alive
- Produce milk (lactate)
- Warm-blooded
- Lungs
- Tails move vertically
- Pods

(differences)

- Ocean habitat
- Excellent swimmers
- Live in groups
- Vertebrates

(similarities)

Ocean Fish

- Born from eggs
- Do not produce milk
- Cold-blooded
- Gills
- Tails move horizontally
- Schools

(differences)

[C]omparative sentences range from simple to complex. Thus, the level of difficulty in a comparison task can be modulated by teaching the mortar vocabulary and sentence structure at levels of complexity appropriate to students' language skills, allowing students to engage in the work regardless of their level of English proficiency.

Another essential point is that these sentence frames can be used for comparing *any* two things. Explicitly teaching mortar vocabulary and how to construct various sentence frames helps students learn not only to compare marine mammals and ocean fish, but how to use language *to compare*, generally. Students will then be more apt to transfer those skills to making comparisons of triangles in mathematics, or of cultures in social studies. Wall charts labeled "Words and Phrases for Comparing" and "Sentence Frames for Comparing" serve as ongoing, practical references and become resources for student writing—and in conjunction with the instruction we have described, they enable students to develop metalinguistic awareness.

How *LANGUAGE!* Teaches Vocabulary Development and Usage

With its various approaches to explicit vocabulary instruction, *LANGUAGE!* reflects the research of Dutro and Moran regarding the teaching of content-specific vocabulary and essential words.

"Brick Words" and *LANGUAGE!*

LANGUAGE! teaches "brick" words—content-specific vocabulary—in multiple ways. Examples of resources include:

- Visual Vocabulary sections in Books A and B
- Systematic previews of vocabulary prior to lesson readings
- Point-of-use margin definitions in reading selections and contextual use to develop paraphrased definitions of key terms
- Word networks activities where students examine relationships between words such as synonyms, antonyms, attributes, and analogies
- Text Connections in the *Interactive Text* where **Comprehend It** or **Take Note** prompts guide the application of metacognitive study skills such as note-taking, paraphrasing, and asking and answering questions to clarify meaning in a passage.

"Mortar Words" and *LANGUAGE!*

LANGUAGE! explicitly teaches the spelling, meaning, and usage of general utility vocabulary—Dutro and Moran's "mortar words." Students encounter what *LANGUAGE!* refers to as "essential words" in the Decodable Text in every unit, as well as in *Interactive Text* activities.

Unit vocabulary words that follow the phonology sequence have also been chosen with an eye on students' "academic language" needs. The utility of essential words and their related structures and patterns quickly becomes apparent as lessons weave among the steps. Examples in *LANGUAGE!* can be found in:

- Step 4: Grammar and Usage where prepositions and prepositional phrases, being verbs, pronouns, and increasingly complex sentence structures are taught systematically and cumulatively
- Step 5: Listening and Reading Comprehension instruction that teaches Bloom's Taxonomy through the **Answer It** exercises

- Additional instructional activities that specifically address these word-level objectives, including:

  - **Choose It** and **Use It** which focus on proper word form for sentence context
  - **Diagram It** that focuses on how high utility words function within a sentence
  - **Find It: Essential Words** exercises that reinforce frequency of use and placement within the context of sentences
  - **Phrase Fluency** where essential word usage is reinforced within decodable phrases.

Function and Form

Instructional design in *LANGUAGE!* explicitly and cumulatively guides students as they practice and learn recurring patterns for putting brick and mortar words together. **Define It**, for example, creates a framework that explicitly links "function and form," as described by Dutro and Moran in their discussion of a rubric for compare and contrast exercises. In the example below, the content-specific "bricks" *bat, mammal, flies,* and *eats insects* are linked together by the "mortar," or essential, words of *A, is a, that,* and *and*.

And so...

word	=	category	+	attributes
bat		mammal	+	flies, eats insects

...becomes...

A *bat* is a *mammal* that *flies* and *eats insects*.

Students are explicitly taught, and quickly learn, that the **Essential Words** often follow similar patterns and work with different content words. As a demonstration, try this **Define It** exercise using these content words, while supplying and identifying the **Essential Words.**

word	=	category	+	attributes
atlas		book	+	contains maps

By understanding and practicing the layering of such "bricks" and "mortar," *LANGUAGE!* students build a solid foundation for reading comprehension.

EXPLICIT INSTRUCTION AND READING COMPREHENSION

The following excerpt reviews studies and draws conclusions regarding the effects of explicit instruction on reading comprehension.

Academic Literacy Instruction for Adolescents: A Guidance Document from the Center on Instruction

Torgesen, J.K., Houston, D.D., Rissman, L.M., Decker, S. M., Roberts, G., Vaughn, S., Wexler, J. Francis, D. J. Rivera, M.O., Lesaux, N. (2007). *Academic literacy instruction for adolescents: A guidance document from the Center on Instruction.* Portsmouth, NH: RMC Research Corporation, Center on Instruction.

The contents of this document were developed under a grant from the Department of Education. However, those contents do not necessarily represent the policy of the Department of Education, and you should not assume endorsement by the Federal Government.

Recommendation 1: Provide Explicit Instruction and Supportive Practice in the Use of Effective Comprehension Strategies Throughout the School Day

comprehension

the ability to understand

Increasing explicit instruction and support for the use of **comprehension** strategies is perhaps the most widely cited current recommendation for improving reading comprehension in all students (National Institute of Child Health and Human Development, 2000), particularly for those who struggle with comprehension (Gersten, Fuchs, Williams, & Baker, 2001). It is based on three kinds of evidence: (1) proficient readers monitor their comprehension more actively and effectively than less proficient readers do (Pressley, 2000); (2) proficient readers are more likely to use a variety of active cognitive strategies to enhance their comprehension and repair it when it breaks down (Nation, 2005); and (3) explicit instruction along with supported, scaffolded practice in the use of multiple comprehension strategies produce consistent improvements in students' reading comprehension (Rosenshine & Meister, 1994; Rosenshine, Meister, & Chapman, 1996).

In fact, in the Report of the National Reading Panel (2000), instruction in comprehension strategies is seen as the core idea, the essence, of comprehension instruction: "The idea behind explicit instruction of text comprehension is that comprehension can be improved by teaching students to use specific cognitive strategies or to reason strategically when they encounter barriers to comprehension when reading" (p. 4–39).

A comprehension strategy can be defined as any activity a student might engage in (including mental activities, conversations with others, or consultation of outside references) to enhance comprehension or repair it when it breaks down. Examples of effective comprehension strategies researchers have studied include:

- active comprehension monitoring that leads to the use of fix-up strategies when comprehension fails;
- use of graphic and semantic organizers, including story maps;
- question generation;
- summarization and paraphrasing; and
- selective rereading.

Evidence for the utility of explicit instruction in comprehension strategies has been found not only in controlled experimental studies but also in benchmark studies of more and less effective schools and teachers. For example, Langer's (2001) influential study of successful and less successful middle and high schools noted that effective teachers were much more likely than less effective teachers to explicitly teach students strategies for accomplishing their reading and writing tasks: "All of the more successful teachers overtly taught their students strategies for organizing their thoughts and completing tasks, whereas only 17% of the less successful teachers did so."

> *"... effective teachers were much more likely than less effective teachers to explicitly teach students strategies for accomplishing their reading and writing tasks ..."*

The reading comprehension strategies that have been studied most broadly to this point have general applicability across content areas and genres. ...

Studies

We now describe ... the strongest experimental studies we were able to identify concerning the effectiveness of explicitly teaching comprehension strategies ...

Dole, J. A., Brown, K.J., & Trathen, W. (1996). The effects of strategy instruction on the comprehension performance of at-risk students. *Reading Research Quarterly*, 31, 62–88.

For a more complete description of the experimental model, see Academic Literacy Instruction for Adolescents, p. 19, at

www.centeroninstruction.org/files/Academic%20Literacy.pdf.

In the strategy instruction condition, [fifth and sixth grade] students were taught how to make predictions about an upcoming selection, how to identify main characters, how to identify the story's central problem, and how to identify a problem's resolution. They were also told why these strategies were valuable and how to use them flexibly. Students were also taught to jot down key words and phrases using a story map provided by the teacher. During each period, the teacher provided some instruction and students read a story and answered practice comprehension questions. Initially, the teachers modeled each strategy and showed how to use it with the story map, then gradually shifted responsibility for using the strategy to the students, first having student leaders model using the strategies, then having students work in small groups, then pairs, and finally on their own. Throughout the process, the teacher acted as a coach, providing students with hints, reminders, and cues. Although new stories were used each day, the strategy instruction was cumulative and repetitive, and students' knowledge and control of the strategies grew over the five-week treatment period.

Outcomes were tested at the end of the intervention and at seven weeks following. For these tests, the students read one story (the instructed story), after receiving instructional supports for the story that were typical of each condition, and then answered 10 open-ended questions, scored by a rubric the researchers developed. Thus, the students in the story knowledge condition first had their teacher introduce critical knowledge for understanding the story, and then they read the story and answered comprehension questions. The next day, the students read another story (the independent story), without any prior instruction from their teacher, and answered 10 comprehension questions. The study's most important finding was that the students in all conditions performed essentially the same on the instructed passages, but the students in the strategy condition did significantly better than students in the other groups on the independent stories. These findings are illustrated graphically below, with comprehension scores derived from the scoring rubric plotted on the vertical axis.

The authors concluded that the study "indicated that at-risk readers who received strategy instruction made superior gains in comprehension performance over their peers who received story content or traditional basal instruction." Although the students performed essentially the same on stories they read after the teacher introduced the story and provided information about its content (in the basal and story content conditions), students in the strategy condition were able to generalize the self-controlled strategies they had learned during the instructional phase to enhance their performance when the teacher was not there to provide support.

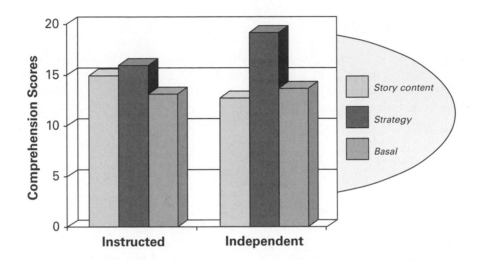

Klingner, J. K., Vaughn, S., & Schumm, J. S. (1998). Collaborative strategic reading during social studies in heterogeneous fourth-grade classrooms. *The Elementary School Journal,* **99, 3–22.**

For a more complete description of the experimental model, see Academic Literacy Instruction for Adolescents, p. 21, at

www.centeroninstruction.org/files/Academic%20Literacy.pdf.

The authors of this study examined "collaborative strategic reading," a method of comprehension strategy instruction that can be used with classrooms that are ethnically, socioeconomically, and academically diverse. The study was conducted in five fourth-grade classrooms in a school whose student population was 68% Hispanic, 24% white, 7% black, and 1% Asian or American Indian. ...

Students in both the instructional and control conditions learned the same content, a social studies topic. Each group received 11 45-minute classroom lessons. Both groups were assigned the same homework activity. Members of the research team provided all the instruction in this study. Students in the instructional condition were taught four reading strategies and given extended opportunities to practice these strategies while learning content in cooperative learning groups of five or six students. The strategies were (1) *preview*—look at the title and headings and make predictions about the passage while thinking about what you already know on the topic; (2) *click and clunk*—monitor comprehension by identifying difficult words and concepts and using fix-up strategies when the text does not make sense; (3) *get the gist*—restate the most important idea from a paragraph; and (4) *wrap up*—summarize what has been learned and ask some questions like those a teacher might ask.

The teacher introduced and modeled the strategies on the first three days, using the social studies text as a basis for the instruction, and also used a think-aloud procedure to help students understand why, how, and when the strategies were beneficial. From the fourth day on, students worked in small groups to learn the textbook content while they practiced using the strategies. A group leader, rotated each day, led the discussion, using the strategies to help the students understand and learn from the text. The authors observed that students generated a great deal of high-quality discussion of the text as they applied the strategies in their groups. The teacher also monitored the cooperative groups and provided additional instruction and support when necessary.

Students in the **control group** were not taught the reading comprehension strategies; rather, they were directly taught the content in the social studies unit. The students read the same content as those in the strategies groups, and the teacher led class discussion and provided additional instruction related to the content.

control group
experimental set, that for compariso purposes, is left unaffected by a process

The intervention effect was assessed with the Gates-MacGinitie test of reading comprehension, administered both before and after the intervention. At the conclusion of the instruction, the students were also administered a 50-question test on the unit's content. The pretest was used to control for small preexisting differences on the Gates-MacGinitie between groups. The analysis showed that the students who received the strategy instruction improved significantly more in general reading comprehension than those who received the traditional instruction. The strategies group improved from a raw score of 21.7 on the pretest to 24.7 on the posttest. Analogous improvement for students in the control group was 20.8 to 21.2. On the test that measured how well the students learned the content, the strategies group achieved a score of 25.1, while the control group obtained an average score of 23.9; neither was reliably different from the other.

> *"The analysis showed that the students who received the strategy instruction improved significantly more in general reading comprehension than those who received the traditional instruction."*

B

The authors concluded that the intervention was more successful than traditional ways of teaching in improving general reading comprehension; at the same time, the students in the strategies condition learned the basic content of the social studies unit just as well as the students who had received more teacher-guided instruction on the topic. Further, the authors' observations suggested that the cooperative learning format had successful drawn typically disengaged (lower-achieving) students into discussions, with resulting increases in their achievement.

Three additional studies are reviewed in the Center on Instruction report.
To download the complete report, go to:

http://www.centeroninstruction.org/files/Academic%20Literacy.pdf.

Conclusions about strategy instruction for adolescent readers

Looking across experimental studies of the effectiveness of comprehension strategies, we found that several common features seem critical to the success of this type of instruction; these features are also noted in the Report of the National Reading Panel (NICHD, 2000).

1. Initial discussions that help students become more aware of their own cognitive processes and learn about strategies they can use to help increase their understanding of what they are reading. Such discussions help establish the purpose of the work the students will be doing to improve their comprehension.

2. Explicit instruction from the teacher about the particular strategies being learned, with frequent think-aloud demonstrations by the teacher to show how the strategy is used during reading. This instruction includes a discussion of why the strategy can be useful, how to do it, and when it is appropriate to use. Teacher modeling of strategy use is essential.

3. Extended opportunities for students to practice using the strategies in meaningful literacy activities. Sometimes this practice is structured as small-group activities that encourage student discussion of both the text's meaning and how they are using the strategy to help them understand; sometimes it involves whole-class discussions. The purpose of this instruction and practice is to gradually transfer responsibility for selecting and using strategies from the teacher to the students.

LANGUAGE! and Explicit Instruction of Comprehension

LANGUAGE! offers extensive lesson-by-lesson guidance and resources to provide explicit instruction of comprehension strategies. Regular exercises and opportunities for modeling self-monitoring, questioning of text, responding to text-related questions, and "repairing" of comprehension are included across each unit's lesson plans, both at the word- and text-level.

In each lesson, point-of-use directions, rationales, and graphics refer teachers to the materials they need. Below are descriptions of a few of the resources in *LANGUAGE!* that support the explicit instruction of comprehension.

Building Academic Language

By teaching signal words from Bloom's Taxonomy and essential phrases, students learn how to accurately interpret and respond to spoken and written language, including comprehension questions. This skill is explicitly taught, modeled, and practiced using scaffolded instruction.

Signal words If the question asks...	How to answer Your answer must include...
Is/are	A "yes" or a "no"
Who	Information about a person or group
Do/does	A "yes" or a "no"
What	An action or name of a thing
When	A specific time, date, or event
Why	A reason or explanation
Where	A general location or specific place
How	The way something is done

From the Handbook Section of Student Text

Transparencies and Templates

LANGUAGE!'s set of Transparencies and Templates contains excellent tools for modeling comprehension for entire classes. These materials can be used to analyze text structures such as main ideas and supporting details (**Map It: Main Ideas**), author purposes such as compare and contrast (**Map It: Compare and Contrast**), story structure (**Story Map**), and character development (**Character Description**, **Character Profile**, **Character Trait**).

Text Connections

Text Connections, located in the back of the *Interactive Text*, pairs text with helpful questions in the margins. This configuration helps students practice self-monitoring of understanding as they read, and is readily incorporated into small-group discussions. Text Connections can also be downloaded from the *Instructional Planning Tools* CD, copied as transparencies, and used on an overhead projector for modeling of effective reading skills.

LANGUAGE!
RESEARCH BASE AND EFFECTIVENESS DATA

Hawthorne School District, California

Middle School — Retrospective Evaluation With State Data

Key Details

Total Participants: 649

Grade Levels: 6–8

Demographics:
- 93% Free/Reduced Lunch (FRL)
- 90% Non-white
- 42% English language learner (ELL)

Instructional Period:
- 2006–2007 school year
- 8 months of implementation

Instructional Time: 90 minutes

English Language Learners and Special Education:
- 59% of sample designated English language learners
- 25% of sample eligible for special education services

Measures:
- California Standards Test—English-Language Arts (CST—ELA)
- Test of Silent Word Reading Fluency (TOSWRF)

Hawthorne School District, located in the Los Angeles County basin in Southern California, is an urban K–12 district. It is composed of approximately 10,000 students.

During the 2006–2007 school year, *LANGUAGE!® The Comprehensive Literacy Curriculum* was implemented at all three of the middle schools in Hawthorne School District. All students in grades 6–8 who performed below the 60th percentile on a test of reading comprehension and fluency were placed in classrooms using *LANGUAGE!* as a core replacement. Approximately 1,000 general education, English language learner (ELL), and/or special education students were enrolled in *LANGUAGE!* classes for struggling readers.

Matched pre- and post-*LANGUAGE!* implementation data from the California Standards Test—English-Language Arts (CST—ELA) and/or the Test of Silent Word Reading Fluency (TOSWRF)—were available and analyzed for 649 students in grades 6 through 8.

Results

Findings from the retrospective evaluation of *LANGUAGE!* in Hawthorne School District suggest that *LANGUAGE!* positively impacted low-performing students' reading gains.

In the 2006–2007 school year, after eight months of *LANGUAGE!* instruction, students in grades 6 through 8 showed an average 5 point gain on the CST—ELA, while the gain for the same grades statewide was only 1.3 points (see Graph 1). By contrast, in the 2005–2006 school year, before receiving *LANGUAGE!* instruction, these same students showed an average loss of 4.7 points on the CST—ELA, while students in the same grades statewide showed an average 3.3 point gain.

The greatest gains were seen in sixth and seventh grades (see Graph 2 and Graph 3). Sixth grade students gained 3.7 points after *LANGUAGE!*, up from a 9.4 point loss observed in the year prior to receiving *LANGUAGE!* instruction. Seventh grade students gained 12.2 points after *LANGUAGE!*, up from a 7.5 point loss in the year prior to receiving *LANGUAGE!* instruction.

Further, the subgroup of Hispanic students—the largest ethnic minority group in the district—also showed significant gains after using *LANGUAGE!* in sixth and seventh grades relative to their performance in the year prior to using *LANGUAGE!* (see Graph 4 and Graph 5). Sixth grade Hispanic students gained 3.1 points after *LANGUAGE!*, up from an 8.4 point loss in the year prior to receiving *LANGUAGE!* instruction. Seventh grade Hispanic students gained 14.6 points after *LANGUAGE!*, up from an 8.3 point loss in the year prior to receiving *LANGUAGE!* instruction.

The percentage of students in grades 6 through 8 performing At or Above Basic on the CST—ELA increased considerably from spring 2006 (prior to *LANGUAGE!*) to spring 2007 (after *LANGUAGE!*) in subgroups of ELL students. Increases were 25 percent for English language learners at Levels 1 and 2 and 12 percent for English language learners at Levels 3, 4, and 5 (see Graph 6). During the same time period, the percentage of students statewide performing At or Above Basic increased by only 1 percent.

Finally, students demonstrated statistically and educationally significant grade equivalent increases in word reading fluency as measured by the Test of Silent Word Reading Fluency (TOSWRF). Over eight months of *LANGUAGE!* instruction, middle school students in sixth, seventh, and eighth grades showed grade equivalent increases of 1.3, 1.7, and 1.5, respectively, on the TOSWRF, indicating accelerated growth in word reading fluency (see Graph 7).

Graph 1.

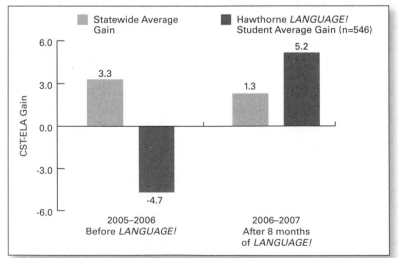

Grades 6–8 Average CST—ELA Scale Score Gain

Graph 2.

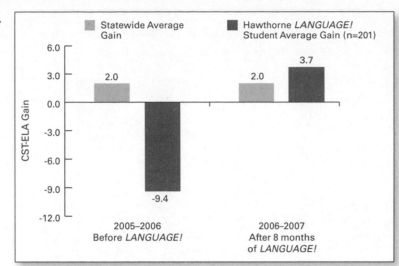

Grade 6 Average CST—ELA Scale Score Gain

Graph 3.

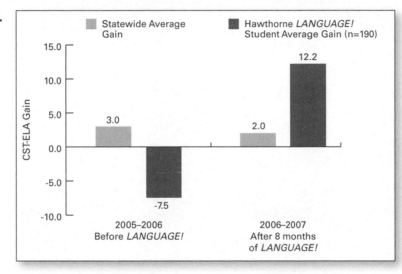

Grade 7 Average CST—ELA Scale Score Gain

Graph 4.

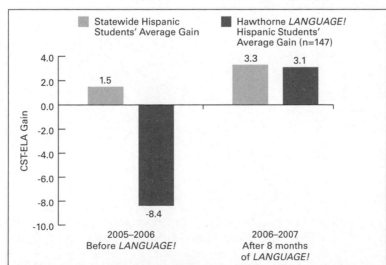

Grade 6 Hispanic Students' Average CST—ELA Scale Score Gain

Graph 5.

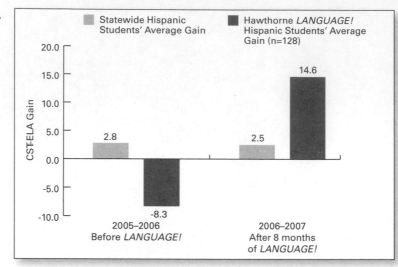

Grade 7 Hispanic Students' Average CST-ELA Scale Score Gain

Graph 6.

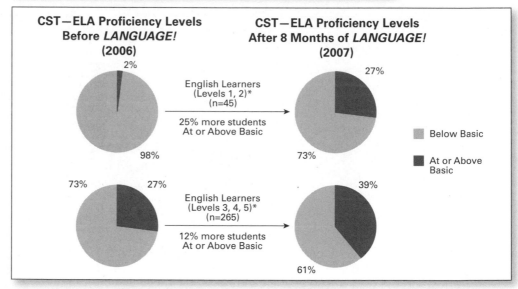

Graph 7.

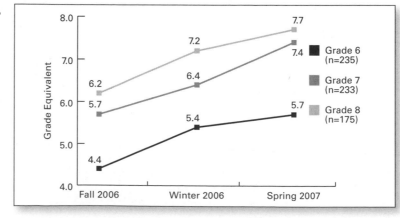

Grades 6–8 Test of Silent Word Reading Fluency (TOSWRF) Growth Over 8 Months

* These levels refer to the English language learners: Level 1 = non-English speaking; Level 2 = beginning; Level 3 = intermediate; Level 4 = basic; and Level 5 = proficient. Source: California English Language Development Test: Technical Report for the California English Language Development Test (CELDT). (2005). Monterey, CA: CTB/McGraw-Hill.

Lee County Public Schools, Florida

Districtwide Middle and High School — Retrospective
Evaluation With State Data

B

Key Details

Total Participants: 7,044

Grade Levels: 6–10

Instructional Period:
- 2005–2006 school year
- 6.5 months of implementation

Instructional Time:
- 45–90 minutes in middle school
- < 90 minutes in high school

Demographics:
- 60% Free/Reduced Lunch (FRL)
- 57% Non-white
- 15% English language learner (ELL)
- 24% Eligible for special education services

Measure: Florida Comprehensive
Assessment Test (FCAT), Reading Subtest

When Florida Comprehensive Assessment Test (FCAT) scores suggested that over half of Lee County's middle and high school students were reading below grade level, the school district responded by implementing *LANGUAGE!® The Comprehensive Literacy Curriculum* as its intensive intervention for 11,400 struggling readers in 84 schools.

Along with implementing a research-based and efficacious literacy curriculum, administrators in Lee County felt it was important to select a curriculum of standardized reading instruction to implement across the district. The aim of the standardized intervention plan was to eliminate disjointed and inconsistent instruction and provide more focused instruction in a district with a high rate of student mobility.

Nearly 275 teachers participated in a modified two-day training in the summer of 2005 and began instruction in the fall with the support of 25 secondary reading coaches. Of these coaches, three became certified area trainers for the *LANGUAGE!* curriculum. The following results demonstrate the progress of 7,044 students receiving *LANGUAGE!* instruction for 6.5 months in grades 6–10.1

Results

Lee County was successful in positively impacting thousands of struggling students across the district.

First, at every grade level, Lee County students who received *LANGUAGE!* instruction made significantly higher average gains on the FCAT than students statewide. The greatest difference was seen in grades 6 and 8, where FCAT Developmental Scale Score (DSS) gains for *LANGUAGE!* students were 87 points greater than statewide DSS gains (see Graph 1).

Second, the gains students made in the year that they received *LANGUAGE!* instruction were generally greater than those the same students made in the year prior to receiving *LANGUAGE!* instruction. Those *LANGUAGE!* students who had matched FCAT DSS data available for three consecutive years—2004, 2005, and 2006—demonstrated greater gains in the year following implementation of the curriculum compared with the year prior to implementation at almost every grade level. The greatest gains were seen in grades 6 and 7. At these levels, the positive gains were more than four times greater after *LANGUAGE!* implementation (see Graph 2). This is meaningful because it suggests that the increase in FCAT DSS gains was associated with the implementation of *LANGUAGE!*

Finally, gains made by *LANGUAGE!* students indicate a step toward closing the achievement gap in Lee County, as they were comparable across all subgroups, including ethnic minorities, English language learners (ELLs), Free/Reduced Lunch (FRL) recipients, and students eligible for special education services. For example, the difference between FCAT DSS gains for *LANGUAGE!* students in grade 7 who were in special education and those in general education was only seven points, whereas the difference between gains for *LANGUAGE!* students in special education and average gains made statewide was 70 (see Graph 3).

All of the above results contributed to significantly increasing the percent of Lee County students performing At or Above Grade Level in Reading on the FCAT. After only 6.5 months of *LANGUAGE!* instruction, 26.5 and 27.7 percent more students in grades 6 and 7, respectively, were performing At or Above Grade Level (see Graph 4).

At every grade level, FCAT average gains made by *LANGUAGE!* students were greater than those made statewide.

Graph 1.

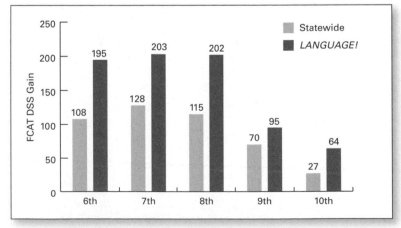

**2005–2006 FCAT Reading Developmental Scale Score (DSS)
Gains by Grade**

In grades 6, 7, and 8, FCAT Reading gains were substantially greater after the implementation of *LANGUAGE!*.

Graph 2.

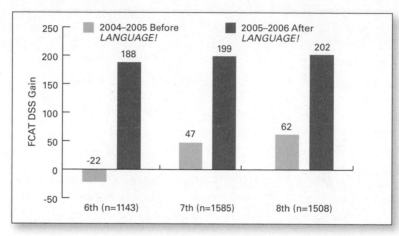

Gain Comparison: 2004–2005 Without *LANGUAGE!*; 2005–2006 With *LANGUAGE!*

Across all subgroups, FCAT Reading gains were, on average, 1.6 times greater for *LANGUAGE!* students than for students statewide.

Graph 3.

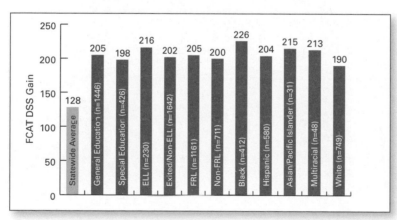

2005–2006 FCAT Reading Developmental Scale Score (DSS) Gains for Grade 7 by Subgroup

More than one-quarter of the district's sixth and seventh grade struggling readers placed At or Above Grade Level in Reading on the FCAT after 6.5 months of *LANGUAGE!* instruction.

Graph 4.

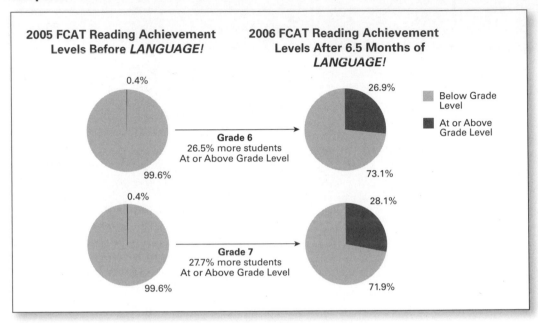

For additional Research and Background materials, including current studies and efficacy data, go to www.teachlanguage.com.

INSTRUCTIONAL PLANNING AND SUPPORT

Table of Contents

C

SCHEDULING OPTIONS

Significant literacy delays require intensive instruction to accelerate learning. *LANGUAGE!* adjusts to fit different schedules. In each schedule below, time is distributed strategically according to the number of minutes in the schedule.

90 Minutes

In a 90-minute lesson, time is distributed strategically across the Six Steps from Sound to Text.

	Minutes per Day
	90
Step 1	10
Step 2	10
Step 3	15
Step 4	15
Step 5	20
Step 6	20

45 Minutes

When less time is available, instruction can be distributed across several days.

	Minutes per Day	
	45	
	Day 1	Day 2
Step 1	10	
Step 2	10	
Step 3	10	
Step 4	15	
Step 5		20
Step 6		25

180 Minutes

When more time is available, additional options are possible. The potential to accelerate learning increases.

	Minutes per Day		
	180		
	Days 1–3	Day 4	Day 5
Step 1	15	15	15
Step 2	15	15	15
Step 3	20	20	20
Step 4	20	20	20
Step 5	30	30	30
Step 6	30	30	30
Independent Reading	20	20	20
Differentiation	30		
Challenge Text		30	
Writing Using the Challenge Text			30

In the same number of days, the number of lessons completed will vary depending on the number of minutes of instruction per day.

90 Minutes

🔔 Challenge Text ✍ Challenge Writing **D** stands for "Differentiation"

45 Minutes

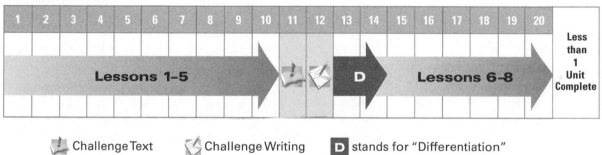

🔔 Challenge Text ✍ Challenge Writing **D** stands for "Differentiation"

180 Minutes

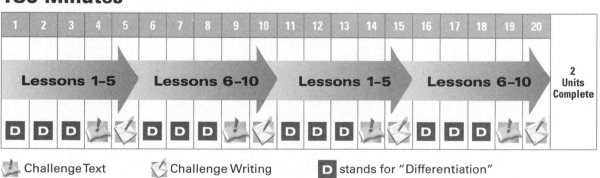

🔔 Challenge Text ✍ Challenge Writing **D** stands for "Differentiation"

180 Days of Instruction in *LANGUAGE!*

Based on your choice of scheduling options, the projected pace of progress through the book levels in *LANGUAGE!* will vary. The relationship between length of time in the instructional block and the number of books projected for completion in a year is as follows: 45-minute instructional block - one book level; 90-minute instructional block – two book levels; 180-minute instructional block – 3 book levels.

If you start in Book A, the chart below illustrates the gain in readability that can be expected in one year.

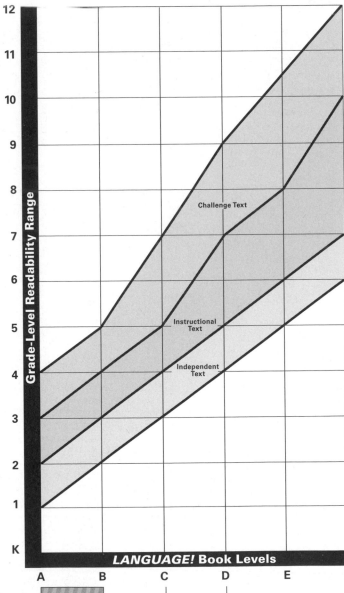

Depending on the scheduling option, in one year students will complete:

45-minute sessions = 1 book >

90-minute sessions = 2 books >

180-minute sessions = 3 books >

TEACHER SUPPORT

The *LANGUAGE!* instructional format provides a clear and organized path through the unit and through the lessons.

Unit 5 1

C

What are the unit objectives?

The **At a Glance for Teachers** provides the **Unit Objectives** that identify the content and skills covered in the unit.

The objectives are closely aligned with areas monitored by assessment and fluency tasks. The grid shows the lesson-by-lesson designation of instruction for each objective.

The icon designates lessons in which **Content Mastery** assessments occur.

Unit 5 — At a Glance for Teachers

Unit Objectives		Lessons 1	2	3	4	5	6	7	8	9	10
STEP 1 Phonemic Awareness and Phonics	Write the letters for the consonant sounds / l /, / f /, / z /, / s /, and the short vowel **o** (/ ŏ /) or / aw /).	•	•	•	•	⬈	•		•	•	•
	Say the sounds for consonants **l, f, z, s**, and short vowel **o** (/ ŏ /) or / aw /).	•	•	•	F	•	•	•	•	•	
	Say the names for consonants **l, f, z, s**, and short vowel **o** (/ ŏ / or / aw /).								F	F	
STEP 2 Word Recognition and Spelling	Read and spell words with double final consonants from this unit (**-ff, -ll, -ss, -zz**).					•			•		⬈
	Spell words with sound-spelling correspondences from this and previous units.	Pretest	•	•	•	⬈	Pretest	•		•	
	Spell the **Essential Words:** *here, there, these, those, where, why.*			•	•						
	Read fluently words composed of sound-spelling correspondences from this and previous units.		F	F	F		F				
	Read fluently the **Essential Words:** *here, there, these, those, where, why.*	•	•	•	•				F		
STEP 3 Vocabulary and Morphology	Identify categories to build word meanings.	•		•		•			⬈	•	•
	Use verb endings **-s** and **-ing** to identify present/present progressive verb forms.		•		•			•	⬈		
STEP 4 Grammar and Usage	Identify adverbs and prepositional phrases that act as adverbs.		•	•		•			•	•	⬈
	Identify present tense verb forms.	•					•		•	•	
STEP 5 Listening and Reading Comprehension	Read fluently phrases and sentences.	F	F	•			F	F	•		
	Preview reading selection using text features.			•					•		
	Make predictions about a reading selection.			•					•		
	Define vocabulary using a reference source or context-based strategies.			•					•		
	Identify factual information by listening to and reading informational text.			•					•		
	Summarize key points from a nonfiction selection.		•								
	Prepare to write an expository (explanatory) paragraph.					•	•				•
	Answer multiple-choice comprehension questions.					•				Ⓒ	
STEP 6 Speaking and Writing	Answer comprehension questions beginning with **where, why, what,** and **when** in complete sentences based on text.								•		
	Write sentences using a six-stage process.	•						•			
	Record information in an informal (two-column) outline.				•						
	Choose E's (examples, evidence, and explanations) to develop supporting detail sentences.		•		•	•					•
	Write a concluding sentence by restating the topic sentence of the paragraph.					•				•	•
	Write an expository (explanatory) paragraph on a nonfiction selection.					•			•	•	

Legend: • Instruction   Ⓒ Comprehension Proficiency   F Fluency   ▨ Benchmark Paper   ⬈ Content Mastery   ▨ Progress Indicator   ▨ End-of-Book Content Mastery

526   Unit 5 • At a Glance for Teachers

Timed fluency tasks are designated with an "F."

Instruction related to an objective is designated with a "•." This includes introductory, reinforcement, and assessment activities.

Ⓒ **Comprehension Proficiency** indicates when comprehension is assessed during the unit.

The **Unit Concepts** column provides teachers with a **brief overview of content** covered in the unit.

Unit Concepts

Unit 5 has a new letter represent vowel sounds. The letter **o** represents two different vowel sounds: short / ŏ / and / aw /. The sounds / f /, / l /, / s /, and / z / are usually represented by double letters **-ff**, **-ll**, **-ss**, **-zz**.
Some two-syllable words have a VC/V pattern. The first syllable is closed; the vowel is short. At the end of one-syllable words, after a short vowel, the sounds / s /, / f /, / l /, and / z / are usually represented by double letters **-ss**, **-ff**, **-ll**, and **-zz**.
Adding **-ing** to a verb means ongoing action and, when used with **am**, **is**, and **are**, ongoing action in the present. Words have **attributes** such as size, parts, color, and function. Attributes refine meaning and build associations.
The **-s** at the end of verbs and the **-ing** at the end of verbs used with **am**, **is**, and **are** signal present tense. Words or phrases (adverbs) that answer the questions *how, when,* and *where* can be moved within the sentence. Different present tense forms of **be** are used with different subject pronouns.
When we listen to and read informational text, we pay attention to the main ideas and supporting details. In order to gather information to use in our writing, we can reread the text and make note of important ideas and facts.
Questions begin with words that signal the kind of information required in the answer. Answers for questions beginning with **where** require a general location or specific place; **why** requires a reason or explanation. An **expository (explanatory) paragraph** explains something. To plan this type of paragraph, writers can create an informal outline. To write an expository paragraph, writers include a topic sentence, supporting details, E's (examples, evidence, and explanations), and a concluding sentence.

Unit Word List

Essential Words

here, there, these, those, where, why

Unit Words

l, f, z, s, o for short / ŏ /

bill	drill	hop	nod	sniff
block	drop	hot	not	sock
blond	fill	ill	odd	spill
blot	fizz	jazz	on	spot
bond	flock	job	pass	stiff
cannot	font	kill	pill	still
class	gill	kiss	pop	stock
clock	glass	lock	pot	stop
cost	golf	lot	rob	top
crop	got	mill	rock	will
dock	grass	miss	rot	
doll	grill	mob	sill	
dot	hill	mop	smog	

o for / aw /

boss	frog	lost
cost	frost	off
cross	log	on
dog		soft

Spelling Lists

Lessons 1–5		Lessons 6–10	
cross	*those*	boss	jazz
here	top	cabin	off
lock	*where*	cannot	profit
there	*why*	classic	rock
these	will	critic	visit

Bonus Words can be found in the *Student Text*, page H76. These are additional words based on the same sound-spelling correspondences from this and previous units. Use these words for expanded reading, spelling, and vocabulary development.

Essential Words are **high- frequency words** needed to read and spell approximately 85 percent of words found in print.

Unit Words are **composed of the sound-spelling correspondences** from the current and previous units.

Two **Spelling Lists** per unit assess students' knowledge of the unit's sound-spelling correspondences, **Essential Words**, and spelling rules.

Bonus Words provide additional words based on cumulative sound-spelling correspondences. These words are used for additional practice.

Unit 5 • At a Glance for Teachers **527**

What are you going to teach in each lesson?

The **Content Map** provides an overview of the specific content addressed throughout the unit. This map identifies the content focus in each lesson.

Unit 5

Content Map

Step	Lesson 1 (TE page 535)	Lesson 2 (TE page 544)	Lesson 3 (TE page 556)	Lesson 4 (TE page 570)	Lesson 5 (TE page 585)
STEP 1 Phonemic Awareness and Phonics	• Sound-spelling correspondences: Consonant sounds / l /, / f /, / z /, / s / represented by -ll, -ff, -zz, -ss Short vowel o (/ ŏ /)	• Sound-spelling correspondences: Consonant sounds / l /, / f /, / z /, / s / represented by -ll, -ff, -zz, -ss Short vowel o (/ ŏ /)	• Sound-spelling correspondences: Consonants l, f, z, s • The letter o represents two sounds: / ŏ / and / aw /	• Sound-spelling correspondences: Consonants l, f, z, s • The letter o represents two sounds: / ŏ / and / aw / • Letter-Sound *Fluency*	Content Mastery: Sound-spelling correspondences from this and previous units
STEP 2 Word Recognition and Spelling	• Words composed of sound-spelling correspondences from this and previous units • Essential Words: **here, there, these why, those, where** • Use of double letters **s, f, l, z**	• Words composed of sound-spelling correspondences from this and previous units • Essential Words: **here, there, these why, those, where** • Word *Fluency*	• Word parts from multisyllable words • Essential Words: **here, there, these why, those, where** • Word *Fluency*	• Words composed of sound-spelling correspondences from this and previous units • Essential Words: **here, there, these why, those, where** • Word *Fluency*	Content Mastery: Unit 5 Spelling Words (Lessons 1–5)
STEP 3 Vocabulary and Morphology	Multiple meanings of word: **jazz**	• Present progressive verb form	• Objects have attributes such as size, parts, color, and function • Idioms	• Present progressive verb forms	Multiple meanings of word: **rock**
STEP 4 Grammar and Usage	• Verbs	• -s means plural noun or singular present tense verb	• Predicate expansion using adverbs or prepositional phrases that act as adverbs • Sentence diagrams: Subject/Verb/Direct Object	• Predicate expanders and their movement to vary sentence structure	• Predicate expansion and punctuation to vary sentence structure
STEP 5 Listening and Reading Comprehension	Decodable Text: **"What is Jazz?" Mega-Dialog** • Phrase *Fluency*	Decodable Text: **"What is Jazz?" Mega-Dialog** • Summaries tell the most important information in a reading selection • Sentence *Fluency*	Instructional Text: **"Jazz: The Recipe"** Context-based vocabulary Factual information	Multiple-choice comprehension questions based on **"Jazz: The Recipe"** Topic sentence (Turn Prompt) for a summary of **"Jazz: The Recipe"**	Writer's Checklist: Expository (explanatory) paragraph
STEP 6 Speaking and Writing	• Sentences: Subjects, predicates (verbs), direct objects, and adverbial phrases based on **"What is Jazz?" Mega-Dialog**	E's (examples, explanations, or evidence) make supporting details clearer	Comprehension questions based on **"Jazz: The Recipe"** (Signal words: **where, why, what, when**)	Graphic organizer: Informal (two-column) outline for the topic, supporting details, and E's based on **"Jazz: The Recipe"**	Expository (explanatory) paragraph based on **"Jazz: The Recipe"**

Challenge Text for Extended Learning: "Growing Up with Jazz"
- Factual information and higher-order thinking questions
- Context-based vocabulary

Writing Using the Challenge Text
- Expository (Explanatory) Paragraph based on **"Growing Up with Jazz"**

| Vocabulary | Comprehension | Reading | Prewrite | Write | Benchmark Paper | Comprehension Proficiency |

528 Unit 5 • Content Map: Lessons 1–5

The Content Map provides the **specific content** covered in each Step of the lesson.

A **pattern of reading and writing activities** is signaled through the use of icons. The progression of activities is predictable across the ten-lesson sequence.

Icons signal when content is assessed throughout the unit.

Instructional Planning and Support • **92**

Fluency is emphasized throughout the curriculum. The type of *fluency* is related to the content of the step.

C

Lesson 6 (TE page 599)	Lesson 7 (TE page 611)	Lesson 8 (TE page 622)	Lesson 9 (TE page 635)	Lesson 10 (TE page 646)
• Sound-spelling correspondences for initial and final blends **sp-, gl-, bl-, -st** • Sound-spelling correspondences from this and previous units	• Sound-spelling correspondences from this and previous units • Syllable awareness	• Sound-spelling correspondences from this and previous units • Syllable awareness • Letter-Name *Fluency*	• Sound-spelling correspondences from this and previous units • Syllable awareness • Letter-Name *Fluency*	• Sound-spelling correspondences from this and previous units
• Words parts from multisyllable words • Word *Fluency*	• Two-syllable words	• Syllables • Short vowel sounds / ă /, / ĭ /, / ŏ /, and / aw / for **o** • Word *Fluency*	• Words composed of sound-spelling correspondences from this and previous units	Content Mastery: Unit 5 Spelling Words (Lessons 6–10)
Compound Words: structure and meaning	• Subject-verb agreement • Present progressive verb forms	• Present tense forms of *be* Content Mastery: Word Meanings and Present Tense Verbs	Multiple meanings of word: **spot**	• Idioms Word definition process
• Predicate expansion and punctuation to vary sentence structure	• Present tense forms of *be* • Subject-verb agreement	• Predicate expansion	• Tense Timeline: Present tense	Content Mastery: Adverbs and Present Tense Verb Forms
Decodable Text: **"What is Jazz?" Mega-Dialog** • Phrase *Fluency*	Decodable Text: **"What is Jazz?" Mega-Dialog** • Sentence *Fluency*	Instructional Text: **"Looking at Jazz"** Context-based vocabulary Factual information	Multiple-choice comprehension questions based on **"Looking at Jazz"**	Graphic Organizer: Informal (two-column) outline • Topic sentence for expository (explanatory) paragraph based on **"Looking at Jazz"**
• Sentences: Expanding the predicate and moving predicate expanders varies sentence structure	Concluding sentences for a paragraph	Comprehension questions based on **"Looking at Jazz"** (Signal words: **why, what, when**)	Graphic Organizer: Informal (two-column) outline based on **"Looking at Jazz"**	Expository (explanatory) paragraph based on **"Looking at Jazz"**

Challenge Text for Extended Learning: "The Duke Jazzes Newport"
   Factual information and higher-order thinking questions
   Context-based vocabulary

Writing Using the Challenge Text
   Expository (Explanatory) Paragraph based on **"The Duke Jazzes Newport"**

| Content Mastery | End-of-Book Content Mastery | Progress Indicator |

The V icon highlights locations across the lessons and steps focusing specifically on **vocabulary** development.

Comprehension proficiency is checked periodically across the units. The C icon indicates when these checks occur.

Unit 5 • Content Map: Lessons 6–10 **529**

How are you going to teach it?

Each unit's lesson planner allows you to see how instruction for the Six Steps unfolds across the lessons and how lessons incorporate each of the Six Steps.

The **Lesson Planner** maps out instruction, activities, and assessment necessary to develop the concepts and skills within and across steps.

The sequence of **instruction, activities**, and **assessment** is outlined in each lesson.

Introduce: Identifies when **new content** is introduced.

The ☆ icon identifies a path for **review or acceleration**. These activities, which are part of the comprehensive curriculum, are essential to address the unit objectives.

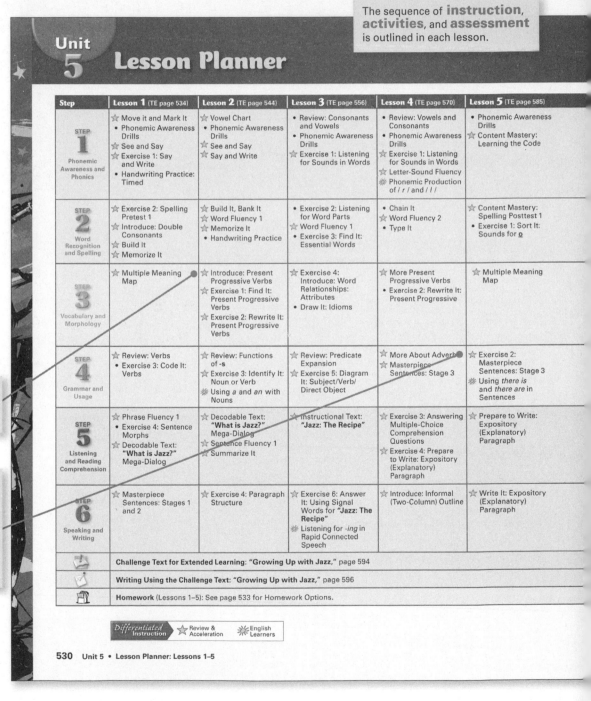

Step	Lesson 1 (TE page 534)	Lesson 2 (TE page 544)	Lesson 3 (TE page 556)	Lesson 4 (TE page 570)	Lesson 5 (TE page 585)
STEP 1 Phonemic Awareness and Phonics	☆ Move it and Mark It • Phonemic Awareness Drills ☆ See and Say ☆ Exercise 1: Say and Write • Handwriting Practice: Timed	☆ Vowel Chart • Phonemic Awareness Drills ☆ See and Say ☆ Say and Write	• Review: Consonants and Vowels • Phonemic Awareness Drills ☆ Exercise 1: Listening for Sounds in Words	• Review: Vowels and Consonants • Phonemic Awareness Drills ☆ Exercise 1: Listening for Sounds in Words ☆ Letter-Sound Fluency ※ Phonemic Production of / r / and / l /	• Phonemic Awareness Drills ☆ Content Mastery: Learning the Code
STEP 2 Word Recognition and Spelling	☆ Exercise 2: Spelling Pretest 1 ☆ Introduce: Double Consonants ☆ Build It ☆ Memorize It	☆ Build It, Bank It ☆ Word Fluency 1 ☆ Memorize It • Handwriting Practice	• Exercise 2: Listening for Word Parts ☆ Word Fluency 1 • Exercise 3: Find It: Essential Words	• Chain It ☆ Word Fluency 2 ☆ Type It	☆ Content Mastery: Spelling Posttest 1 • Exercise 1: Sort It: Sounds for o
STEP 3 Vocabulary and Morphology	☆ Multiple Meaning Map	☆ Introduce: Present Progressive Verbs ☆ Exercise 1: Find It: Present Progressive Verbs ☆ Exercise 2: Rewrite It: Present Progressive Verbs	☆ Exercise 4: Introduce: Word Relationships: Attributes • Draw It: Idioms	※ More Present Progressive Verbs • Exercise 2: Rewrite It: Present Progressive	☆ Multiple Meaning Map
STEP 4 Grammar and Usage	☆ Review: Verbs • Exercise 3: Code It: Verbs	☆ Review: Functions of -s ☆ Exercise 3: Identify It: Noun or Verb ※ Using a and an with Nouns	☆ Review: Predicate Expansion ☆ Exercise 5: Diagram It: Subject/Verb/Direct Object	※ More About Adverbs ☆ Masterpiece Sentences: Stage 3	☆ Exercise 2: Masterpiece Sentences: Stage 3 ※ Using there is and there are in Sentences
STEP 5 Listening and Reading Comprehension	☆ Phrase Fluency 1 • Exercise 4: Sentence Morphs ☆ Decodable Text: "What is Jazz?" Mega-Dialog	☆ Decodable Text: "What is Jazz?" Mega-Dialog ☆ Sentence Fluency 1 ☆ Summarize It	☆ Instructional Text: "Jazz: The Recipe"	☆ Exercise 3: Answering Multiple-Choice Comprehension Questions ☆ Exercise 4: Prepare to Write: Expository (Explanatory) Paragraph	☆ Prepare to Write: Expository (Explanatory) Paragraph
STEP 6 Speaking and Writing	☆ Masterpiece Sentences: Stages 1 and 2	☆ Exercise 4: Paragraph Structure	☆ Exercise 6: Answer It: Using Signal Words for "Jazz: The Recipe" ※ Listening for -ing in Rapid Connected Speech	☆ Introduce: Informal (Two-Column) Outline	☆ Write It: Expository (Explanatory) Paragraph

Challenge Text for Extended Learning: "Growing Up with Jazz," page 594

Writing Using the Challenge Text: "Growing Up with Jazz," page 596

Homework (Lessons 1–5): See page 533 for Homework Options.

Differentiated Instruction ☆ Review & Acceleration ※ English Learners

530   Unit 5 • Lesson Planner: Lessons 1–5

The ☀ icon identifies where the **Focus on Academic Language** activities occur. These activities target content often difficult for English learners and provide additional instruction and practice.

Lesson 6 (TE page 599)	Lesson 7 (TE page 611)	Lesson 8 (TE page 622)	Lesson 9 (TE page 635)	Lesson 10 (TE page 646)
• Phonemic Awareness Drills • Move It and Mark It ☀ Pronouncing Words Ending in a Consonant Sound	• Phonemic Awareness Drills ☆ See and Name ☆ Name and Write ☆ Syllable Awareness ☀ Phonemic Production of / z /	• Phonemic Awareness Drills ☆ Letter-Name Fluency • Exercise 1: Syllable Awareness	• Phonemic Awareness Drills ☆ Letter-Name Fluency • Exercise 1: Syllable Awareness	• Exercise 1: Listening for Sounds in Words
☆ Exercise 1: Spelling Pretest 2 • Exercise 2: Listening for Word Parts ☆ Word Fluency 3	• Build It	• Review: Syllables • Exercise 2: Sort It: Vowel Sounds ☆ Word Fluency 4	• Chain It	☆ Content Mastery: Spelling Posttest 2
• More About Compound Words ☆ Exercise 3: Sort It: Meaning Categories	• Exercise 1: Rewrite It: From Plural to Singular • Exercise 2: Find It: Present Progressive	☆ Exercise 3: Rewrite It: Forms of the Verb *Be* ☆ Content Mastery: Word Meanings and Present Tense Verbs ☀ Practice Using the Verb *Be* with Progressive Verbs	• Multiple Meaning Map	• Draw It: Idioms • Define It
☆ Review: Moving the Predicate Painters ☆ Exercise 4: Masterpiece Sentences: Stage 3	☆ Introduce: The Verb *Be* ☆ Exercise 3: Identify It: Forms of the Verb *Be* • Exercise 4: Choose It and Use It	• Exercise 4: Sentence Dictation	☆ Tense Timeline • Exercise 2: Masterpiece Sentences: Stage 3	☆ Content Mastery: Adverbs and Present Tense Verb Forms
☆ Phrase Fluency 2 • Exercise 5: Sentence Morphs ☆ Decodable Text: **"What is Jazz?"** Mega-Dialog	☆ Decodable Text: **"What is Jazz?"** Mega-Dialog ☆ Sentence Fluency 2	☆ Instructional Text: **"Looking at Jazz"**	☆ Exercise 3: Answering Multiple-Choice and Open-Ended Comprehension Questions	☆ Prepare to Write: Expository (Explanatory) Paragraph
☆ Masterpiece Sentences: Stages 1, 2, and 3	☆ Exercise 5: Concluding Sentences	☆ Exercise 5: Answer It: Using Signal Words from **"Looking at Jazz"**	☆ Prepare to Write: Expository (Explanatory) Paragraph	☆ Write It: Expository (Explanatory) Paragraph
Challenge Text for Extended Learning: **"The Duke Jazzes Newport"** page 654				
Writing Using the Challenge Text: **"The Duke Jazzes Newport"** page 656				
Homework (Lessons 6–10): See page 533 for Homework Options.				

The *Instructional Planning Tools* **CD** makes it possible for teachers to tailor and print the Lesson Planner. The CD allows teachers to incorporate parts of the **Planning and Pacing Guides** into their Lesson Planner, according to their students' needs.

Assessment Materials: Content Mastery tasks, **Summative Tests**, and **Progress Indicators** are distributed throughout the units.

Review: Indicates when to **review content**.

How can you differentiate instruction?

Three **Planning and Pacing Guides** provide ways to tailor the curriculum to address specific instructional needs.

Unit 5 — Planning and Pacing Guides
Differentiated Instruction

☆ **Review & Acceleration** activities designated with a ☆ in this Teacher Edition include new concepts, fluency and assessment tasks, and activities related to the Instructional Text in Steps 5 and 6. These activities form the core of this program's comprehensive curriculum. In the following two scenarios, use *only* the starred activities. Data from the assessment measures will help you determine whether students fit one of these scenarios.

1. **To address weaknesses in student performance.** Students whose performance falls below the cutoff test scores can repeat these activities to practice basic skills that need strengthening.

2. **To accelerate instruction for students who are demonstrating strong growth.** Students demonstrating strong performance can accelerate progress by focusing on the designated activities.

> The ☆ icon identifies activities for **review** or **acceleration** in the curriculum. Use of these **preselected activities** depends on student performance.

☀ **Focus on Academic Language** activities expand on and enhance unit-specific content. These activities appear at the point of use throughout the unit.

Lesson 1	Lesson 2	Lesson 3	Lesson 4	Lesson 5
	Step 4: Using *a* and *an* with Nouns	**Step 6:** Listening for *-ing* in Rapid Connected Speech	**Step 1:** Phonemic Production of / r / and / l /	**Step 4:** Using *there is* and *there are* in Sentences

Lesson 6	Lesson 7	Lesson 8	Lesson 9	Lesson 10
Step 1: Pronouncing Words Ending in a Consonant Sound	**Step 1:** Phonemic Production of / z /	**Step 3:** Practice Using the Verb *Be* with Progressive Verbs		

> The **Focus on Academic Language** activities are based on the content of the unit. They provide instruction and practice in areas identified in the **Contrastive Analyses** that can be of difficulty in learning Academic English. This chart displays all of the Academic Language learning lessons in the unit at a glance.

✓ **Special Instructional Support** activities customize teaching materials and provide opportunities for individualized instruction.

Lesson 1	Lesson 2	Lesson 3	Lesson 4	Lesson 5
Step 1: *Sortegories* CD: Sound Count **Step 2:** *Words for Teachers* CD: Word Card Generator *Words for Teachers* CD: Word Study Guide	**Step 1:** Folder Activity: Phoneme Discrimination—Short / a / vs. / o / **Step 2:** *Sortegories* CD: Sort It *Words for Teachers* CD: Fluency Builder Grid	**Step 2:** Folder Activity: Alphabetize Essential Words Units 3–5 *Sortegories* CD: Build It **Step 5:** *LANGUAGE! eReader* CD: **"Jazz: The Recipe"**	**Step 2:** Folder Activity: Tic-Tac-Toe with Essential Words **Step 3:** *Sortegories* CD: Morph It	**Step 2:** *Words for Teachers* CD: Word Card Generator—Sort Present and Present Progressive Verb Forms **Step 3:** *Sortegories* CD: Categorize It

Lesson 6	Lesson 7	Lesson 8	Lesson 9	Lesson 10
Step 2: *Words for Teachers* CD: Word Unscramble **Step 3:** *Sortegories* CD: Relate It **Step 4:** *Sortegories* CD: Phrase Building	**Step 2:** *Words for Teachers* CD: Word Search **Step 4:** *Sortegories* CD: Grammar Sort	**Step 4:** *Words for Teachers* CD: Word Card Generator—Build Sentences, Move Adverbial Information **Step 5:** *LANGUAGE! eReader* CD: **"Looking**	**Step 3:** *Sortegories* CD: Analogy Building **Step 4:** Folder Activity: Sentence Unscramble with Adverbs	

> The activities for **Special Instructional Support** feature the use of technology to provide reinforcement. The technology allows students to practice content and skills in a variety of formats, with teacher support or independently.
> - *Sortegories* CD
> - *eReader* CD
> - *LANGUAGE! Words for Teachers* CD

532   Unit 5 • Planning and Pacing Guides

How is daily instruction supported?

The lesson pages in the *LANGUAGE!* Teacher Editions bring the objectives, content, activities, and instructional directions together to guide and support teachers.

The **Transition Statement** identifies the focus for the step and provides links from step to step and from lesson to lesson within a unit.

The ☆ icon indicates that this activity is part of the **Review & Acceleration** path through the lesson.

Materials for each activity are listed at point of use.

The **level of scaffolding** is signaled by icons.

Explicit guidance is provided to deliver content.

When a new activity appears, a **Why Do/ How To** introductory explanation is provided.

The **Activity purpose** is stated in a "use" statement at the beginning of the activity.

Thumbnails of *Interactive Text* and *Student Text* pages guide teachers to the correct materials.

Key content is provided at point of use in the lesson.

Answers are provided for all activities.

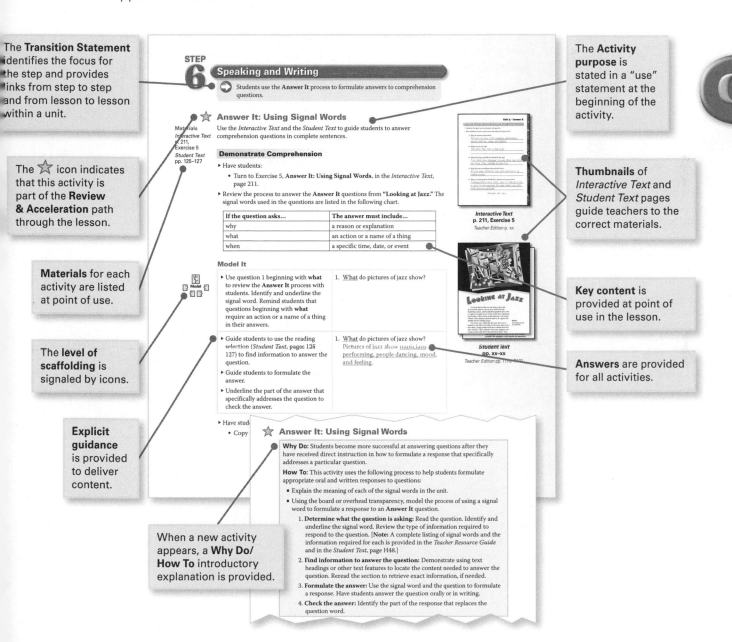

STEP 6 Speaking and Writing

Students use the **Answer It** process to formulate answers to comprehension questions.

Answer It: Using Signal Words

Use the *Interactive Text* and the *Student Text* to guide students to answer comprehension questions in complete sentences.

Materials
Interactive Text p. 211, Exercise 5
Student Text pp. 125–127

Demonstrate Comprehension

▶ Have students:
• Turn to Exercise 5, Answer It: Using Signal Words, in the *Interactive Text*, page 211.
▶ Review the process to answer the **Answer It** questions from "Looking at Jazz." The signal words used in the questions are listed in the following chart.

If the question asks...	The answer must include...
why	a reason or explanation
what	an action or a name of a thing
when	a specific time, date, or event

Model It

▶ Use question 1 beginning with **what** to review the **Answer It** process with students. Identify and underline the signal word. Remind students that questions beginning with **what** require an action or a name of a thing in their answers.	1. What do pictures of jazz show?
▶ Guide students to use the reading selection (*Student Text*, pages 125–127) to find information to answer the question. ▶ Guide students to formulate the answer. ▶ Underline the part of the answer that specifically addresses the question to check the answer.	1. What do pictures of jazz show? Pictures of jazz show musicians performing, people dancing, mood, and feeling.

▶ Have students:
• Copy

Interactive Text
p. 211, Exercise 5
Teacher Edition p. xx

Student Text
pp. xx–xx
Teacher Edition pp. 117 & T431

☆ Answer It: Using Signal Words

Why Do: Students become more successful at answering questions after they have received direct instruction in how to formulate a response that specifically addresses a particular question.

How To: This activity uses the following process to help students formulate appropriate oral and written responses to questions:

■ Explain the meaning of each of the signal words in the unit.

■ Using the board or overhead transparency, model the process of using a signal word to formulate a response to an **Answer It** question.

1. **Determine what the question is asking:** Read the question. Identify and underline the signal word. Review the type of information required to respond to the question. [**Note:** A complete listing of signal words and the information required for each is provided in the *Teacher Resource Guide* and in the *Student Text*, page H48.]

2. **Find information to answer the question:** Demonstrate using text headings or other text features to locate the content needed to answer the question. Reread the section to retrieve exact information, if needed.

3. **Formulate the answer:** Use the signal word and the question to formulate a response. Have students answer the question orally or in writing.

4. **Check the answer:** Identify the part of the response that replaces the question word.

LANGUAGE! LAUNCH: THE FIRST THREE WEEKS

A Three-Week Timeline for Implementing *LANGUAGE!*

This three-week timeline takes into consideration many of the issues that impact implementation of *LANGUAGE!* that are not addressed in the lesson plans. Its purpose is to help you tackle the task of learning a new curriculum through a series of small steps. As you gain familiarity with different aspects of the curriculum and all of its tools, you will be better positioned to monitor your pacing. This timeline offers reminders of important tasks that need to be completed during the first weeks of implementation. Explaining the research and clearly outlining expectations are key steps that help develop student acceptance of the program. The more familiar you are with the curriculum before walking into that first day of class, of course, the more confident and effective your teaching of *LANGUAGE!* will be.

Bridge for Books C and E

The Bridges for Books C and E are designed for use prior to beginning instruction when the results of the *LANGUAGE!* Reading Scale Placement Test indicate entry into Book C or Book E.

Purpose

The Bridge, a 15-day sequence of 90 minute lessons:

- Helps establish prerequisite content and skills for the first unit in Book C or E.

- Introduces you and your students to the components of the *LANGUAGE!* instructional materials.

- Creates familiarity with key instructional activities in the curriculum.

Instructional Focus

The *LANGUAGE!* Reading Scale Placement Test information provides a measure of the students' current reading level using a Lexile-based assessment tool. This measure provides an accurate indicator of students' level of reading comprehension therefore the content and skill emphasized in the Bridges focus on areas of literacy content and skills other than reading comprehension. In particular the focus is on prerequisite concepts and skills for success in Unit 13, the first unit in Book C; or Unit 25, the first unit in Book E. These prerequisites focus on major building blocks of the English language.

Book C Bridge Emphases	Book E Bridge Emphases
• Letter-sound correspondences • Sentence development • Paragraph structure	• Sound and syllable structure of words • Sentence development • Paragraph structure

Each of these building blocks deals with increasingly more complex demands of language literacy learning.

Required Materials

The main tools for teaching these 15 lessons are:

Book C Bridge	Book E Bridge
• The *Book C Bridge Teacher Edition* • *Bridge Interactive Text* • Book *C Student Text*, Handbook section	• The *Book E Bridge Teacher Edition* • *Bridge Interactive Text* • Book E *Student Text*, Handbook section

After you administer the Book C or Book E Baseline Assessment (see *Book C* or *Book E Assessment Teacher Edition*) and enter the data into the *LANGUAGE! Online Assessment System*, you should follow the lesson progression outlined in this Bridge to orient students to prerequisite content and skills while also familiarizing them with several of the frequently-used instructional activities they will use in the first unit of the book.

Week 1

Student Assessment

Before classes begin, go into the *LANGUAGE! Online Assessment System* to set up your class roster. (The pamphlet in the teacher's kit has the product registration key that is necessary to access the system; arrange a common password with your colleagues.) This will require some background information on each student, but you will only need to enter this information once.

Once classes start, immediately administer the four baseline measures. A master set of these tests is in the teacher kit and your district should have ordered classroom sets. Take two days to administer all four tests and begin scoring them.

The online system will track your students' progress during the year and from year to year. Enter the raw scores from the baseline measures. The online system will convert these scores into standard scores.

Introducing *LANGUAGE!* to Your Students

Most students benefit from understanding how they were placed in a *LANGUAGE!* classroom. Explain the school's placement criteria to the students. Go on to outline how *LANGUAGE!* looks different, sounds different, feels different, and truly is different from traditional English or literacy instruction. Because of these differences, students can expect a much more successful and satisfying experience. For more ideas on motivating the reluctant reader, see the section on Classroom Management on p. 293.

LANGUAGE! embraces an approach to learning that has proven its effectiveness. Share research on the brain with your students. Help them understand the role of the left hemisphere in language learning, the role of hemispheric integration, and the power of kinesthetic movement and multisensory activities that enhance learning and remembering. For more information on brain research and reading, see the Research and Background section on page 47.

Classroom Procedures

To set up your classroom, consider all of the equipment and tools necessary for teaching *LANGUAGE!* Students need to be able to see the overhead projector screen or Smart Board, for example. The pocketchart needs to be visible and readily accessible. Desks need to be arranged so that students can easily move from whole-group instruction to follow-up activities with partners and small groups. You should have easy access to all areas of your classroom to answer questions and to keep inappropriate behaviors in check.

Guide your students in developing routines in your classroom, including entrance and exit practices that maximize instructional time. Establish how students access the materials they need for the various activities. When use of these materials are first called for, model where and how to use them.

Students need to take responsibility for their behavior in your class. Establish simple positive reinforcements for good behavior, attitude, and class participation. For many *LANGUAGE!* students, it has been a long time since they experienced success in a classroom. For many, their academic frustrations have contributed to behavioral problems. They need to feel it is worthwhile for them to make the effort, and believe that they can make progress and succeed. For more information on establishing classroom routines see Classroom Management page 293.

Curriculum Preparation

Before you start teaching the units in a book, take the End-of-Book Content Mastery test. These tasks reflect the central objectives from the six units of instruction. Taking the test is a great way for you to preview what will be taught, know what mastery "looks like," and measure personal comfort in teaching the content.

Completing all of that unit's Content Mastery tasks before teaching that unit is excellent preparation for teaching the content.

Teaching the Curriculum

Instruction should begin as soon as possible. As you introduce instructional routines, teach them within the framework of a lesson; for example, teach the movements for the phonemic awareness drills as they occur within the lesson. Even in a 90-minute block, finishing a lesson in one day will be a challenge, especially at first. As your familiarity and comfort level with teaching strategies and routines increases, you will move through the lessons more quickly.

In a very real sense, students placed in a *LANGUAGE!* classroom are running out of time. Every day should be focused on advancing their literacy skills, building academic momentum, and encouraging their progress.

TEACHER'S TIP

For insights and suggestions on corrective feedback for behavioral and academic performance, see the section on Classroom Management on p. 293.

Week 1

Week 1 Checklist ✔

Student Assessment

☐ Set up your class roster and enter baseline data into the *LANGUAGE! Online Assessment System*

☐ Administer baseline measures in Fluency, Spelling, Comprehension, and Writing

Research/Rationale

☐ Help students understand how they were placed in a *LANGUAGE!* classroom

☐ Explain the research that is the basis for the phonemic awareness drills

Classroom Management

☐ Set up a classroom conducive to *LANGUAGE!*

☐ Establish entrance/exit routines

☐ Create student accountability for behavior

Curriculum Preparation

☐ Preview Content Mastery materials

Teaching the Curriculum

☐ Begin teaching Lesson 1

Week 2

Student Assessment

Use the letters that are available on our Web site to inform parents about their children's placement in *LANGUAGE!* (You will find an example on page 320.) These letters will help introduce *LANGUAGE!* to your students' families, provide information about how their child is performing, as well as establish a positive link between your classroom and your students' homes. Use the *On line Assessment System* to print a class report using the baseline data. Looking at your class as a whole will help you anticipate what it will take to move them forward!

Scaffolded Instruction

As instruction progresses, the lesson plan calls for frequent fluency practice. Take the time to explain the power of repeated readings. Students will be asked to reread fluency passages as well as the instructional with a focus on improving fluency and enhancing comprehension. You need to silence the age-old cry: "We've already read this!" As students begin to chart their fluency, they will see their rising fluency rates as one of the first real signs of progress.

Make sure students know the fluency goal for their respective books. (See page 34 in *Assessment: Teacher Edition* for each book's "Target Number of Words Correct Per Minute.") Explain that it is important that they practice individual words—along with phrases , sentences, and passages—to improve their fluency.

Your students also need to understand that fluency is more than rate. They need to be reading with **prosody** . Activities like Sentence Morphs and Phrase It give your students practice in determining the meaningful chunks within a sentence. From the very beginning, your modeling of smooth, even reading will be essential.

> **prosody**
> stress and intonation

Classroom Procedures

Because of the frequent nature of fluency practice, it is important to establish a routine to move smoothly in and out of fluency drills. Model the role of the reader and the monitor and reinforce behavioral expectations. Students need to be charting fluency rates, but this does not necessarily have to happen at the same time as the practice.

Fluency practice is designed as a partner activity. As instruction progresses, there are more opportunities for partner and small group work. Set up behavioral expectations for any partner or small group assignment. Assigning jobs within a small group helps each person take responsibility for the work done by the group. Use the timer for independent work sessions. *Hint: Always underestimate the amount of time needed to complete the assigned task!*

Week 2

Curriculum Preparation

Load the *Sortegories* and *eReader* CDs on at least one classroom computer. Once the software is up and running, you can begin to familiarize yourself with the potential of each program as an instructional tool. The easiest way to introduce the software is to demonstrate an activity to the whole class. An LCD projector or a Smart Board, if available, allows the activities to be experienced by the entire class while you demonstrate the use of the programs.

Teaching the Curriculum

By the end of week 2, students should have finished a minimum of four lessons. While it may still take more than one day to teach a lesson, with any luck, you should also be feeling more comfortable with the curriculum. Make sure you are giving daily feedback on the completed *Interactive Text* pages. It is not necessary to collect these pages each day and grade them. By circulating around the classroom, you should be checking their work and issuing daily participation grades that reflect your students' efforts.

Week 2 Checklist ✔

Student Assessment

- ☐ Send out parent letters with baseline data
- ☐ Print out report of class baseline data

Research/Rationale

- ☐ Explain purpose of fluency practice
- ☐ Set fluency goals for class

Classroom Procedures

- ☐ Teach students procedures for fluency activities
- ☐ Set up behavioral expectations for any partner or small group assignment

Curriculum Preparation

- ☐ Load *Sortegories* and *eReader* CDs on classroom computer
- ☐ Introduce *Sortegories* and *eReader* activities to students

Teaching the Curriculum

- ☐ Complete Lessons 1–4

Week 3

Student Assessment

By week 3, you should have administered and scored the first set of Content Mastery tasks. Make every effort to score the tests the same day as they are administered. These scores should then be entered into the *On line Assessment System.* Timely entry of the data keeps the task manageable. The *On line Assessment System* will highlight those students whose scores suggest a need for reinforcement or reteaching.

Research/Rationale

Provide explicit feedback to your students on each Content Mastery task. Help students understand the purpose of reviewing the Content Mastery tasks and the power of putting their thought process into words. This also provides one more opportunity to reinforce the skills being assessed.

As you become more comfortable in managing the curriculum, homework may become an appropriate tool to reinforce classroom learning. Students may benefit from understanding the rationale for homework assignments and how these exercises benefit them. (See the section on Classroom Management for research-based suggestions on best practices for homework; and review Homework Options before each unit and on the *Instructional Planning Tool* CD.)

Curriculum Preparation

Begin using the *LANGUAGE! Words for Teachers* CD to create supplemental activities. With this CD, you can make worksheets tied to unit concepts in minutes. You can create meaningful homework activities that reinforce skills taught in the classroom. As students learn the procedures for completing some of these activities, you can use this CD—along with other activities—to create lesson plans for substitute teachers and not lose an entire day of instruction.

Classroom Procedures

Review Content Mastery tasks with students after these tasks have been administered and scored.

As classroom procedures develop, students will need to learn how to do certain independent activities. This will allow you to work with small groups of students or individuals who need reteaching or have make-up work to complete. Folder activities and independent reading are two independent activities that will become easy to prepare, model, and reinforce.

Students should be gaining familiarity with the Six Traits writing rubric used in this curriculum. (See the Student Handbook, page H64.) Consider putting a copy of this rubric in your students' notebooks as well as up on your wall. Research reinforces the need for students to know how their writing will be evaluated.

Week 3

Teaching the Curriculum

Share **Content Mastery** tasks with students. This feedback not only reinforces the skills being assessed, but also values the activity and the effort required to complete them. Students need to recognize the need to put forth their best efforts. A whole group review is a simple way to reinforce learning and solidify their skill base. This feedback is most effective when it follows the assessment task in a timely manner. By this point, homework should be part of the daily routine.

You should feel increasing confidence with *LANGUAGE!*'s instructional flow. Your goal should be to move through the curriculum with great fidelity and appropriate pacing. Trust the curriculum. Fifteen days per unit will help you and your students stay on track to complete a book in a semester.

Week 3 Checklist ✔

Student Assessment
- ☐ Administer **Content Mastery** tasks
- ☐ Enter scores into the *Online Assessment System*

Research/Rationale
- ☐ Explain the purpose of "think aloud" activity with **Content Mastery** tasks
- ☐ Share rationale and guidelines for all homework assignments

Classroom Procedures
- ☐ Teach procedures for reviewing **Content Mastery** scores
- ☐ Model independent review activity
- ☐ Share the writing rubric with students

Curriculum Preparation
- ☐ Create a worksheet with *LANGUAGE! Words for Teachers* CD

Teaching the Curriculum
- ☐ Share **Content Mastery** tasks with students
- ☐ Assign homework on a regular basis
- ☐ Continue moving forward with lessons in the initial unit

A Perfect World

In a perfect world, all students would reach mastery in each unit, all students would end a book conveniently at the end of the year, and all students would move out of intervention. But this isn't a perfect world, so we often have to negotiate solutions. Here are some thoughts for a couple of the more frequently asked questions in our less-than-perfect world:

Managing the meaning of mastery... Data from the **Content Mastery** tests should inform instruction and not be an impediment to movement through the curriculum. Keep these steps in mind each time you administer the mastery tasks in a unit:

- Teach the unit.
- Administer the Content Mastery tasks as directed in the *LANGUAGE!* Teacher Editions, score the tasks, and reinforce and/or re-teach as indicated according to the guidelines.
- Re-administer the missed items. This is an important step to see if further reinforcement or re-teaching improves student performance.
- Aim for 80% of the students in the class to get 80% or better on the Content Mastery.
- Move on to the next unit.
- Monitor closely the 20% of the students who didn't reach 80%. Scaffold instruction and provide extra practice to those students.

When the end of the school year does not coincide with the end of a book ... While the ideal pacing of instruction in *LANGUAGE!* should bring students to the end of a book as the end of the school year arrives, this type of pacing nirvana doesn't always occur. There are several options for managing this imperfection in timing—each with advantages and disadvantages. These options are outlined on the attached PDF. The bottom line recommendation is that the *LANGUAGE!* Summative Tests and Progress Indicators are to be administered at the end of each book as mapped out in the *LANGUAGE!* Teacher Editions. When this is not possible, the advantages and disadvantages outlined in the chart should help decision-makes to make informed choices.

Thinking ahead... Since many students in *LANGUAGE!* will continue in the curriculum in the coming year, we encourage teachers to enter data for Content Mastery, Summative Test, and Progress Indicator data into the *LANGUAGE!* Online Assessment System (LOLA). This system is designed to capture longitudinal performance data electronically for ease of transmission from year-to year. The good news is that there have been many changes to LOLA this year making it easier to both collect and report individual, class, and district-level information.

Nancy Eberhardt
Editorial Director, *LANGUAGE!*

When the end of the school year does not coincide with the end of a book in *LANGUAGE!*...While it would be ideal if the end of a school year lined up perfectly with the completion of a book in *LANGUAGE!,* this perfection in timing often does not happen. The imperfection of timing presents some options for *LANGUAGE!* users to consider. Each option has its advantages and disadvantages.

Option	Advantage	Disadvantage
Use local or state data to measure changes in learning.	The use of local or state data, rather than *LANGUAGE!*-related measures, preserves the measures associated with the curriculum for use at the end of the book.	State or local test content and skills may not be related to the content or skills in the *LANGUAGE!* curriculum. Often the content is different than what the students are prepared to handle based on instruction.
Administer the Progress Indicator (*LANGUAGE!* Reading Scale, TOSCRF, and TWS-4) at the end of the year	The use of the Progress Indicators allows for calculable changes from previous administration. If students do not complete the book by the end of the year and the Progress Indicators are administered, use caution in interpreting the results.	The use of the Progress Indicators at the end of the year, in addition to the end of the book, increases the potential impact of a practice effect by using the test more frequently than intended. The practice effect, in turn, impacts the interpretation of the results.
Administer the End-of-Book Content Mastery Tests at the end of the year	The use of the End-of-Book Content Mastery Tests can inform the instructional process for the following year when students resume instruction, factoring in the impact of the summer as well. Teachers need to be able to evaluate student performance in light of the content that has and has not been covered instructionally at the time of test-taking.	The End-of-Book Content Mastery Tests are curriculum-based, which means that performance is based on the opportunity to learn the specific content and skills in the curriculum. The use of these measures at the end of the year rather than the end of the book is problematic, because the assessment includes material for all units in the book. Students asked to take the Summative Tests before completing all of the units are vulnerable to weaker performance than when having the opportunity to complete all of the units before taking these measures.
Use the Content Mastery and fluency data	The use of the Content Mastery tasks and fluency can inform the instructional process for the following year when students resume instruction, factoring in the impact of the summer as well.	There is no point of comparison for interpreting the results.

The recommendation is that the Summative Tests and Progress Indicators be administered at the end of each book as mapped out in the *LANGUAGE!* Teacher Editions. When that is not possible, the advantages and disadvantages outlined above for each option allows decision-makers to make an informed choice.

Table of Contents

D

RESEARCH BITE

"Results from large and well-studied populations with reading disability confirm that in young school-aged children, as well as in adolescents, a deficit in phonology represents the most robust and specific correlate of reading disability. Such findings form the basis for the most successful and evidence-based interventions designed to improve reading" [1]

Shaywitz & Shaywitz, 2007

RESEARCH: WHY DO STEP 1

Phonemic awareness refers to the recognition of sounds in spoken, not written, language. It is the understanding that speech is made up of a series of individual sounds that can be manipulated to affect meaning. The ability to use phonics as a means to decode printed words is dependent upon students understanding that speech is made up of individual sounds—that is, students' phonemic awareness.

Poor readers' mental representations of the internal details of spoken words tend to be incomplete, nonspecific, or erroneous (Stone & Brady, 1995). Recognizing all the consonants in blends, distinguishing similar vowels while spelling words and learning their meanings, and repeating the sounds of similar words such as *reintegrate* and *reiterate* is especially problematic for students with weak phonological processing (Moats, 1996; 2000). Therefore, students often need practice with the same phonological awareness tasks that facilitate reading and spelling acquisition in young children, but with different methods, timing, and conversation about phonology. Even though the approach may be different for older children, phonemic awareness is a critical building block for comprehension (Curtis, 2004). Curtis has found that there are middle and high school students who have reading problems that result from not having mastered the alphabetic principle. It is estimated that at least one out of every ten adolescents has serious word identification difficulties stemming from problems associated with the phonological aspects of word analysis (Curtis & Longo,1999; 2004).

How *LANGUAGE!* Does It

LANGUAGE! addresses phonemic awareness and phonics by:

- Explicit instruction in phoneme awareness and manipulation
- Developing letter-sound and letter-name fluency and automaticity
- Explicit instruction and extended practice of the alphabetic principle
- Instruction focused on morpheme awareness, including prefixes, suffixes, and inflectional endings
- Instruction and practice of syllable awareness and identification.

Sound it Out

	Read It!	Hint	Answer
1.	SHOCKED CUSSED TOE	*person*	
2.	SAND TACKLE LAWS	*fictional character*	
3.	MY GULCH HOARD UN	*person*	
4.	MOW BEAD HICK	*book*	
5.	TALL MISCHIEF HER SUN	*person*	
6.	CHICK HE TUB AN AN US	*product*	
7.	THOUGH TIGHT AN HICK	*thing*	
8.	AISLE OH VIEW	*phrase*	
9.	TUB RAID HEAP HUNCH	*TV show*	
10.	CARESS TOUGHER CLUMP US	*person*	
11.	DOCKED HEARSE WHOSE	*person*	
12.	THUMB ILL KEY WAKE OWL LICKS HE	*place*	
13.	AGE ANT HUB BLOWS HEAVEN	*fictional character*	
14.	THESE HOUND DOVE MOO SICK	*movie*	
15.	BUCKS SPUN HE	*fictional character*	

Key Terms

digraphs combinations of two consonants that together represent one sound; examples *sh, ch, th, gh*

blends phonemes where two or more consonants appear together in a word, with each consonant retaining its sound; examples: *str-* in the word *straight*

phonograms letter-sound combinations that include more than one grapheme or phoneme; examples *-ack, -oke, -ump.*

diphthongs phonemes where one vowel sound glides into another in the same syllable; examples: *oi, oy, ow, ou*

What do you want students to learn?

- Phoneme awareness
- Short, long, and variant vowel sounds
- Consonant sounds: stable, **digraphs** , **blends** , and clusters
- Schwa
- Common **phonograms**
- Syllable awareness
- Syllable types: closed, final silent **-e**, **r**-controlled, open vowel **digraphs** , consonant + **le**, and **diphthongs**
- The syllabication process
- Suffixation: pronunciation and spelling.

In Books A and B, students manipulate sounds in spoken words. Then they use letter cards to represent sounds.

In Books C–F, students identify and apply syllable types to decode words.

What You Need to Know

What is the difference between phonemes, phonemic awareness, and phonics?

Distinguishing between sounds within words and establishing the relationship between sounds and letters are essential for beginning and struggling readers. For reading teachers, knowledge of the various *ph* words is helpful in creating a conceptual framework for teaching these vital skills.

As defined by the International Dyslexia Association:

> "Phonology is the study of sounds and how they work within their environment. A **phoneme** is the smallest unit of sound in a given language that can be recognized as being distinct from other sounds in the language. Phonological awareness is the understanding of the internal linguistic structure of words. An important aspect of phonological awareness is **phonemic awareness** or the ability to segment words into their component sounds."

*While **phonics**, or sound-symbol association, is explained as:*

> "the knowledge of the various sounds in the English language and their correspondence to the letters and combinations of letters which represent those sounds. Sound-symbol association must be taught (and mastered) in two directions: visual to auditory and auditory to visual. Additionally, students must master the blending of sounds and letters into words as well as the segmenting whole words into the individual sounds."

 Define these key terms and offer examples.

phoneme _____

_____

phonemic awareness _____

_____

phonics _____

_____

What is the difference between a consonant sound and a vowel sound?

The sounds of English are categorized as either consonants or vowels. Of the 40 or more speech sounds in our language, 25 are consonant sounds and 15 are vowel sounds. What is the difference between these types of sounds?

Consonant sounds restrict the flow of air during production. Consonants are **closed** sounds because they close off the flow of air. A part of our vocal apparatus that allows us to speak, such as lips, teeth, and/or tongue, closes off the flow of air when consonant sounds are produced.

Each category of consonant sound is labeled according to the degree to which the air is stopped. For example, **stops** are characterized by closure of the airflow with the lips, teeth, or tongue (e.g., / m /, / b /, / t /). In contrast, **fricatives** narrow the distance between the articulators but do not stop the airflow completely (e.g., / s /, / z /, / f /). The following chart shows the relationship between the mouth position and air restriction for the production of consonant sounds.

		Mouth Position						
		Lips	Lips/Teeth	Tongue Between Teeth	Tongue Behind Teeth	Roof of Mouth	Back of Mouth	Throat
Type of Consonant Sound	Stops	/p/ /b/			/t/ /d/		/k/ /g/	
	Fricatives		/f/ /v/	/th/ /_th_/	/s/ /z/	/sh/ /zh/		/h/
	Affricatives					/ch/ /j/		
	Nasals	/m/			/n/		/ng/	
	Lateral				/i/			
	Semivowels	/hw/ /w/			/r/	/y/		

Adapted with permission from Bolinger, D. (1975). *Aspects of Language* (2nd ed.) (p. 41). New York: Harcourt Brace Jovanovich.

Consonant Chart

Vowel Sounds do not restrict the flow of air during production. Vowel sounds are **open** sounds because the airflow is not restricted. The vowel is the nucleus of the syllable. If there is no vowel sound, there is no syllable. A single vowel sound can be a word, as in the word *I*, or a syllable as with the *o* in *omit*. Usually the vowel combines with one or more consonant sounds to form words and syllables.

Vowels are produced by varying tongue positions and tongue heights (high to low and front to back). Different vowel sounds are made with subtle changes in the mouth position. Vowel sounds are more difficult to learn than consonant sounds because changes in the mouth are so small that they are difficult to feel or discriminate.

D

Vowel Chart

Vowel Chart

ē
1. me
2. these
3. see
4. eat
5. chief
6. happy
7. key
8. either

ĭ
1. sit
2. gym

ā
1. baby
2. make
3. rain
4. play
5. eight
6. vein
7. they
8. great
9. straight

ě
1. pet
2. head

ă
1. cat

ī
1. item
2. time
3. pie
4. my
5. right

ŏ
1. fox
2. swap

ŭ
1. cup
2. cover
3. flood
4. tough
5. among

ə
1. about
2. lesson
3. elect
4. definition
5. circus

aw
1. saw
2. pause
3. call
4. dog
5. wall

ō
1. go
2. vote
3. boat
4. show
5. toe

o͝o
1. took
2. put
3. could

o͞o
1. moo
2. ruby
3. tube
4. chew
5. blue
6. suit
7. soup

er her / fur / sir

ar cart

or sport

Vowel Chart (completed)

oi	oy	oil / boy
ou	ow	out / cow

What is schwa? ə

Stress in words and the **schwa** go together. Stress is the emphasis that syllables have in words.

- If a syllable is stressed, the vowel is usually long or short.

- If the syllable is not stressed, the vowel is usually reduced to a schwa. Schwa sounds like / ŭ /, but is more reduced.

- An *a* that begins or ends a word is often reduced to schwa.

Schwa for the Letter *a*
a like' / ə-līk' /

- The *a* in *alike* is reduced to schwa. The *a* sounds like / ŭ /.

- In a multisyllable word, the second syllable is often reduced to ə.

Schwa in Multisyllable Words
mul' ti ply' / mŭl' tə-plī' /
The second syllable *ti* is reduced schwa.
The *i* sounds like / ŭ /.

What You Need to Know

What is a syllable?

Words are made up of larger sound bites called syllables. A syllable is a word, or a word part, that has one vowel sound. Every word has at least one syllable type, determined by its vowel sound and representational pattern(s). Recognizing syllable types helps students pronounce unfamiliar words.

Syllabication, or the process of dividing words into their syllable units, is a critical structural analysis skill. The ability to segment a word into syllable units helps readers access the pronunciation of longer, more complex vocabulary. The syllabication process focuses on the pattern of vowels and consonants in the word. Using these patterns, readers identify the syllable types, which they can pronounce. In *LANGUAGE!* this process is taught beginning in Book C, Unit 13, using the strategy called **Divide It**.

Syllable Type*	Pattern	Vowel Sound
Closed (U13)	A syllable that ends with a consonant sound (**dig, trans-mit**).	The vowel sound is short. / ă /
r-controlled (U14)	A syllable that has a vowel followed by **r** (**car, mar-**ket).	The vowel sound is **r**-controlled: / âr /, / ôr /, or / êr /.
Open (U15)	A syllable that ends with a vowel (**she, my, o-**pen).	The vowel sound is long. / ā /
Final silent e (U16)	A syllable that ends in a final silent **e** (**made**, in-**flate**).	The vowel sound is long. / ā /
Vowel digraph (U19)	A syllable that contains a vowel digraph (r**ai**n, pl**ay**).	The vowel sound is usually long. / ā /
Final consonant + le (U22)	A **final** syllable that ends in a consonant followed by **le** (puz-**zle**).	The vowel sound is schwa. / ə /
Vowel diphthong (U23)	A syllable that contains a vowel diphthong (**oi**l, b**oy**; **ou**t, c**ow**).	The vowel sound is a glide, sounding like two sounds.

*The *LANGUAGE!* unit in which the concept is introduced is indicated in parentheses.

INSTRUCTIONAL FOCUS

Instructional activities in Step 1: Phonemic Awareness and Phonics are designed to make abstract phonological concepts concrete. First, students learn how to manipulate sounds in order to strengthen phonemic awareness before incorporating phonics instruction. Next, students learn about the graphemes that represent those sounds. Accurate and automatic sound-spelling correspondences lay the groundwork for syllables and morphemes in later units.

How will you maximize student learning?

- Use charts to teach the sounds of the English language
- Demonstrate multisensory techniques to practice phonemic awareness
- Use manipulatives to teach phonemic awareness and phonics
- Provide opportunities to practice fluency.

D

"*I couldn't put it down.*"

Step 1 Why Do/How To Activities

More complete descriptions and instructions for these activities can be found in the Appendix. See page 362 for the table of contents.

Sounds	Activity Snapshot
Anchor the Word	This multisensory technique lets you guide class-wide practice of phonemic awareness.
Move It and Mark It	Uses manipulatives to practice a variety of phonemic awareness sklIls.
Consonant Chart	Students analyze and recognize differing qualities of consonant sounds.
Vowel Chart	Students analyze and recognize differing qualities of vowel sounds.
Listening for Sounds in Words	Sudents practice identifying where a particular phoneme is located in a word or syllable.
Production/Replication	Students copy teacher modeling of phonemic production.
Isolation	Students identify target phonemes in words.
Segmentation	Adds a kinesthetic element to combining phonemes to create words.
Blending	Explicitly teaches the blending of constituent sounds.
Rhyming	Students recognize and generate rhyming phonemes.
Deletion	Students recognize and separate individual sounds in words by deleting specific phonemes.
Reversal	Students manipulate phonemes by moving them within words.
Substitution	Students manipulate sounds through the replacement of phonemes.
Syllables	
Syllable Awareness	Students practice identifying the number of syllables and vowel sounds in multisyllabic words.
Listening for Stressed Syllables	Practices identification of stressed syllables in multisyllabic words.
Discover It	Guides students in identifying underlying sound-spelling patterns, syllable types, and morpheme units.
Fluency	
See and Say	Develops the visual-to-auditory memory link for letter-sound associations.
Say and Write	Reinforces the connection between sounds and letters.
See and Name	Drills letter-name recall.
Name and Write	Practices sound-letter association.
Letter-Sound Fluency	Develops accurate and automatic retrieval of letter-name association.
Letter-Name Fluency	Develops accurate and automatic retrieval of letter-name associations.
Handwriting Fluency	Reinforces letter-name associations while practicing proper letter formation.

Interactive Text

This consumable text provides ready-made materials—unit-by-unit, lesson-by-lesson, step-by-step—to develop phonemic awareness and phonics skills. Exercises include **Letter-Sound** and **Letter-Name Fluencies, Spelling Pretests, Say and Write** dictation, and many other activities that support Step 1 objectives.

Letter Cards

These alphabetic manipulatives allow hands-on activities and games to practice letter-name and letter-sound association, and other phonemic awareness and phonics skills.

Example of *Interactive Text*

LANGUAGE! Presents the Speech Sounds of English: A Video Tutorial with Louisa Moats

This 46-minute DVD provides modeling and reinforcement of modeling, replication, and production of speech sounds. Presented by Dr. Louisa Moats, a leading researcher and expert in language development and reading instruction, this video includes lively demonstrations of:

- How to teach articulation of each sound as it relates to other sounds
- The system of speech formation
- Understanding basic phonology
- Correct pronunciation of English phonemes for phonemic awareness, phonic decoding, and spelling.

You Try It!

Using the *Teacher Edition* for Step 1

Unit lessons in the *Teacher Edition* provide the "steps within a *step*" to guide development of phonemic awareness and phonics mastery. Examples from *LANGUAGE!*'s three entry points—Unit 1, Unit 13, and Unit 25—are shown on this and the next two pages to demonstrate the range of exercises, activities, and objectives.

Preparations

What materials/equipment do you need to teach this lesson?

_____

_____

How will you store and distribute the materials your students need for this lesson?

_____

Directions

Are the directions clear?

_____

_____

Do you think you will need to practice?

_____

_____

Connections

What foundation is being laid with **Move It and Mark It?**

_____

_____

Where do you think the sounds come from?

_____

_____

Unit 1

Lesson 1

STEP 1

Phonemic Awareness and Phonics

Students establish sound-spelling correspondences for consonants **b**, **c**, **f**, **m**, **s**, and **t**, and the short sound for the vowel **a**.

Lesson 1 Materials
See the Book A *Instructional Planning Tools* CD for a complete list of materials for this lesson.

One of the first skills needed to read and spell English words is awareness of their component sounds. This is called **phoneme awareness**. In each unit **Step 1: Phonemic Awareness and Phonics** focuses on this skill.

☆ Move It and Mark It

Why Do: Visual and concrete representations of phonemes in words help students learn to manipulate phonemes in words.

How To: Use colored tiles to represent the sounds in a particular word. Say the word, moving one tile represented by the arrow as you say each sound. Blend the sounds represented by the tiles. Move your index finger under the tiles from left to right. Say the word. Have students follow your model.

Materials
Colored tiles or pieces of paper (3 per student)

Use this activity to develop students' phonemic awareness of the sounds / ā / (short **a**), / b /, / k /, / f /, / m /, / s /, and / t /.

With single sounds:
▶ Have students arrange three colored tiles or pieces of paper in a row.
▶ Say / m /.
▶ Repeat the sound as you move a tile down.
▶ Have students practice these sounds with you: / ā /, / t /, / s /, / b /, / k /, / f /. Avoid adding "uh" to the ends of the sounds.

With words:
▶ Repeat activity using **am**.
▶ For each sound in **am** (/ ā / / m /), move one tile down as you say each sound.
▶ Blend sounds represented by the tiles: Move your index finger under the tiles from left to right. Say the word **am**.
▶ Replace the tiles.
▶ Have students:
  • Practice these words with you: **at**, **bat**, **cat**, **sat**, **fat**, **ab**, **tab**, **cab**.

/ ā /   / m /

| *Differentiated Instruction* | ☆ Review & Acceleration | ✓ Special Instructional Support | ☀ English Learners | 🌐 Technology | Challenge Text |

10 Unit 1 • Lesson 1

From Book A, Unit 1, Lesson 1

You Try It!

Unit 13 — Lesson 7

STEP 1

Phonemic Awareness and Phonics

➡️ Students learn to shift the stress in multisyllable words. They also learn to identify the schwa sound in unstressed syllables.

Lesson 7 Materials
See the Book C *Instructional Planning Tools* CD for a complete list of materials for this lesson.

⭐ **Introduce: Shifting the Syllable Stress**

Materials
Colored tiles or pieces of paper

▸ Explain to students that a word may be pronounced differently when it functions as a different part of speech, and that the pronunciation change is usually a shift in syllable stress.

▸ Demonstrate shifting syllable stress with this procedure:

1. Place two different colored tiles or pieces of paper in a row on the overhead transparency.
2. Say the target word to students, moving up the tiles corresponding to the stressed syllable when you say it.
3. Move the tiles back in a row.
4. Say the alternate pronunciation of the word, moving up the tile corresponding to the newly stressed syllable.
5. Use each word form in a sentence to demonstrate the link between pronunciation and usage.

Example: Say **con′ flict**.
The **conflict** was resolved.

Example: Say **con flict′**.
Music will **conflict** with my schedule.

▸ Explain to students:

Sometimes a word can look the same but be pronounced in two different ways by shifting the syllable stress.

Shifting the stress can change the meaning and the function of the word.

The word is a noun when the stress is on the first syllable. In the first example, **con′ flict** is a noun.

The word is a verb when the stress is on the second syllable. In the second example, **con flict′** is a verb.

Differentiated Instruction ⭐ Review & Acceleration | ✓ Special Instructional Support | ✳️ English Learners | 🌐 Technology | 📘 Challenge Text

98 Unit 13 • Lesson 7

From Book C, Unit 13, Lesson 7

Preparations

What is the *Instructional Planning Tool* and how is it referenced in this lesson?

_____

_____

How will you display the colored tiles in your classroom?

_____

_____

D

Directions

What does the star indicate?

_____

_____

Where are the directions for Introduce: Shifting the Syllable Stress?

_____

_____

Connections

Compare and contrast the use of colored tiles in this lesson and the previous lesson from Unit 1, Lesson 1.

_____

_____

What is the power of making this activity manipulative and multisensory?

_____

_____

You Try It!

Preparations

How will you prepare to lead the review?

_____

_____

Do you know what is meant by "voiced/voiceless?" Where can you go for more information?

_____

_____

Directions

How much of this exercise should you do with your students?

_____

_____

When and how should you check it?

_____

_____

Connections

How will the focus of this lesson help students in Step 2: Spelling and Word Recognition?

_____

_____

Compare how manipulatives are used in this lesson and the two previous lessons.

_____

_____

Unit 25 Lesson 1

STEP 1

Phonemic Awareness and Phonics

➡ Students review the two sounds for **s** and learn the sound-spelling pattern for **c** when it is pronounced / s /.

Lesson 1 Materials

See the Book E *Instructional Planning Tools* CD for a complete list of materials for this lesson.

Review: Two Sounds for s

Use this activity to review the two sounds for the letter **s**: / s / and / z /.

▸ Remind students that **s** can represent two sounds, / s / and / z /. Recall with students that sometimes the letter that comes before **s** indicates how to pronounce **s**.

  If **s** is preceded by a voiced consonant sound, then the **s** is voiced and sounds like / z /, as in **cabs** and **curves**.

  If **s** is preceded by a voiceless consonant sound, then the **s** is voiceless and sounds like / s /, as in **maps** and **poets**.

  When **s** begins a word, it usually sounds like / s /, as in **send** and **sound**.

Sort It: Two Sounds for s

Materials
Interactive Text p. 6, Exercise 1

Use this activity in the *Interactive Text* to review the conditions for the **s** pronunciations, / s / and / z /.

▸ Have students:

  • Turn to Exercise 1, **Sort It: Two Sounds for s**, in the *Interactive Text*, page 6.

  • Read the example word with you.

  • Listen for the pronunciation of **s** at the end of the word.

  • Mark an X in the column that indicates the correct pronunciation of **s** in that word.

  • Follow this procedure for each of the remaining words.

Review: The Sound / k / for c

Materials
Letter cards or transparency pieces

Use this activity to review the sound / k / for **c**.

▸ Use overhead tiles, pieces of transparency, or letter cards to represent the sounds in the word **count**.

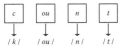

▸ Say the word **count**.

Interactive Text
p. 6, Exercise 1
Teacher Edition p. 22

Differentiated Instruction ★ Review & Acceleration ✓ Special Instructional Support ☀ English Learners ⊙ Technology ◆ Challenge Text

10 Unit 25 • Lesson 1

From Book E, Unit 25, Lesson 1

ONGOING ASSESSMENT

How will you evaluate student learning?

- Monitor fluency practice.
- Monitor **Content Mastery**.

Fluency Practice

Fluency practice provides ongoing information about automatic sound and letter recognition. Letter-sound and letter-name fluency practice is a part of the instructional sequence in Books A and B. Fluency tasks help monitor the level of automaticity of the letter-sound and letter-name correspondences. **Letter-Sound Fluency**, **Letter-Name Fluency**, and **Fluency Charts** are provided in the Resources section of each *Interactive Text*.

- Fluency Tasks
- Content Mastery
- Benchmark Paper
- Comprehension Proficiency

adjust · instruct · assess

Since the focus of Books A and B is on sound-letter correspondences, there are letter-sound and letter-name fluency tasks for those levels. In Books C–F the focus of the content in Step 1 shifts to syllables. Therefore, letter-sound and letter-name fluency is no longer assessed.

Letter-name and letter-sound fluency resources in *LANGUAGE!* include:

- One letter-sound fluency per unit
- One letter-name fluency per unit
- Fluency charts to record progress
- Target fluency rate goals in books A and B of 50 correct letters/sounds per minute.

Content Mastery

Content Mastery Tasks in Step 1 focus on:

- Phoneme recognition
- Sound-spelling correspondences
- Syllable awareness.

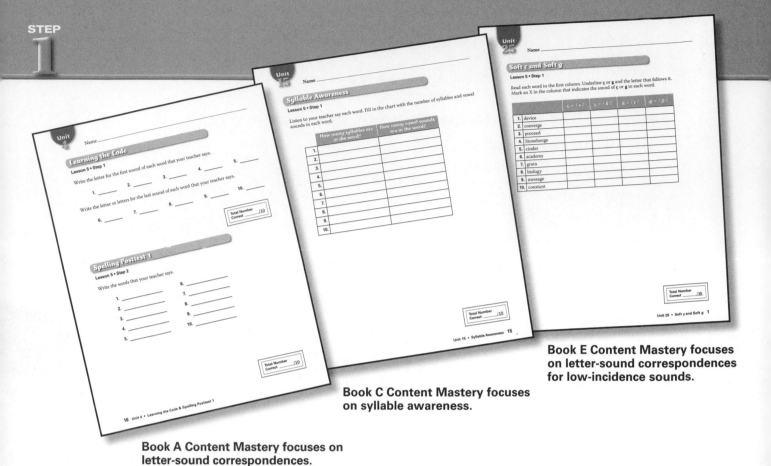

Book A Content Mastery focuses on letter-sound correspondences.

Book C Content Mastery focuses on syllable awareness.

Book E Content Mastery focuses on letter-sound correspondences for low-incidence sounds.

Prescriptive Teaching Boxes

A **Prescriptive Teaching Box** follows every **Content Mastery** task at point of use in the Teacher Edition. These *If… Then…* Boxes guide teachers to reinforce if students do not reach 80% mastery, or reteach if students score below 60% mastery on a **Content Mastery** task.

If . . .	Then . . .
Students score below 80%	Reinforce: • Sound Spelling Correspondences: Use **Say and Write** in Unit 5, Lesson 1, Step 1.
Students score at or below 60%	Reteach: • Sound Spelling Correspondences: Use **Segmentation, See and Say**, and **Say and Write** in Unit 5, Lesson 1, Step 1.

Prescriptive Teaching Box

Retesting based on student performance

Once the appropriate measures have been taken to reinforce or reteach concepts based on student scores, it is advisable to retest students to ensure they are performing at 80% proficiency or above before moving on. For more information on retesting, refer to the **Content Mastery** section of the *Assessment: Teacher Edition.*

DIFFERENTIATED INSTRUCTION FOR STEP 1

How will you respond when a student experiences difficulty in learning?

 Use **Special Instructional Support** activities to customize teaching materials and provide opportunities for individualized instruction.

Lesson 1	Lesson 2	Lesson 3	Lesson 4	Lesson 5
Step 1: *Sortegories* CD: Sound Count	**Step 1:** Folder Activity: Phoneme Sort: Words with Short Vowels	**Step 2:** Folder Activity: Tic-Tac-Toe With Essential Words	**Step 2:** Folder Activity: Syllable Sort: Number of Syllables in a Word	**Step 3:** *Sortegories* CD: Morph It
Step 2: *Words for Teachers* CD: Word Card Generator—Essential Words	**Step 2:** *Sortegories* CD: Sort It	*Sortegories* CD: Build It	**Step 3:** *Sortegories* CD: Categorize It	
Words for Teachers CD: Word Study Guide—Spelling Words	*Words for Teachers* CD: Fluency Builder Grid—Essential Words	**Step 5:** *LANGUAGE! eReader* CD: **"It'll Never Work"**		

The *Sortegories* CD ...

- Provides interactive phonemic awareness activities
- Helps monitor student performance.

bath	sniff	whim
theft	quest	

ă	ĕ	ĭ
bath		

Pacing Based on Student Performance

For students whose assessment results show strong phonemic performance, instruction can be accelerated by focusing on only the **Review and Acceleration** activities in Step 1. These activities are designated with a ☆ on the unit Lesson Planner pages.

For students needing more attention in this content area, these starred activities can be repeated for additional reinforcement.

> *For further discussion about Differentiated Instruction, please see the section on page 267–292.*

You Try It!

Complete the exercises on this and the next three pages to see how *LANGUAGE!* offers explicit instruction for developing phonemic awareness and phonics skills.

What problems do you anticipate students having with this excercise?

_____

_____

_____

_____

Unit 3 Lesson 8

Exercise 1 · Syllable Awareness

▸ Listen to the word.

▸ Count the syllables.

▸ Write the letter for each vowel sound you hear.

	How many syllables do you hear?	1st Vowel Sound	2nd Vowel Sound	3rd Vowel Sound
1.				
2.				
3.				
4.				
5.				
6.				
7.				
8.				
9.				
10.				

From Book A *Interactive Text*

How can you measure student understanding during the completion of this activity?

_____

_____

_____

_____

_____

D

Unit 13 · Lesson 7

Exercise 1 · Listening for Stressed Syllables

▸ Listen to each word and sentence your teacher says.

▸ Repeat the word.

▸ Listen for the stressed, or accented, syllable.

▸ Put an X in the box to mark the position of the stressed syllable.

▸ Do the first two with your teacher.

1. | X | | 6. | | |

2. | | X | 7. | | |

3. | | | 8. | | |

4. | | | 9. | | |

5. | | | 10. | | |

42   Unit 13 • Lesson 7

From Book C *Interactive Text*

You Try It!

Consonant Chart

Unit _____

Student _____

Date _____

		Mouth Position						
		Lips	Lips/Teeth	Tongue Between Teeth	Tongue Behind Teeth	Roof of Mouth	Back of Mouth	Throat
Type of Consonant Sound	Stops							
	Fricatives							
	Affricatives							
	Nasals							
	Lateral							
	Semivowels							

Adapted with permission from Bolinger, D. (1975). *Aspects of Language* (2nd ed.) (p. 41). New York: Harcourt Brace Jovanovich.

From Transparencies and Templates

How important is modeling when reviewing these sounds?

_____

_____

_____

_____

_____

![You Try It!]

Vowel Chart

Unit _____ Student _____ Date _____

Vowel Chart (blank)   61

From Transparencies and Templates

How does this knowledge impact higher level skills?

_____

_____

_____

_____

_____

From the *LANGUAGE!* Classroom

As a young man, Demetrius knew how to spell his name, but didn't know any of the sounds of the alphabet, how to make the letters not in his name, and couldn't read even the simplest word. He was nervous, self-conscious, insecure, and convinced that no matter what he did, reading wouldn't be a thing he could ever do. (He'd been through several teachers by this time, one of whom told him he was "hopeless".) I started him in LANGUAGE! with the phonemic awareness drills and phonics. Within three days he was building words and starting to decode them, and on the fourth day, he read the first "book" of his life: the Unit 1 decodable mini-dialog out of the Student Text. This young man was so excited, he burst into tears, and asked to take the Student Book home so he could read it to his girlfriend. (Which he did!)

Siri Stenberg *Reading Coordinator,* Adult Basic Education Program
Rochester Public Schools #535; Rochester, Minnesota

Table of Contents

E

RESEARCH BITE

"Fluency and automatic reading frees up 'cognitive space' so that conscious attention can be devoted to textual meaning."

Reid Lyon, 2005

In Step 2: Word Recognition and Spelling, students use sound-to-letter correspondence as the basis to build words to spell and read, and practice sound-spelling correspondences to promote the **fluent** *spelling and reading of words.*

"Science is clear. Becoming a good reader requires rapid, fluent, and automatic decoding of isolated words" (Chard, D.J. Vaughn, S., & Tyler, B.J. 2002). Students with learning and reading weaknesses often fail to develop sufficient decoding speed at the word level (Berninger, 1999; Ehri & Soffer, 1999; Wagner & Barker, 1994). Focusing first on the alphabetic principle and then on word-level **automaticity**, fluency practice often is the key to distinguishing skilled from less-skilled readers through adolescence (Shaywitz et al.,1999). It is particularly important for older struggling students to become fluent with irregular words, as these words do not follow the regular rules for pronunciation (Shaywitz, 2003). In fact, children should not be removed from a reading intervention program until they can read words and passages fluently at their grade level (Shaywitz, 2003). Spelling and reading are associated, and their interconnectedness suggests that these skills should be developed reciprocally (Ehri, 1994; 1989; 1987; 1986). Learning composition (the content and organization of writing) will be limited in the intermediate grades if students' spelling and handwriting are poor (Berninger et al., 1999).

How *LANGUAGE!* Does It

LANGUAGE! addresses word recognition and spelling by:

- Emphasizing recognition of high-frequency words
- Differentiating instruction according to sound-spelling predictability (e.g., *cat*) or nondecodability (e.g., *the*)
- Including fluency drills focused on reading lists of phonologically predictable words and irregular words
- Teaching word recognition and spelling reciprocally
- Developing spelling generalizations.

What do you want students to learn?
Students will learn how to:

- Read and spell words based on sound-spelling correspondences
- Read and spell high-frequency words
- Recognize words accurately and automatically
- Read and spell words based on syllable patterns
- Use syllabication strategies to decode unknown words
- Apply spelling rules
- Spell contractions.

In Books A and B students combine **graphemes** from current and previous units to build words to read and spell.

graphemes
units of a writing system

E

w + e + b = web

In Books C and D students will combine all syllable types to build multisyllabic words.

spi + der = spider

In Books D—F students also use prefixes, roots, and suffixes to build multisyllable words.

in + flec + tion + al = inflectional

What You Need to Know

Content in Step 2: Word Recognition and Spelling is based on building and decoding words. *LANGUAGE!* presents words from three distinct categories in each of the 36 units.

Unit Words

Unit Words are 100 percent decodable. They are based on the sound-spelling correspondence concepts taught in the current and previous steps. Since about 87 percent of English words are phonologically predictable (Hanna, Hanna, Hodges, and Rudoft, 1996), learning the words based on the sound-spelling correspondences makes it possible for students to read a large percentage of words accurately. **Unit Words** are also taught in order to explore their multiple meanings, contextual usage, semantic variation, and use in composition.

Unit Words were chosen from four resources:

1. First 1000 (Edward Fry)
2. Core Vocabulary (Andrew Biemiller)
3. Academic Word Lists (Averil Coxhead)
4. Second 1000 Words of the General Service List (Paul Nation)

"Why do I have to keep writin' in these K's when they don't make any noise anyway?"

FAMILY CIRCUS © BIL KEANE, INC. KING FEATURES SYNDICATE

Essential Words

Essential Words are high-frequency English words.
Essential Words are not decodable in the unit in which they are introduced; some become decodable in later units. For example, the word *that*, which is taught in Unit 1, becomes decodable in Unit 8 when *th* for /*th*/ is taught. Since it is a high-frequency word used extensively in spoken and written language, it is introduced at an earlier unit as an **Essential Word**. Some words, such as *was* and *said*, are never decodable but are explicitly taught to mastery because of their high utility in English.

LANGUAGE! emphasizes High-Frequency Words in English that encompass a high percentage of words that we read and write.

The top **25** words comprise of 33% of all written English

The top **100** words comprise of 50% of all written English

The top **300** words comprise of 65% of all written English

(Fry, Kress, and Fountoukidis, 2002)

This chart shows how High-Frequency Words are rolled out across the *LANGUAGE!* program.

High-Frequency English Words	Book A	Book B	Book C	Book D	Book E	Book F
Top 100	49%	81%	100%	-	-	-
Top 500	18%	43%	70%	83%	94%	100%
Top 1000	13%	36%	60%	80%	94%	100%

(Fry, Kress, and Fountoukidis, 2002)

*For the complete **Essential Word List**, see pages 343–344 in the Appendix.*

Bonus Words

Similar to **Unit Words, Bonus Words** are 100 percent decodable. **Bonus Words** provide an expanded word list that teachers can use to accelerate vocabulary instruction for students who quickly master the unit words. **Bonus Words** are not assessed.

You Try It!

Using the Unit Word List

The **Unit Word List** appears as part of the At a Glance for Teachers for each unit. The list provides easy access to the unit's **Essential Words, Unit Words Bonus Words,** and **Spelling Lists,** and word-level objectives.

Essential Words

Unit Words

Spelling List

Bonus Words

Unit Word List

Essential Words

gone, look, most, people, see, water

Unit Words

Syllabication

above	blanket	commend	finish	melon	salad
across	blossom	commit	gallon	method	second
adapt	bonnet	common	gallop	minutes	select
adult	bottom	connect	happen	panel	seven
album	bucket	consent	hundred	planet	status
along	button	consist	husband	pocket	sudden
amend	cannon	constant	intense	prison	suspend
append	channel	cotton	involve	problem	ticket
assess	chicken	cricket	jacket	radish	vanish
assist	children	dentist	kitten	random	visit
atlas	collect	dozen	lemon	rascal	wagon
attach	comma	dragon	linen	ribbon	woman
basket	command	expand	magnet	rocket	

Shifting Stress

affect	conflict	content	present
compact	construct	contrast	subject
complex	consult	extract	suspect
conduct	contact	object	

Words with Prefixes

disrupt	instruct	nonfat	unlock
distinct	invent	nonstop	unplug

Spelling Lists

Lesson 1–5		Lesson 6–10	
across	*most*	blanket	method
atlas	*people*	bottom	nonstop
command	problem	common	object
cotton	ribbon	disrupt	present
gone	rocket	I'm	suspect
invent	*see*	infant	ticket
look	*water*	it's	upset
magnet		kitten	

Bonus Words can be found in the *Student Text*, page H118. These are additional words based on the same sound-spelling correspondences from this and previous units. Use these words for expanded reading, spelling, and vocabulary development.

Unit 13 • At a Glance for Teachers   3

From Book C Unit 13

Instructional activities in Step 2: Word Recognition and Spelling are designed for students to apply the sound-spelling associations to read and spell words, as well as to learn words that are of high utility, but not phonologically decodable.

How will you maximize student learning?

- Explain orthographic rules and spelling conventions.
- Provide opportunities to practice fluency.
- Use templates to generalize spelling rules.
- Demonstrate multisensory techniques to apply the sound-spelling associations to read (decode) and spell (encode) words.
  - Decoding strategies
  - Encoding strategies
  - Strategies to memorize **Essential Words**.

Teacher's Tip

For missed spelling words, I give the students 3 x 5 cards for each word missed. Students use color to remind them of the part they missed. For example, if they forgot the "r" in "through," they would write the "r" in red, but the other letters in black.

Linda Manning, *Teacher*
Dundee Middle School, Dundee, Illinois

For "Guide to Orthography," see pages 345–351 in the Appendix.

Why Do/How To Activities for Step 2

More complete descriptions and instructions for these activities can be found in the Appendix. See page 362 for the table of contents.

Decoding	Activity Snapshot
Build It	Students use letter-manipulatives to work on multisensory tasks that reveal the parts-to-whole structure of the English language.
Find It	Students locate and identify target letters, words, and concepts in text.
Folder Activities	Folder activities can be used for alphabetization and other spelling exercises.
Chain It	To build familiarity with sound-spelling correspondences, students form new words by changing single letters.
Sort It	Students sort letter and word cards into categories.
Word Fluency	These exercises develop word recognition and reading automaticity.
Divide It	This useful decoding strategy helps students systematically identify syllabic patterns.
Encoding	
Add It	This exercise lets students practice spelling rules when endings are added to words.
Contract It	Students practice the challenging task of forming and decoding contractions.
Double It	Students develop word analysis skills related to the doubling of the final consonant before an ending.
Drop It	Students explore rules about dropping the final **e** before an ending.
Change It	This exercise provides a step-by-step guide to help students learn the rules governing the final **y** before a suffix.
Spelling Pretest	Spelling dictation exercise promotes decoding and encoding automaticity.
Essential Words	
Memorize It	This activity drills automatic recognition of frequently used English words.
Type It	Students keyboard **Essential Words** to reinforce the encoding of sight words.
Handwriting Practice	Students practice recognition and written formation of letters.
Find It	Students locate and identify **Essential Words** in text.
Word Fluency	These exercises develop word recognition and reading automaticity of **Essential Words**.

Using the Teacher Edition for Step 2

Unit lessons in your *Teacher Edition* provide the "steps within a Step" to guide development of word recognition and spelling. Examples from *LANGUAGE!*'s three entry points—Unit 1, Unit 13, and Unit 25—are shown on the next three pages to demonstrate the range of exercises, activities, and objectives.

STEP
2 **Word Recognition and Spelling**

 Students build words using the sound-spelling correspondences for **a**, **b**, **c**, **f**, **m**, **s**, and **t**. Students also read and spell high-frequency words.

☆ **Spelling Pretest 1**

Why Do: Students need direct spelling instruction to develop as writers. Spelling lists comprising words with instructed patterns are provided with each unit. Italics designate **Essential Words**.

How To: Dictate each word on the list, say it in a sentence, and then repeat the word. Have students write the word. Check answers with students.

Materials
Interactive Text
p. 6, Exercise 3

Use **Spelling Pretest 1** in the *Interactive Text* to identify the words students need to practice throughout the unit.

▶ Have students:
• Turn to Exercise 3, **Spelling Pretest 1**.

▶ Dictate the list below for students; say the word in the sentence; repeat the word. (**Essential Words** appear in italics.)

1. *a*   You are *a* student.
2. *I*   *I* am at bat.
3. *is*   This *is* my lunch.
4. fat   Some meat has lots of **fat**.
5. *that*   Is *that* your pencil?
6. *this*   *This* is my best friend.
7. *the*   *The* answer is correct.
8. *are*   You *are* very funny!
9. sat   The class **sat** in a group.
10. tab   He turned to the page with the **tab**.

Interactive Text
p. 6, Exercise 3
Teacher Edition p. 24

Unit 1 • Lesson 1   **15**

From Book A, Unit 1, Lesson 1

Preparations
How can the transition statement help frame your preparations?

Should you practice spelling these words with your students before administering the pre-test?

Directions
What does the Why Do/HowTo box signify and where else can you find it?

Where do students take the spelling pre-test? How will you check it?

Connections
What is the advantage for students to have the **Essential Words** in the first spelling test?

How does mastery of Step 1 skills lead to mastery in Step 2?

Preparations

What materials do you need to work with to prepare for this lesson?

_____

_____

How would a visual model help move your students successfully through these activities?

_____

_____

Directions

How are you to use the words in Exercise 2 for Exercise 3?

_____

_____

How are you to use Bank It and what purpose does it serve?

_____

_____

Connections

In this step, the focus is on the spelling patterns for prefixes. How do you think this will be connected to instruction in Step 3 (word meaning) and Step 4 (word usage)?

_____

_____

How can a focus on prefixes influence reading fluency?

_____

_____

STEP 2 — Word Recognition and Spelling

Students identify and categorize prefixes in words. They also read and spell high-frequency words and practice fluent single-word reading.

⭐ **Review: Prefixes**

▸ Review with students:

A **prefix** is a syllable that is added at the beginning of a base word. Examples of prefixes include **dis-**, **in-**, **un-**, and **non-**.

A prefix changes the meaning of the base word.

⭐ **Find It: Prefixes**

Materials
Interactive Text
p. 26,
Exercise 2

Use this activity in the *Interactive Text* to provide practice in identifying and blending prefixes in words.

▸ Write the following prefixes on the board: **dis-**, **in-**, **un-**, **non-**.

▸ Have students:

• Turn to Exercise 2, **Find It: Prefixes**, in the *Interactive Text*, page 26.

▸ Model this activity on the board using the first word, **nonfat**.

1. Write **nonfat** on the board or an overhead transparency.
2. Ask a student to come up and circle the prefix in **nonfat**. non
3. Model how to read the word by blending the prefix and the base word.

▸ Repeat the process with the next three words.

(un)clasp   (in)land   (dis)trust

▸ Have students:

• Circle the prefix in each of the remaining words.
• Blend the prefix and the base word to read the entire word.

⭐ **Sort It: Prefixes**

Materials
Interactive Text
p. 26,
Exercise 3
Interactive Text
p. R58

Use this activity in the *Interactive Text* to provide practice in distinguishing prefixes.

▸ Have students:

• Turn to Exercise 3, **Sort It: Prefixes**, in the *Interactive Text*, page 26.
• Look at the words from Unit 13, Lesson 4, Exercise 2, **Find It: Prefixes**.
• Sort the words by prefix and write them in the chart.
• Read the words to a partner.
• Choose three words with each prefix and record them in the **Prefixes** section of **Bank It** in the *Interactive Text*, page R58. Label the columns: **dis-**, **in-**, **non-**, and **un-**.

Interactive Text
p. 26, Exercises 2 and 3
Teacher Edition p. 68

Interactive Text
p. R58

Unit 13 • Lesson 4 **57**

From Book C, Unit 13, Lesson 4

 STEP

2 **Word Recognition and Spelling**

Students use syllable division as a strategy to decode compound words in context. They also build words with **-dge** and practice fluent single-word reading.

⭐ **Build It: Words with -dge**

Materials
Letter cards
Pocket chart
Interactive Text
p. R69

Use this activity and the *Interactive Text* to provide practice in using sound-spelling correspondences to build words.

▸ Display these letter cards in the pocket chart.

| tr- | br- | b | j | f | **i** | **u** | -dge |

▸ Have students:

- Locate and remove the same letter cards from the *Interactive Text*, page xxx.
- Turn to the **Sound-Spelling Correspondences** section of **Bank It** in the *Interactive Text*, page R69.
- Label a column **-dge**.
- Combine letter cards to build words that end with **-dge**.
- Record those words in the correct column of **Bank It**.
- Share and compare words with a partner.

Possible words ending with **-dge** include bridge, budge, trudge, fudge, and judge.

Divide It

Materials
Interactive Text
pp. C1–C6, Text
Connection 1
Interactive Text
p. R7, Syllable
Division
Patterns
Interactive Text
p. R6, Divide It
Checklist
Self-stick notes

Use this activity with **Text Connection 1, "Circle Poems Take Many Forms,"** in the *Interactive Text* to practice a strategy for decoding multisyllable words in context.

▸ Remind students that dividing words into syllables will help them read unfamiliar words.

▸ Write **fulfillment** on the board or an overhead transparency.

Note: Do *not* read the word since the pronunciation of the word is the answer.

▸ Model how to follow the steps of **Divide It** using an accelerated process to break this word into syllables.

1. Circle all prefixes, roots, and suffixes within the word. ment (suffix)
2. Underline the first vowel. u
3. Underline the next vowel. i
4. Divide the word into syllables. Determine the syllable type of each syllable to determine the vowel sound in it. closed, closed
5. Blend the syllables to form a word that makes sense in context. Read the word.
   ful / fill ment

Note: Refer students to these reference pages in the *Interactive Text* if more support is needed:
   Divide It Checklist, page R6
   Syllable Division Patterns, page R7

Interactive Text
p. R69

Interactive Text
p. R6

From Book E, Unit 25, Lesson 3

Preparations

How will you organize the materials needed for these activities?

_____

Why is providing a visual model for these activities so important for moving successfully through these activities?

_____

E

Directions

How will you direct students to move between the Text Connections (at the back of the IT) and the other IT activities?

_____

Where do you place the letter cards for word building and what is important about their display?

_____

Connections

How is Divide It, as a strategy, dependent on student mastery of prefixes?

_____

How does student knowledge of vowel sounds help students successfully use Divide It?

_____

Activity Materials

Interactive Text

This consumable provides ready-made materials—unit-by-unit, lesson-by-lesson, step-by-step—so students can practice word recognition and spelling skills. Word fluencies and **manipulatives** are located in the back of each book's *Interactive Text*.

manipulatives

learning tools that may be handled and moved

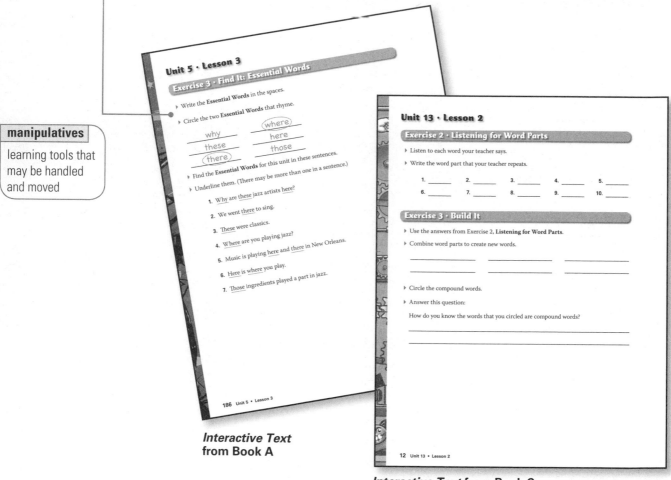

Unit 5 · Lesson 3

Exercise 3 · Find It: Essential Words

▸ Write the **Essential Words** in the spaces.

▸ Circle the two **Essential Words** that rhyme.

why   where
these   here
there   those

▸ Find the **Essential Words** for this unit in these sentences.

▸ Underline them. (There may be more than one in a sentence.)

1. Why are these jazz artists here?
2. We went there to sing.
3. These were classics.
4. Where are you playing jazz?
5. Music is playing here and there in New Orleans.
6. Here is where you play.
7. Those ingredients played a part in jazz.

186 Unit 5 · Lesson 3

Interactive Text from Book A

Unit 13 · Lesson 2

Exercise 2 · Listening for Word Parts

▸ Listen to each word your teacher says.

▸ Write the word part that your teacher repeats.

1. _____   2. _____   3. _____   4. _____   5. _____
6. _____   7. _____   8. _____   9. _____   10. _____

Exercise 3 · Build It

▸ Use the answers from Exercise 2, **Listening for Word Parts**.

▸ Combine word parts to create new words.

_____   _____   _____
_____   _____   _____

▸ Circle the compound words.

▸ Answer this question:

How do you know the words that you circled are compound words?

_____
_____

12 Unit 13 · Lesson 2

Interactive Text from Book C

Word-Building Letter Cards

These alphabetic manipulatives allow hands-on practice in building words. They are also located in the back of the *Interactive Text*.

Essential Word Cards

Excellent for drills and activities, **Essential Word Cards** are located in the back of students' *Interactive Text*.

Word Bank

The **Word Bank** in the back of the *Interactive Text* allows students to record words as they build them.

Teacher's Tip

To increase durability of manipulatives, teachers might consider laminating the materials before students cut them up. Cut up pieces can be stored in an envelope or plastic sleeve in the students' binders or folders.

E

You Try It!

Complete these exercises to see how *LANGUAGE!* offers explicit instruction for challenging spelling concepts.

Double It

	Write the Base Word	One Vowel?	One Consonant After the Vowel?	One Syllable?	1 - 1 - 1	Not 1 - 1 - 1	Suffix	Write the Base · Suffix
1.	spell	1		1		✓	-ing	spelling
2.	stop	1	1	1	✓		-ing	stopping
3.	sort						-ing	
4.	form						-ing	
5.	step						-ing	
6.	sit						-ing	
7.	win						-ing	
8.	bat						-ing	
9.	miss						-ing	
10.	drop						-ing	
11.								

Drop It

	Write the Base Word	Ends in e	Does Not End in e	Write the Ending	Ending Begins with Vowel?	Ending Begins with Consonant?	Put the Base · Ending Together
1.	hope	✓		ing	✓		hoping
2.	wave	✓		ed	✓		waved
3.	love			ing			
4.	need			less			
5.	wish			ing			
6.	crack			ed			
7.	smile			ing			
8.	vote			ed			
9.	will			ful			
10.	grade			ing			
11.							
12.							

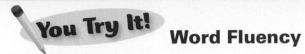 **Word Fluency**

	Correct	Errors
1st Try		
2nd Try		

there	these	those	here	where	why	these	here	why	there	10
those	where	there	those	why	these	here	where	why	here	20
where	there	those	here	these	why	those	there	where	these	30
why	where	there	here	those	where	these	why	those	here	40
those	why	here	where	there	these	why	those	where	there	50
here	those	where	why	these	there	those	here	there	where	60
these	where	why	those	there	here	where	why	those	there	70
where	these	here	there	why	those	there	where	why	here	80
these	where	there	why	here	there	those	here	those	why	90
where	these	why	here	there	those	here	where	why	there	100

Word Fluency 4

E

Unit 5 • Fluency   R45

Word Fluency from Book A *Interactive Text*

How will you establish routines for fluency drills, including partnering, time keeping, recording data and other considerations?

_____

_____

_____

_____

_____

How will you evaluate student learning?

- Monitor word fluency.
- Monitor Content Mastery.

Word Fluencies

Word Fluency tasks are a part of the instructional sequence in every unit. While not an assessment tool, fluency practice provides ongoing information about automatic word recognition. **Word Fluency Builders** and **Fluency Charts** are provided in the Appendix of each *Interactive Text*.

To promote word fluency, the *LANGUAGE!* curriculum provides:

- Three phonetic word fluencies per unit
- One nonphonetic word fluency per unit
- One nonphonetic review per book
- Frequent one-minute timings in every unit
- Individualized goals
- **Fluency Charts** to record progress
- Target goals that vary by book.

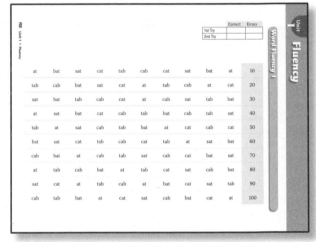

Word Fluencies 1–3 include phonetic words

There is a strong relationship between how fast students read and how well they comprehend. Research supports that 120 Words Correct Per Minute (WCPM) is the score expected for the end of third grade on passage reading. Given that older students typically read isolated words at a slower rate than connected text, expect that students' performance on **Word Fluency** may be slower than their performance on **Sentence Fluency** as practiced in Step 5.

LANGUAGE! Book	Target Number of WCPM
A	120
B	130
C	140
D	145
E	150
F	150-180

Content Mastery

Two spelling tests make up the **Content Mastery** for Step 2 in every unit. The first test assesses spelling knowledge of phonology and high-frequency words. The second test assesses advanced phonology concepts and spelling rules. Students are held responsible for spelling words correctly in their written work after the orthographic pattern has been introduced and assessed.

Spelling Test 1

occurs in Lesson 5 and tests:

- Unit phonology
- Essential words
- Words in isolation

Spelling Test 2

occurs in Lesson 10 and tests:

- Advanced phonology
- Spelling rules
- Words with morphological endings
- Dictated sentences

Prescriptive Teaching Boxes

A **Prescriptive Teaching Box** follows every **Content Mastery** task at point of use in the *Teacher Edition*. These *If... Then...* boxes guide teachers to reinforce if students do not reach 80% mastery, or reteach if students score below 60% mastery on a **Content Mastery** task.

If . . .	Then . . .
Students score below 80%	Reinforce: • Unit 5 Spelling Words: Use *LANGUAGE! Words for Teachers* **Word Card Generator** for missed words.
Students score at or below 60%	Reteach: • Unit 5 Decodable Spelling Words: Use **Build It** in Unit 5, Lesson 1, Step 2. • Unit 5 **Essential Words**: Use **Memorize It** in Unit 5, Lesson 1, Step 2.

Prescriptive Teaching Box From Unit 5

Retesting based on student performance

Once the appropriate measures have been taken to reinforce or reteach concepts based on student scores, it is advisable to retest students to ensure they are performating at 80% proficiency or above before moving on. For more information on retesting, refer to the Content Mastery section of the *Assessment: Teacher Edition*.

DIFFERENTIATED INSTRUCTION FOR STEP 2

How will you respond when a student experiences difficulty in learning?

 Use **Special Instructional Support** activities to customize teaching materials and provide opportunities for individualized instruction.

Lesson 1	Lesson 2	Lesson 3	Lesson 4	Lesson 5
Step 1: *Sortegories* CD: Sound Count **Step 2:** *Words for Teachers* CD: Word Card Generator—Essential Words *Words for Teachers* CD: Word Study Guide—Spelling Words	**Step 1:** Folder Activity: Phoneme Sort: Words with Short Vowels **Step 2:** *Sortegories* CD: Sort It *Words for Teachers* CD: Fluency Builder Grid—Essential Words	**Step 2:** Folder Activity: Tic-Tac-Toe With Essential Words *Sortegories* CD: Build It **Step 5:** *LANGUAGE!* eReader CD: **"It'll Never Work"**	**Step 2:** Folder Activity: Syllable Sort: Number of Syllables in a Word **Step 3:** *Sortegories* CD: Categorize It	**Step 3:** *Sortegories* CD: Morph It

Lesson 6	Lesson 7	Lesson 8	Lesson 9	Lesson 10
Step 2: *Words for Teachers* CD: Word Unscramble **Step 3:** *Sortegories* CD: Relate It	**Step 2:** *Words for Teachers* CD: Word Search—Words with Schwa **Step 3:** *Sortegories* CD: Analogy Building **Step 4:** *Sortegories* CD: Grammar Sort	**Step 4:** *Words for Teachers* CD: Word Card Generator—Build Sentences with Direct Objects **Step 5:** *LANGUAGE!* eReader CD: **"Way to Go!"**	**Step 3:** *Words for Teachers* CD: Word Card Generator—Sort Words with Prefixes **Step 4:** Folder Activity: Grammar Sort—Present and Future Tense Verb Phrases	

Syllable Sort Folder Activity for Unit 1

Unit 14

mar	bar	bit
rab	ket	ber
test	con	

Closed   r- Controlled

?

The *Sortegories* Interactive CD ...	The *Words for Teachers* CD ...

• Ways to monitor student performance.
• Interactive decoding and encoding activities.
• Timed or untimed activities, including
   ▪ Sort It
   ▪ Build It
   ▪ Recognize It.
	• Software for creating customized activities.
	• A database of 4000+ words.
	• The ability to choose words according to content areas.
	• A range of activities, including
	   ▪ Word Card Generator
	   ▪ Word Study Guide
	   ▪ Fluency Builder Grid
	   ▪ Double It
	   ▪ Drop It.

Homework

Folder Activities and other Why Do/How To exercises provide additional ways to differentiate instruction before or after assessment. Students can play Tic-Tac-Toe using **Essential Words**, for example, or alphabetize **Unit Words** using self-stick notes.

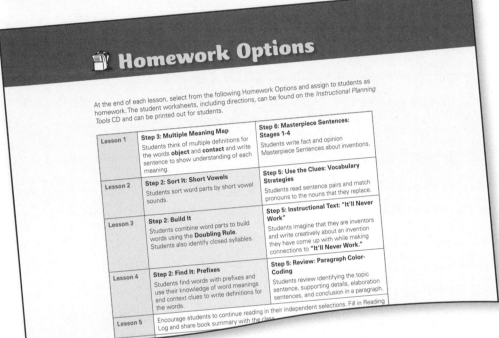

At the end of each lesson, select from the following Homework Options and assign to students as homework. The student worksheets, including directions, can be found on the *Instructional Planning Tools* CD and can be printed out for students.

Lesson 1	**Step 3: Multiple Meaning Map** Students think of multiple definitions for the words **object** and **contact** and write sentence to show understanding of each meaning.	**Step 6: Masterpiece Sentences: Stages 1-4** Students write fact and opinion Masterpiece Sentences about inventions.
Lesson 2	**Step 2: Sort It: Short Vowels** Students sort word parts by short vowel sounds.	**Step 5: Use the Clues: Vocabulary Strategies** Students read sentence pairs and match pronouns to the nouns that they replace.
Lesson 3	**Step 2: Build It** Students combine word parts to build words using the **Doubling Rule**. Students also identify closed syllables.	**Step 5: Instructional Text: "It'll Never Work"** Students imagine that they are inventors and write creatively about an invention they have come up with while making connections to **"It'll Never Work."**
Lesson 4	**Step 2: Find It: Prefixes** Students find words with prefixes and use their knowledge of word meanings and context clues to write definitions for the words.	**Step 5: Review: Paragraph Color-Coding** Students review identifying the topic sentence, supporting details, elaboration sentences, and conclusion in a paragraph.
Lesson 5	Encourage students to continue reading in their independent selections. Fill in Reading Log and share book summary with the class.	

The *Words for Teachers* CD allows you to create customized homework materials to meet the individual needs of your students.

Unit 13 Word Search homework for Step 2

Word Search *Use your highlighter to mark all of the words listed in the Word Bank in the puzzle below*

UNIT 13   STUDENT _____   DATE _____

Word Bank:			
conduct	discuss	inflict	unbend
conflict	disgust	nonfat	unbent
congress	infect	nonsense	unclad
discredit	inflect	nonskid	subject

```
Y P N I N F E C T B D T F Y F J R O N O N S N O N
D X Q M H J G U N B E N D Z C O N I N F L I C T G
L O R U V C M F Y D C O N F L I C T I S G U I N F
A Y L L P L O X O E N Z L R T I A R J M R K F R B
Z K C M W H U N C L A D U N B E D I S C U S S N T
M J Y V D I S C R E D I T E A S W B A K D J S T A
S K L F M W E C D E H F X J Q I Y L M A W I J C H
D N F V N U N O N P A T E W V A L S K U W B U E Q
X R F H Y E X Y O E Z T L U M E E J M H Z R H L K
U U C Z F M U C G D M K M V M E H M L E X A H G V
W Y F H V Q D Z O I X D A K D O A C F B F S B P W
M L A G Y W B F J X J J A F C E A O O I F E C T E
Q I D X U Y S J O O U G C U W O P Y T T R M I W U
C C W T Y C F U U Z I Q Z Q P X S O S L X F Z F J
M B L R D D P E J D X K Q L P N S G J Z F V T U H
O G W O I N C P Z T E A B A F X U G A T H U B M R
```

© 2005 Jane Fell Greene. All rights reserved. Published by Sopris West Educational Services.   Word Search

From the *LANGUAGE!* Classroom

Several of my special education high school students were struggling with their spelling mastery tasks as we approached Book D. In order to motivate them to do better, I rewarded those who got a 100% on their pretest by making them spelling teachers for the rest of the week. After checking the pretests, I had students with less than a perfect paper pick a spelling teacher from those who scored 100%. Students worked together for 5-6 minutes per day studying their words according to their peer's instructions. They could choose from an oral quiz, practicing on white boards, building words, etc. When it was time to take the mastery task, all students—including spelling teachers—took the spelling mastery test. Spelling teachers couldn't wait to find out how their students performed. Reteaching is no longer necessary after a mastery task because all of my students pass their spelling tests on the first try! Poor spellers are working harder to become teachers. More advanced spellers are taking more responsibility to teach their friends how to spell during peer editing, interactive text book assignments, and spelling tests. If no one gets 100% on the pretest, everyone studies and I give them another pretest the next day to determine the next round of teachers. Students love being spelling teachers!

Janice Kai, *Special Education Teacher*
St. Vrain Valley School District, Colorado

Table of Contents

RESEARCH BITE

Words are learned incrementally over time as a consequence of multiple exposures. As each exposure to the word occurs, depth of word knowledge increases along a continuum from shallow word knowledge to deep word knowledge. In general, the development of understanding of a term's meaning follows these steps:

1. Never saw it before.

2. Heard it but don't know the meaning.

3. Recognize it in context as having something to do with ...

4. Know the meaning well.

5. Can use the word in a sentence.

Paribakht & Wesche, 1997

Vocabulary knowledge is different from word recognition. Vocabulary refers to the reservoir of word meanings that we draw from in order to understand what we hear, express, or read. The term refers to the number of words in the cognitive bank of word meanings to which the student has access. All too often, students may be able to pronounce words accurately without knowing their meanings. Ultimately, it is the fluent access to these meanings that allows students to comprehend what they read.

Research: Why Do?

"Vocabulary serves as the bridge between the word-level processes of phonics and the cognitive processes of comprehension" (Hiebert & Kamil, 2005). Vocabulary learning must entail active engagement in learning vocabulary words (Dole, Sloan, & Trathen, 1995). Helping students develop a curiosity about words is an important aspect of vocabulary instruction. Providing instruction in **morphology**, word relationships, evolving meanings of new words in the language, figurative language, and content specific vocabulary builds students' awareness of word meanings (Hiebert & Kamil, 2005). Vocabulary should be taught both directly and indirectly, and direct instruction of vocabulary should be included in reading lessons (Kamil, 2004). Vocabulary and word meanings are best learned in relation to other known words and ideas (Beck & McKeown, 1991; Stahl, 1998). A direct approach to teaching word definitions, **connotation**, and **denotation** should complement a contextual approach in which students are asked to speculate about possible meanings for new words they encounter in text. There is direct evidence of the strong relationship between vocabulary knowledge and the ability to read at higher readability levels. Thus, to a considerable degree, vocabulary knowledge determines language comprehension and literacy (Biemiller, 1999).

morphology
the structure and formation patterns of words

connotation
implied meaning or association

denotation
literal meaning

How *LANGUAGE!* Does It

LANGUAGE! addresses vocabulary and morphology by:

- Building word knowledge through the exploration of multiple meanings, strategies for defining words, and study of word relationships, including antonyms, synonyms, homophones, and analogies.

- Developing vocabulary knowledge in context along with strategies to use the context to determine word meanings.

- Including instruction with idioms, expressions, and figurative language.

- Teaching common morphemes, beginning with inflectional endings *-ed*, *-s*, and *-ing*.

- Emphasizing the existence of large word families connected by a root. Anglo-Saxon, Latin, and Greek roots and **affixes** are taught sequentially and cumulatively.

affixes
additions to word roots, including prefixes and suffixes

What is Vocabulary?

> *"The term vocabulary refers to the storehouse of word meanings that we draw on to comprehend what is said to us, express our thoughts, or interpret what we read."*
>
> Moats, 2004
>
> *"Vocabulary is not a developmental skill or one that can ever be seen as fully mastered. The expansion and elaboration of vocabularies is something that extends across a lifetime."*
>
> Hiebert & Kamil, 2005

F

CALVIN AND HOBBES ©1989 Watterson. Dist. By UNIVERSAL PRESS SYNDICATE.
Reprinted with permission. All rights reserved.

Vocabulary and Morphology • **153**

What do you want students to learn?

- Word relationships: antonyms, synonyms, attributes, homophones, and analogies
- Multiple meanings, multiple uses
- Definition development
- Context-based vocabulary strategies
- Idioms and common expressions
- Use of dictionary and thesaurus
- Compound words
- Verb tense: irregular forms
- Nouns: irregular plural forms
- Inflectional and derivational endings
- Latin prefixes, roots, suffixes
- Greek combining forms.

attributes
qualities or characteristics

analogies
comparisons of words that are related in some way

idioms
distinctive expression that cannot be deciphered literally

In *Books A* and *B*, students learn word relationships such as synonyms, antonyms, attributes, and homophones. In addition, students learn multiple meanings of words and how to write authentic definitions using categories and **attributes** . They learn that inflectional endings add to the meaning of the word, but not its function. Idiomatic and common expressions are also discussed using unit vocabulary.

In *Books C* and *D*, word relationships continue with the addition of **analogies** in Book C and degrees of meaning in Book D. The study of derivational suffixes and their impact on word function also occurs in Books C and D. Vocabulary is expanded through the use of Latin roots, prefixes, and suffixes.

In *Books E* and *F*, vocabulary expansion with Latin roots, prefixes, and suffixes continue with the addition of Greek combining forms in Book F. Multiple meanings are studied in context. Figurative language such as similes, metaphors, and symbols are gradually introduced beginning in Book C, while **idioms** and common expressions continue to be discussed through book F.

What You Need to Know

What are the Layers of Word Knowledge

The vocabulary in English is vast. Linguists estimate there are approximately 1,000,000 English words. Many English words have multiple meanings and multiple functions that add to their complexity. Students who exhibit delays in vocabulary acquisition need an *efficient* means to gain vocabulary knowledge.

LANGUAGE! provides three layers of word learning. At the most basic level, that of the word, it is essential for students to move from speech to print (spelling) and from print to speech (reading). The next layer involves understanding the literal meanings of words and using the context in which words appear to assign the correct meaning to a word when that word has multiple meanings. The final layer involves mastering the nuances in meaning presented by figurative language. In this layer of word meaning, the reader or listener must interpret the meaning of a word or words in idioms, similes, metaphors, and other more abstract uses of language.

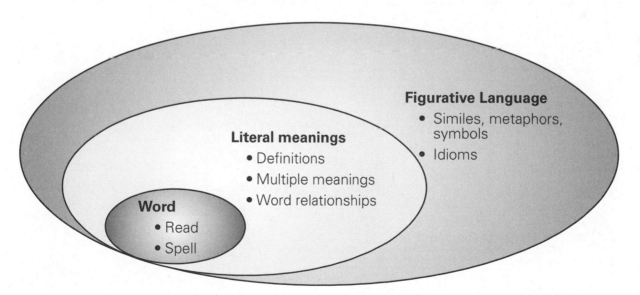

Figurative Language
- Similes, metaphors, symbols
- Idioms

Literal meanings
- Definitions
- Multiple meanings
- Word relationships

Word
- Read
- Spell

You Try It! Depth of Word Knowledge Exercise

Shallow Word Knowledge: partial understanding of a word because the word has been encountered in a limited context.

Deep Word Knowledge: deep understanding of a word is demonstrated when 1) multiple meanings and usages are understood; 2) the word can be used with accuracy in written and spoken language; 3) the word's definition can be generated (Moats, 2004).

Practice a Degrees of Meaning exercise by placing these adjectives in order of degree along the continuum from least amount of knowledge to greatest.

Word Bank				
recognizable	intimate	unknown	foreign	familiar

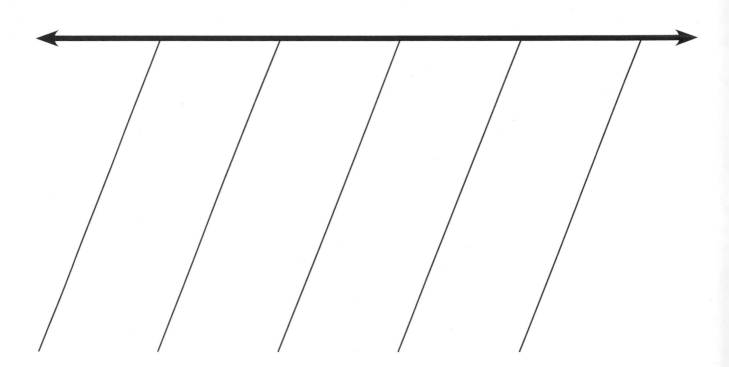

Three Sources of Vocabulary

Vocabulary throughout *LANGUAGE!* is developed from three sources in the curriculum:

Unit Words	Words in Context	Morphology
• Unit Words (decodable) • Essential Words (high frequency)	• Highlighted vocabulary words • Embedded vocabulary words	• Inflectional/derivational endings • Latin roots, prefixes, suffixes • Greek combining forms

Taught together, vocabulary based on the phonological scope and sequence and new words encountered in reading selections allow students to practice a range of vocabulary development strategies.

Unit Words

The Unit Words listed in the Handbook section of the Student Text are decodable. This means that they are constructed from the spelling patterns taught in each unit. These patterns follow the phonology scope and sequence. Furthermore, each Unit includes six "Essential Words"—high frequency terms with high utility in spoken and written language.

Step 3 objectives in teaching the Unit Vocabulary include:

- Understanding and creating meaningful definitions
- Generating multiple meanings of words
- Identifying and categorizing word relationships, including antonyms, synonyms, homophones, and analogies.

F

What You Need to Know

Content-based Vocabulary

The words from the student Instructional and Challenge Text selections were chosen largely according to the work of Isabel Beck (2002). Beck categorized vocabulary words into three tiers according to their academic utility in the language.

- Tier 1—most basic words rarely requiring an instructional explanation. Examples: *happy, school, boy, run*

- Tier 2—high utility words that appear across broad range of content areas; once learned these words are known in a wide variety of settings. Examples: *generally, simultaneous, productive, fortunate*

- Tier 3—content specific words with low frequency or utility outside of a specific content area. Examples: *isotope, isthmus, lathe.*

In *LANGUAGE!*, the words highlighted in the reading selections are largely Tier 2 words, though some Tier 3 words are introduced to guarantee the comprehension of content. These words, highlighted in yellow in the *Student Text* with definitions inserted in the margins, have been selected to enhance the current reading selection but will have applicability in other reading contexts as well. Selection of words for their esoteric or unique attributes has been minimized in order to provide students with the most useful word meanings.

Step 3 teaches context-based vocabulary through:

- Direct instruction of highlighted vocabulary words

- Context-based strategies that use context clues to infer the meanings of words encountered in text.

What You Need to Know

Morphology

Another Step 3 content strand builds word meaning through the study of morphology—meaningful segments of language, or morphemes, including roots, prefixes, suffixes, and combining forms.

***LANGUAGE!* features four dimensions of morphology:**

1. Inflectional Endings (Introduced in Books A and B)
2. Derivational Endings (Introduced in Books D–F)
3. Latin Roots (Introduced in Books D–F)
4. Greek Combining Forms (Introduced in Book F)

The Endings

There are two types of suffixes studied in *LANGUAGE!*—inflectional and derivational.

Inflectional suffixes are those that change the form of the word but not the part of speech. Inflectional endings are learned in early childhood, usually between ages four and seven, as children develop speech patterns that include the majority of inflectional forms. Inflectional endings show:

- Number   *-s, -es*
- Possession   *-'s, -s'*
- Time   *-ed, -ing*

Derivational suffixes change the form of the word. They can also change the function—the grammatical form, or part of speech. For example, derivational endings can transform:

- a noun to a verb   *human* to *humanize*   *-ize*
- a noun to an adjective   *fame* to *famous*   *-ous*
- a verb to a noun   *dictate* to *dictator*   *-or*

Key Term

Morpheme: is the smallest unit of meaning in language. Words from "bat" to "elephant" are morphemes, because they are units of meaning. However, a unit of meaning isn't always a stand-alone word. Prefixes and suffixes, for example, modify a word's meaning but are not stand-alone words. One of the most common morphemes is *s*, the English marker for plural in many words.

Example of morpheme counting:

bat=	1 morpheme:	bat
bats=	2 morphemes:	bat + s
bat's=	2 morphemes:	bat + 's
bats'=	3 morphemes:	bat + s +'

What You Need to Know

The Roots

There are two types of roots studied in *LANGUAGE!*—Latin roots and Greek combining forms.

Latin roots provide clues to the meanings of hundreds of thousands of English words. For example, the Latin root *mit* (go, send) is the root in the following words:

- *transmission*
- *emit*
- *permit*

Greek combining forms constitute the majority of words in the scientific and technological vocabulary of English. Examples of Greek combining forms:

- *dermatology*
  - *dermato* = skin
  - *logy* = science of
- *arachnophobia*
  - *arachno* = spider
  - *phobia* = fear of

RESEARCH BITE

Prefixes and suffixes, along with Latin roots and Greek combining forms, open doors to the meanings of the majority of English words. About 60 percent of English vocabulary is derived from Latin and Greek. Most scientific and technological vocabulary comes from Greek. Teaching the meaning of one root can provide the key to the meanings of hundreds of English words. Therefore, teaching meaning via the study of word parts proves efficient in helping students master the massive vocabulary of English.

Henry, 2005

3 INSTRUCTIONAL FOCUS

Instructional activities in Step 3: Vocabulary and Morphology emphasize explicit attention to word meanings and vocabulary enhancement.

How will you maximize student learning?

- Employ a variety of strategies and graphic organizers to accurately determine, define, and utilize word meanings

- Enhance word knowledge via instruction in word relationships: synonyms, antonyms, and homophones

- Incorporate vocabulary instruction in Step 5: Listening and Reading Comprehension by directly teaching the meanings of critical, academic words in text as well as teaching students how to use contextual clues to decipher unfamiliar terms

TEACHER'S TIP

For the "Expression of the Day," I write the expression on a 3 x 5 card. The students do a drum roll and a cymbal clap preceding it. This gives it an importance and helps students remember it. One of the games we play on Friday is for students to 1) use the expression in a sentence so that I can tell they know what it means or 2) to define it.

Linda Morning, *LANGUAGE! Teacher,*
Dundee Middle School; Dundee, Illinois

F

Why Do/How To Activities for Step 3

More complete descriptions and instructions for these activities can be found in the Appendix. See page 362 for the table of contents.

Preteaching Vocabulary	Activity Snapshot
Multiple Meaning Map	This graphic organizer helps build rich word associations.
Define It	This graphic organizer guides students in developing word definitions.
Draw It	Drawing vocabulary terms, expressions, and idioms allows students to nonverbally express their understanding.
Explore It	This exercise helps students explore a words denotations, connotations, functions, and usage.
Write It: Attributes	Specific Write It activities guide the application of concepts, content, and skills.
Relate It: Synonyms and Antonyms	This exercise helps develop understandings of word relationships, aiding word recall.
Context-Based Vocabulary	
Direct Instruction of Highlighted Words	Highlighted words in *Student Text* selections provide point-of-use vocabulary development.
Answer It	These exercises aid students in recognizing and responding to signal words.
Use the Clues	Context-based strategies help students develop vocabulary and comprehension.
Word Relationships	Students learn to recognize relationships between words, including antonyms, synonyms, homophones, and attributes.
Morphology	
Sort It	These activities add a kinesthetic element to recognizing words and developing definitions and meanings.
Rewrite It	These writing exercises let students practice manipulations of plural formation, verb endings, and other morphological changes.
Match It	Students match related elements, such as words with their definitions.
Define It: Prefixes	This exercise investigates prefix meanings, reinforcing recognition and usage.
Choose It	This activity calls on students to select appropriate word forms to complete sentences.
Using a Dictionary: Word Origins	This reference exercise lets students probe where English words originated.
Find It: Word Derivations	This activity calls on students to recognize and identify word forms.
Build It: Using Morphemes	Using manipulatives, students create words by assembling prefixes, roots, and suffixes.

Step 3 Activity Materials

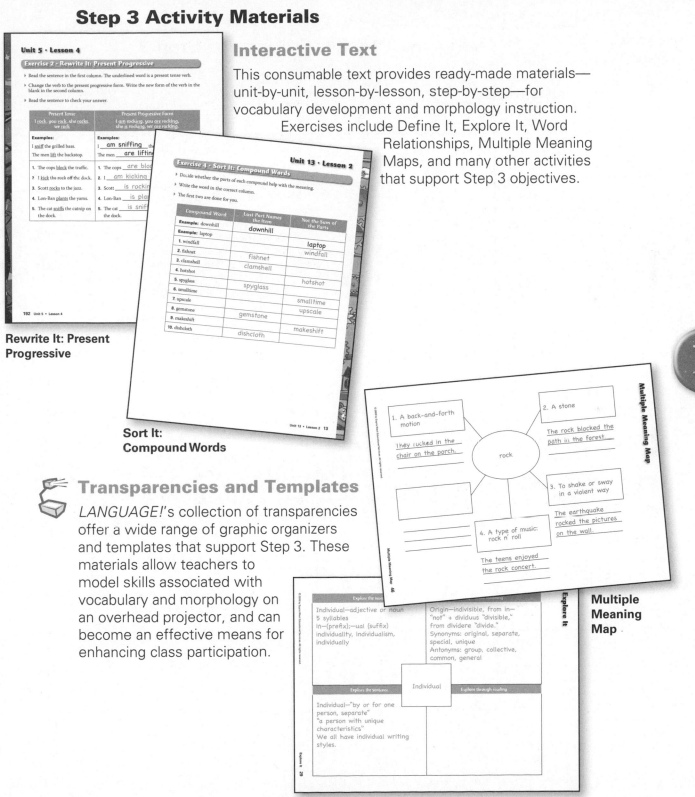

Interactive Text

This consumable text provides ready-made materials—unit-by-unit, lesson-by-lesson, step-by-step—for vocabulary development and morphology instruction. Exercises include Define It, Explore It, Word Relationships, Multiple Meaning Maps, and many other activities that support Step 3 objectives.

Rewrite It: Present Progressive

Sort It: Compound Words

Transparencies and Templates

LANGUAGE!'s collection of transparencies offer a wide range of graphic organizers and templates that support Step 3. These materials allow teachers to model skills associated with vocabulary and morphology on an overhead projector, and can become an effective means for enhancing class participation.

Multiple Meaning Map

Explore It

You Try It!

Using the Teacher Edition for Step 3

Lesson plans from *LANGUAGE!*'s three entry points—Unit 1, Unit 13, and Unit 25—are shown here to demonstrate Step 3 objectives, exercises, and activities across the curriculum.

Preparations

What does the icon signify?

_____

_____

What could you do to make sure your students always have the materials needed for a given lesson?

_____

_____

Directions

Do you think you need to read these directions more than once before teaching this activity? Why?

_____

_____

What directions could you give your students to ensure they copied the information onto the template?

_____

_____

Connections

How can you reinforce your focus on handwriting (steps 1 and 2) with this activity?

_____

_____

How can learning how to categorize a word help students develop a topic sentence?

_____

_____

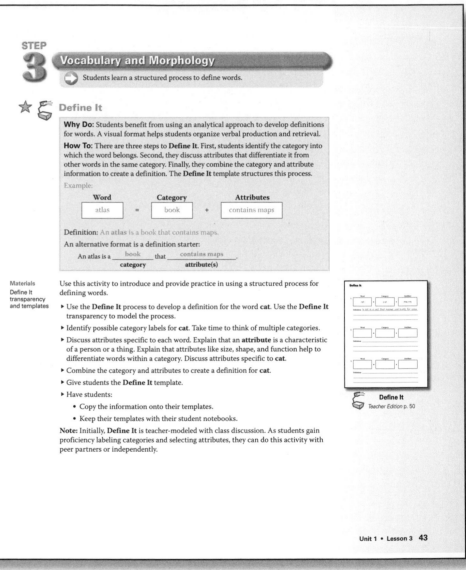

From Book A, Unit 1, Lesson 3

 You Try It!

How will you handle the need for dictionaries and thesauri in your classroom?

_____

_____

What are ways to help students remember what is being asked for in the first three quadrants that would affect your preparation of student materials?

_____

_____

Directions

After reading the directions, how will you introduce this activity to your students?

_____

_____

How will you ensure your students have their templates for Lesson 3?

_____

_____

Connections

How does this activity validate the work of syllable patterns in steps 1 and 2?

_____

_____

How does this activity create a bridge between vocabulary and reading comprehension?

_____

_____

STEP

3 **Vocabulary and Morphology**

Students complete word study for the Unit 13 target word (**invent**) at three levels: word, meaning, and sentence context. They also develop rich associations through common expressions.

★ **Explore It**

Why Do: The acquisition of literacy involves gaining cumulative and comprehensive knowledge of vocabulary words.

How To: This activity uses a graphic organizer to structure word exploration. Each cell of the organizer explores a different dimension of the word.

> **Word:** This cell focuses on the structural and grammatical features of the words. Students indicate the number of syllables and grammar functions for the word.

> **Meaning:** This cell captures information about the meaning parts (i.e., roots, prefixes, suffixes) and word relationships.

> **Sentence:** Use of the word in the sentence moves word knowledge to the application level.

> **Reading:** Information from reading selections expands the connections to meaning. Reading material is the source of examples and other facts related to the word.

The graphic organizer can be used to direct whole-class discussion or small-group work. Students should be encouraged to use the dictionary, thesaurus, and other resources.

Materials
Explore It transparency and templates
Dictionary
Thesaurus

Use this activity to build cumulative and comprehensive knowledge of the word **invent**.

▸ Display the **Explore It** transparency on the overhead.

▸ Give students copies of the **Explore It** template.

▸ Write the target word, **invent**, in the center space of the transparency.

▸ Use a dictionary, thesaurus, and other resource materials to complete the template with students.

▸ Model how to fill out each cell of the template.

▸ Have students:

• Work with you to research each cell of the template.

• Fill out the first three cells ("Explore the word," "Explore the meaning," and "Explore the sentence") of the template with you.

• Save the graphic organizer in their student notebooks to complete the last box, "Explore through reading," in Unit 13, Lesson 10, Step 3.

Explore It
Teacher Edition p. 24

Unit 13 • Lesson 1 **15**

From Book C, Unit 13, Lesson 1

You Try It!

Preparations

How will you prepare to teach the expression of the day?

_____

_____

Where will your students keep their work on idioms and expressions of the day?

_____

_____

Directions

What are your two reference points for directing this activity?

_____

_____

How will you direct your students to move from **Use the Clues** to the expression of the day?

_____

_____

Connections

How is the expression of the day connected to this unit?

_____

_____

How does Use the Clues help build the bridge between vocabulary and reading comprehension?

_____

_____

Vocabulary and Morphology

Students learn the meanings of selected vocabulary words before reading the text. They also apply context-based strategies to determine the meanings of words.

Vocabulary Focus

Materials
Interactive Text pp. C1–C6, Text Connection 1

Use this activity with **Text Connection 1**, "Circle Poems Take Many Forms," in the *Interactive Text* to preteach vocabulary.

▶ Have students:
- Turn to **Text Connection 1**, in the *Interactive Text*, pages C1–C6.

▶ Locate with students the highlighted words **sparingly**, **flout**, **convey**, **profound**, and **gaping** and their definitions at the bottom of the page.

▶ Read and discuss the definitions.

Build Vocabulary

▶ Work with students to clarify the meanings of these words in the context of the selection.

Use the Clues: Vocabulary Strategies

Materials
Interactive Text pp. C1–C6, Text Connection 1

Use this activity with **Text Connection 1** in the *Interactive Text* to help students identify the meanings of words with suffixes in context.

▶ Read lines 7–10 with students.

▶ Have students:
- Turn to **Text Connection 1, Use the Clues A: Vocabulary Strategies**, page C1.
- Use meaning signals and context clues to define the word **poetry**.

▶ Read lines 17–23 with students.

▶ Have students:
- Turn to **Use the Clues B: Vocabulary Strategies**, page C2.
- Use meaning signals to define the phrase **closed form**.

▶ Read text lines 59–63 with students.

▶ Have students:
- Turn to **Use the Clues C: Vocabulary Strategies**, page C4.
- Use meaning signals to define the phrase **open form**.

Expression of the Day

Use this activity to practice a new common expression daily.

▶ On the board or an overhead transparency, display this common expression: **the inner circle**.

▶ Discuss the meaning of the expression: *the small group of people who control an organization or political party*.

▶ Model the expression in a sentence.

Example: Dr. Simpson was a member of **the inner circle** of government officials.

Interactive Text pp. C1–C6, Text Connection 1

Teacher Edition pp. TC1–TC4

Unit 25 • Lesson 3   43

From Book E, Unit 25, Lesson 3

How will you evaluate student learning?

- Monitor Content Mastery

Content Mastery Tasks in Step 3 focus on:

- Word relationships
- Definitions
- Morphological concepts

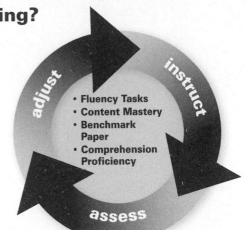

- Fluency Tasks
- Content Mastery
- Benchmark Paper
- Comprehension Proficiency

TEACHER'S TIP

Review the Content Mastery task for a given unit prior to teaching it in order to familiarize yourself with the content emphasis.

Prescriptive Teaching Boxes

A Prescriptive Teaching Box follows the directions for every Content Mastery task at point of use in the Teacher Edition. These *If... Then... Boxes* guide teachers to reinforce or reteach specific content if students do not achieve 80% mastery or reteach if students score below 60% mastery on a Content Mastery task. Prescriptive Teaching Boxes make tips for differentiation readily accessible.

F

If . . .	Then . . .
Students score below 80%	Reinforce: • Use **Word Relationships: Antonyms** in Unit 3, Lesson 3, Step 3; **Classify It** in Unit 3, Lesson 6, Step 3; and **Word Relationships: Synonyms** in Unit 3, Lesson 8, Step 3.
Students score at or below 60%	Reteach: • Use **Multiple Meaning Map** in Unit 3, Lesson 1, Step 3; **Word Relationships: Antonyms** in Unit 3, Lesson 3, Step 3; and **Word Relationships: Synonyms** in Unit 3, Lesson 8, Step 3.

From Unit 3, Lesson 8

You Try It!

Complete these exercises to see how *LANGUAGE!* provides instruction and practice for vocabulary development and development of encoding and decoding skills related to morphology.

Unit 5 · Lesson 7

Exercise 2 · Find It: Present Progressive

▶ Listen as your teacher reads the passage out loud.

▶ Look for the verb in each sentence.

▶ Underline the verbs that are in the present progressive form.

> Frogs are fond of ponds. A mob of them is hopping from the grass into the pond. They are swimming. The frogs swim to the land and hop on the sand. Some frogs are basking on the dock. Some frogs are sitting on a rock. Some frogs are plopping on the damp moss. They trill in the soft grass.
>
> A swift dog is running into the soft grass. It sniffs the grass. It is tracking frogs. Dogs are fond of tracking frogs. The frogs are panicking. They are hopping fast to the pond. They are spilling back into the pond. The tracking dog is gone.

Find It: Present Progressive

Why is this activity of finding present progressive verbs in Step 3: Vocabulary and Morphology?

_____

_____

_____

_____

_____

_____

Unit 13 · Lesson 6

Exercise 3 · Word Relationships: Antonyms, Synonyms, and Attributes

▶ Read each pair of words.

▶ Sort word pairs according to their relationship. Write the word pairs in the correct column.

▶ Discuss answers with your partner.

base : bottom   bottom : top

ribbon : thin   end : finish   jacket : buttons   disconnect : connect

over : above   eggs : dozen   common : uncommon   disappear : vanish

cotton : soft   nonstop : stop

Antonyms (Opposite)	Synonyms (Same)	Attributes

Word Relationships: Antonyms, Synonyms, and Attributes

How does this activity reinforce the work students do with Define It?

_____

_____

_____

_____

_____

You Try It!

Draw It

Draw the figurative meaning of each idiom. *Use* the idiom in a sentence to help describe what is happening in your picture.

UNIT 13   STUDENT _____   DATE _____

string someone along	look down your nose at someone
bite the bullet	be in hot water

Draw It

Draw It customized homework for Unit 13, from the *Words for Teachers* CD

Draw It

Brainstorm other ways/times to use the Draw It template to reinforce the meaning of idioms.

_____

_____

_____

_____

_____

F

DIFFERENTIATED INSTRUCTION FOR STEP 3

How will you respond when students are experiencing difficulty?

 Use **Special Instructional Support** activities to customize teaching materials and provide opportunities for individualized instruction.

Lesson 1	Lesson 2	Lesson 3	Lesson 4	Lesson 5
Step 1: *Sortegories* CD: Sound Count **Step 2:** *Words for Teachers* CD: Word Card Generator—Essential Words *Words for Teachers* CD: Word Study Guide—Spelling Words	**Step 1:** Folder Activity: Phoneme Sort: Words with Short Vowels **Step 2:** *Sortegories* CD: Sort It *Words for Teachers* CD: Fluency Builder Grid—Essential Words	**Step 2:** Folder Activity: Tic-Tac-Toe With Essential Words *Sortegories* CD: Build It **Step 5:** *LANGUAGE! eReader* CD: **"It'll Never Work"**	**Step 2:** Folder Activity: Syllable Sort: Number of Syllables in a Word **Step 3:** *Sortegories* CD: Categorize It	**Step 3:** *Sortegories* CD: Morph It
Lesson 6	Lesson 7	Lesson 8	Lesson 9	Lesson 10
Step 2: *Words for Teachers* CD: Word Unscramble **Step 3:** *Sortegories* CD: Relate It	**Step 2:** *Words for Teachers* CD: Word Search—Words with Schwa **Step 3:** *Sortegories* CD: Analogy Building **Step 4:** *Sortegories* CD: Grammar Sort	**Step 4:** *Words for Teachers* CD: Word Card Generator—Build Sentences with Direct Objects **Step 5:** *LANGUAGE! eReader* CD: **"Way to Go!"**	**Step 3:** *Words for Teachers* CD: Word Card Generator—Sort Words with Prefixes **Step 4:** Folder Activity: Grammar Sort—Present and Future Tense Verb Phrases	

From Unit 13

Sortegories CD ...	WORDS *for Teachers* CD offers ...

• monitors student performance
• offers interactive vocabulary activities
• provides open sorting activities that vary in difficulty
• suggests ways to scaffold instruction through exercises like
  ■ Morph It
  ■ Categorize It
  ■ Relate It
  ■ AnalogyBuilding
  ■ Multiple Meaning Maps
  ■ Cloze It.
	• the the ability to create customized activities
	• a database of 4000+ words
	• the ability to choose words according to content areas
	• a Word Study Guide.

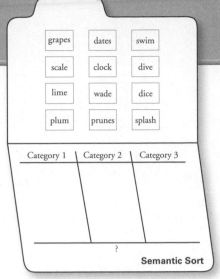

Folder Activities

Folder Activities provide an easy method for differentiating instruction before or after assessment. For example, students can sort words into categories using the Semantic Sort. This exercise challenges students to group vocabulary words according to meaning. For a closed sort, the category labels are provided. For an open sort, students generate the category labels on their own.

Semantic Sort

Homework

The *Words for Teachers* CD allows you to create customized homework materials that focus on Step 3 skills.

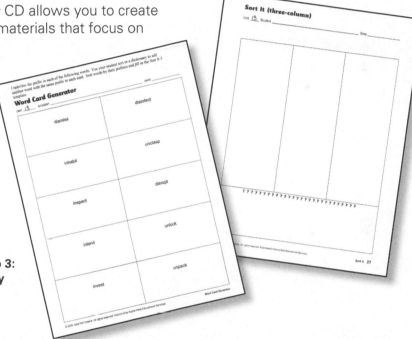

Examples of customized homework for Unit 13, Step 3: Vocabulary and Morphology

F

RESEARCH BITE

The root mit means "to send." Knowing this, students can derive the meanings of words using the same Latin root. Furthermore, Latin roots in English words are often the same as those in Spanish words thereby increasing the level of access to English for Spanish-speaking students who are learning English as a second language.

Henry, 2003

From the *LANGUAGE!* Classroom

Do you have access to a SMART Board? Try using Sortegories on a SMART Board with teams of students. When done with a timer, *Sortegories* becomes more like a game show when word building or word sorting. Teams can keep score based on their percentage correct and time used.

Janice Kai, *Special Education Teacher*
St Vrain School District, Colorado

Table of Contents

RESEARCH BITE

"Grammar need not be dry, arcane, pointless; it can be alive, entertaining, relevant. As with so many subjects, it depends only on how it is put across ... discovery first, definitions of terms last."

David Crystal, *Honorary Professor of Linguistics*
University of Wales, Bangor

G

RESEARCH: WHY DO STEP 4

Understanding grammatical rules makes accurate reading and communication possible, and a solid grasp of their form and function is vital if students are to achieve academically. Textbooks, tests, and most curricular content are written in academic language, language that emphasizes specific rules of grammar and usage. In the longer term, most employment opportunities benefit from this knowledge and these skills. Students who do not master academic language are likely to experience limited life opportunities.

Research: Why Do?

syntax
phrase and sentence structure

As students progress to reading text, a solid grasp of punctuation, **syntax**, and other grammatical "rules of the road" grows in importance. Interpreting embedded clauses, passive voice, verb tenses, and pronoun referents are among the recurring challenges for students with language weaknesses (Westby, 2004). "Syntax has always been viewed as a core deficit in children with the high incidence diagnosis of specific language impairment," writes Cheryl Scott in *The Handbook of Language and Literacy*, "and these same children are at high risk for reading and writing disorders" (Stone, Silliman, Ehren, Apel, eds., 2004). According to David Mulroy, author of *The War Against Grammar*: "Often the confusion is grammatical. To understand the meaning, you need to understand the structure" (Mulroy, 2003).

As mentioned above, the language of literacy—books, tests, and formal writing—is called "academic language." Along with the vocabulary dimension, text structure and syntactic complexity contribute to the difficulties many students experience when struggling to understand their textbooks (Shefelbine, California Frameworks, 1999). In other words, mastery of Step 4: Grammar and Usage will benefit your students across the school curriculum.

How *LANGUAGE!* Does It

LANGUAGE! addresses grammar and usage by:

- Providing the building blocks for comprehension and writing.
- Teaching the form and function of words in sentences, progressing from nouns to verbs to modifiers to function words.
- Emphasizing through explicit instruction the relationship between morphological features and grammatical function; for example, that the inflectional ending –*ed* signals a past tense verb.
- Teaching, modeling, and practicing sentence structure, syntax, elaboration, and combining.
- Making the abstract relationship between sentence parts concrete through the use of diagramming.

You Try It!

Got Grammar?

These high school exit exam questions, the first from California and the second from Illinois, demonstrate the importance of grammatical knowledge in high-stakes testing.

Choose the most effective substitute for each underlined part of the sentence.

1. <u>Akia told us about her safari across the plains of East Africa in our geography class.</u>

   a. In our geography class, Akia told us about her safari across the plains of East Africa.

   b. Akia told us about her safari in our geography class across the plains of East Africa.

   c. In our geography class Akia told about her safari across the plains of East Africa to us.

   d. Leave as is.

2. After <u>the final performance of one last</u> practice landing, the French instructor nodded to the young African-American woman at the controls and jumped down to the ground.

   a. no change   b. one finally ultimate

   c. one final

   d. one last final

What are the grammatical structures students need to know to answer these questions?

_____

_____

_____

_____

_____

What do you want students to learn?

- Identify the parts of speech, their forms, and their grammatical functions.

- Decipher and construct compound sentences

- Understand and accurately form subject-verb agreement.

- Identify punctuation marks and their contributions to comprehension and writing.

- Form increasingly complex and grammatically correct sentences.

In Step 4: Grammar and Usage, instruction focuses on the function of words, syntax (grammatical arrangement of words), and the mechanics that signal word forms and sentences.

- Grammar parallels the vocabulary strand. It focuses on the function that words have in sentences. For example, -s is introduced in Step 3: Vocabulary and Morphology to mean plural; -s is revisited in Step 4: Grammar and Usage with its function in subject agreement.

- Syntax and sentence structure are taught systematically and cumulatively to expand spoken language first and then written language.

- Sentence signals are taught explicitly including capitalization and punctuation. Emphasis is placed on the role of these mechanics to signal meaning.

What Is Grammar?

According to Webster's *New World College Dictionary, 4th Edition,* grammar is the set of rules that govern our speech and writing based on the study of its system of word structures (morphology) and word arrangements (syntax). In practice, grammar provides the linguistic conventions and clues—such as noun-pronoun agreement and punctuation—that help us navigate what we read, and communicate more effectively in spoken and written language.

> ## What You Need to Know

Vocabulary Connection: When Form Meets Function

Words serve specific functions in sentences. Their forms help determine their meanings, but their functions in sentences determine their meanings as well. To determine the function of a word, and often its meaning, the word must be studied in context. Context is critical in determining function.

Here is a common example. Think about the word *bat* in the following three sentences. How does the word *bat* function in each?

>The **bat** flew into the cave.

>They **bat** at the piñata at the party.

>She swings the **bat**.

In the first sentence, the word *bat* answers the question "What did it?" It is functioning as the subject. In the second sentence, the word *bat* answers the question "What did they do?" *bat* functions as the predicate in this second sentence. In the third sentence, it answers the question "Who (what) did she do it to?" and functions as the direct object. While it looks the same in each sentence, *bat* functions differently in each sentence.

A word's form does not necessarily reveal its function. Consider *batted* in these two sentences.

>In the first inning, the players *batted* poorly.

>The *batted* balls were scattered in the field.

In the first sentence, the word *batted* functions as the predicate, answering the question "What did they do?" In the second sentence, the word batted answers the question "What kind of balls?" In this case, *batted* functions as an adjective.

LANGUAGE! explicitly guides students to attend to both the form and function of words. This awareness improves students' comprehension and writing. Understanding how words function lays the foundation for learning grammar, which is the focus of Step 4.

What You Need to Know

Unlocking Syntax

"Syntax is the way in which words are arranged to show relationships of meaning within and sometimes between sentences" (Crystal, 2005). Students must be able to interpret the syntax or word order of a sentence in order to comprehend it. *LANGUAGE!* teaches students how to "unpack" a syntactically embedded sentence, such as the following:

During the show, a talented newcomer with his saxophone in hand, stepped nervously onto the stage.

Students learn, through explicit instruction and modeling, to ask a series of questions to unlock the meaning of a sentence.

Who is doing it?	newcomer
What did he do?	stepped
How did he step?	nervously
Where did he step?	onto the stage
When did he step?	during the show
What kind of newcomer?	talented
How many newcomers?	a
Which newcomer?	with his saxophone in hand

As students ask and answer these questions, they learn to focus on order and function to better understand each sentence they read.

Punctuation Matters

In Step 4: Grammar and Usage, students learn explicitly to note punctuation when they read and include punctuation when they write. You might explain punctuation to students, in the words of Lynne Truss in *Eats, Shoots & Leaves,* as "a courtesy designed to help readers to understand a story without stumbling.... [W]ithout it, there is no reliable way of communicating meaning. Punctuation herds words together, keeps others apart. Punctuation directs you how to read, in the way a musical notation directs a musician how to play."

As an example, placing commas correctly reflects comprehension of a given sentence. Note how punctuation alters the meaning of the following sentences:

> *A panda eats shoots and leaves.*
>
> *A panda eats, shoots, and leaves.*
> (Truss, 2003)

The first sentence tells us what a panda eats, while the second sentence tells us about three actions a panda takes.

Another example:

> *A woman, without her man, is nothing.*
>
> *A woman: without her, man is nothing.*
> (Truss, 2003)

In the first sentence, a woman is nothing without her man. In the second sentence, the addition of a colon and a comma reverses the meaning completely!

RESEARCH BITE

"As we discover more about the way we each use grammar as part of our daily linguistic survival, we inevitably sharpen our individual sense of styles, and thus promote our abilities to handle more complex constructions, both in speaking/ listening and in reading/writing. We become more likely to spot ambiguities and loose constructions, and to do something about it."

David Crystal, *Honorary Professor of Linguistics*
University of Wales, Bangor

G

What You Need to Know

Essential Phrases

In Step 3, students are introduced to fixed and regularly occurring groups of words that often defy understanding: idioms and common expressions. Students learn that idioms and common expressions have figurative meanings as opposed to the literal meaning of each individual word.

In Step 4, students are introduced to another type of frequently recurring sequences of words that are not grammatically complete structural units. Usually they are combinations of noun phrase fragments and/or prepositional phrase fragments that frequently appear together in written academic texts (Biber & Conrad, 1999). These sequences of words, like idiomatic and fixed expressions, are stored and retrieved from memory as a whole (Wray, 2002).

Biber and Conrad identified these kinds of recurring sequences in academic writing and referred to them as *lexical bundles*. Examples of these bundles are such phrases as *one of the most, the end of the*, and *the fact that the*. While these bundles are pervasive in academic writing, their frequency of use makes them easy to overlook. They are, however, "building blocks" for academic writing (Biber & Conrad, 1999).

Examples of "Essential Phrases" in *LANGUAGE!*

Essential Phrases are presented in the Focus On Academic Language boxes in the Teacher Edition. Here are examples and the unit and lesson where they are introduced.

- *for the rest of the* (Unit 7, Lesson 9)
- *I don't know what/where/why/how/if ...* (Unit 11, Lesson 6)
- *at the end of the* (Unit 7, Lesson 9)
- *one of the most* (Unit 13, Lesson 7)
- *the results of the* (Unit 15, Lesson 7)

English learners, as well as English speakers, need to be taught to recognize these lexical bundles during reading and to use them in writing. The lexical bundles identified by Biber and Conrad (1999) are explicitly taught in *LANGUAGE!* and are referred to as **Essential Phrases**. Like **Essential Words**, these **Essential Phrases** cannot be easily understood by looking at their constituent parts; they need to be recognized as a "whole" when reading, and retrieved as a "whole" in writing. Doing so will assist students' reading fluency and, in turn, comprehension when reading academic writing.

The introduction of **Essential Phrases** is controlled by the students' ability to decode and spell the constituent words. Students are taught the meaning of each phrase, and more importantly, how these **Essential Phrases** are used in written academic texts. Finally, they practice using **Essential Phrases** in their own speaking and writing.

Wray (2002) points out two clear benefits of this focus of explicit instruction. Once students learn the meanings of these phrases, learn how they are used in academic writing, and are comfortable with using them in their own writing, it will reduce the processing efforts required in reading and writing. It will also increase their ability to participate in the world of academic writing—both as reader and writer.

LANGUAGE! teaches students that both informal language (the language used at home and with friends) and formal, or academic language (the language of school and work), are viable means of communication. By mastering academic language, students possess the ability to "code-switch" in order to present themselves and their ideas in the most effective manner whatever the situation.

Step 4: Grammar and Usage also introduces students to the idiosyncrasies of English usage. English incorporates vast arrays of figures of speech and other problematic language conventions. *LANGUAGE!* directly teaches idiomatic expressions, figurative language, and other nonliteral usage.

How will you maximize student learning?

- Provide explicit instruction and modeling about parts of speech, sentence structure, the way words work together in context, and punctuation.

- Teach and demonstration strategies for sentence decoding and building, identifying the function of words in sentences, and recognizing the impact of word order on meaning.

- Guide the exploration, recognition, and understanding of essential phrases, idiomatic expressions, and other forms of figurative language.

CALVIN AND HOBBES ©1986 Watterson. Dist. By UNIVERSAL PRESS SYNDICATE. Reprinted with permission. All rights reserved.

Why Do/How To Activities for Step 4

More complete descriptions and instructions for these activities can be found in the Appendix. See page 362 for the table of contents.

Grammar	Activity Snapshot
Code It	This exercise provides structured practice analyzing grammar components in text.
Sort It	These exercises help reader's recognize parts of speech, types of nouns and verbs, and other grammatical concepts.
Identify It	Students tell apart parts of speech by distinguishing nouns from verbs, common nouns from proper nouns, main verbs from helping verbs, etc.
Find It	Readers locate parts of speech and other grammar-related concepts in text.
Text Connection	A variety of text-centered activities guide students in using grammar to better understand text selections.
Syntax	
Masterpiece Sentences	This highly structured writing practice lets students explore grammar as they create sentences.
Diagram It	Students use sentence diagramming to analyze grammar concepts.
Sentence Structure	
Rewrite It	These exercises provide opportunities to apply grammar knowledge
Combine It	This structured practice explicitly teaches students how to create more syntactically complex sentences.
Sentence Dictation	This writing activity helps students recognize syntactic structure and content.
Punctuate It	These exercises allow targeted practice of specific punctuation marks.

TEACHER'S TIP

Use a permanent marker to write the Masterpiece Sentence questions on laminated sentence strips and then apply magnetic tape to the back of the strips. These can then be placed on a large classroom whiteboard. Students love coming up to the board to contribute words to the sentence and then manipulate the words/phrases around for sentence variety. The use of dry erase markers makes for a quick clean up. While a student is at the board, the other class members are using either sticky notes or laminated pieces of cardstock at their desks to record their words and manipulate word order.

Charlene Allred, *Junior High Reading Coach*
Mesa Public Schools; Mesa, Arizona

STEP 4

Activity Materials

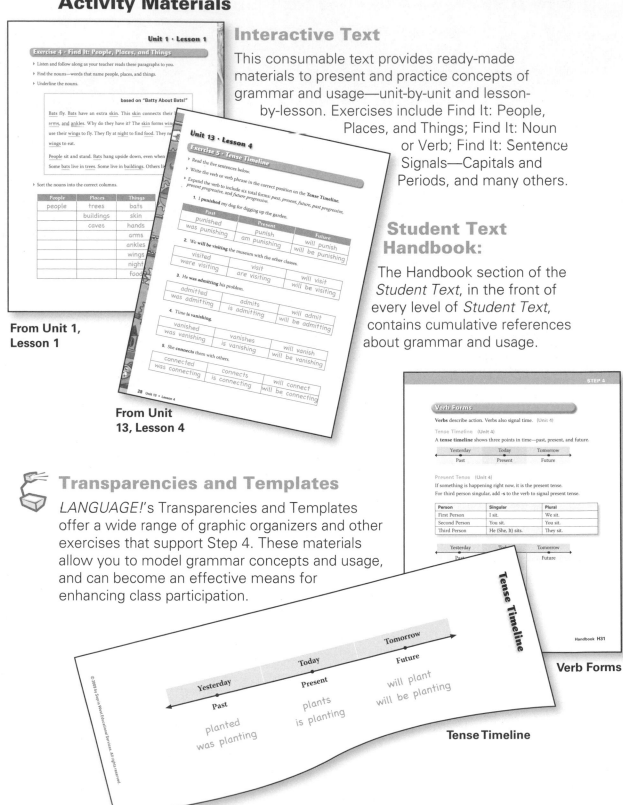

Interactive Text

This consumable text provides ready-made materials to present and practice concepts of grammar and usage—unit-by-unit and lesson-by-lesson. Exercises include Find It: People, Places, and Things; Find It: Noun or Verb; Find It: Sentence Signals—Capitals and Periods, and many others.

Student Text Handbook:

The Handbook section of the *Student Text*, in the front of every level of *Student Text*, contains cumulative references about grammar and usage.

From Unit 1, Lesson 1

From Unit 13, Lesson 4

Transparencies and Templates

LANGUAGE!'s Transparencies and Templates offer a wide range of graphic organizers and other exercises that support Step 4. These materials allow you to model grammar concepts and usage, and can become an effective means for enhancing class participation.

Verb Forms

Tense Timeline

Using the Teacher Edition for Step 4

Lesson plans for Step 4: Grammar and Usage from *LANGUAGE!*'s three entry points—Unit 1, Unit 13, and Unit 25—are shown here to demonstrate the range of objectives, exercises, and activities across the curriculum.

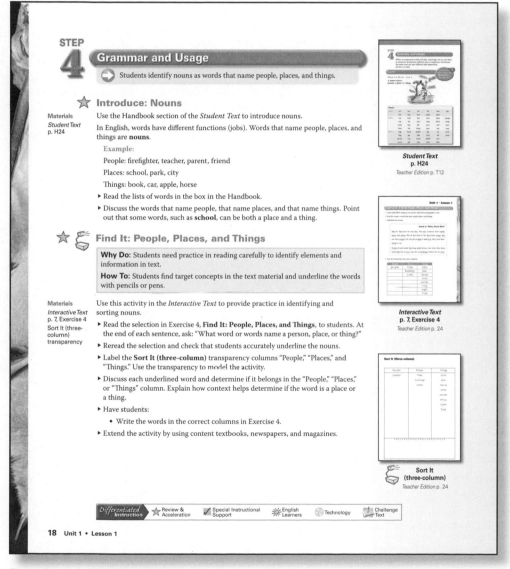

From Book A, Unit 1, Lesson 1

Preparations

How could you prepare the examples to display ahead of time?

_____

_____

What materials do you need to prepare and what equipment will you need to teach these activities?

_____

_____

Directions

Where are the students working when you are introducing nouns?

_____

_____

How do you know where to direct the students for completing different activities?

_____

_____

Connections

How is sorting nouns related to reading comprehension?

_____

_____

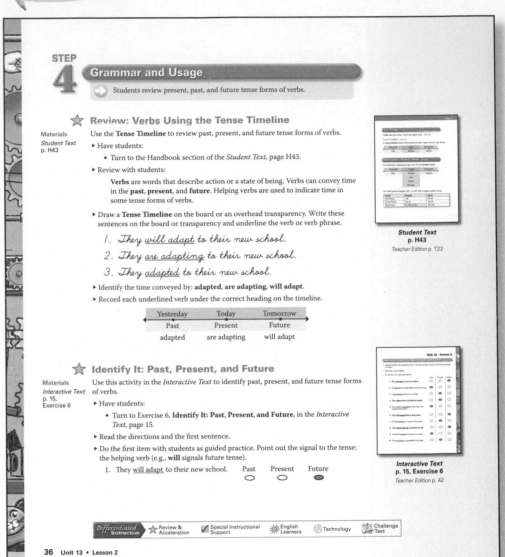

You Try It!

Preparations

What do you need to have ready to teach the Tense Timeline?

_____

_____

What materials will students need for these two activities?

_____

_____

Directions

How can you make the review of the **Tense Timeline** interactive?

_____

_____

How will you monitor student understanding as they complete **Identify It**?

_____

_____

Connections

How does the **Tense Timeline** make the abstract concept of verb tense more concrete?

_____

_____

How could you make the **Tense Timeline** more interactive if students are struggling to understand verb tense?

_____

_____

From Book C, Unit 13, Lesson 2

You Try It!

STEP 4

Grammar and Usage

➡ Students distinguish between phrases and independent clauses. They also recognize run-on sentences and learn strategies to correct them.

Review: Phrases and Simple Sentences

Use this activity to review the difference between a phrase and a simple sentence.

▸ Review with students:

A **phrase** is a group of words that functions as a single word.

A phrase does not have a subject and predicate.
Examples: in each line, about the theme, to recite the poem

A **simple sentence** is a group of words that has one subject and one predicate and conveys a complete thought.
Examples: The poet wrote quickly.

The subject is **poet** (Who did it?); the predicate is **wrote** (What did the poet do?).

Introduce: Independent Clauses

Materials
Student Text
p. H73

Use the Handbook section of the *Student Text* to introduce the concept that a simple sentence is an independent clause.

▸ Have students:

• Turn to the Handbook section of the *Student Text*, page H73.

▸ Explain to students:

A **clause** is a group of words that contains a subject and a predicate.

An **independent clause** has one subject and one predicate; it represents a complete thought.

A **simple sentence** contains one subject and one predicate and represents a complete thought. Therefore, a simple sentence can also be called an independent clause.

▸ Write the following words on the board or an overhead transparency, omitting the capital letter and punctuation:

poets make music with words

▸ Have students:

• Read the words aloud.

• Decide if they make a sentence. yes

• Identify the subject by asking themselves "Who does it?" poets

• Identify the predicate by asking themselves "What do they do?" make

• Tell where to place the capital letter and punctuation. Poets; words.

▸ Ask students if this is an independent clause. yes Why? because the sentence has one subject and one predicate, and is a complete thought

Student Text
p. H73
Teacher Edition p. T37

Differentiated Instruction ★ Review & Acceleration | ✓ Special Instructional Support | ☀ English Learners | ◉ Technology | ⬥ Challenge Text

56 Unit 25 • Lesson 4

From Book E, Unit 25, Lesson 4

Preparations
How will you prepare to teach these activities?

_____

_____

This lesson introduces "independent clauses." Do you need to teach this concept to mastery in this lesson?

_____

_____

Directions
How will you use the *Student Text* in this lesson?

_____

_____

How will you check student comprehension of the concepts reviewed here?

_____

_____

Connections
How can you use the Masterpiece Sentence questions to help students determine the difference between a phrase and an independent clause?

_____

_____

How will this activity impact your students' writing skills?

_____

You Try It!

Complete these exercises to see how *LANGUAGE!* offers explicit instruction for teaching Step 4: Grammar and Usage.

How can you help your students remember to do both steps in the directions?

_____

_____

_____

How many items do you model for students?

_____

_____

_____

Do the activity.
Did you use the context? Why?

_____

_____

_____

Unit 1 · Lesson 5

Exercise 2 · Review: Noun or Verb

▸ Listen to your teacher read this information to you.

based on "Batty About Bats!"

Bats have wings. They have skin that connects parts of their bodies.
$\overline{1}$ $\overline{2}$
The skin makes wings. Bats use their wings to fly. They fly at night
$\overline{3}$ $\overline{4}$ $\overline{5}$
to find food. Flying takes energy. Food makes energy. Bats eat a lot.
$\overline{6}$ $\overline{7}$ $\overline{8}$
Some eat fruits and flowers. Some eat frogs, fish, and lizards. Some
$\overline{9}$
eat flies and other bugs.
$\overline{10}$

▸ Put an X to show if the word is a noun or verb.

▸ If it is a noun, put an X to show if it is singular or plural.

	The word is a		If it is a noun, it is	
	Noun	Verb	Singular	Plural
1. bats				
2. skin				
3. makes				
4. use				
5. fly				
6. food				
7. energy				
8. eat				
9. fruits				
10. flies				

Model

Pair/Share

22 Unit 1 • Lesson 5

***Interactive Text* from Book A**

You Try It!

Unit 13 · Lesson 4

Exercise 5 · Tense Timeline

▶ Read the five sentences below.

▶ Write the verb or verb phrase in the correct position on the **Tense Timeline**.

▶ Expand the verb to include six total forms: *past, present, future, past progressive, present progressive,* and *future progressive.*

1. I **punished** my dog for digging up the garden.

Past	Present	Future

2. We **will be visiting** the museum with the other classes.

3. He **was admitting** his problem.

4. Time **is vanishing**.

5. She **connects** them with others.

28 Unit 13 · Lesson 4

How can you get students to actively engage in this activity?

_____

_____

_____

_____

_____

G

Interactive Text from Book C

You Try It!

How could you make this
activity more interactive
and manipulative?

_____

_____

_____

_____

_____

Unit 25 · Lesson 4

Exercise 5 · Combine It: Compound Sentences

▸ Read each pair of independent clauses.

▸ Decide whether to use **and**, **but**, or **or** to join the clauses.

▸ Write the compound sentence on the line.

▸ Add sentence signals—capital letters, commas, and end punctuation.

▸ Circle the conjunction used to join the independent clauses.

1. My father loves reading poetry.
   My mother prefers to read science journals.

   _____

   _____

2. The class went to a play.
   They also went backstage to meet the actors.

   _____

   _____

3. The student may start to write his poem tonight.
   He may postpone his work until the weekend.

   _____

   _____

4. The poem had an organized rhythm.
   It had a regular rhyme pattern, too.

   _____

   _____

5. The students could choose to read their poems aloud.
   They could choose to post their poems on the bulletin board.

   _____

   _____

Interactive Text **from Book E**

What You Need to Know

Structure and Function of English

The structure and function of the English language are directly taught to mastery in *LANGUAGE!* Why? Textbooks and tests are written in academic language. Employment opportunities require academic language. Students who do not master academic language have limited life opportunities.

LANGUAGE! teaches students that both informal language (the language used at home and with friends) and formal, or academic language (the language of school and work) are viable means of communication. Students master academic language so that they, like most educated adults, have the ability to code-switch.

English incorporates vast arrays of figures of speech and other problematic language usage devices. Idiomatic expressions, figurative language, and other unusual usages are directly taught.

Teacher's Tip

Use a permanent marker to write the Masterpiece Sentence questions on laminated sentence strips and then apply magnetic tape to the back of the strips. These can then be placed on a large classroom whiteboard. Students love coming up to the board to contribute words to the sentence and then manipulate the words/phrases around for sentence variety. The use of dry erase markers makes for a quick clean up. While a student is at the board, the other class members are using either sticky notes or laminated pieces of cardstock at their desks to record their words and manipulate word order.

Charlene Allred, *Junior High Reading Coach*
Mesa Public Schools; Mesa, Arizona

What You Need to Know

What are Masterpiece Sentences?

The **Masterpiece Sentences** process guides students to construct sentences, element by element. Through six stages, students build and then expand a base sentence. This sentence expansion process is a vehicle to develop the understanding of grammatical and syntactic structures and to apply it to speaking and writing. In this process, students generate components of sentences and record them on pieces of paper. By manipulating the sentence components, students learn to write increasingly more complex sentences. For example, the process begins with the base sentence: **The lion crept.**

What did it? The lion	What did it do? crept.

Using a series of questions about the subject and predicate, the base is expanded. As part of the process, word choice is refined.

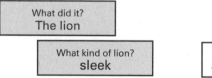
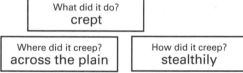

Finally, the sentence components are rearranged for variety and interest.

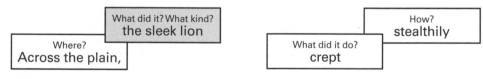

The **Masterpiece Sentence** process uses concrete manipulation of sentence parts as one way to explain the development of complete sentences. This process complements sentence diagramming.

Why Diagram Sentences?

Students who have not read widely in English have not developed the "sense of a sentence" necessary for developing comprehension and composition skills. Explaining that a sentence is a group of words that expresses a complete thought is an elusive abstraction. Defining a sentence, using words like *subject* and *predicate*, no matter how well explained, does not help most students. We need to make the abstract concrete.

Who (what) did it?   *What did they (he, she, it) do?*

| simple subject | simple predicate |

In the initial developmental stages of composition and grammar, diagramming sets the stage. It ensures that: a) students can actually see the elements necessary for a complete sentence; and b) students can recognize a complete or incomplete sentence.

The lion crept.

Who (what) did it?   *What did they (he, she, it) do?*

| lion | crept |

The

As students' abilities develop, diagramming illustrates interrelationships among sentence parts. It doesn't help to explain that one part "modifies" another part. This, too, is grossly abstract. Diagramming explicitly shows function. It illustrates how words relate to each other to create meaning. Below, note how the adjective sleek is positioned beneath *lion*—the noun that functions as the simple subject of the sentence. Note how the adverb *stealthily* and the adverbial prepositional phrase *across the plain* are positioned beneath *crept*— the verb that functions as the simple predicate of the sentence.

The sleek lion crept stealthily across the plain.

Who (what) did it?   *What did they (he, she, it) do?*

Which lion? What kind of lion? Crept how? when? where?

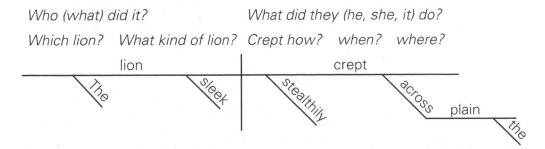

STEP 4

As students begin to develop composition skills, we often advise them as follows: "Vary your sentence structure" or "Expand your sentences." Students with limited reading and writing experience simply don't know how. Diagramming more complex sentences provides concrete and multisensory experience and practice with the versatility of English and illustrates the myriad variations of basic sentence patterns.

Across the plain, the sleek lion crept stealthily.

Advancing reading comprehension to higher levels requires more than vocabulary. It requires the explicit teaching of syntax. Teaching the interrelationships among words and phrases within sentences ultimately improves reading comprehension. When we make these abstractions concrete, students see the interrelationships. A visual complement to an explanation, combined with the hands-on opportunities to manipulate sentence parts through diagramming and **Masterpiece Sentences**, provides the concrete experiences that many students need. Below, note that a prepositional phrase (*in the pale moonlight*) that is part of the *predicate* is positioned at the beginning of the sentence. Manipulating sentence parts helps students to see the ways in which English sentences can be modified.

In the pale moonlight, the sleek, ravenous lion crept stealthily, across the wild savannah.

Who (what) did it?   *What did they (he, she, it) do?*

Which lion?   What kind of lion?   *Crept how?   when?   where?*

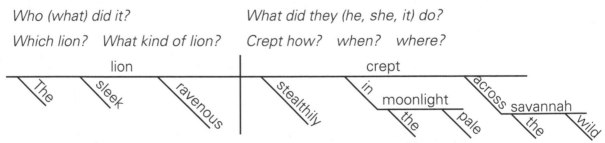

Consider this: many students have adequate vocabulary and decoding to comprehend a passage. But when sentences have embedded syntax—as they do in textbooks—comprehension fizzles. This is because students often lose meaning as the sentence becomes more complex or as sentence elements shift position. These students require explicit teaching of the *variety of structures* of English sentences.

In answer to the question: Why teach diagramming? The answer is clear. We teach diagramming to make clear the critical interrelationships among *grammar*, *composition*, and *comprehension*. (See *Teacher Resource Guide*, page 352, for the progression of sentence diagramming.)

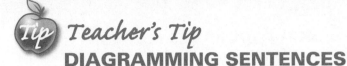

Teacher's Tip
DIAGRAMMING SENTENCES

Here are basic rules for diagramming sentences:

- *A "base sentence" is placed on a horizontal line, separated by a vertical line that dissects the main horizontal line. This will be the only line that completely dissects the baseline.*

- *Direct objects are placed on the baseline separated from the predicate by a vertical line that stops at the baseline.*

- *Adjectives, articles, and adverbs are placed on diagonal lines below the subject, predicate, or direct object that they modify.*

- *Prepositional phrases are broken down into the preposition on the slanted line, the object of the preposition on a line horizontal to the baseline, and the article on a slanted line below the object of the preposition.*

- *Compounded subjects, predicates, and direct objects are placed on horizontal lines that run parallel to the baseline and are joined by a triangle. The article is placed inside the triangle.*

- *The position on a diagram is completely related to the function of the word or groups of words as opposed to the order of the words in a sentence.*

"Sorry, but I'm going to have to issue you a summons for reckless grammar and driving without an apostrophe."

Diagram It: Compare Form and Function

Diagramming helps you see how the position of a word in a sentence changes its function. Note the form and function of the word **bat** in each of the sentences.

1. The **bat** flew into the cave

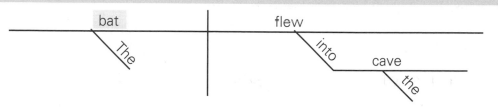

2. They **bat** at the piñata at the party.

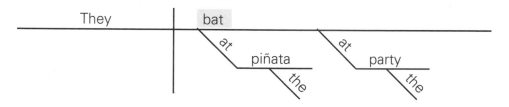

3. She swings the **bat**.

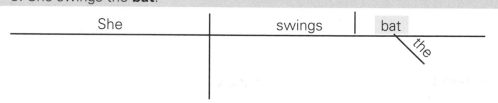

4. In the first inning, the players **batted** poorly.

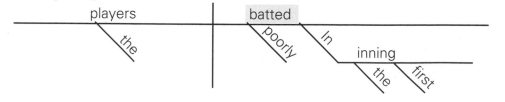

5. The **batted** balls were scattered across the field.

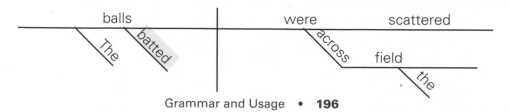

1. **Bat** is functioning as a **subject**.

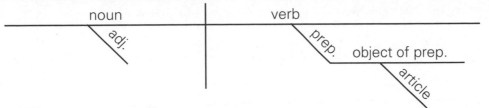

2. **Bat** is functioning as the **predicate**.

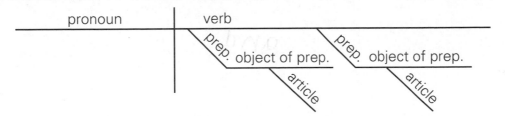

3. **Bat** is functioning as the **direct object**.

4. **Batted** is functioning as the **predicate**.

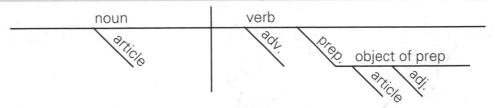

5. **Batted** is functioning as an **adjective** modifying the subject.

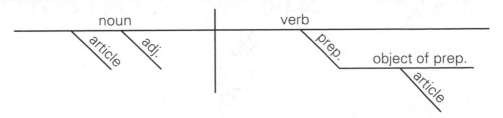

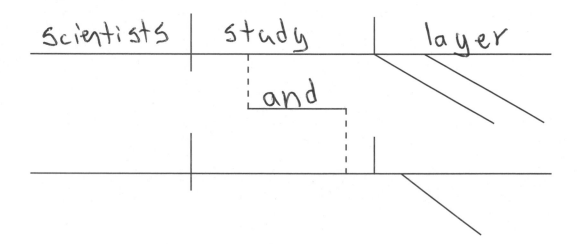

You Try It! Diagram It: Compound Sentences

Here is your opportunity to practice your diagramming skills. The first exercise comes from your students' Book D *Interactive Text*, Unit 18, Lesson 7. The second is from the same lesson, but uses the Diagram It 6 transparency. This allows class-wide modeling of the skill.

Scientists study the ozone layer, and they conduct many experiments.

Scientists | study | layer

and

Many countries govern Antarctica, and they send researchers there.

(noun / pronoun)   (verb)   (noun/pronoun)

countries | govern | Antarctica

(adj.)

conj.
and

(subject)   (action state of being)   (Direct object)

they | send | researchers

there
adverb

STEP 4 ONGOING ASSESSMENT

How will you evaluate student learning?

- Monitor Content Mastery

Content Mastery tasks in Step 4 focus on:

- Grammar concepts
- Sentence structure
- Mechanics

Vocabulary from the unit and excerpts from the text selections are used for these assessment tasks. This allows students to focus on the grammar and syntax concepts rather than decoding demands. Question formats include open-ended, identification, and multiple choice.

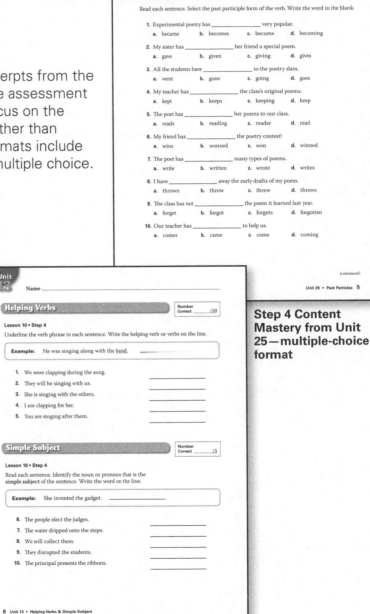

Unit 25

Name _____

Past Participles

Lesson 9 • Step 4

Number Correct _____ /10

Read each sentence. Select the past participle form of the verb. Write the word in the blank.

1. Experimental poetry has _____ very popular.
   a. became   b. becomes   c. become   d. becoming

2. My sister has _____ her friend a special poem.
   a. gave   b. given   c. giving   d. gives

3. All the students have _____ to the poetry slam.
   a. went   b. gone   c. going   d. goes

4. My teacher has _____ the class's original poems.
   a. kept   b. keeps   c. keeping   d. keep

5. The poet has _____ her poems to our class.
   a. reads   b. reading   c. reader   d. read

6. My friend has _____ the poetry contest!
   a. wins   b. wonned   c. won   d. winned

7. The poet has _____ many types of poems.
   a. write   b. written   c. wrote   d. writes

8. I have _____ away the early drafts of my poem.
   a. thrown   b. throw   c. threw   d. throws

9. The class has not _____ the poem it learned last year.
   a. forget   b. forgot   c. forgets   d. forgotten

10. Our teacher has _____ to help us.
    a. comes   b. came   c. come   d. coming

(continued)

Unit 25 • Past Participles **5**

Step 4 Content Mastery from Unit 25—multiple-choice format

Unit 3

Name _____

Subject or Direct Object

Lesson 10 • Step 4

Listen to your teacher read this information to you.

Wrap It Up!

Scientists made jackets for the bones. The jackets protect the fossils. They use paper or foil. They cut burlap strips. They dip the strips in plaster. They wrap each bone. First, they cover the top and side. The strip dries. Then, they turn it over. Next, they cover the other side. They cover it with strips. This cover creates the jacket. The scientists number the jackets. The log keeps track of the bones in jackets. Dr. Sereno keeps the dig's log book. The bones head back to the lab in Chicago for more study.

Put an X to show if the noun is a subject or a direct object.

	Is the noun a	
	Subject	Direct Object
1. scientists		
2. jackets		
3. jackets		
4. fossils		
5. strips		
6. bone		
7. side		
8. cover		
9. log		
10. log book		

Total Number Correct _____ /10

Unit 3 • Subject or Direct Object **15**

Step 4 Content Mastery from Unit 3—open-ended format

Unit 13

Name _____

Helping Verbs

Lesson 10 • Step 4

Number Correct _____ /10

Underline the verb phrase in each sentence. Write the helping verb or verbs on the line.

Example: He was singing along with the band. _____

1. We were clapping during the song. _____
2. They will be singing with us. _____
3. She is singing with the others. _____
4. I am clapping for her. _____
5. You are singing after them. _____

Simple Subject

Lesson 10 • Step 4

Number Correct _____ /5

Read each sentence. Identify the noun or pronoun that is the **simple subject** of the sentence. Write the word on the line.

Example: She invented the gadget. _____

6. The people elect the judges. _____
7. The water dripped onto the steps. _____
8. We will collect them. _____
9. They disrupted the students. _____
10. The principal presents the ribbons. _____

6 Unit 13 • Helping Verbs & Simple Subject

Step 4 Content Mastery from Unit 13—identification format

Prescriptive Teaching Boxes

A Prescriptive Teaching Box follows every Content Mastery task at point of use in the Teacher Edition. These *If... Then...* Boxes guide teachers to reinforce if students do not reach 80% mastery, or reteach if students score below 60% mastery, on a Content Mastery Task.

If . . .	Then . . .
Students score below 80%	Reinforce: • Verbs: Use the **Folder Activity:** Grammar Sort—Present and Past Tense Verbs. See the *Teacher Resource Guide.* • Simple Subjects and Direct Objects: Use **Code It: Direct Object**, Unit 13, Lesson 6, Step 4.
Students score at or below 60%	Reteach: • Helping Verbs: Use **Identify It: Main Verb or Helping Verb**, Unit 13, Lesson 3, Step 4. • Verbs: Use **Identify It: Past, Present, Future Verbs**, Unit 13, Lesson 2, Step 4. • Simple Subjects: Use **Review: Simple Subject and Simple Predicate**, Unit 13, Lesson 6, Step 4. • Direct Objects: Use **Review: Direct Objects**, Unit 13, Lesson 6, Step 4.

Step 4 Prescriptive Teaching Box from Unit 13, Lesson 10

Retesting based on student performance

Once the appropriate measures have been taken to reinforce or reteach concepts based on student scores, it is advisable to retest students to ensure they are performing at 80% proficiency or above before moving on. For more information on retesting, refer to the Content Mastery section of the *Assessment*: Teacher Edition.

DIFFERENTIATED INSTRUCTION FOR STEP

How will teachers respond when a student experiences difficulty in learning?

 Use Special Instructional Support activities to customize teaching materials and provide opportunities for individualized instruction.

Lesson 1	Lesson 2	Lesson 3	Lesson 4	Lesson 5
Step 1: *Sortegories* CD: Sound Count **Step 2:** *Words for Teachers* CD: Word Card Generator *Words for Teachers* CD: Word Study Guide	**Step 1:** Folder Activity: Phoneme Discrimination **Step 2:** *Sortegories* CD: Sort It *Words for Teachers* CD: Fluency Builder Grid	**Step 2:** *Sortegories* CD: Build It Folder Activity: Alphabetize Essential Words Units 1–3 **Step 5:** *LANGUAGE! eReader* CD: **"Africa Digs"**	**Step 2:** Folder Activity: Tic-Tac-Toe with Essential Words **Step 3:** *Sortegories* CD: Morph It	**Step 2:** *Words for Teachers* CD: Word Card Generator—Sort Plural and Possessive Nouns **Step 3:** *Sortegories* CD: Categorize It
Lesson 6	**Lesson 7**	**Lesson 8**	**Lesson 9**	**Lesson 10**
Step 2: *Words for Teachers* CD: Word Unscramble **Step 3:** *Sortegories* CD: Relate It **Step 4:** *Sortegories* CD: Phrase Building	**Step 2:** *Words for Teachers* CD: Word Search **Step 4:** *Sortegories* CD: Grammar Sort	**Step 4:** *Words for Teachers* CD: Word Card Generator—Build Sentences with a Direct Object **Step 5:** *LANGUAGE! eReader* CD: **"Africa Digs"**	**Step 3:** *Sortegories* CD: Analogy Building **Step 4:** Folder Activity: Sentence Unscramble—Direct Objects	

Special Instructional Support grid for Unit 3, with Step 4 activities highlighted

Sortegories CD	*Words for Teachers* CD
Activities that support Step 4 instruction include: • Phrase Building • Sentence Building • Grammar Sort	Activities that support Step 4 instruction include: • Word Card Generator • Word Study Guide

Step 4 and English Learners

The explicit attention to grammar and sentence structure through *LANGUAGE!*
is very beneficial to English learners. Teachers of English learners are advised
to provide many opportunities for oral practice of proper grammar and
sentence structure. Focus on Academic Language, indicated by the ☀ icon
on the Planning and Pacing Guide of each unit and at point of use, provides
activities with the English learner in mind. With attention to each of the Six
Steps, the activities support instruction of unit-specific content.

 Focus on Academic Language activities expand on and enhance unit-specific content.
These activities appear at the point of use throughout the unit.

Lesson 1	Lesson 2	Lesson 3	Lesson 4	Lesson 5
	Step 1: Syllable Awareness	**Step 4:** Meaning and Use of Quantity Adjective *much*	**Step 4:** Meaning and Use of Prepositions *above* and *across*	**Step 3:** Idiom *"Be in hot water"*
Lesson 6	**Lesson 7**	**Lesson 8**	**Lesson 9**	**Lesson 10**
Step 6: Practice with Word Prominence in Spoken English	**Step 4:** Essential Phrase *one of the most*	**Step 1:** Pronunciation of Contractions Formed with *am* and *is*	**Step 4:** Practice with Negative Present Tense Statements	

Unit 13 Focus on Academic Language chart, with Step 4 objectives highlighted

For more information on Differentiated Instruction see p. 267.

STEP 5 LISTENING AND READING COMPREHENSION

Table of Contents

RESEARCH BITE

"Effective teachers don't stop at describing a [reading] strategy—they model how the strategy works and tell students why they should use particular strategies in particular situations."

Biancarosa, 2005

In Step 5: Listening and Reading Comprehension, students apply the skills they have developed at the word and sentence levels through Steps 1-4 to text-level comprehension. LANGUAGE! guides the development of comprehension by teaching a variety of strategies. These include explicit instruction of reading strategies, the modeling of effective self-monitoring habits, and liberal use of graphic organizers to help students unlock the meaning in the text.

Direct instruction in strategies such as summarizing, self-questioning, identifying text structure and features, linking content to prior knowledge, graphic and semantic organizers, and comprehension monitoring promotes reading comprehension (Pressley, 2000; Taylor, Pearson, Garcia, Stahl & Bauer, 2006). Proficient readers are actively engaged during the reading process. They constantly monitor comprehension, make predictions about upcoming content, and apply comprehension to reading objectives (Pressley, 2002). Constructing or engaging existing background knowledge greatly assists reading comprehension especially when connections between text content and prior knowledge are made explicit (Anderson, 1984; Pressley, 2001; Hill & Flynn, 2006; Shaywitz, TK). Authors organize text according to predictable structures. Identifying text structure and reciprocally utilizing that structure to summarize text has been found to greatly assist reading comprehension (Meyer & Poon, 2001). In addition, using available text features prior to and during reading benefits comprehension (Surber & Schroeder, 2007). Finally, comprehension is enhanced by the amount of reading performed by a child. Students who read large amounts of text across a wide range of subject matter experience growth in comprehension (Guthrie, Wigfield, Metsala, & Cox, 1999).

Incidental exposure to words alone is not enough to facilitate growth in the many sub-skills that constitute reading either for decoding (Gillon & Dodd, 1995) or comprehension (Williams, 1998). Teachers use graphic organizers extensively to elicit input from students (Goldman & Rakestraw, 2000) and to demonstrate the structure of narrative and expository text. Students are able to learn higher-order reasoning skills when teachers model, discuss, and connect what students already know with what they need to know through careful questioning that leads to both factual and inferential interpretations of text (Pressley & Wharton-McDonnald, 1997; Williams 1998). There is also a clear relationship between reading rate (fluency) and comprehension; as readers become more fluent, comprehension of what they read increases. Finally, through direct instruction, it is important for teachers to make a distinction between the topic of the passage (what the passage is about) and the main idea (what the author says about the topic) since main idea identification affects student performance on reading comprehension activities such as summarizing and outlining (Longo, 2001).

How *LANGUAGE!* Does It

LANGUAGE! addresses Listening and Reading Comprehension by:

- Emphasizing strategies to improve fluent reading, including phrasing and repeated readings.

- Teaching context-based vocabulary strategies to enhance comprehension.

- Teaching comprehension strategies explicitly, including predicting, clarifying, and summarizing.

- Stressing identification of the hierarchy of information in text (i.e., topic, main idea, details).

- Using graphic organizers to represent the structure and organization of information in text.

- Providing text selections that are based on decodability criteria and readability values to guide the gradual increase of difficulty for all levels of text.

- Providing reading material in a wide range of genres on a wide range of topics at multiple reading levels in each unit.

- Emphasizing the use of informational text to build vocabulary and background knowledge to prepare for academic texts.

- Systematically teaching the signal words associated with the levels of Bloom's Taxonomy to increase understanding of comprehension questions.

- Explicitly teach the structure of fictional text, including plot, setting, character development, and other characteristic features

H

RESEARCH BITE

"Good comprehenders link the ideas presented in print to their own experiences. Good comprehenders have a knack for summarizing, predicting, and clarifying what they have read, and many are adept at asking themselves guide questions to enhance understanding."

Lyon, 1998

What You Need to Know

Comprehension and Chall's Stages of Reading Development

Below are ways that listening and reading comprehension are expressed across Chall's 5 Stages of Reading Development. (Associated grade levels are indicated in parentheses.)

Stage 0 **Prereading/Emergent Literacy** (Pre-K—K)
- Familiarity with sounds and letters
- Recognition of same sounds in different words
- Ability to predict parts of familiar stories
- Ability to recognize a few words in print

Stage 1 **Decoding** (K-2)
- Awareness of alphabetic principle—that sounds correspond to letters
- Ability to decode words with different sound-spelling correspondences

Stage 2 **Confirmation and Fluency** (3)
- Increase in reading speed and accuracy
- Increase in automatic recognition (ungluing from print)
- Ability to attend to both print and meaning

Stage 3 **Reading to Learn** (4-8)
- Motivation to read changes from mastering the reading process to gaining information from text
- Increase in vocabulary

Stage 4 **Reading for Multiple Viewpoints** (9-12)
- Increase in ability to analyze text, consider different viewpoints, and apply knowledge to unfamiliar settings
- Ability to understand literary devices
- Ability to respond critically to text

Stage 5 **Reading to Construct New Knowledge** (post-secondary)
- Construction of new knowledge delivered by text, not teacher
- Ability to form judgments about text content
- Selectivity in types of text

CONTENT EMPHASIS

What do you want students to learn?

- Context-based vocabulary strategies to enhance comprehension
- Comprehension strategies to question, clarify, summarize, and predict while reading
- Analysis of text by identifying topic, main idea, details, and elements of overall structure
- Distinguishing among the various genres of informational text and literature
- Note taking to aid comprehension and recall
- Interpretation of signal words to aid understanding of academic language in speech and text, and practice suitable responses
- Self-monitoring of comprehension while reading
- Fluent reading with prosody and accuracy.

The content of Step 5: Listening and Reading Comprehension focuses on comprehension development in both spoken and written English. Central to the instructional strategy of Step 5 is providing high-quality reading selections that cross a range of readability levels—Decodable, Instructional, and Challenge text—in every unit. Step 5 emphasizes explicit instruction in teaching, modeling, and practicing useful comprehension strategies. These strategies are designed specifically to teach struggling readers effective self-monitoring techniques to enhance comprehension, including questioning, predicting, clarifying, and summarizing.

What You Need to Know

Reading Comprehension and Scaffolded Instruction

As students progress beyond word-level comprehension, it is easy to assume that those skills translate to text-level comprehension. The understanding of connected text, though, is improved significantly by the development of a discrete and particular set of skills. Like the teaching of word-level skills, the teaching of text-level comprehension requires scaffolded instruction, including direct explanation, modeling, and monitoring (Alfassi, M., 2004).

Mastery emerges as students become capable of monitoring their own comprehension. This includes the development of "repair" strategies to use when understanding falters. These skills, of course, apply well beyond reading instruction and will benefit students throughout their education.

LANGUAGE! teaches students four distinct comprehension strategies. Again, each requires the teacher to provide direct explanation, modeling, and monitoring.

- **Questioning:** Keeping tabs on what is happening through constant questioning of who, what, where, when, how, and why while reading. When something is unclear or does not make sense, students must be taught to acknowledge this, pause, and seek clarification.

- **Clarifying:** When puzzled by a passage, seeking clarification by doing selective rereading, forming and asking questions, and/or accessing additional resources such as a dictionary.

- **Summarizing:** Demonstrating an understanding of text by generating regular summaries of what has been read up to that point.

- **Predicting:** Using clues from a story's title, images, captions, previously read text, and other text features—an excellent exercise in itself—to inform thinking about what they expect to read or what may happen next.

Over time, these discrete skills inform and reinforce each other, and become increasingly automatic.

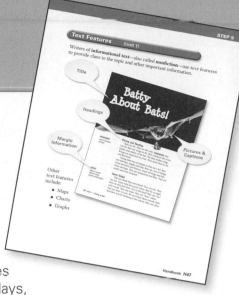

What You Need to Know

Understanding a Range of Text Types and Features

Students are exposed to a wide variety of text in *LANGUAGE!* and learn to identify unique features. Text selections include expository, narrative text, and poetry, as well as nonfiction and fiction. Genres range from newspaper and magazine articles, to plays, science fiction, and folktales.

Explicit instruction teaches students the elements of these different forms, and helps them explore the information contained in titles, headlines, captions, charts, tables of contents, stage directions, and other text features.

Handbook section of *Student Text*, Book A

Recognizing Signal Words

Signal words are introduced gradually in each unit beginning in Book A and continuing through Book D. These words are introduced sequentially according to the levels of Bloom's Taxonomy. Initially the signal words are words like *who* or *when*. These words, which are used frequently, require literal information to answer. As students progress through the units in *LANGUAGE!*, the signal words require more inferential or evaluative thinking. Words like critique and *hypothesize* are representative of signal words that are taught in later units in the curriculum. The Handbook section of the *Student Text* provides a cumulative listing of signal words organized by Bloom's levels and with corresponding information to answer them. The complete list appears in Book D.

From the Handbook section of the *Student Text*, Book D

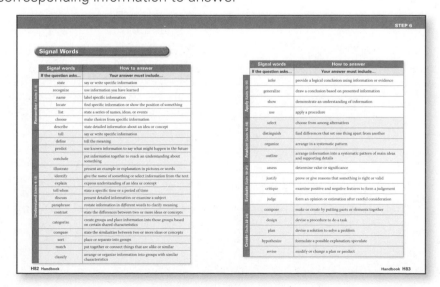

Listening and Reading Comprehension • 209

What You Need to Know

Text Selections and Readability Levels

Decodable Text—Independent Reading

The Decodable Text is at the easiest readability level. This text is written with 75 percent decodable words based on *LANGUAGE!*'s phonology Scope and Sequence for Books A through C. This text is used to apply decoding skills and build fluency. Decodable text preteaches vocabulary and provides background information for Instructional Text. Beginning in Book C, this level of text is referred to as Independent Text.

In Book D, the Independent Text also incorporates a visual—a chart, illustration, or other graphic—as part of the selection. At this point, interpreting the visual information becomes part of the instructional focus. The answers to comprehension questions require the use of both the text and visuals.

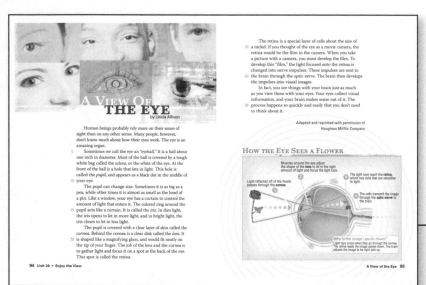

Target Words

Each unit in *LANGUAGE!* has a target word. The reading selections for each unit are connected through the unit's target word and illustrate its multiple meanings. The target word, selected from the decodable **Unit Words**, is the common denominator for all the reading material in the unit. In every unit, students experience multiple meanings for the target word across multiple contexts. In Unit 9, for example, the target word **bug** is explored in selections about insects, information about a scientific discovery of a rare insect, its idiomatic usage, and a story about a computer **bug**. Each selection contributes to a deeper understanding of the range of meanings of a target word **bug**.

What You Need to Know

Instructional Text—Shared and Supported Reading

With its mid-range readability for the unit, Instructional Text is designed to develop vocabulary, comprehension strategies and skills, and content knowledge while it explicitly teaches text structures. The Instructional Text selections are used extensively as the basis for writing both as a model of the different types of writing that students are expected to do and as an information source for content and ideas of their writing.

Beginning in Book D, the Instructional Text selections are also provided in the back of the *Interactive Text* in a section called the **Text Connections**. This format for the text selections allows students to analyze and mark the text, take notes, and answer comprehension questions designed to help students improve their independence in understanding text. Additionally, vocabulary and grammar activities are embedded in the **Text Connections** to provide an opportunity for application of the skills and strategies from Steps 3 and 4 to the text selections.

Instructional Text from Book E, Unit 28

Challenge Text— Read Aloud

Challenge Text features reading selections with the most difficult readability level in each unit. Depending on the reading ability of your students, these selections can be read to students or by them. These selections provide additional exposure to a variety of literary genres supported by comprehension questions geared toward higher-order thinking skills. Challenge Text selections also feature discussion topics so that students learn to think and discuss topics beyond the literal information in the text. Additionally, each Challenge Text reading selection has a related writing or speaking activity. The writing activities provide more opportunities for students to apply the writing skills that they are learning through other parts of the Six-Step lesson process. Challenge Text–focused lessons are included in the Teacher Editions at the end of Lessons 5 and 10 in every unit.

What You Need to Know

Step 5 Text Selection Readability Levels

The three levels of reading selections follow a prescribed sequence for optimum learning. First, students read the Decodable (Books A and B) or Independent (Books C–F) level text material. Then they read the Instructional level text material. In addition, they read the Challenge level text material. There is an instructional relationship between the three levels and consistent pattern of use. This is outlined on the Content Map at the beginning of each unit.

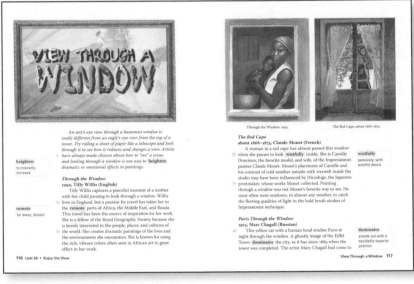

Challenge Text, Book E, Unit 28

Percent of Expository and Literature Reading Selections per Book in LANGUAGE! 4th Edition

Book	Percent	
	Expository	Literature
A	75	25
B	79	21
C	82	18
D	50	50
E	34	66
F	48	52

What You Need to Know

The Lexile Readability Scale

The readability level of each text selection, based on the Lexile readability scale, increases incrementally throughout the curriculum . Lexile measures are calculated based on two main criteria—word frequency (semantic difficulty) and sentence length (syntactic complexity). A text selection's Lexile provides a useful tool for monitoring students' reading and comprehension skills, as well as for guiding their choice of independent reading material. (For a more complete examination of the Lexile Framework® visit www.lexile.com on the Web.)

LANGUAGE! Readability Levels for Text Selections

Book	Lexile® Text Measure Ranges and Corresponding Grade Ranges		
	Decodable	**Instructional**	**Challenge**
A	200–400 (1–2)	300–700 (2–3)	650–950 (4–5)
B	300–700 (2–3)	500–850 (3–4)	750–1050 (5–6)
C	500–850 (3–4)	650–950 (4–5)	850–1075 (6–7)
	Independent	**Instructional**	**Challenge**
D	650–950 (4–5)	750–1075 (5–7)	950–1150 (7–9)
E	750–1050 (5–6)	850–1100 (6–8)	1000–1200 (8–10)
F	850–1075 (6–7)	950–1200 (7–10)	1100–1300 (10–12)

INSTRUCTIONAL FOCUS

Instruction in Step 5: Listening and Reading Comprehension develops strategies to increase fluency, build vocabulary, identify text elements and organization, interpret and respond to questions, and improve overall engagement while listening to and reading text. These objectives are addressed by means of explicit instruction that introduces concepts and models strategies that lead to self-monitoring of comprehension.

How will you maximize student learning?

- Provide opportunities to practice fluency, including phrase fluency
- Introduce students to a variety of texts and their features, including such important concepts as topic, main idea, topic sentences, and supporting details
- Model specific comprehension strategies, including questioning, clarifying, summarizing, and predicting
- Model "repair" strategies to use when understanding falters, including selective rereading, questioning, and seeking out additional resources such as dictionaries and encyclopedias
- Encourage and maximize opportunities for student reading of high-interest text of appropriate readability.

TEACHER'S TIP

Using Visuals

Interpreting visual information is a new instructional focus for independent text that starts in Book D. It needs to be taught explicitly. Many students struggle with interpreting graphs and charts, so teachers need to demonstrate the process. Projecting this text using an overhead or LCD projector is a simple but effective way to model the strategies for students. At first, assign one question at a time, set the timer, and then check each answer immediately. Slowly release students to work more independently—but always check answers. Until students demonstrate mastery of these skills, model finding the correct answer using the displayed text or visual.

Jenny Hamilton, National *LANGUAGE!* Trainer, Daphne, Alabama

Step 5 Why Do/How To Activities

More complete descriptions and instructions for these activities can be found in the Appendix. See page 362 for the table of contents.

Comprehension	Activity Snapshot
Use the Clues	Lets students practice context-based strategies to develop vocabulary and comprehension.
Blueprint for Reading	Guides students in examining text structure to promote comprehension and prepare for writing tasks.
Answer It	Provides explicit instruction and practice in interpreting question signal words and formulating responses.
Think About It	Asks students to engage open-ended questions in response to text.
Map It	Different Map It exercises allow students to deconstruct an article or story by Main Idea, Plot, or Reasons to aid comprehension.
Comprehend It	Helps students practice self-monitoring of their comprehension by having them ask themselves specific questions as they read.
Text Connections	These exercises in *Interactive Texts* offer guided practice in analyzing text structure and context-based use of vocabulary and grammar skills.
Identify It	These activities can be applied to finding main ideas, topic sentences, supporting details, and other features of text structure.
Fluency	
Phrase Fluency	Explicit instruction in phrasing enhances comprehension, promotes automatic word recognition, and helps students move beyond word-by-word reading.
Scoop It	Adds a kinesthetic element to promote proper and automatic phrasing. It is the basis for • Sentence Morphs • Phrase It
Sentence Fluency	Timed readings of sentences help students develop automatic and accurate word recognition in sentence structures.
Passage Fluency	Repeated timed readings of text help students build fluency by improving their reading speed, accuracy, and phrasing skills.

H

You Try It!

Using the Teacher Edition for Step 5

Lesson plans from Unit 1, Unit 13, and Unit 25—the three entry points for *LANGUAGE!*—reflect the range of Step 5 instructional objectives, exercises, and activities across the curriculum.

Preparations

Where are the phrase fluencies and the corresponding charts?

_____

_____

How will you introduce phrase fluency to your students and establish its purpose?

_____

_____

Directions

Why is it important to explicitly teach and model **Phrase Fluency** and **Sentence Morphs?**

_____

_____

What are ways to develop consistent procedures and behavioral expectations for all fluency drills?

_____

_____

Connections

How can you use Phrase Fluency to reinforce the concept of **Scoop It?**

_____

_____

How can students use Masterpiece Sentence painter questions to help them master **Scoop It?**

_____

_____

STEP
5
Listening and Reading Comprehension

Students read phrases accurately, automatically, and fluently. Students also read **Mini-Dialogs 1–4** to practice decoding and develop fluency.

 Phrase *Fluency* **1**

Why Do: Students need to be able to read phrases with accuracy and appropriate intonation. The **Phrase Fluency** process enhances comprehension, increases automatic word recognition, and discourages word-by-word reading.

How To: The **Phrase Fluency** activity has two steps. First, students learn to read the words accurately. Second, they learn to say the phrases as if speaking them. **Phrase Fluency** sections for each unit are located in the back of the *Interactive Text*.

Note: If students reach the end of the **Phrase Fluency** sheet before the time is up, instruct them to continue reading by starting over at the beginning.

Goal setting is discussed in *Assessment: Teacher Edition*.

Materials
Interactive Text
p. R12, Phrase
Fluency 1

Use this activity in the *Interactive Text* to help students develop automatic phrase recognition.

▸ Read a phrase and have students repeat it. Emphasize accurate word recognition, and saying words in meaningful groups, as you would speak them.

▸ Have students:

• Read the **Phrase Fluency 1** page to themselves.

• Take turns reading the phrases to a partner.

Interactive Text
p. R12

Scoop It

Why Do: Students benefit from opportunities to practice reading with proper phrasing. The physical motion of "scooping" provides multisensory reinforcement of meaning.

How To: Students use a pencil or eraser to "scoop" words from left to right while reading the phrases. Starting at the left dot, they drag the pencil point or eraser to the right dot while reading the group of words.

Example: • some inventions •

Note: Scoop It is a multisensory technique that can be used by students whenever they are reading text material. It is used as part of the **Sentence Morphs** activity to facilitate phrasing and fluency.

Unit 1 • Lesson 1   **19**

From Book A, Unit 1, Lesson 1

STEP 5 — Listening and Reading Comprehension

Students apply phrasing techniques while reading **"Off-the-Wall Inventions"** accurately, automatically, and fluently with expression.

⭐ Independent Text: "Off-the-Wall Inventions"

Materials
Student Text
p. 4

Use this activity in the *Student Text* to help students read decodable vocabulary in connected text.

Activate and Build Knowledge

**Build
Knowledge**

▸ Have students:

  • Turn to **"Off-the-Wall Inventions"** in the *Student Text*, page 4.

▸ Ask for volunteers to list some inventions that changed the world. If students have difficulty, list some common inventions, such as the light bulb or the computer, and ask them to think of more inventions.

▸ Tell students that some inventions are silly or strange. Some of them are meant to be funny, and some just turn out that way. Tell students they will learn more about both useful and unusual inventions as they read the selections in this unit.

▸ Read **"Off-the-Wall Inventions"** in the *Student Text*, page 4, to students.

▸ Model expression based on meaning, inflection at punctuation, and phrasing of meaningful word groups.

▸ Have students:

  • Choral read the selection with you.

  • Use the scooping technique with their fingers or erasers to enhance prosody and fluency.

  • Read the selection again with partners, using proper expression, inflection, and phrasing.

Student Text
p. 4
Teacher Edition p. T65

⭐ Find It: Closed Syllables

Materials
Interactive Text
p. 10,
Exercise 5
Highlighters

Use this activity in the *Interactive Text* to identify words with closed syllables in context.

▸ Read the excerpt based on **"Off-the-Wall Inventions"** in Exercise 5, **Find It: Closed Syllables**, to students.

▸ Have students:

  • Turn to Exercise 5, **Find It: Closed Syllables**, in the *Interactive Text*, page 10.

  • Reread the text silently or quietly to themselves.

  • Highlight closed syllables with short vowels.

  • Sort each syllable or word according to its short vowel sound.

  • Record nonphonetic syllables and syllables that they're unsure of in the last column under the "?".

Interactive Text
p. 10, Exercise 5
Teacher Edition p. 25

Differentiated Instruction | ⭐ Review & Acceleration | ✓ Special Instructional Support | ✳ English Learners | Technology | Challenge Text

From Book C, Unit 13, Lesson 1

Preparations

What will you use to read the independent text to your students and incorporate the prompts from the TE?

_____

_____

How could you prepare the independent text selection to enable students to do **Scoop It?**

_____

_____

Directions

How will you establish behavioral expectations for reading the independent text selections?

_____

_____

How can you help your students understand the directions for **Find It?**

H

_____

_____

Connections

How do **Sentence Morphs** help students prepare for using **Scoop It** with connected text?

_____

_____

How does the work in **Find It** rely on student knowledge of vowel sounds?

_____

_____

You Try It!

Preparations

How might you prepare the questions suggested in the TE to help students better understand the task?

_____

What do you need to prepare to share the Speaking Tips for Students?

_____

Directions

How will you determine if students understand the assignment and its purpose?

_____

Will you include directions for marking their poem to help with prosody?

_____

Connections

How will knowledge and awareness of Sentence Signals help students when they practice reading their poems?

_____

How does reading the poem with expression and prosody improve students' understanding the poem?

_____

STEP
5 **Listening and Reading Comprehension**

→ Students select a poem from **"Circle Poems Take Many Forms"** or **"Circles in Nature"** and prepare for a presentation of that poem.

Present It: Poetry

Materials
Interactive Text pp. C1–C12, Text Connections 1 and 2

Use this activity to help students practice reading a poem in preparation to present a poem.

▶ Explain to students that they will read a poem to the class in Unit 25, Lesson 9. Tell them that in this lesson they will select a poem and practice reading it aloud in preparation for that presentation.

▶ Review the **Speaking Tips** with students.

▶ Help students understand what is meant by **mood**. Offer this selection of terms as examples of mood: peaceful, somber, joyous, sorrowful, hopeful, pensive, gloomy, longing, hopeful, wistful, or contemplative.

▶ Have students:

• Select a poem from **"Circle Poems Take Many Forms"** or **"Circles in Nature."**

• Consider the following question: What is the emotion, or mood, of the poem you selected?

• Read the poem aloud, making sure to read smoothly and pause at appropriate places, trying to convey the mood of the poem.

▶ Remind students that readers should not necessarily pause at the end of every line of the poem; readers must pay attention to the punctuation and to the meaning of a poem to determine when to pause.

▶ Have pairs of students:

• Take turns reading their poem to each other. (Each student should practice reading her or his poem aloud three or four times.)

• Give feedback to each other on the delivery of the poem.

✓ **Special Instructional Support**

An oral presentation of this selection can be found in the following:
• *LANGUAGE! eReader* CD:
  "Circles in Nature"

Speaking Tips *for Students*

Organization and Content
• Stay on topic.
• Organize content.
• Provide a beginning, middle, and end.
• Emphasize important points.
• Use examples.
• Use specific vocabulary.
• Support opinions with evidence.

Delivery
• Speak clearly.
• Use facial expressions and gestures.
• Use volume, pitch, and phrasing.
• Make eye contact.
• Use correct grammar.
• Use props and media.

Interactive Text pp. C1–C12, Text Connections 1 and 2
Teacher Edition pp. TC1–TC7

Differentiated Instruction ★ Review & Acceleration | Special Instructional Support | English Learners | Technology | Challenge Text

108 Unit 25 • Lesson 8

From Unit 25, Lesson 8

Activity Materials

Student Text

The *Student Text* contains two main components that are essential to instruction in Step 5: (1) the Handbook and (2) the Text Selections. The Handbook provides resources for use during and after instruction. Key strategies, including how to answer questions and use the context to figure out the meaning of unfamiliar vocabulary words, are provided in the Handbook. The Teacher Edition guides the use of both sections of the *Student Text*.

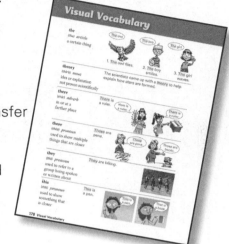

Visual Vocabulary—A Vocabulary Reference Tool

- Uses visual images to facilitate English learners transfer of vocabulary knowledge from their first language.

- Supplies student-friendly definition and context sentences with each vocabulary word, making word meanings accessible to all learners.

- Provides visual images for highlighted Instructional Text, Challenge Text, and Essential Words in Books A and B.

Interactive Text

This consumable text provides ready-made exercises and activities for Step 5: Listening and Reading Comprehension. Exercises include tasks designed to improve phrasing, fluency, vocabulary development and comprehension.

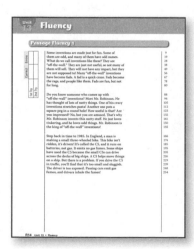

From Book A Interactive Text for Unit 3

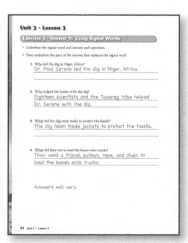

From Book A Interactive Text for Unit 3

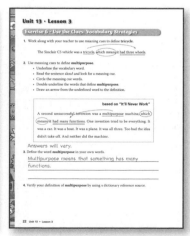

From Book C Interactive Text for Unit 13

LANGUAGE! Book List for Independent Reading

LANGUAGE! includes recommendations of high-quality books for your students' independent reading needs. Guided by subject descriptions and the Lexile Scale, you can assign and encourage students to read these books with confidence. See page 437 for more information on the Book List for Independent Reading selections.

See Book List for Independent Reading on page 437

The Variety of Literature in *LANGUAGE!*

Contemporary and classic literature is the basis of the student text selections in *LANGUAGE!*. These selections represent diverse cultural populations and interests. Here are some examples of the literary excerpts included in *LANGUAGE!*: "The Disappearing Man" (Isaac Asimov); "The Freedom Dreamer" (Martin Luther King Jr.); "Nashes Bashes, Word Play" (Ogden Nash); "The House on Mango Street" (Sandra Cisneros); "Rules of the Game" (Amy Tam); "The Raven" and "The Tell Tale Heart" (Edgar Allan Poe); "Nothing Gold Can Stay" (Robert Frost).

In addition to the *Student Text* text selections, *LANGUAGE!* offers a variety of extended reading opportunities:

- **The *LANGUAGE!* Book List for Independent Reading** provides a suggested list of titles for independent reading, organized by grade level range and readability level. See pages 437–453.

- **The *LANGUAGE!* Access to Literature CD** (using Kurzweil 3000) provides 1,800 classic literature selections in a read aloud format from authors including Jane Austin, Charles Dickens, Jack London, William Shakespeare, Mark Twain, and H.G. Wells.

- **The *LANGUAGE!* Nonfiction eVersion CD** provides 20 nonfiction selections exploring content areas of science and social studies, read aloud in a natural voice. Print forms of these selections are also available.

You Try It!

Complete these exercises to see how *LANGUAGE!* promotes listening and reading comprehension.

Unit 1: Phrase Fluency from Book A *Interactive Text*

Discuss ways students could revisit phrase fluency.

_____

_____

_____

_____

_____

_____

Unit 1 Fluency

Phrase Fluency 1

Correct / Errors		a cat	2	sat on a cab	73
		a fat cat	5	sat on a mat	77
		a cab	7	that bat	79
		a bat	9	that cat	81
		at bat	11	that cab	83
1st Try / 2nd Try		fat cats	13	that mat	85
		fat bats	15	that fat cat	88
		bats at	17	the mat	90
		bat at a ball	21	the cat	92
		bats at the ball	25	the bat	94
		has a cab	28	the cab	96
		has a mat	31	the cats	98
		has a cat	34	the mats	100
		has a fat cat	38	the fat cats	103
		has a cat	41	the fat bats	106
		has cats	43	the bats	108
		has bats	45	the cabs	110
		a bat	47	this cat	112
		a cab	49	this fat cat	115
		in the cab	52	this bat	117
		Casey in a cab	56	this fat bat	120
		sat in a cab	60	this cab	122
		on the cat	63	this mat	124
		on the mat	66	the mat	126
		in the cab	69	the bat	128

R12   Unit 1 • Fluency

Phrase Fluency from Book A *Interactive Text*

Unit 13, Lesson 5: Use the Clues: Vocabulary Strategies

What are other meaning cues? (Hint: Use the glossary of Why Do/How To's.)

_____

_____

_____

_____

_____

Unit 13 · Lesson 3

Exercise 6 · Use the Clues: Vocabulary Strategies

1. Work along with your teacher to use meaning cues to define **tricycle**.

   The Sinclair C5 vehicle was a tricycle, which means it had three wheels.

2. Use meaning cues to define **multipurpose**.
   - Underline the vocabulary word.
   - Read the sentence aloud and look for a meaning cue.
   - Circle the meaning cue words.
   - Double underline the words that define **multipurpose**.
   - Draw an arrow from the underlined word to the definition.

   > **based on "It'll Never Work"**
   >
   > A second unsuccessful invention was a multipurpose machine, which means it had many functions. One invention tried to be everything. It was a car. It was a boat. It was a plane. It was all three. Too bad the idea didn't take off. And neither did the machine.

3. Define the word **multipurpose** in your own words.

   _____

   _____

   _____

4. Verify your definition of **multipurpose** by using a dictionary reference source.

Phrase It activity from Book C _Interactive Text_

You Try It!

Unit 25, Lesson 25: Text Connections

Brainstorm ways to maneuver students and prepare yourself for using the Text Connections.

_____

_____

_____

_____

_____

_____

Unit 25 Text Connections

Text Connection 1

Circle Poems Take Many Forms

1 *A poem begins with a lump in the throat, a home-sickness or a love-sickness. It is a reaching-out toward expression; an effort to find fulfillment. A complete poem is one where the emotion has found its thought and the thought has found the*
5 *words.*
Robert Frost, 20th century poet

What Is Poetry?

Poetry is a special kind of literature. A poem uses words sparingly[1] and imaginatively. Most poems are meant to be read out loud because the language of poetry combines the
10 qualities of speech and song.

> **Use the Clues A: Vocabulary Strategies**
> - Read lines 7–10.
> - Use meaning signals and context clues to answer the question in the bold heading, **What Is Poetry?**
> - Circle the meaning signal.
> - Highlight the context clues that helped you define **poetry**.
>
> _____
>
> _____
>
> _____

Poetry often includes six major elements: thought, form, imagery, melody, meter, and mood. In this unit, we will be learning about two elements: thought and form. The thought is the sum of the poet's ideas. One element of a poem's
15 thought is its theme. A poem's theme may be stated as a universal truth, a truth that is not limited by time and space.

---

[1] **sparingly:** in a limited manner

(continued)

Unit 25 • Text Connection 1   **C1**

Comprehend It

Answer the questions below in the space provided.

1. What does Robert Frost think is the purpose of a poem?

_____

_____

2. Why is the sense of hearing important to poetry?

_____

_____

_____

_____

_____

_____

_____

H

Circle Poems Take Many Forms from Book E *Interactive Text*

TEACHER'S TIP
Using Text Connections

Text Connections are located in the back of the Interactive Text, *making it necessary for students to move between these back pages and specific unit/step pages. Flipping back and forth can be a problem, but here are ways to smooth out the transitions: (1) use colored paper clips or sticky notes to mark different pages in the Interactive Text—unit/step specific pages, fluency pages, and Text Connection pages; (2) have students remove Text Connection pages for the current unit and place them in their student notebooks.*

To make sure students are on the correct page and to maximize instruction using the Text Connections consider: (1) writing the current page number on the board; (2) projecting the Text Connection pages using an overhead or LCD projector.

Explicit instruction using Text Connections—including modeling, scaffolded practice, and corrective feedback—will improve your students' comprehension. Guaranteed.

Jenny Hamilton, National *LANGUAGE! Trainer,*
Daphne, Alabama

"And what's the story behind the story?"

Background Information for Text Selections

The following chart provides background information for all text selections in book levels A–F.

Book	Unit	Target Word	Selection	Author	Content Area	Context	Illustrations
A	1	bat	Batty About Bats!	Kathi M. Kowalksi (adaptation)	Science	Why we need bats and bats need us	photos of different species of bat
			Bats in China		Social Studies	Chinese folklore: How Chinese people value bats	Examples of bats in Chinese art
			Casey at the Bat	Based on the poem by Ernest Lawrence Thayer	Literature—poetry	Explores the famous poem "Casey at the Bat"	
			At Bat	Jacqueline Hechtkopf	Literature—poetry	Explores different choices and fears in the context of baseball	
	2	map	A Map is a Sandwich	Jeanne Miller (adaptation)	Social Studies	Explains how maps are made	Examples of maps and a map key
			The Hardest Maps to Make		Social Studies	How people explore and map the ocean	Diagram of sonar as used in undersea mapping
			Mapping the Unknown		Social Studies	How early explorers mapped the earth	Historical map from Herodotus
			Atlas: A Book of Maps	Judy Rosenbaum	Humanities, Literature	Explains the Greek myth of Atlas	
			Floki: Sailor Without a Map		Social Studies	How an early explorer found Iceland without a map	
	3	dig	Africa Digs	Michelle Laliberte (adaptation)	Science	How a few scientists discovered a new dinosaur	Image of a dig site from the sky
			The Big Dig	Laurie Ann Toupin (adaptation)	Social Studies	Explores the infrastructure changes in Boston called the "Big Dig"	
			Dig This	Shureice Kornegay (adaptation)	Science	A tenth grader writes about her experience on a paleontological expedition	
	4	twins	Facts About Twins (Mega-Dialog)		Social Studies	Explores the experience of being twins	
			The Vast Sky (Mega-Dialog)		Science	How constellations are sometimes twins	Persian illustration of Gemini
			Remarkable Twins	Craig Sanders (adaptation)	Social Studies	Famous and not-so-famous twins	

H

Book	Unit	Target Word	Selection	Author	Content Area	Context	Illustrations
A			Gemini: The Twins		Science	How a constellation was named after two brothers	Diagram of the constellation Gemini.
			Conjoined Twins		Science	Explores the mysterious death of conjoined twins from Siam	Picture of Chang and Eng Bunker
			Twin Towers: Two Perspectives		Social Studies, Literature	A twin reflects on the memory of 9/11.	
	5	jazz	What is Jazz?		Humanities	Explains the present and past fascination with jazz	
			Jazz: The Recipe	Heather Mitchell Amey (adaptation)	Humanities	Explores the elements that make jazz	
			Looking at Jazz	Marc H. Miller (adaptation)	Humanities	How jazz influences visual art	Images of jazz-influenced visual art
			Growing Up With Jazz	Virginia A. Spatz (adaptation)	Humanities, Literature	The life and music of Louis Armstrong	
			The Duke Jazzes Newport	Brandon Marie Miller (adaptation)	Humanities, Literature	Recalls a night at the Newport Jazz Festival with Duke Ellington	
	6	toxic	Toxic Pollutants		Science	How to raise awareness about toxic pollutants	
			Rachel Carson		Science, Literature	How a writer and scientist protected nature with her talents	
			Coming Clean About Toxic Pollution		Science	Explores different types of toxic pollution	
			Riddle of the Frogs	Judy Rosenbaum (adaptation)	Science	A group of students discovered that toxins had deformed frogs	
			Amazon Toxins	Bernice E. Magee (adaptation)	Science	How toxic plants can be deadly and beneficial	
B	7	web	The World on the Web		Science	How the Internet has changed the world	
			Log On		Social Studies	What kids do online and what parents should do for their kids	
			World Wide Web		Science	Explores the elements and uses of the Internet	
			Web of Lies	Emilio Garcia (review)	Humanities, Literature	Gives a review and summary of a movie	

Book	Unit	Target Word	Selection	Author	Content Area	Context	Illustrations
B			Web Wins!		Humanities, Literature	Compares teenagers' use of the Internet to their use of television	
			Super Webs	Steve Miller (adaptation)	Science	Explains the construction and material of spider webs	
			The Spider's Thread	Akutagawa Ryunosuke (adaptation and translation by Dean Durber)	Humanities, Literature	Japanese folktale about a spider and his thread	
			Spider Woman	Karen M. Leet	Humanities, Literature—poetry	Explains a poem about how the Navajo became great weavers	
	8	whale	Singing Wales		Science	Explores some of the behaviors of whales	
			A Man and His Songs		Humanities	The life of Woody Guthrie	
			Whale Song	Australian Broadcasting Corporation (adaptation)	Science	Explores the meaning of and reason for whale songs	
			Woody's Song	Barbara Hall (adaptation)	Humanities, Literature	The life, songs, and era of Woody Guthrie	
			Hmong Song		Social Studies	Explores how the Hmong people make their traditional music	
			The Power of Song	Bob Black (adaptation)	Social Studies	How a song helped a soccer team win the big game	
	9	bug	Bugs Live!		Science	Where bed bugs and dust mites live	Image of a bed bug coming out of a pillow
			Bad Bugs		Science	What bugs do to the yard, plants, and other bugs	
			How Bugs Bug Us	Creative Publishing, Intl. (adaptation)	Science	How bugs live in people's homes and bodies	Images of bugs with arrows to the human body parts where they live
			New Old Insects		Science	Explains a recent discovery of an old insect	Image of the insect with an arrow to where it lives on a map
			Buggy English		Humanities	Explores the multiple meanings of the word bug	

Book	Unit	Target Word	Selection	Author	Content Area	Context	Illustrations
B			Lighting Bugs		Humanities, Literature	Story about a computer program problem and how two kids solved it	
	10	time	Past Time		Science	How people told time before clocks	
			It's About Time		Social Studies	Explains time zones and different kinds of clocks	
			Telling Time		Social Studies	History of telling time before clocks	
			Time Zones		Science	Explains geography behind time zones	Image of a map with different time zones marked
			Creating the Calendar	Robert S. Bianchi, Karen Kane, Kelly Musselman, and David Stuart (adaptation)	Humanities	How different civilizations developed a calendar	Image of 5 time periods on the Mayan calendar
			The Time Machine	H.G. Wells (adaptation by Les Martin)	Literature	Story about a scientist's time travel to the future	
			Time Traveler		Humanities, Literature— poetry	Poem about time travel	
	11	wind	Facts About Kites		Science	What kites do and what they were used for in the past	
			Kites: Shapes and Uses		Humanities	What kites are and how they have been used	
			Hurricane!		Science	Defines and explains hurricanes	Chart categorizing hurricanes
			A Kite's Tale	Rebecca Higbee (adaptation)	Social Studies	How kites were used for military and scientific purposes	Image of the Chinese letters for kite
			The Dust Bowl	Peter Roop and Jane Fell Greene (adaptation)	Social Studies	Discusses a historical period in the Great Plains	
			Wind Sports		Humanities	Explores different wind and water sports	
	12	sandwich	What's for Lunch?		Humanities	Discusses the invention and use of sandwiches	
			Making Hero Sandwiches		Humanities	Hero sandwich history and how a hero sandwich is made	

Book	Unit	Target Word	Selection	Author	Content Area	Context	Illustrations
B			Eponymous Sandwiches		Social Studies	How sandwiches and elements got their names	Maps that show where certain foods got their names
			Sandwiches + Hero = Success		Social Studies	How one chef became a hero in her community	
			A World of Sandwiches		Social Studies	Different types of sandwiches in various cultures	
C	13	invent	Off-the-Wall Inventions		Social Studies	Explores some odd inventions	
			Solving Problems		Science	How inventions might solve some world problems	
			It'll Never Work	Nick Griffiths (adaptation)	Science	Explains some strange inventions	Image of the Dynasphere
			Way to Go!	Steve Miller (adaptation)	Science	Some different inventions for transportation	
			Leonardo da Vinci: The Inventor	Nick D'Alto, Milan Kralik, Jr., and the Museum of Science, Boston (adaptation)	Humanities	Different inventions created by Leonardo da Vinci	
			Podway Bound: A Science Fiction Story	Justin Werfel	Literature	A science fiction story about an escape from prison	
	14	art	Making Art		Humanities	How sketching from boredom can lead to artistic success	
			Art at Home and Art in Caves	Patricia M. Newman (adaptation)	Social Studies	How some art is made and how art began	
			From Rock Art to Graffiti	Paul Bahn (adaptation)	Social Studies	Art history and modern art	
			Becoming an Artist	Patricia Wild, Louise L. Greene, Patricia M. Newman, Sally Crandall (adaptation)	Humanities	How various artists developed their talents at young ages	
			Leonardo the Artist	Museum of Science, Boston; Katherine S. Balch; and Denise Budd (adaptation)	Humanities	Explores Leonardo da Vinci's artistic achievements	

Book	Unit	Target Word	Selection	Author	Content Area	Context	Illustrations
C			Art in Space	Roger Malina and Frank Pietronigro (adaptation)	Science	Explores the influence of space on art forms	
	15	hero	Mythical Heroes		Humanities	Explanation of super-heroes, myths, and Roman gods	
			Unsung Heroes		Social Studies	Ordinary people who are heroes	
			Legendary Superheroes	Claire Watts and Robert Nicholson (adaptation)	Humanities	A look at what makes a superhero	
			These Shoes are Mine	Gary Soto	Humanities	A play that explores the qualities of heroes	
			Navajo Code Talkers	Nancy E. Cluff and Bruce Watson (adaptation)	Social Studies	How the Navajo people helped by using code in World War II	
			The Ride of Her Life	Rose Andrews (adaptation)	Social Studies, Literature	Story of a girl who warned local citizens of the approaching enemy	
	16	athlete	The Complete Athlete		Humanities	Explains the idea behind the Special Olympics	
			Extreme Athletes		Social Studies	What extreme athletes do and how they stay safe	
			A Special Kind of Athlete	Gary Crooker (adaptation)	Humanities	How people volunteer to participate in the Special Olympics	
			Swifter, Higher, Stronger	Ann Stalcup (adaptation)	Humanities	Explains the history of the Olympic Games	
			Tony Hawk: Extreme Athlete	Tony Hawk Official Web site (adaptation)	Social Studies	Explores the life and accomplishments of skater Tony Hawk	
			Roberto Clemente: The Heart of the Diamond	Joanne Loftus (adaptation)	Humanities, Literature	The life and achievements of Roberto Clemente	
	17	Egypt	The Pyramids		Science	Introduction to the use and construction of the pyramids	
			Living in Egypt		Social Studies	Two portraits of students living in ancient Egypt	
			Building a Pyramid	Miriam Ayad (adaptation)	Social Studies	How the pyramids were built	Image of tools used to cut the rock

Book	Unit	Target Word	Selection	Author	Content Area	Context	Illustrations
C			Growing Up Egyptian	Peggy Wigus Wymore and Joyce Haynes (adaptation)	Humanities	How children grew up in ancient Egypt	
			The Study of Mummies	Joyce Haynes (adaptation)	Science	How, why, and when scientists study mummies	
			King Tut: Egyptian Pharaoh	Jane Scherer and Susan Washburn (adaptation)	Social Studies, Literature	Explores King Tutankhamen's legacy and tomb	Images of the tomb and its location
	18	explore	Life at the Pole		Science	Explains what life is like in Antarctica	
			Mysteries of Antarctica	Karen E. Lewis (adaptation)	Social Studies	Explains the many reasons Antarctica is a mysterious place	
			The First Transcontinental Railroad	Charlotte Gemmell (adaptation)	Social Studies	History of the Transcontinental Railroad and the people who built it	
			Continental Drift	Gretchen Noyes-Hull and Mary Reina (adaptation)	Science	Explains how the earth's land developed into its continents	
			The Quest for a Continent	Beth Weston (adaptation)	Social Studies, Literature	The life of Christopher Columbus and his voyages	
D	19	speed	Early Olympic Speeders		Humanities	How three Olympic athletes excelled in their fast sports	Chart of recent Olympic results
			Fiber Optics: High Speed Highways for Light	Nancy Day (adaptation)	Science	Explains how fiber optics work and why they're important	
			Raymond's Run	Toni Cade Bambara	Humanities, Literature	Story of a young girl who loves to run	
			A Slow Take on Fast Food	Diane Vuyatzis (adaptation)	Social Studies	Explains the history of and negative side to fast food	
			The Tortoise and the Hare: A Fable	Aesop's Fables (adaptation)	Humanities, Literature	The fable of the race between the tortoise and the hare	
	20	play	Nash's Bashes: Word Play		Science, Literature—poetry	Explains the poetry and life of Ogden Nash	
			The Marble Champ	Gary Soto	Humanities, Literature	A story of a young girl who discovers her talent for marbles	

Listening and Reading Comprehension • 231

Book	Unit	Target Word	Selection	Author	Content Area	Context	Illustrations
D			A Game of Catch	Richard Wilbur	Humanities, Literature	A story about a game of catch that ends in painful consequences	
			Yo-Yo Ma Plays the World	Janet Tassel (adaptation)	Social Sciences, Literature	Explains the history and life achievements of the famous cellist	Map of the Silk Road
			Young Playwright on Broadway: Lorraine Hansberry's A Raisin in the Sun	Vicki Hambleton (adaptation)	Humanities, Literature	Gives a history, summary, and early review of Hansberry's play	
	21	family	Plant Families		Science	Explores plant families and how they are classified	
			A Family in Hiding: Anne Frank's Diary	Anne Frank (adaptation from The Definitive Edition)	Humanities, Literature	Life and history of the Frank family during the Holocaust	
			Bringing Up Baby: Family Life in the Animal World		Science	Explores different ways animals raise their babies	Chart of how long childhood lasts for certain animals
			Who Cares About Great-Uncle Edgar	Lila Perl (adaptation)	Science, Humanities	Explores the genealogy and science behind heritage	
	22	puzzle	How to Make a Crossword Puzzle		Humanities	History of crossword puzzles and steps on how to make one	Images of crossword puzzles
			A Collection of Puzzling Tales	George Shannon (adaptation)	Social Studies, Humanities	Tales from different cultures that have puzzles to solve within	
			The Disappearing Man	Isaac Asimov	Literature	A story about a boy whose father is a detective tracking down a thief	
			Puzzle People		Social Studies, Humanities	Three puzzle inventors and their inventions	
			The Rosetta Stone		Social Studies, Humanities	History of the Rosetta Stone and how it is the key to reading Egyptian hieroglyphics	
	23	power	Horsepower		Science	How the horsepower measurement came to be	Graph that shows the horsepower of different modes of transportation

Book	Unit	Target Word	Selection	Author	Content Area	Context	Illustrations
D			Zaaaaaaaap!	Jennifer A. Ratliff	Science, Literature	A story about an energy crisis in the future brought on by the loss of natural resources	
			Satyagraha: Power for Change	Alden R. Carter	Humanities, Literature	How one brave kid used nonviolence to change the minds of his peers	
			Mohandas Gandhi: Soul Force		Social Studies	How one man used nonviolence to change the world	
			Blackout	Kathiann M. Kowalski	Science	Documents the reason for and consequences of the power outage in 2003.	Diagram that shows how power outlets receive power
	24	dream	Dream While You Sleep	Faith Hickman Brynie	Science	Explores the experiences of sleeping and dreaming	Image of a sleep cycle chart
			Dreaming the Night Away	Judith Herbst (adaptation)	Science	How people dream and what happens in dreams	
			Dream Team	Ron Jones	Humanities, Literature	A story about a basketball coach who finds talent in an unlikely place	
			Pursuit of a Dream	Barbara Eaglesham (adaptation)	Science	How scientists discovered the structure of DNA	Diagram of DNA structure
			Martin Luther King, Jr.: The Freedom Dreamer	Jim Haskins, Peter Roop, and Sylvia Whitman (adaptation)	Humanities, Literature	The history and "I Have a Dream" speech of Martin Luther King, Jr.	
E	25	circle	Stonehenge: Secrets of an Ancient Circle		Science, Social Studies	Explores the mysteries of Stonehenge	
			Circle Poems Take Many Forms	Edwin Markham, John G. Niehardt, Richard Wright, Jack Prelutsky	Humanities, Literature—poetry	Explores different kinds of poetry	
			Circles In Nature	E. E. Cummings, Barbara Juster Esbensen	Literature—poetry	Different poems that use circles found in nature	
			Living in a Circle		Science, Social Studies	How different civilizations in history have lived in circular structures	Diagram of a tipi

H

Book	Unit	Target Word	Selection	Author	Content Area	Context	Illustrations
E			The Circle of Life		Humanities, Literature— poetry	The life and works of William Shakespeare	
	26	move	Tsunamis		Science	What a Tsunami is and how it is caused	Diagram of the cause of a Tsunami
			The House on Mango Street	Sandra Cisneros	Social Studies, Literature	A story about a young girl's struggle with where she comes from	
			Rules of the Game	Amy Tan	Social Studies, Literature	How a young girl became a chess champion	
			The Women's Suffrage Movement		Social Studies	How Susan B. Anthony and Elizabeth Cady Stanton fought for the right to vote	
			Savion Glover: The Man Can Move	Sylviane Gold, Savion Glover, and Bruce Weber	Humanities	How one man's creativity brought him success in music and dance	
	27	social	Wolf Society		Science	The hierarchy of power in wolf packs	
			David Copperfield	Charles Dickens	Social Studies, Literature	A story about an orphan who works in a factory	
			Stand Alone or Join the Crowd		Social Studies, Literature	How following the crowd is not always a good idea	
			Youth Activists Work for Social Change		Social Studies, Literature	How a group of students worked for social change	
	28	view	A View of the Eye	Linda Allison (adaptation)	Science	How the eye functions	Diagram of how the eye works
			My First View of Ellis Island	Edward Corsi (adaptation)	Social Studies, Literature	An immigrant's first impression of Ellis Island	
			Amigo Brothers	Piri Thomas	Humanities, Literature	A story of two friends who have to box each other and both leave the ring as champions	
			Ansel Adams: View Through a Lens	Mary Street Alinder (adaptation)	Humanities, Literature	Ansel Adams writes about his art	Photograph of Half Dome in Yosemite National Park
			View Through Windows	Marjorie Jackson	Humanities	Examines paintings that use windows as a way to see a scene	Images of paintings of window scenes
	29	call	Cell Phone Radio Commercial		Humanities	Transcribes a radio commercial for cell phones	

Book	Unit	Target Word	Selection	Author	Content Area	Context	Illustrations
E			Advertisements: It's Your Call		Humanities	How advertisements work and who they target	Image of a magazine advertisement
			Cell Phone Print Ad		Humanities		
			Cell Phones For Teens: A Good Call For Safety?		Humanities	A persuasive essay that argues for teens needing cell phones for safety	
			A Call to Poetry	Naomi Shihab Nye, Lori M. Carlson, Leslie Marmon Silko	Literature— poetry	Group of poems that discuss the calling of different poets	
			The Call of the Wild: For the Love of Man	Jack London	Literature	A story about a dog and his master	
			The Call of the Wild: The Sounding of the Call	Jack London	Literature	A story about a dog and his decision to stay with the master or retreat into the wild	
	30	individual	The Eighteenth Camel	Thelma Schmidhauser (adaptation)	Humanities	Examines the need for and value of camels in the Arabian deserts	
			The Pig: An Individual Dilemma	Barbara Kimenye	Social Studies, Literature	A story about an elderly man and his pig.	
			A Remarkable Individual	Erik Weihenmayer (adaptation)	Social Studies, Literature	How a blind man climbed all of the Seven Summits	
F	31	heart	The Heart of Our Land		Social Studies	The geography and history of the heartland	
			Dear Rosita	Nash Candelaria	Humanities, Literature	A correspondence of letters between a woman in college and her father	
			The Tell-Tale Heart	Edgar Allan Poe	Literature	A story about the extreme thoughts of the criminal mind	
			Heroes of the Heart		Science	Explains the medical advances in cardiac care	
			Language of the Heart: A Collection of Poems	Emily Dickenson, Thomas H. Johnson, William Wordsworth, C.K. Williams, Joseph Bruchac	Humanities, Literature	A collection of poems that speak about the heart	
	32	gold	Good As Gold		Science	Examines the value of gold through history	

Book	Unit	Target Word	Selection	Author	Content Area	Context	Illustrations
F			Nothing Gold Can Stay	Robert Frost	Humanities, Literature—poetry	The life and works of Robert Frost	
			The Treasure of the Sierra Madre	John Huston, B. Traven	Social Studies, Literature	A play about three men searching for gold	
			Blue Gold: Earth's Liquid Asset	John Vidal	Science	Examines the valuc of water as it becomes more and more scarce	
			The Golden Mean: How the Universe Adds Up		Math	Explores the mathematical sequence that recurs throughout the universe	Diagrams of the golden proportion in architecture and design
	33	right	Playing with the Logic of Space: The Art of M.C. Escher		Math, Humanities	How M.C. Escher used shapes to create surprising images	Images of Escher's drawings
			The First Amendment	Lucy Bledsoe	Social Studies	Definition, history and current relevance of the First Amendment	
			A Printer's Journal in Revolutionary America		Social Studies, Humanities	How printing technology influenced the Revolution	Timeline of the American Revolution
			The Right Choice		Humanities, Literature—poetry	Examines how people choose certain paths	
			'Right Brain or 'Left Brain': Myth or Reality	John McCrone	Science	Explores the idea that the left and right sides of the brain have specific qualities	
	34	knowledge	The Value of Knowledge		Humanities	How education influences an income in the work force	Graphs that show level of income compared to education
			Mrs. Flowers	Maya Angelou	Social Studies, Literature	How a woman influenced the direction of a writer's life	
			Apollo 13: Ingenuity Saves the Mission	Jim Lovell, Jeffrey Kluger	Science, Literature	How a rescuers navigated danger and landed a spacecraft safely on Earth	
			Alvar Nuñez Cabeza de Vaca: A Man of Knowledge	Alvar Nuñez Cabeza de Vaca	Social Studies, Literature	Journal excerpts from Cabeza de Vaca's journey to the New World	
			Majory Stoneman Douglas: Knowing the River of Life		Social Studies, Literature	Profile of an activist for the Everglades	

Book	Unit	Target Word	Selection	Author	Content Area	Context	Illustrations
F	35	imagination	The Tech of Shrek: Imagination Animated		Science, Humanities	How the movie Shrek was made	
			The Raven: A Romantic Imagination	Edgar Allen Poe	Literature—poetry	A dark and mysterious poem	
			La Vida Robot: Imagination Rules!	Joshua Davis (adaptation)	Science	How a team of high school students created a robot for a competition	
			Don Quixote	Miguel de Cervantes	Literature	A story of an idealistic knight and his squire	
	36	brilliance	Brilliance Through Time and Space		Science	How a star shines at night	
			Sequoyah: Brilliant Code-Maker		Humanities, Literature	How a man developed a written code for his people	
			The Miracle Worker: Brilliance Unbound	William Gibson	Humanities, Literature	A play that tells of the life of Helen Keller and her relationship with her teacher	

What You Need to Know

"Mirror" and "Window" Text in *LANGUAGE!*

"Students should be able to find themselves in the available books, but they should also be able to find representatives of others about whom they wish to learn" (Biancarosa, G., and Snow, C.E., 2004).

Most *LANGUAGE!* students have had limited exposure to text or literature that explores a range of subjects. They may also have had limited contact with stories that reflect their lives and experiences. For these reasons, *LANGUAGE!* text selections emphasize "Mirror" and "Window" text.

Mirror Text "reflects" students' background and allows them to connect to text through gender, ethnicity, and culture. This allows them to draw on personal background knowledge to aid in comprehension.

Window Text, in contrast, provides openings for students to learn about the world beyond their own life experience. They have often missed large amounts of content knowledge because of their reading struggles. In their content, *LANGUAGE!* text selections seek to replace lost learning opportunities by including text from a wide range of subjects.

H

How will you evaluate student learning?

Fluency Practice

Fluency practice helps you monitor student progress in regards to automatic word recognition and phrasing. As noted earlier, the ability to read fluently has a direct correlation to reading comprehension. Phrase, Sentence, and Passage Fluencies are spaced throughout units, as indicated in each unit's Content Map.

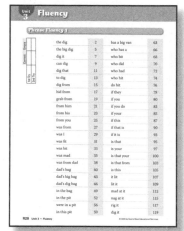

Phrase Fluency
from Unit 3, Lesson 1

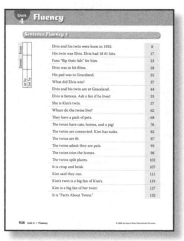

Sentence Fluency
from Unit 4

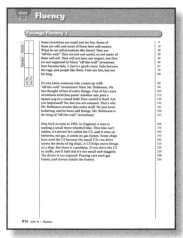

Passage Fluency
from Unit 13, Lesson 2

Comprehension Proficiency

In Step 5, Comprehension Proficiency activities in the *Interactive Text* help you monitor students' ability to interpret and answer multiple choice and open-ended comprehension questions. Occurring twice per book, one Comprehension Proficiency activity includes modeling and guiding students through the process of answering multiple choice questions. A second activity provides students with an opportunity to apply the process independently. While not included in the Content Mastery data collection, students' proficiency answering the questions will provide you with feedback about your students' ability to interpret questions and use the text to answer them.

Progress Monitoring

At the end of the book, students demonstrate proficiency in reading comprehension by taking the Progress Indicator for the *LANGUAGE!* Reading Scale. Refer to the *LANGUAGE!* Reading Scale section in any *LANGUAGE! Assessment: Teacher Edition* for more information about the administration, scoring and interpretation of this measure.

5 DIFFERENTIATED INSTRUCTION

How will teachers respond when a student experiences difficulty in learning?

 Use **Special Instructional Support** activities to customize teaching materials and provide opportunities for individualized instruction.

Lesson 1	Lesson 2	Lesson 3	Lesson 4	Lesson 5
Step 1: *Sortegories* CD: Sound Count **Step 2:** *Words for Teachers* CD: Word Card Generator—Essential Words *Words for Teachers* CD: Word Study Guide—Spelling Words	**Step 1:** Folder Activity: Phoneme Sort: Words with Short Vowels **Step 2:** *Sortegories* CD: Sort It *Words for Teachers* CD: Fluency Builder Grid—Essential Words	**Step 2:** Folder Activity: Tic-Tac-Toe With Essential Words *Sortegories* CD: Build It **Step 5:** *LANGUAGE! eReader* CD: **"It'll Never Work"**	**Step 2:** Folder Activity: Syllable Sort: Number of Syllables in a Word **Step 3:** *Sortegories* CD: Categorize It	**Step 3:** *Sortegories* CD: Morph It
Lesson 6	**Lesson 7**	**Lesson 8**	**Lesson 9**	**Lesson 10**
Step 2: *Words for Teachers* CD: Word Unscramble **Step 3:** *Sortegories* CD: Relate It	**Step 2:** *Words for Teachers* CD: Word Search—Words with Schwa **Step 3:** *Sortegories* CD: Analogy Building **Step 4:** *Sortegories* CD: Grammar Sort	**Step 4:** *Words for Teachers* CD: Word Card Generator—Build Sentences with Direct Objects **Step 5:** *LANGUAGE! eReader* CD: **"Way to Go!"**	**Step 3:** *Words for Teachers* CD: Word Card Generator—Sort Words with Prefixes **Step 4:** Folder Activity: Grammar Sort—Present and Future Tense Verb Phrases	

Technology Tools for Differentiation

Sortegories CD...	*e-Reader* CD...	*Words for Teachers* CD...
The Phrase Building /Sentence Building and Analogies exercises on the Sortegories CD model and reinforce comprehension skills.	This technology tool provides an oral presentation of selected stories, supported by comprehension questions. eReader helps English learners practice listening comprehension while offering a good model of spoken English.	With the ability to generate vocabulary specific to content areas (science, social studies, etc.), this tool aids development of student comprehension across the curriculum.

From the *LANGUAGE!* Classroom

Student reader "Self-Reflections" from a *LANGUAGE!* classroom:

"When I read in my head I can concentrate more on the book than I do reading it aloud. Even since I started Ms. Metelak's class I started to enjoy reading more amd more. Reading is a good thing. One day I might want to be a reader for kids or some kind of thing like that so I will practice reading every day and get better one step at a time."

"I now realize the following things about myself as a reader. One of the things is that I actually like it and that I understand it. Another thing is that the books I read capture me and I don't want to stop reading until the book is finished."

"Something new I tried as a reader was if I did not understand what I was reading I will go back and read it again."

"Something new that I tried as a reader was the genres. I never liked action but I tried action books and now I like that genre a lot."

"I now realize the following things about myself as a reader is that if I put my mind to it I can actually finish a book."

"A new thing I tried as a reader is reading a big Harry Potter book... I thought that I couldn't read those kinds of books but I could."

"I now realize the following things about myself as a reader. It cool because I know how to read faster and know how to be a good reader and I can read to my younger brothers."

Hali Metelak, *7th & 8th Grade Teacher and Certified LANGUAGE! Instructor*
Vista Middle School; Los Angeles Unified School District; Los Angeles, California

STEP

6 SPEAKING AND WRITING

Table of Contents

RESEARCH BITE

"Effective writing instruction acknowledges that the smooth deployment of the higher-level writing strategies needed to plan, generate, and review text depends on easy use of lower-level skills such as handwriting, keyboarding, spelling, grammar and punctuation, and access to appropriate vocabulary."

Graham & Perin, 2007

I

RESEARCH: WHY DO STEP 6

At first glance, the link between spoken and written expression might seem quite direct. Research, though, suggests that the two abilities require very different skills and actually call on distinct language centers of the brain. Writing is a truly complex activity requiring explicit instruction. "Writing is a skill that draws on subskills and processes such as handwriting and spelling; a rich knowledge of vocabulary; mastery of the conventions of punctuation, capitalization, word usage, and grammar; and the use of strategies such as planning, evaluating and revising text (Graham & Perin, 2007).

The benefits of communicating effectively through written expression reach well beyond the classroom. Most contexts of life require a level of writing proficiency. Unfortunately, 70 percent of students in grades 4-12 are low-achieving writers (Graham & Perin, 2007). Educators need to examine current practices in light of the research on effective writing strategies if schools want to consistently produce proficient writers.
To become proficient, students need the ability to adapt their writing to its context and move flexibly among a variety of formats—e.g., outlines, lists, sentences, paragraphs, and
essays (Graham & Perin, 2007).

According to the research, teaching explicit strategies for planning and organizing the writing process is the key to helping students achieve self-directed writing. Some of these techniques are genre-specific and all should be coordinated with curriculum (Graham & Perin, 2007; Berninger & Richards, 2002; De La Paz & Graham, 1996; Feretti, MacArthur, & Dowdy, 2000; Page-Voth & Grahma, 1999; Wong, 1997).

Student writing improves when models are provided and students emulate the critical elements and patterns of these examples (Graham & Perin, 2007). Prewriting activities are an additional tactic that lets students generate and organize their ideas for their compositions before facing the blank page. Explicit and step-by-step preparations such as these have a positive effect on the quality of their writing (Graham & Perin, 2007).

Writing instruction also improves reading comprehension. Research shows it extends and deepens students' knowledge and is a valuable tool for learning content (Graham & Perin, 2007; Biancarosa & Snow, 2004). The use of graphic organizers to clarify organizational patterns or structures of the text for writing instruction, for example, has proven an effective means for improving comprehension of adolescent poor readers (Longo 2001; Taylor & Beach, 1984) as well as dyslexic readers and those with other learning disabilities (Shaywitz, 2003). Instruction in a combination of study skill strategies proves most effective in improving the ability of students to gain information from text. These include main idea instruction, summarizing, note taking, and outlining. Explicit and systematic instruction of these reading strategies makes a dramatic difference in the quality of students' writing (Graham & Perin, 2007; Mastropieri & Scruggs, 1997).

Vocabulary Connection

Developing writers often have difficulty generating language to express their ideas, including selecting words that convey their intended message in a precise, interesting, and natural way. Others can express themselves orally, but lack knowledge of how to represent language in writing (Berninger et. al., 1992). Students develop academic language through writing in response to their reading. Analyzing literature and composing essays and reports on different topics helps to incorporate the more sophisticated vocabulary and complex language structure that typifies academic language (California Frameworks, 1999).

Grammar Connection

Traditional grammar instruction does not appear to improve the quality of students' writing. However, "teaching students to focus on the function and practical application of grammar within the context of writing (versus teaching grammar as an independent activity) produced strong and positive effects on students' writing" (Graham & Perin, 2007).

I

How *LANGUAGE!* Does It

LANGUAGE! teaches the skills of speaking and writing by:

- Directly linking instruction from Step 3: Vocabulary and Morphology and Step 4: Grammar and Usage to the writing process in Step 6

- Directly linking the Step 6 instruction to the Step 5 reading selections.

- Presenting text selections as models for writing

- Using graphic organizers to demonstrate text features, structures, and component parts of sentences, paragraphs, and reports

- Explicit teaching and modeling of prewriting strategies, including outlines and lists, with support from graphic guides and checklists

- Emphasis and explicit instruction on the drafting and revision process, with support of graphic guides and checklists

- Teaching grammar in the context of function and practical application within the writing process

- Developing automaticity with written language conventions including spelling, punctuation, and capitalization.

"'What I Did on My Summer Vacation—A Prequel.'"

The content of Step 6 addresses two objectives simultaneously: 1) it serves as a complement to Step 5 by using oral and written responses to monitor comprehension, and 2) it develops strategies and skills unique to composition. To reach these goals, students will:

- Learn to correctly interpret questions and provide complete, accurate answers, first orally and then in written form.

- Engage in brainstorming and other strategies involved in the prewriting process.

- Use outlines and graphic organizers to organize content and ideas in preparation write.

- Express themselves in a variety of written formats ranging from sentences to multiparagraph pieces, including narratives and reports.

- Write different types of paragraphs including expository, sequence, reasons, compare/contrast, narrative, literar analysis, and persuasive.

- Use checklists based on the Six Traits of Effective Writing to guide the writing process, especially the revision phase.

- Actively engage in peer review to refine knowledge of writing process.

- Learn the Six Traits of Effective Writing and use them as a framework.

Just as listening comprehension precedes reading comprehension, speaking precedes writing. Using the content and skills taught in previous steps, Step 6 focuses on written expression as a means of reflecting understanding. In fact, Step 5: Listening and Reading Comprehension and Step 6are taught reciprocally.

What You Need to Know

LANGUAGE! and the Six Traits of Effective Writing

No other act of communication equals the demand of writing. To write well, we must juggle multiple concepts and skills simultaneously. In fact, we must use the building blocks taught in all of the steps of the curriculum to write. Writing is a cumulative and culminating task.

The Six Traits of Effective Writing capture the multi-dimensional aspect of writing. The traits are both the foundation of the students' Writer's Checklists, and the basis of the rating rubrics tailored for use in the evaluation process. The Six Traits are the common denominator of all the aspects of the evaluation process for writing and reflect content and skills from all Steps in the *LANGUAGE!* curriculum.

This chart reflects the alignment of *LANGUAGE!* with the Six Traits of Effective Writing.

Trait	Strategies	Steps
Ideas and Content	• Collection of information from text selections • Activation of prior knowledge	Step 5: Listening and Reading Comprehension
Organization	• Analysis of models • Graphic organizers and outlines • Transition words • Text structures and characteristics	Step 5: Listening and Reading Comprehension Step 6: Speaking and Writing
Voice and Audience Awareness	• Purposes of text • Language within text that engages reader	Step 5: Listening and Reading Comprehension Step 6: Speaking and Writing
Word Choice	• Deeper word knowledge • Proper grammatical usage • Revising/rewriting sentences	Step 3: Vocabulary and Morphology Step 4: Grammar and Usage Step 5: Listening and Reading Comprehension Step 6: Speaking and Writing
Sentence Fluency	• Sentence combining • Variation of sentence syntax and length	Step 4: Grammar and Usage Step 6: Speaking and Writing
Conventions of Written Language	• Correct and legible formation of letters • Accurate spelling • Application of punctuation and capitalization rules • Usage of correct grammar • Development of writing, editing, and revision processes	Step 1: Phonemic Awareness and Phonics Step 2: Word Recognition and Spelling Step 4: Grammar and Usage Step 6: Speaking and Writing

Use of Text in Writing

LANGUAGE! begins with an emphasis on expository writing, the type of writing most frequently required of students. For this reason, a large percentage of text selections in the first three books are informational. Research confirms that exposure to such text can deepen comprehension, offer background knowledge, and strengthen writing skills by using content vocabulary, while modeling the processes involved in planning, evaluating, and revising text (Graham & Perin, 2007). Students use the content from their reading selections as a source of content and ideas for their written responses. Responses reflect comprehension of the text as well as students' growth in a number of skills that contribute to improved writing.

Types of Writing Tasks

Students will learn—in a scaffolded progression—to write for varied purposes, including but not limited to:

- Complete, accurate answers to questions according to Bloom's Taxonomy
- Basic paragraphs
- Simple and expanded summary paragraphs
- Multiple paragraph essays
- Reports and presentations
- Personal narratives
- Fictional narratives
- Research papers
- Literary analysis essays.

RESEARCH BITE

Each of the critical steps in the writing process must be taught directly (Gersten and Baker, 2001) and practiced repeatedly (Swanson, Hoskyn, and Lee, 1999) if students are to write coherently and fluently.

Even for accomplished writers, writing can be an intimidating task. Research confirms that how students feel about writing impacts their response to writing intervention. Furthermore, repeated writing practice prevents work-avoidance, and scaffolded instruction increases children's learning (Berninger et al., 1995).

How will you maximize student learning?

- Employ explicit instruction and modeling of effective writing practices at the sentence, paragraph, and multiparagraph levels.

- Use graphic organizers and other forms of planning to promote prewriting strategies.

- Use checklists to guide students' writing and revision process.

Answering Questions: A Difficult Writing Task

In an academic setting, written responses to questions is one of the most frequently required writing tasks. *LANGUAGE!* is intently focused on teaching this complicated and essential skill. In the Answer It activity, students turn questions into statements and identify signal words that indicate the information necessary to answer the questions. Knowledge of the question signal words helps students master this skill. The signal words are taught in accordance to the hierarchy established in Bloom's Taxonomy. (To review Bloom's Taxonomy for signal words, see page 355 in the Appendix.)

Reading and Writing: A Reciprocal Process

LANGUAGE! develops reading and writing as reciprocal processes. The Instructional and Challenge Texts both provide models of varying complexities, text structures, and genres for students to refer to while writing.

Explicit instruction using text selections plays a helpful role in pointing out the features of effective writing. By highlighting and modeling the components of introductions and conclusions, sentence and paragraph structures, main ideas, topic sentences, and supporting details, students can begin to practice and incorporate them into their own writing.

Writing and Speaking Using the Challenge Text

The Challenge Text in each unit features a Writing and Speaking Using the Challenge Text lesson plan. This lesson provides useful practice in responding to text through writing and speaking, while developing written academic language skills.

Writing: A Construction Project

The demands of writing are impressive because of the need to manage and coordinate numerous processes at the same time. Using an architectural analogy may help your students understand the needs and complexities of a writing project.

Like a building project, writing requires planning, good materials, and quality control. Before construction can begin on a house, for instance, blueprints have to be drawn. In a similar fashion, writers must organize their thoughts before they can effectively develop them on paper.

Once composition begins, writers must craft their project from the ground up, with words that are organized in a grammatically and syntactically correct fashion. The content must be accurate, the sentences varied and thoughtfully crafted. When connected, the sentences effectively build a composition that reflects the writer's thoughts and ideas (Singer & Bashir, 2004).

Lastly, writers must learn how to direct an evaluative eye on their own work. As with all jobs, good construction requires the identification and repair of oversights and shoddy work along the way. In composition this "quality control" takes the form of rewriting, editing, and revision. All of these elements are needed in good written work, just as they are necessary in building a solid house.

Teacher's Tip

I use the Unit Essential words, Unit Spelling Lists, and Unit Vocabulary words to create 5 sentences that I dictate to my students. I have the students write them on a mini white board with an Expo marker. The students compete with each other to see who can finish the sentence correctly first. They have a blast competing with each other and the winner for each sentence gets a piece of candy. This activity stresses: Word recognition and spelling, vocabulary, capitalization, end punctuation, proper sentence structure, listening skills, and speaking and writing. The students are improving greatly and really look forward to this activity.

Julie Harfield, *Special Education Teacher*
St. Vrain Valley School District, Colorado

Step 6 Why Do/How To Activities

More complete descriptions and instructions for these activities can be found in the Appendix. See page 362 for the table of contents.

Answering Questions	Activity Snapshot
Answer It	These recurring exercises let you model, and your students practice, academic language as it applies to constructing answers to different levels of questions and demonstrating their understanding of the text.
Think About It	This activity prompts oral responses through class discussion. These questions require students to use higher order thinking skills. They appear at the end of each Challenge Text selection.
Graphic Organizers	
Blueprints for Writing	These templates—in graphic and outline forms— provide opportunities for explicit instruction of prewriting planning.
Informal (Two-Column) Outline	Through the use of this informal outline, students practice organizing main ideas and the corresponding details.
Map It	Map It templates allow you and your class to explore text structure, including Main Ideas, Plot, and Reasons as part of prewriting strategies.
Writing Process	
Masterpiece Sentences	These step-by-step guides for developing sentence structure grow in sophistication using a six-stage process.
Take Note	Provides guided practice in gathering information from text for use in writing activities.
Revise It	This scaffolded activity helps students develop skills in analyzing, editing, and revising text.

Activity Materials

Interactive Text

This consumable text provides ready-made materials to present and practice speaking and writing concepts and skills—unit-by-unit, lesson-by-lesson. Exercises range from recognizing and responding to signal words to guided writing activities.

Guided writing exercise from Book C *Interactive Text*

Student Text: Handbook

The Handbook section of the *Student Text*, in the front of every level of *Student Text*, contains easily accessible and cummulative references for writing strategies, tips and conventions that students have learned in the current and prior books.

From the Handbook section beginning in Book A

Transparencies and Templates

The program's set of transparencies and templates allows you to model the range of prewriting and writing concepts and skills for your entire class.

Masterpiece Sentence Work Strips template

You Try It! Using the Teacher's Edition

Lesson plans for Step 6: Speaking and Writing from Unit 1, Unit 13, and Unit 28—*LANGUAGE!*'s three entry points— are shown here to demonstrate the range of objectives, exercises, and activities linked to the Instructional Text across the curriculum.

Preparations

What do you need to do to prepare to teach this activity?

_____

_____

How might your students benefit from a way to keep these signal words organized?

_____

_____

Directions

Do you think your students need a visual model for this activity?

_____

_____

How will you introduce this activity and its value?

_____

_____

Connections

How might **Answer It** help your students in other classrooms?

_____

_____

What skills from earlier steps are reinforced with this activity?

_____

_____

STEP

6   **Speaking and Writing**

Students learn the **Answer It** process to formulate answers to comprehension questions.

☆ **Answer It: Using Signal Words**

Why Do: Students become more successful at answering questions after they have received direct instruction in how to formulate a response that specifically addresses a particular question.

How To: This activity uses the following process to help students formulate appropriate oral and written responses to questions:

- Explain the meaning of each of the signal words in the unit.
- Using the board or overhead transparency, model the process of using a signal word to formulate a response to an **Answer It** question.

  1. **Determine what the question is asking:** Read the question. Identify and underline the signal word. Review the type of information required to respond to the question. [**Note:** A complete listing of signal words and the information required for each is provided in the *Teacher Resource Guide* and in the Handbook section of the *Student Text*, page H48.]

  2. **Find information to answer the question:** Demonstrate using text headings or other text features to locate the content needed to answer the question. Reread the section to retrieve exact information, if needed.

  3. **Formulate the answer:** Use the signal word and the question to formulate a response. Have students answer the question orally or in writing.

  4. **Check the answer:** Identify the part of the response that replaces the question word.

Materials
Student Text
p. H48,
pp. 20–22
Interactive Text
p. 14, Exercise 5

Use the Handbook section of the *Student Text* to introduce students to a process to answer comprehension questions in complete sentences.

Demonstrate Comprehension

▶ Have students turn to Exercise 5, **Answer It**, in the *Interactive Text*, page 14, and demonstrate the process to answer the **Answer It** questions using question 1 from "Batty About Bats."

Model It

▶ Show students how to determine what the question is asking. Identify and underline the signal words. Then, review the type of information required to respond to the question.

1. Is a bat a mammal?

If the question asks....	The answer must include...
is/are	A "yes" or "no"

Interactive Text
p. 14, Exercise 5
Teacher Edition p. 51

Unit 1 • Lesson 3 **47**

From Book A Unit 1, Lesson 3

STEP

Speaking and Writing

Students review how to add transitional words and phrases to topic sentences to create transition topic sentences.

✓ Pre-write
Write
Revise

**Student Text
p. H95**
Teacher Edition p. T48

⭐ Report Structure

Materials
Student Text
p. H95

Interactive Text
p. 29,
Exercise 6
(Unit 13,
Lesson 4,
Step 6)

Interactive Text
pp. 48–50,
Exercise 7

Use this activity to review the structure of a report and show how to create transition topic sentences that link information in the report.

Topic Sentences: Adding Transitions

▸ Have students:
  • Turn to the Handbook section of the *Student Text*, page H95.
  • Locate the transition topic sentences highlighted in yellow in the report.
  • Identify the circled transition words.
▸ Remind students that each body paragraph in a report usually begins with a transition topic sentence.
▸ Explain to students that they can use what they know about writing a topic sentence for a single paragraph and apply it to the topic sentence of each paragraph in a report.
▸ Have students:
  • Turn to Exercise 6, **Write It: Expository Paragraph**, from Unit 13, Lesson 4, Step 6, on page 29 of the *Interactive Text*.
  • Review the two ideas with the stars in front of them.
▸ Remind students that when they write their report, each of the star ideas will become the topic sentence of a body paragraph.
▸ Explain that in the body paragraphs of the report, the **IVF topic sentence** is a good type of topic sentence to use initially.
▸ Explain that in a multiparagraph report, writers add transitional words or phrases to transition topic sentences to introduce the new ideas in that body paragraph and to create links between body paragraphs.

**Interactive Text
p. 29, Exercise 6
(Unit 13, Lesson 4, Step 6)**
Teacher Edition p. 111

Transition Topic Sentences

▸ Have students:
  • Turn to Exercise 7, **Write It: Transition Topic Sentence**, in the *Interactive Text*, pages 48–50.
▸ Guide students to select transition words to create links between the body paragraphs in a report. Point out that more than one transition word may be correct in any given sentence.

**Interactive Text
pp. 48–50, Exercise 7**
Teacher Edition pp. 111–112

Unit 13 • Lesson 7   **107**

From Book C, Unit 13, Lesson 7

Preparations

What specific writing skill is the focus of this lesson?

_____

_____

How might a visual model contribute to this activity?

_____

_____

Directions

What materials will your students be working out of?

_____

_____

How will you keep their writing activities organized and accessible?

_____

_____

Connections

How does this approach help reluctant writers become more proficient?

_____

_____

How does this process help students in other core curriculum classes?

_____

_____

I

STEP 6

You Try It!

Preparations

What procedures and behavioral expectations do your students need to know to ensure the success of this activity?

_____

_____

What materials do you need to have available to your students as they prepare their final copy?

_____

_____

Directions

How might you demonstrate to students the value of revision?

_____

_____

What are the potential benefits and pitfalls of **Peer Writing Reviews?**

_____

_____

Connections

How do undeveloped cognitive skills affect your students' willingness to revise and rewrite their narrative?

_____

_____

How are Benchmark Papers used in the comprehensive assessment system?

_____

_____

STEP 6 Speaking and Writing

Students use peer reviews to revise and finalize their personal narratives.

Revising and Editing: Personal Narrative

Materials

Peer Writing Review transparency and templates

Interactive Text p. R9, Personal Narrative Writer's Checklist

Six Traits Writing Rubric

Personal Narrative Planner templates (Unit 28, Lesson 8, Step 6)

Use this activity to help students critique their draft personal narratives prior to writing a final copy.

▸ Arrange students in groups of three and provide two copies of the **Peer Writing Review** template for each student.

▸ Explain that one way to help revise written work is to get feedback from others. The **Peer Writing Review** template helps to organize the feedback you want to give.

▸ Display the **Peer Writing Review** transparency and review each category of information with students. Point out the structure of the template, which includes space for both positive ("Things That Work Well") and constructive feedback ("Things You Might Improve").

▸ Have each group member:

• Listen as each author reads his or her narrative aloud to the group. Then complete a **Peer Writing Review** template for the author. Each listener should complete a review.

• Pay attention to the way the author followed the structure of a personal narrative.

• Share the completed **Peer Writing Review** with the author.

▸ Have students:

• Use the **Peer Writing Review** feedback along with the **Personal Narrative Writer's Checklist** in the *Interactive Text* to revise their paragraphs.

• Use editor's marks or word-process capabilities to make any necessary revision or corrections to their draft.

Write the Final Copy

▸ Once students have finished reviewing, have them:

• Write or word process a final draft of their narrative based on the **Peer Writing Review** input and the **Personal Narrative Writer's Checklist** review.

▸ Collect students' essays to evaluate.

• Use the **Six Traits Writing Rubric** for Book E to evaluate students' narratives. Then hold conferences with students to discuss their progress.

Peer Writing Review

Interactive Text p. R9, Personal Narrative Writer's Checklist

Six Traits Writing Rubric

Differentiated Instruction Review & Acceleration Special Instructional Support English Learners Technology Challenge Text

544 Unit 28 • Lesson 10

From Book E, Unit 28, Lesson 10

Writing *Using the* Challenge Text

Students write an expository (compare/contrast) paragraph based on the selections "**Atlas: A Book of Maps**" and "**Floki: Sailor Without a Map.**"

✔ Pre-write
✔ Write
✔ Revise

Write It: Compare/Contrast Paragraph

Materials
Interactive Text back cover, Writer's Checklist Paper

Set the Stage

▶ Write the following topic on the board or on an overhead:

How were Hercules in "Atlas: A Book of Maps" and Floki in "Floki: Sailor Without a Map" the same and how were they different?

▶ Make sure each student has two sheets of lined paper and a pencil with an eraser.

Guide the Writing Process

Pre-write

▶ Discuss the writing assignment with the students, making sure they understand the concepts of same and different.

▶ Ask students to turn and talk with a partner about how Hercules and Floki are the same and different, with each partner making a Venn diagram that illustrates the similarities and differences. (An example of a completed Venn diagram might look like the graphic below.)

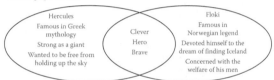

Hercules		Floki
Famous in Greek mythology	Clever	Famous in Norwegian legend
Strong as a giant	Hero	Devoted himself to the dream of finding Iceland
Wanted to be free from holding up the sky	Brave	Concerned with the welfare of his men

▶ Write the following topic sentence on the board or an overhead:

Hercules and Floki are similar in some ways and different in others.

▶ Review with students the Book A **Writer's Checklist** on the inside back cover of the *Interactive Text*, pointing out the skills for which they will be held responsible in their paragraphs.

Write

▶ Ask the students to copy the topic sentence on the board onto their papers.

▶ Tell students to use information from their Venn diagrams and complete their paragraphs by writing two complete sentences about how Hercules and Floki are the same and two complete sentences about how they are different.

Revise and Edit

▶ Ask students to re-read their work using the Book A **Writer's Checklist** and make any revisions and/or corrections.

▶ After reviewing the students' paragraphs, ask them to put their work in their student notebooks.

Interactive Text back cover, Writer's Checklist

Unit 2 • Writing Using the Challenge Text **255**

From Book A, Unit 2, Writing Using the Challenge Text

Preparations

What concept do students need to clearly understand before undertaking this writing exercise?

_____

_____

How might you model the effective use of the Writer's Checklist?

_____

_____

Directions

What role does the Venn Diagram play in this activity?

_____

_____

How long will students' finished paragraphs be?

_____

_____

Connections

What are ways to acknowledge good student work from this activity?

_____

_____

How might you connect this writing exercise to students' personal interests?

_____

_____

STEP
6 ONGOING ASSESSMENT

Given the complex nature of writing and its development, assessment looks very different for Step 6 when compared to the other Steps. The initial writing assessment provides the baseline from which to measure a student's writing development.

Using the Six Traits of Effective Writing

LANGUAGE! bases the evaluation of student writing on the Six Traits of Effective Writing. Students are explicitly taught to write with these elements in mind. They use a Writer's Checklist for prewriting, first drafts, revision, and final drafts. One of the strengths of the Six Traits rubric is that it incorporates all aspects of the writing process. Often poor writers are heavily penalized for their poor spelling and grammar. Because of their paper's appearance, their creativity and idea development is often overlooked. A better approach is one that honors other aspects of good writing (Graham & Perin, 2007).

- Fluency Tasks
- Content Mastery
- Benchmark Paper
- Comprehension Proficiency

adjust · instruct · assess

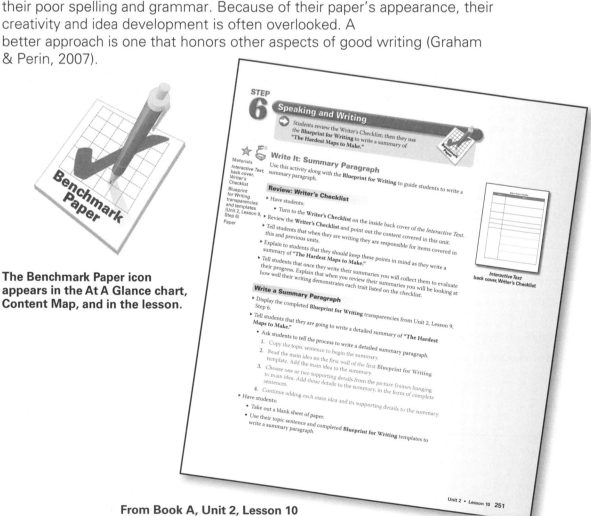

The Benchmark Paper icon appears in the At A Glance chart, Content Map, and in the lesson.

From Book A, Unit 2, Lesson 10

The Writer's Checklist that students use to evaluate and revise their drafts is based on The Six Traits of Effective Writing. The book-level 4-point rubrics that teachers use to evaluate students' Benchmark papers and Progress Indicator papers are also based on the Six Traits of Effective Writing.

Benchmark Papers occur in the second and fourth unit of every book, when students' writing is evaluated. Directions to administer these tasks are included at point of use in the *Teacher Edition*. See any *Assessment:Teacher Edition* pages 32–33 for more information on Benchmark Papers.

Progress Monitoring

At the end of each book, students demonstrate proficiency in writing by taking the Progress Indicator: Writing. Refer to the Progress Indicator: writing section of any *LANGUAGE! Assessment:Teacher Edition*, for more information about the administration, scoring, and interpretation of this measure.

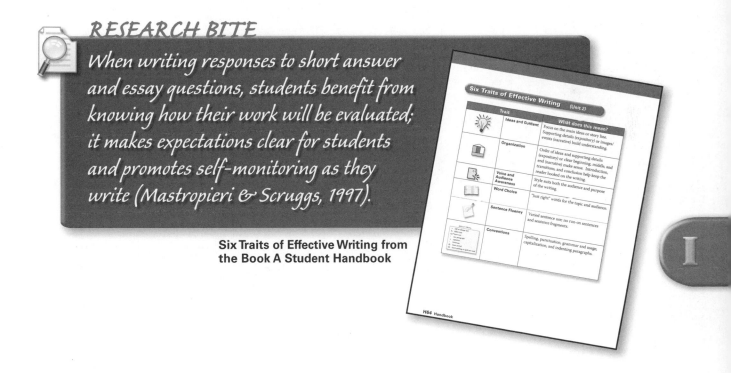

RESEARCH BITE

When writing responses to short answer and essay questions, students benefit from knowing how their work will be evaluated; it makes expectations clear for students and promotes self-monitoring as they write (Mastropieri & Scruggs, 1997).

Six Traits of Effective Writing from the Book A Student Handbook

You Try It! Writer's Checklists

How might you model the use of this checklist?

_____

_____

_____

The Student Handbooks in all *Student Texts* feature a "Writer's Checklist" that increases in complexity from Book A through Book F. (The same checklist also appears in all *Interactive Texts*.) These checklists align with the Six Traits of Effective Writing.

STEP 6

Writer's Checklist for Book A   (Unit 2)

Trait	Did I...?	Unit
Ideas and Content	❏ Focus all sentences on the topic	1
	❏ Provide supporting details for my topic sentence	1
	❏ Include examples, evidence, and/or explanations to develop the supporting detail sentences	5
Organization	❏ Write a topic sentence	1
	❏ Tell things in an order that makes sense	1
	❏ Use transition words and/or phrases	4
	❏ Write a concluding sentence	5
Voice and Audience Awareness	❏ Think about my audience and purpose for writing	6
	❏ Write in a clear and engaging way that makes my audience want to read my work; can my reader "hear" me speaking	6
Word Choice	❏ Try to find my own way to say things	2
	❏ Use words that are lively and specific to the content	2
Sentence Fluency	❏ Write complete sentences	1
	❏ Expand some of my sentences by painting the subject and/or predicate	3, 6
Conventions	Capitalize words correctly:	
	❏ Capitalize the first word of each sentence	1
	❏ Capitalize proper nouns, including people's names	3
	Punctuate correctly:	
	❏ Put a period or question mark at the end of each sentence	1
	❏ Put an apostrophe before the **s** for a singular possessive noun	2
	❏ Use a comma after a long adverb phrase at the beginning of a sentence	5
	Use grammar correctly:	
	❏ Use the correct verb tense	4
	❏ Make sure the verb agrees with the subject in number	4
	Spell correctly:	
	❏ Spell all **Essential Words** correctly	1
	Apply spelling rules	
	❏ The doubling rule (1-1-1)	6

Handbook H65

Book A Writing Rubric

Name_____   Date_____

Grade_____   Teacher_____   Holistic Score_____

Trait	4	3	2	1	Value	Teacher Comments
Ideas and Content	Focuses on the topic. Main idea (topic sentence) is well supported with details and elaboration (examples, evidence, and explanations).	Mostly focuses on the topic. Sentences supporting the main idea (topic sentence) may be general rather than detailed and specific.	Main idea (topic sentence) is unclear and/or lacks sufficient support.	Does not address prompt and/or lacks a topic sentence. Supporting details are absent or do not relate to topic.	____	
Organization	Topic sentence clearly states main idea. Ideas are clear and logically organized. Contains concluding sentence.	Topic sentence states main idea. Organization mostly clear and logical. May contain concluding sentence.	Structure may not be entirely clear or logical. Paragraph may seem more like a list and/or be hard to follow.	No evident structure. Lack of organization seriously interferes with meaning.	____	
Voice and Audience Awareness	Strong sense of a person and purpose behind the words. Brings topic to life.	Some sense of person and purpose behind the words.	Little sense of person and purpose behind the words.	No sense of person or purpose behind the words.	____	
Word Choice	Words are specific to the content, accurate, and vivid. Words enhance meaning and the reader's enjoyment of the writing.	Words are correctly used but may be somewhat general.	Words may be used inaccurately and/or repetitively.	Extremely limited range of words.	____	
Sentence Fluency	Writes complete sentences and varies sentence structure.	Writes in complete sentences and attempts to use sentences with expanded predicates.	Writes mostly simple sentences. May include some run-ons and fragments.	Numerous run-ons and/or fragments interfere with the message.	____	
Conventions	*Mechanics:* No errors in capitalization and punctuation. Paragraph is indented.	*Mechanics:* Few errors in capitalization and punctuation. Paragraph is indented.	*Mechanics:* Some errors in capitalization and punctuation. Paragraph may not be indented.	*Mechanics:* Many capitalization and punctuation errors. Paragraph not indented.	____	
	Grammar/Usage: No errors in grammar and usage.	*Grammar/Usage:* Few errors in grammar and usage.	*Grammar/Usage:* Some grammar and usage errors.	*Grammar/Usage:* Errors in grammar and usage interfere with meaning.	____	
	Spelling: All **Essential Words** and most other words spelled correctly.	*Spelling:* Most **Essential Words** and most other words spelled correctly.	*Spelling:* Some **Essential Words** and other words misspelled.	*Spelling:* Many spelling errors.	____	
				TOTAL POINTS	____	

Book A Writer's Rubric

How might this writing rubric differ from traditional writing instructions?

_____

_____

_____

How will teachers respond when students experience difficulty in learning?

In Steps 1-4, measurable skills are taught that lend themselves to tangible slivers of assessment. Because writing is a compilation of those skills, its assessment and remediation require a different approach. The most important aspect of improving student writing is corrective feedback. Students need to see examples of good writing, opportunities to emulate aspects and elements of good writing, and constructive feedback on their writing.

Practice does not make perfect if the practice does not incorporate corrective feedback. If students practice writing poorly, they will continue to do so unless teachers intervene with constructive criticism and corrective strategies (Sousa, 2001).

Corrective Feedback for Writing

In response to rubric scores, teachers may need to provide opportunities for more modeling and practice. The compilation of skills required in writing gives assessment of Step 6 tasks a very different structure than the other steps. As weaknesses appear in student writing, you can revisit activities to practice smaller skill sets.

Corrective feedback for student writing might include the following:

- When answers to questions fall short of expectations, teachers may want to use a poor example and work with the class to rewrite it. Teachers need to "think out loud" to let students hear their thoughts and process as they work to revise the answer. Then, students can choose one of their weaker answers and revise it.

- When revising longer pieces of writing, focus on one aspect for revision. For example, a student might focus only on sentence fluency even thought other traits may also be weak; or, a student might work on only the conclusion paragraph even though the body of the paper is also weak. By guiding students to rewrite with a limited focus, students are not so overwhelmed with the process.

- If the majority of your students are weak in a specific skill, provide opportunities for extra practice. For example, to work on word choice students could use strategies from Masterpiece Sentences to upgrade basic sentences provided by the teacher.

Focus on Academic Language

As part of each unit's Planning and Pacing Guide, this chart outlines focused instruction related to Step 6 instruction. Skills such as English Intonation in Questions and Word Prominence in Spoken English are of particular benefit to English learners.

☀ Focus on Academic Language activities expand on and enhance unit-specific content. These activities appear at the point of use throughout the unit.

Lesson 1	Lesson 2	Lesson 3	Lesson 4	Lesson 5
Step 1: Phonemic Production of / t /	**Step 1:** Phonemic Production of / m /	**Step 6:** English Intonation: Introduction	**Step 1:** Pronunciation of *I am* and *I'm* in Spoken English **Step 3:** Pronunciation of Plural-Marker **-s**: / s / or / z /	

Lesson 6	Lesson 7	Lesson 8	Lesson 9	Lesson 10
Step 1: Phonemic Production of / t /		**Step 6:** Practice with English Intonation in Questions		

Focus on Academic Language chart from Unit 1

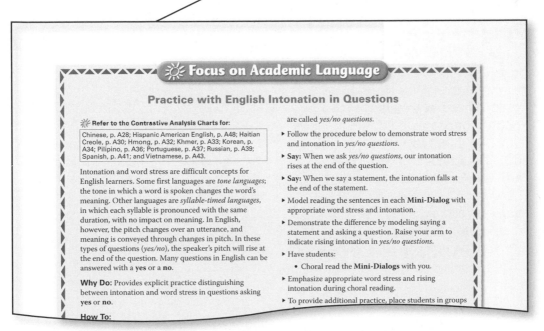

Focus on Academic Language lesson at point-of-use in Book A, Unit 1, Lesson 8

The *eReader* CD

The *eReader* allows students ...

- To revisit Instructional Text with a teacher-directed purpose
- To select, copy and paste, and organize text material to prepare for writing.
- To develop the Blueprint for Writing outline on the computer.

Homework Options

Homework materials for Step 6, printable from the *Instructional Planning Tools* CD, are available at different points in each unit to aid review and differentiation. The Homework Options chart at the beginning of each unit can aid you in incorporating homework into your planning and pacing.

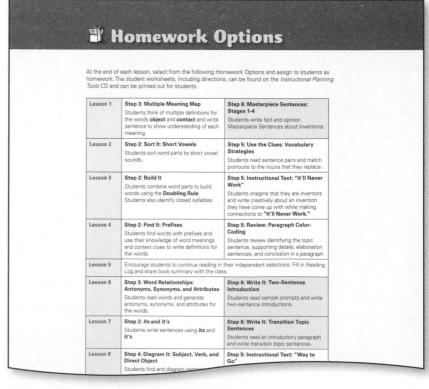

📋 **Homework Options**

At the end of each lesson, select from the following Homework Options and assign to students as homework. The student worksheets, including directions, can be found on the *Instructional Planning Tools* CD and can be printed out for students.

Lesson 1	**Step 3: Multiple Meaning Map** Students think of multiple definitions for the words **object** and **contact** and write sentence to show understanding of each meaning.	**Step 6: Masterpiece Sentences: Stages 1-4** Students write fact and opinion Masterpiece Sentences about inventions.
Lesson 2	**Step 2: Sort It: Short Vowels** Students sort word parts by short vowel sounds.	**Step 5: Use the Clues: Vocabulary Strategies** Students read sentence pairs and match pronouns to the nouns that they replace.
Lesson 3	**Step 2: Build It** Students combine word parts to build words using the **Doubling Rule**. Students also identify closed syllables.	**Step 5: Instructional Text: "It'll Never Work"** Students imagine that they are inventors and write creatively about an invention they have come up with while making connections to **"It'll Never Work."**
Lesson 4	**Step 2: Find It: Prefixes** Students find words with prefixes and use their knowledge of word meanings and context clues to write definitions for the words.	**Step 5: Review: Paragraph Color-Coding** Students review identifying the topic sentence, supporting details, elaboration sentences, and conclusion in a paragraph.
Lesson 5	Encourage students to continue reading in their independent selections. Fill in Reading Log and share book summary with the class.	
Lesson 6	**Step 3: Word Relationships: Antonyms, Synonyms, and Attributes** Students read words and generate antonyms, synonyms, and attributes for the words.	**Step 6: Write It: Two-Sentence Introduction** Students read sample prompts and write two-sentence introductions.
Lesson 7	**Step 2: *Its* and *It's*** Students write sentences using **its** and **it's**.	**Step 6: Write It: Transition Topic Sentences** Students read an introductory paragraph and write transition topic sentences.
Lesson 8	**Step 4: Diagram It: Subject, Verb, and Direct Object** Students find and diagram sentences.	**Step 5: Instructional Text: "Way to Go"**

Homework Options chart from Unit 13

 **You Try It!**

Complete these exercises to see how *LANGUAGE!* offers explicit instruction for Step 6: Speaking and Writing.

Why are activities involving signal words included regularly as part of Step 6?

_____

_____

_____

_____

_____

_____

Unit 2 · Lesson 8

Exercise 4 · Answer It: Using Signal Words

▸ Underline the signal words and answer each question.

▸ Then underline the part of the answer that replaces the signal word.

1. Who learned about using sound and echoes from bats?

   _____

   _____

2. Do echoes from all places in the ocean sound alike?

   _____

   _____

3. Are there limits to sonar?

Interactive Text from Book A, Unit 2, Lesson 8

You Try It!

What are effective ways to model **Rewrite It** and other revision-related exercises.

_____

_____

_____

_____

_____

_____

Unit 13 · Lesson 6

Exercise 6 · Use the Clues: Vocabulary Strategies

▶ Read each pair of sentences.

▶ Find the pronoun that is circled.

▶ Underline the noun that the pronoun replaces.

▶ Draw an arrow to show the link between the pronoun and the noun it replaced.

1. Inventors have quick minds. (They) think about problems.

2. Inventions impact our lives. (They) make our lives better.

3. A patent confirms your ownership. (It) means that your invention belongs to you.

4. Inventors begin with a problem. They think about (it).

5. Inventors begin with a problem. This is how (they) think.

Exercise 7 · Rewrite It

▶ Read each sentence pair in Exercise 6, **Use the Clues: Vocabulary Strategies**.

▶ Replace the circled pronoun with the noun that it represents.

▶ Rewrite the sentence using the noun.

▶ Check for sentence signals—capital letters, commas, and end punctuation.

▶ Read the new sentence.

1. _____

2. _____

3. _____

4. _____

5. _____

Map It: Persuasive Writing

How might you model this activity for students?

Example that gets readers' attention: _____

_____

_____

Statement of position: _____

_____

_____

First reason: _____

_____

_____

Supporting facts or examples: _____

_____

_____

Second reason: _____

_____

_____

Supporting facts or examples: _____

_____

_____

Anticipated objection:

Your response to this objection:

Call to action:

Map It: Persuasive Writing   **46**

I

From the *LANGUAGE!* Classroom

We piloted *LANGUAGE!* 4th edition with elementary, middle, and high school students. Teachers used daily timed writings as directed in the Teacher Resource Guide. Our goal was to increase the level of automaticity so that students could think about what they were writing, rather than how they were writing. Teachers did 30 second timed writings daily, beginning with lower case letters. Students worked to write the complete alphabet without errors in 30 seconds or less. After completing that goal, they moved from Essential Words to phrases and sentences using the fluencies in the back of their Student Interactive Text. Elementary teachers saw the biggest improvement in content of students' writing. We also heard from these students' general education teachers that they were seeing improvement too—in legibility, and most importantly, the content of students' writing.

Donna Lutz, *National LANGUAGE! Trainer / Coach*
Elk Grove, California

DIFFERENTIATED INSTRUCTION

Table of Contents

INTRODUCTION TO DIFFERENTIATION

What is differentiated instruction? It is the key to shoring up student deficiencies and providing students with manageable challenges. Differentiation involves meeting students wherever they are in their educational journey and teaming with them to promote, plan, and guide their next steps.

At the practical level, Carol Ann Tomlinson, in her book *The Differentiated Classroom: Responding to the Needs of All Learners*, defines differentiation this way:

> Differentiated instruction is an approach to teaching in which the teacher strives to do whatever is necessary to ensure that struggling and advanced learners, students of varied cultural heritages, and children with differing backgrounds of experiences learn to their greatest potential. Differentiation is the tool to providing rigorous, challenging, and coherent curriculum for all students.

Planning and Pacing Guides for Unit 13

This section details *LANGUAGE!*'s approach to differentiated instruction and the variety of differentiation tools that the curriculum provides, including the technology tools *Sortegories*, *eReader*, and *Words for Teachers*. It describes how the curriculum uses assessment to tailor differentiation with explicit, responsive prescriptions. The section also explores what differentiation looks like for the three main student populations that *LANGUAGE!* serves: English learners, Curriculum Casualties, and students with language-based learning disabilities.

The *LANGUAGE!* Assessment System

The *LANGUAGE!* Assessment System is a well-designed, efficient assessment program that provides you with the measures you need to accurately place students into the curriculum; and to monitor, in a timely manner, their progress through the curriculum. It furnishes you with the data necessary to inform instruction and to ensure students meet their goals.

This system is comprised of formative and summative tests designed to capture skill development in the critical areas of literacy. Consistent use of these assessments is critical to each student's success and will make your teaching more efficient and fruitful.

The *LANGUAGE!* Assessment System

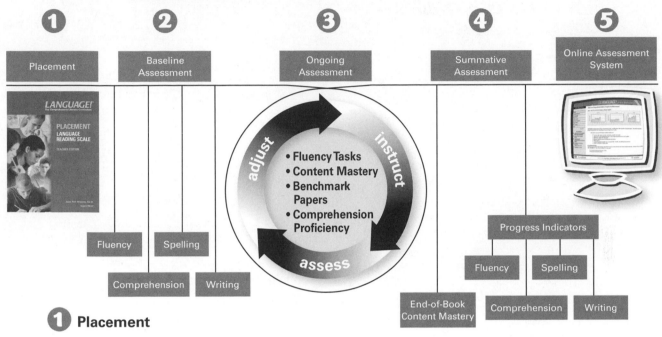

1 Placement

Data from the *LANGUAGE! Reading Scale Placement* Test indicates which of the three *LANGUAGE!* entry points is appropriate for each student.

2 Baseline Assessments

Administered only once after a student's placement in Book A, C, or E and prior to entering the *LANGUAGE!* curriculum, scores on baseline tests constitute the starting point for measuring a student's progress through the curriculum.

3 Ongoing Assessments

Regular testing of student mastery of the content, concepts, and skills taught in the curriculum ensures that teachers have current information about each student in order to adjust pacing or provide instructional support activities for individual students.

4 Summative Assessments

Given at the end of each book, the *Summative Assessments* assess the critical skills of literacy through both norm-referenced and curriculum-based measures.

5 The Online Assessment System

This easy-to-use database allows teachers and administrators to record, track, and report student test results. Teachers and administrators can monitor student growth through reports that can be generated at the individual, class, building, and district levels.

Differentiation and the *LANGUAGE! Online Assessment System* (LOLA)

The *LANGUAGE! Online Assessment System (LOLA)* is your valuable ally in managing data regarding student performance. It is a key tool for linking assessment to instruction and gives you the information you need to make differentiation work for you and your students. It supports placement, progress, monitoring, and instructional pacing.

With the *Online Assessment System,* you can:

1. Obtain recommendations for student placement and pacing based on the raw scores entered

2. Automatically convert raw scores to grade equivalents and save them for easy access

3. Track and monitor each student's performance from unit to unit

4. Create easy-to-read charts showing a student's growth in different target areas

5. Customize instruction to meet individual objectives and learning needs

6. Customize, generate, and print reports for parents, students, teachers, and administrators.

To access the *The LANGUAGE! Online Assessment System (LOLA),* go to data.teachlanguage.com.

Snapshots from the *LANGUAGE! Online Assessment System*

The following reports are just two examples of the kind of information available to you and your students through *LOLA*.

Content Mastery Data

The data and charts help you measure and monitor student performance in the first four steps. This information can help you target areas where your students may benefit from review or acceleration.

Summative Assessment

This data allows you to monitor student gains in reading comprehension and other literacy skills as the progress through the curriculum.

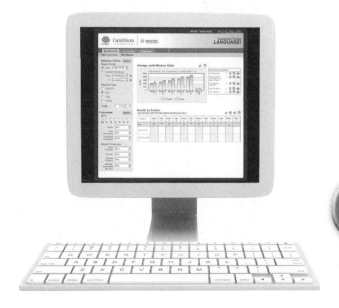

Road Signs for Differentiated Instruction in *LANGUAGE!*

Charts in the *LANGUAGE! Teacher Edition* make it easy to link student deficiencies with specific exercises and activities to address them. These charts include Prescriptive Teaching Boxes, Special Instructional Support, and Homework Options.

Prescriptive Teaching Boxes

Prescriptive Teaching Boxes appear immediately after **Content Mastery** tasks. They prescribe specific exercises that can help shore up demonstrated areas of student difficulty—based on mastery thresholds of 80% and 60%—through review, reinforcement, and reteaching.

Special Instructional Support

An element in the Planning and Pacing Guides of each unit, the Special Instructional Support (SIS) chart allows you to anticipate or respond to student difficulties by inserting step-specific reinforcement activities.

Homework Options

The Homework Options chart offers suggestions for additional practice after each lesson. Worksheets can be printed from the *Instructional Planning Tools* and the *Words for Teachers* CDs. For a discussion of effective homework practices, see the section on Classroom Management.

Prescriptive Teaching Box for Step 2: Word Recognition and Spelling from Unit 13, Lesson 5

Special Instructional Support suggestions for Unit 13

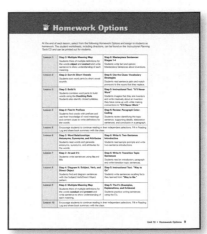

Homework Options for Unit 13

The Six Degrees of Differentiation

Effective differentiation is one of the keys to keeping *LANGUAGE!* students engaged and on track. Proceed too quickly and a reluctant learner may grow discouraged. Move too slowly and a student ready for acceleration may lose motivation. *LANGUAGE!*'s comprehensive assessment system loses effectiveness if it is not consistently guiding instruction. (See the Assessment section for a more detailed discussion.)

The differentiation model in *LANGUAGE!* could be described as falling into six categories. These range from explicit instruction to independent student work. The progression takes into account two major factors: 1) the amount of lesson preparation required; and 2) the level of behavior management required.

From an instructional standpoint, these two factors increase in complexity from the 1st to the 6th degree. In the 1st degree of differentiation, for example, lessons are class-wide and teacher-focused. In contrast, the 6th degree of differentiation might involve a variety of small groups or individuals tackling independent work with a teacher-led group. The technology tools and other resources may be useful at any degree. By beginning with the 1st degree, you can ease your way into differentiation. This approach gives you the opportunity to teach procedures and behavioral expectations before students are expected to perform them with increasing independence.

Degree of Differentiation	Differentiation Content	Instructional Style
1st Degree	Think Aloud exercises and activities based on **Content Mastery** tasks	Class-wide, teacher-focused
2nd Degree	Whole group activities, such as *Sortegories* and Sentence Sorting, in which students respond to teacher prompts	Class-wide, but with more interaction
3rd Degree	Common independent activities such as Folder Activities and independent reading. Provides the opportunity to begin teaching procedural and behavioral expectations.	Teacher circulates and monitors student practice, reinforcing expectations and procedures.
4th Degree	Common independent activity such as independent reading	Teacher conferencing with individual students to provide one-on-one instruction
5th Degree	Different but simultaneous classroom activities, such as Folder Activities, independent reading, or a writing activity; again reinforcing procedural and behavioral expectations.	Teacher circulates and monitors student practice, reinforcing expectations and procedures.
6th Degree	Different but simultaneous classroom activities	Teacher working with small groups of students, offering reinforcements and enrichment in addition to working with students who have been absent.

Visualizing Differentiation By Degree

Using small groups to help differentiate instruction can be challenging and require appropriate behavior on the part of the students and a level of preparation on the part of the teacher. To maximize differention time blocks, it is necessary to establish these routines. The following graphic illustrates the Six Degrees of Differentation as outlined on page 7.

Once procedures and expectations have been established, be sure to use all data available to you for building independent work stations and determining groups: classroom observations, *Interactive Text* activities, fluency measures and **Content Mastery**. Consider the possible configurations and activities for delivering differentiated instruction.

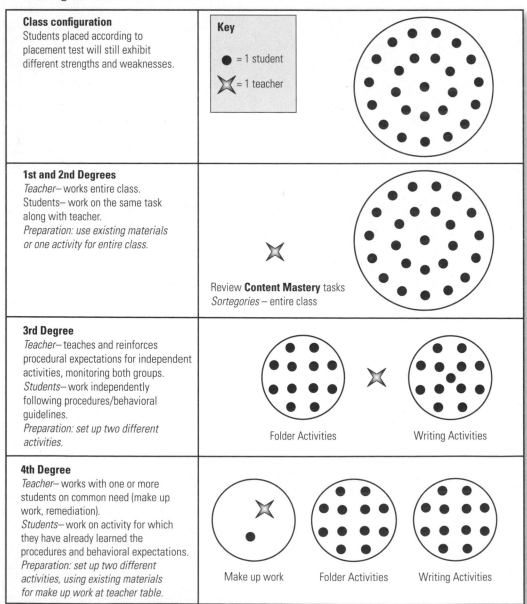

Class configuration Students placed according to placement test will still exhibit different strengths and weaknesses.	**Key** ● = 1 student ✕ = 1 teacher
1st and 2nd Degrees *Teacher*– works entire class. Students– work on the same task along with teacher. *Preparation: use existing materials or one activity for entire class.*	Review **Content Mastery** tasks *Sortegories* – entire class
3rd Degree *Teacher*– teaches and reinforces procedural expectations for independent activities, monitoring both groups. *Students*– work independently following procedures/behavioral guidelines. *Preparation: set up two different activities.*	Folder Activities Writing Activities
4th Degree *Teacher*– works with one or more students on common need (make up work, remediation). *Students*– work on activity for which they have already learned the procedures and behavioral expectations. *Preparation: set up two different activities, using existing materials for make up work at teacher table.*	Make up work Folder Activities Writing Activities

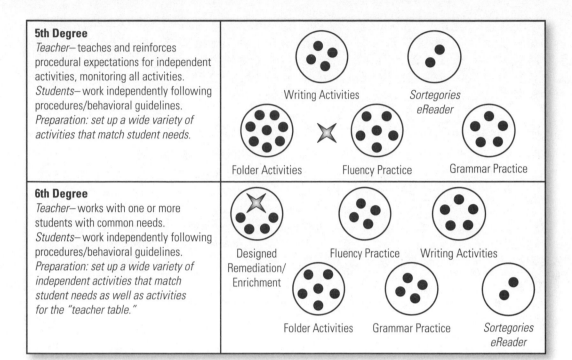

5th Degree *Teacher*–teaches and reinforces procedural expectations for independent activities, monitoring all activities. *Students*–work independently following procedures/behavioral guidelines. *Preparation: set up a wide variety of activities that match student needs.*	Writing Activities Sortegories eReader Folder Activities Fluency Practice Grammar Practice
6th Degree *Teacher*–works with one or more students with common needs. *Students*–work independently following procedures/behavioral guidelines. *Preparation: set up a wide variety of independent activities that match student needs as well as activities for the "teacher table."*	Designed Remediation/ Enrichment Fluency Practice Writing Activities Folder Activities Grammar Practice Sortegories eReader

Differentiation Offers Solutions

Regular and thoughtful differentiation does more than keep the curriculum clicking. It offers solutions to a variety of classroom issues. These include:

- **Absenteeism**: By planning a regular day of differentiation—the day after each lesson that contains **Content Mastery** material—you can have students make up work missed due to absences. If they miss a class, they have to work with you instead of taking part in small group activities with classmates. This alone might reduce absenteeism! It also honors the commitment of the students who get to class every day.

- **Motivation**: Including differentiation days that feature special activities can be fun and engaging for students.

- **Creativity**: Days scheduled for differentiation (usually two days per unit) can include opportunities for more independent reading and follow-up writing activities.

- **Time for Technology Tools**: Lesson plans do not schedule time for the use of technology tools and other support pieces. Differentiated instruction provides you with protected time to routinely incorporate these resources into your classroom.

TOOLS FOR DIFFERENTIATION IN *LANGUAGE!*

The variety of technology tools and other resources available in *LANGUAGE!* make for smooth and effective insertion of differentiated instruction into your lesson planning. The different tools are described here, and your familiarity with their features will continue to grow as you use them in the classroom and explore them on your own.

LANGUAGE! Online Assessment System

The *Online Assessment System* aids record-keeping of Placement Test scores, **Content Mastery** tasks, **End-of-book Content Mastery** tasks and **Fluency** scores along with **Progress Indicator** data. It also serves as a differentiation tool by charting individual progress over time and drawing attention to students falling below proficiency as well as those students who are excelling.

Instructional Planning Tools CD

This CD contains various ways to customize your lessons and support differentiation. Resources here include:

- **Customizable lesson plans**: With the TE lesson plan text as a starting point, this IPT feature helps you plan for multiple classes, insert exercises for review and reteaching, and highlight or replace specific activities for substitute teachers.

- **Printable *Interactive Text* pages**: *Interactive Text* pages also exist in digital form on the IPT. This allows you to print pages for reteaching and review, acceleration and homework, or to replace lost pages.

- **Homework**: Worksheets and other student homework materials are printable from the IPT.

- **Transparencies and Templates**: In addition to the set of transparencies and templates provided, printable versions of these materials are contained on the IPT for creating differentiated instruction for whole-class and small-group review and reteaching. Examples of Transparencies and Templates for each step include:
  - For Step 1: Chain It, Consonant and Vowel Charts;
  - For Step 2: Change It, Drop It;
  - For Step 3: Define It, Double It, Explore It, Word Wheel;
  - For Step 4: Diagram It 1–6, Tense Timeline;
  - For Step 5: Book Report Organizer Chart, Character Description, K-W-L, Six Elements of Poetry, Map It: Plot Analysis;
  - For Step 6: Blueprint for Writing, Checklist for Revising, Map It: Main Ideas.

Sortegories CD

The *Sortegories* CD contains reading activities that support instruction across Steps 1–4. This technology tool allows students to work independently using decodable vocabulary, and it tracks each student's work, providing a grade for each completed activity. If your classroom has a SMART board, *Sortegories* can also be used for whole-class instruction.

Using *Sortegories*, you can customize differentiated instruction by selecting particular activities or clusters of activities that target student needs. The Special Instructional Support (SIS) chart before each unit offers specific suggestions of *Sortegories* activities that address specific skills for Steps 1–4. These include such exercises as:

- Sound Count
- Sort It
- Morph It
- Categorize It
- Phrase Building
- Grammar Sort
- Analogy Building
- Relate It

eReader CD

With a CD that accompanies each level of the *Student Text, eReader* is a text-to-speech software program that supports students as they read the Instructional Text selections. The Planning and Pacing Guides before each unit offer specific suggestions on how to use *eReader* to differentiate instruction.

With *eReader*, students can:

- Follow along as Instructional Text selections are read using a human or synthetic voice
- Access and have key vocabulary words and definitions read aloud
- Access the complete *LANGUAGE!* glossary
- Highlight text and have it read by word, sentence, or paragraph
- Copy and paste segments as part of their writing research.
- Type notes about what they are reading and have their work read aloud.
- Control the size, font, color, and background color of their notes.

Words for Teachers CD

The *Words for Teachers* CD allows you to create unit-specific worksheets tailored to individual student needs. The Special Instructional Support and Homework Options charts before each unit in the *Teacher Edition* (TE) suggest specific exercises for Steps 1–4 available on this CD. Organized by unit, these materials can be used for in-class practice or reinforcement as homework. Exercises include:

- **Word Card Generator**: This format allows you to customize a worksheet to review **Unit Words**, practice identifying different verb forms, provide vocabulary for sentence building, and many other exercises.

- **Draw It**: This customizable worksheet allows students to review and explore vocabulary and idioms through drawing.

- **Word Unscramble and Word Search**: These popular activities practice letter and word recognition, decoding and encoding skills, handwriting, and other word-level skills for customized word lists.

- **Word Study Guide**: Word Study Guides can be tailored to review and reteach vocabulary by asking students to alphabetize, sort unit vocabulary from **Essential Words**, and write sentences of different tenses using the words.

- **Fluency Builder Grid**: This exercise is effective for reviewing and practicing recognition of specific words with which students may have struggled.

- **Spelling Rules Practice**: Exercises such as **Drop It**, **Double It**, and **Change It** offer guided practice in word morphology.

Folder Activities

LANGUAGE! Folder Activities offer hands-on exercises to differentiate instruction. Using file folders and sticky notes, you can prepare exercises that focus on specific areas of difficulty for individual students. For students who are ready for enrichment, folder activities can also include more challenging words and tasks. Specific folder activities are described in the Why Do/How To section, starting on page 362. Folder activities provide students with practice in alphabetizing, phoneme discrimination, sound-spelling correspondence, grammar and syllable sorts, semantic sorts, word and phrase sorts, sentence unscramble, and many other literacy skills.

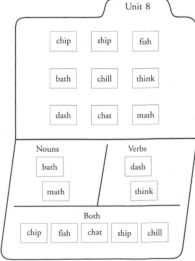

Grammar Sort

LANGUAGE! AND
UNIVERSAL ACCESS

Differentiation is an integral part of the *LANGUAGE!* curriculum. The program's blend of teaching strategies and resources is designed to be dynamic and flexible in addressing students' changing instructional needs. Regular assessment paired with clear prescriptions based on the results help keep students on track toward educational goals. Whatever learning challenges students may face, *LANGUAGE!* meets students where they are and guides them where they need to go.

Providing Universal Access

"Simply providing physical access to general education does not ensure that students with disabilities will gain cognitive access to the content of the curriculum," says reading researcher Ed Kame'enui of the University of Oregon. "To gain cognitive access to the general education content, attention must be given to the architectural requirements of that content."

In instructional design and resources, *LANGUAGE!* specifically addresses these "architectural requirements" for all learners—not only students with disabilities. It provides universal access to its content by means of accurate placement based on assessment, explicit instruction that is mastery-based, multisensory instruction to promote retention and student engagement, and the use of technology to aid student comprehension and expression.

The especially strong linkage between assessment, instruction, and differentiation provides a continuum of appropriate responses to student performance. By following the program's design, your teaching is guided by flexible prescriptions that keep students of differing abilities engaged and learning.

Following are specific ways in which the curriculum meets the differentiated instructional needs of diverse student populations.

Differentiation for English Learners

LANGUAGE! offers multiple modes of differentiated instruction to promote the language acquisition of English learners. Beginning with newcomers who possess virtually no English skills, the goal of the curriculum is to bring English learners to full fluency in spoken and written English simultaneously.

In the core *LANGUAGE!* curriculum, differentiated instruction for English learners is supported in various ways. These include:

- The Visual Vocabulary section that appears in the *Student Text* for Books A and B. This resource promotes vocabulary acquisition, including sentences that offer examples of proper usage.

- Focus on Academic Language lessons. Detailed lesson plans guide practice of accurate phonemic production in English, English intonation, correct use of articles and other points of grammar, common and idiomatic expressions, and many other skills that are vital in spoken and written English. These lesson plans appear in each unit, and are noted in the Focus on Academic Language chart as part of each unit's Planning and Pacing Guides.

- Special Instructional Support and Homework charts in the Planning and Pacing Guides for each unit. These charts point out specific exercises and activities for any student who needs extra practice, drawing from the Why Do/How To activities (see page 362) and materials on the various technology tools (*Sortegories* CD, *eReader* CD, *Words for Teachers* CD, and *Instructional Planning Tools*).

- Contrastive Analyses in the back of each TE. These charts point out points of phonological, morphological, orthographic, and syntactic variation requiring particular attention when teaching English learners. Ten languages are contrasted with English: Chinese (Cantonese, Mandarin, Wu, and other dialects), Haitian Creole, Hmong, Khmer (Cambodian), Korean, Pilipino (Tagalog), Portuguese, Russian, Spanish, and Vietnamese. Lessons that practice the point of difference are noted in each Contrastive Analysis.

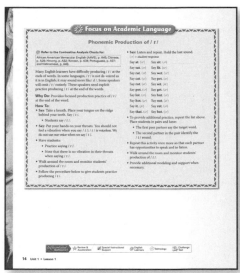

Focus on Academic Language Lesson From Unit 1

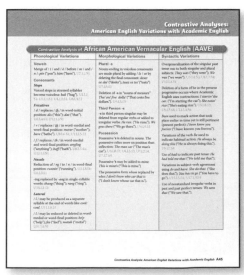

Contrastive Analysis for African American Vernacular English (AAVE)

Everyday English for Newcomers to English

For students with essentially no English skills, *LANGUAGE! Everyday English for Newcomers to English* is available as a separate program. Each week of this six-week course is built around a common scenario—School, Home, Neighborhood, Grocery Store, The Mall, and My Day. *Everyday English for Newcomers to English* provides an entry point for newcomers by:

- increasing their oral fluency
- introducing them to the sounds of the English language
- strengthening their use of everyday words and phrases
- fostering their knowledge of core vocabulary
- presenting key characteristics of how English works
- practicing common exchanges of spoken English.

The teacher edition for *Everyday English for Newcomers to English* uses the same step-by-step process as the core *LANGUAGE!* curriculum. This structure not only ensures students a foundation of basic English, but also prepares them for advancing into the regular *LANGUAGE!* classroom.

Everyday English for Newcomers to English is available as a separate program.

Differentiation for Curriculum Casualties

The term "Curriculum Casualties" encompasses students whose education has suffered for a variety of reasons. They may have moved often or been "lost" in overcrowded classes. They may have faced personal family issues that undercut their attitude toward learning. For some, their learning style may simply not have meshed with traditional instruction.

Differentiation in *LANGUAGE!* provides the mode and resources to help get these students' education back on track. The strong assessment component provides accurate data on their baseline starting points and therefore offers accurate measurements of their progress. When students struggle, the strong linkage to differentiation through Prescriptive Teaching Boxes, Special Instructional Support activities, plus the Homework Options chart, put individualized instruction within reach.

In addition, Curriculum Casualties have often missed vital elements of general content knowledge. They may have reached middle school with no idea how to read a map or a chart, or basic knowledge about history, geography, or science. The range of high-interest subjects in *LANGUAGE!* text selections can help students fill in these gaps of background knowledge. They will encounter "mirror text," reflecting their lives and community, and "window text," exposing them to other lives, cultures, and worlds.

Placement and **Content Mastery** scores may also indicate the need to move more quickly through certain aspects of the curriculum. The starred activities chart the "review and accelerate" path enabling teachers to effectively move students toward complete literacy. True differentiation embraces acceleration as well as deceleration.

Differentiation for Students with Language-Based Learning Disabilities

The *LANGUAGE!* curriculum includes features that address the particular needs of students with language-based learning disabilities. These learning disabilities affect a student's success with reading, spelling, and writing at an age-appropriate level. Many children with learning disabilities related to literacy also struggle with spoken language.

Students wrestling with language-based learning disabilities may experience these difficulties:

- Students may struggle with expression and be vague and hard to understand. They may have difficulty recalling the exact word they want and often resort to unspecific terms such as "stuff," "thing," or "um";

- They might find it hard to understand questions, follow directions, tell time, memorize rhymes, memorize the times tables, tell left from right, recall or retell a story's plot, and other memory-related tasks;

- They may lag behind other students in learning the alphabet and numbers, spelling, and vocabulary acquisition.

Often these frustrations lead to emotional and behavioral problems, as well. If you think one of your students may have an unidentified language-based learning disability, consult with your school's special education specialist.

In addressing language-based learning disabilities, *LANGUAGE!* follows the edict of Jane Fell Greene, Ed.D.—"As quickly as we can, as slowly as we must." Regular assessment matched with clear prescriptions for differentiation provide multiple opportunities for extra practice, review, and reteaching. The carefully scaffolded curriculum creates many opportunities for students to revisit skills and truly develop long-term retention of essential literacy concepts. Instruction also embraces the need for these students to practice skills through multisensory activities.

Features of the curriculum that support differentiated instruction for students with language-based learning disabilities include:

Read-Aloud Text Selections

Written in decodable text, **Mini-Dialogs** and **Mega-Dialogs** in the *Student Text* are designed to be read aloud in a conversational exchange. This approach supports scaffolded instruction, allowing you to actively monitor student fluency and comprehension. Teacher-read Challenge Text is part of each unit, and class read-alouds appear in the *Teacher Edition*. All of the read-aloud text selections relate to and reinforce the content and language of the unit in which they appear.

Technology Tools

- The *eReader* CD: This CD features a read-aloud function for Instructional Text that lets students listen to the story as they follow along in the text. With *eReader*, students can:

  - Adjust formatting to change the font, background color, and the size and color of text for reading ease.

  - Have *eReader* read aloud vocabulary and definitions from the text selection or the program glossary.

  - Highlight text for rereading of words, sentences, and paragraphs.

  - Copy and paste text as part of the research process.

- *Sortegories, Instructional Planning Tools*, and *Words for Teachers* CDs. These CDs allow you to provide ample opportunities for repeated practice, in a variety of formats, to develop skill mastery. While *Sortegories* provides interactive feedback and practice for students, *Instructional Planning Tools* and *LANGUAGE! Words for Teachers* offer quick access to templates and a wide variety of worksheets that you can customize for independent practice.

Manipulatives and Multisensory Instruction

Many of the exercises and activities in the *LANGUAGE!* curriculum feature manipulative tools and multisensory instruction that reveal and reinforce the parts-to-whole structure of the English language. When delivered through the Response to Intervention model, this approach reinforces the ability of dyslexic students to be successful learners when these strategies are incorporated into instruction. (For more on this learning disability, see the section "The Dyslexic Student").

Manipulative materials featured in the *LANGUAGE!* curriculum include:

- Letter Cards. These manipulatives facilitate the teaching of word building, sound-to-letter correspondence, and the alphabetic principle in general.

- Morphemes for Meaning Cards. These manipulatives promote the development of syllabic identification, understanding of word structure, encoding and decoding, word building at the syllabic level, and other word-level skills and strategies.

Letter Cards

- Overhead Tiles. These colored tiles aid explicit instruction and modeling of phonemic awareness skills.

Multisensory instruction is frequently incorporated in general lessons, instructional activities, and suggestions for differentiated instruction highlighted in the Special Instructional Support boxes. Activities that emphasize this approach to learning include:

- **Phonemic Awareness Drills**. These exercises incorporate kinesthetic, auditory, and verbal elements to develop phonemic awareness.

- **Listening for Sounds in Words**. Based on the Elkonin procedure, this activity adds a visual and concrete element for developing phonemic awareness and phonics skills.

- **Build It**. Using letter cards or self-stick notes, students physically create words by manipulating letters or syllables.

- **Combine It**. Using **Masterpiece Sentence Work Strips**, students physically move words and phrases to create more syntactically sophisticated sentences.

- **Folder Activities**. The use of self-stick notes in a variety of formatted file folders creates opportunities to repeatedly practice skills across all Six Steps from Sound to Text.

What You Need to Know

The Dyslexic Student

Dyslexia is the most common form of language-based learning disability. Sally Shaywitz, M.D., and Bennett Shaywitz, M.D., in their article "The Neurobiology of Reading and Dyslexia," report that dyslexia affects 5 to 17 percent of school-aged children in the United States. Of those identified as having a learning disability, 80 percent are identified as having dyslexia. At one time, dyslexia was thought to be primarily prevalent among males, but recent investigations show there is no significant difference between the number of males and females affected. Nor do children outgrow the condition—another belief that has been overturned (Shaywitz & Shaywitz, 2002).

Studies indicate that dyslexia is neurobiological in origin. Brain imaging research has revealed that dyslexic readers use different portions of the brain than those brain regions used by non-dyslexic readers. Higher-order cognitive and linguistic abilities of dyslexic individuals, though, are typically sound—a circumstance that has often confounded educators and frustrated dyslexics themselves. As with other struggling readers, dyslexic students may need support to overcome feelings of inadequacy and the fear of failure in the classroom.

As discussed in the Research and Background section, deciphering the reading code requires the ability to recognize and manipulate phonemes. This ability often eludes dyslexic readers, to greater and lesser degrees. "In order to read," write Drs. Shaywitz, "a child has to develop the insight that spoken words can be pulled apart into phonemes and that the letters in a written word represent these sounds. This so-called phonemic awareness is largely missing in dyslexic children and adults."

Multisensory instruction has proven the most effective strategy in addressing the learning needs of dyslexic readers. The concept is to recruit additional parts of the brain to help support phonemic awareness, sound-spelling correspondence, and other essential reading skills. This may take the form of kinesthetic learning, such as forming extra large letters on a carpet square or tracing sandpaper letters with a finger. Text-to-voice and voice-to-text software may also prove useful in assisting dyslexic students with reading-based tasks and writing assignments.

Dyslexia may also express itself as difficulty with organizing information in general. Explicit instruction and modeling in the use of graphic organizers may prove particularly useful in helping dyslexic students manage reading tasks.

Teacher's Tip

The World Wide Web is rich with ideas and resources to help differentiate instruction for dyslexic readers.

What You Need to Know

Differentiation for Deaf and Hard-of-Hearing Students

To develop literacy in children who are deaf or hard of hearing, educators must recognize the parallels for literacy development in hearing children to those elements unique to the deaf or hard-of-hearing child (Ewoldt 1985; Padden and Ramsey 1993; Rottenberg 2001; Rottenberg and Searfoss 1992, 1993). Such understanding will aid teachers in planning more appropriate and meaningful literacy instruction and activities in their classrooms.

Deaf students can benefit from literacy activities that already exist within a regular classroom. It is crucial for younger students, hearing or deaf, to have time to explore writing, drawing, books, and environmental print. Story time and journal writing are also appropriate activities for all students. Deaf and hard-of-hearing children and youth can participate in many literacy events and use written language just as their full-hearing peers do.

The deaf and hard-of-hearing students interact socially while writing, provide information about written text, label writing creations, and monitor text construction like their full-hearing peers. Overall, deaf and hard-of-hearing students can draw from literacy experiences with reading. If they are within print-rich classrooms and supportive homes, their deafness will not significantly differentiate their literacy development (Ewoldt 1985; Padden and Ramsey 1993; Rottenberg 2001; Rottenberg and Searfoss 1992, 1993).

When considering the classroom learning environment, it is important to provide hard-of-hearing and deaf students with opportunities to read and enjoy books along with their friends and teachers. It is also beneficial to explore the written word through drawing (e.g. idioms, **Mini-Dialogs**, **Expressions of the Day**) and writing. Oral discussions of literacy experiences are also helpful in developing spoken language (Briggle 2005).

RESEARCH BITE

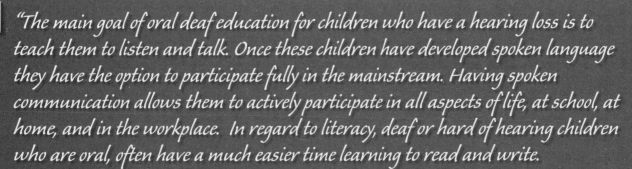

"The main goal of oral deaf education for children who have a hearing loss is to teach them to listen and talk. Once these children have developed spoken language they have the option to participate fully in the mainstream. Having spoken communication allows them to actively participate in all aspects of life, at school, at home, and in the workplace. In regard to literacy, deaf or hard of hearing children who are oral, often have a much easier time learning to read and write.

**From the Alexander Graham Bell Association
for the Deaf and Hard of Hearing Web site**

LANGUAGE! in the Hearing Impaired Classroom

I was introduced to LANGUAGE! while serving as executive director for an oral school for deaf and hard-of-hearing students in pre-Katrina New Orleans. The students were having success with basic reading skills, but their language and writing skills were weak. These 4th- through 6th-graders were to be mainstreamed but were having difficulties that held them back within our support program because of inadequate literacy skills.

After attending a *LANGUAGE!* training, I realized that this curriculum could fill the gap for these students. We implemented *LANGUAGE!* on a very small scale in grades 4-6, in addition to our regular reading program. Being an oral school for the deaf, we found that the phonemic awareness drills in Step 1 increased students' sound discrimination skills and helped to improve their articulation of the vowel and consonant sounds. The phonics component bridged the gap between the sound–symbol relationships. The nice transition into spelling and vocabulary connected the sounds and symbols into meaningful words used in their everyday language and within the textbooks they were reading. Everything began to make sense to them and their overall reading and literacy skills began to improve.

Pacing was somewhat slow and some modifications had to be made because the "language" within the lessons had to be pre-taught. For example, using a **Multiple Meaning Map** required pre-teaching of graphic organizers so the students could understand the purpose and use, the term "multiple" had to be taught in advance, and then the three terms used in combination had to become meaningful to the students. Following this preteaching, the students were able to use the **Multiple Meaning Map** as intended.

Teachers in our *LANGUAGE!* classrooms noted their students' improved comprehension during the spoken language piece, discussions, and working through the comprehension questions at the end of the text selections. Students showed marked improvement in unlocking the meanings of words within the text as well as better insights overall into what they were reading.

Susan Rampp-Niette, M.C.D., CCC-SLP; National LANGUAGE! Trainer
Houma, Louisiana

High-Functioning Autism and Asperger's Syndrome

What is autism?

The Autism Society of America describes autism as: "the result of a neurological disorder that affects the normal functioning of the brain, impacting development in the areas of social interaction and communication skills. Both children and adults with autism typically show difficulties in verbal and non-verbal communication, social interactions, and leisure or play activities. One should keep in mind however, that autism is a spectrum disorder and it affects each individual differently and at varying degrees ..."

"High-functioning autism" is not a specific diagnosis in itself; rather, it describes autistic individuals who are more capable of active participation in the classroom or other social setting.

What is Asperger's Syndrome? Like autism, Asperger's Syndrome is neurobiological in nature. The Autism Society of America distinguishes Asperger's Syndrome (or Asperger's Disorder) from high-functioning autism in that people with the former lack language delays, and the disorder's other expressions are less pronounced.

In expression, the ASA describes children with Asperger's Syndrome as "... only mildly affected and frequently have good language and cognitive skills. To the untrained observer, a child with Asperger's Disorder may just seem like a normal child behaving differently.

"Children with autism are frequently seen as aloof and uninterested in others. This is not the case with Asperger's Disorder. Individuals with Asperger's Disorder usually want to fit in and have interaction with others; they simply don't know how to do it. They may be socially awkward, not understanding of conventional social rules, or may show a lack of empathy. ..."

The following passages, quoted from "A Unique Mind Learning Style Differences in Asperger's Syndrome and High-Functioning Autism" (*The ASHA Leader*, Vol. 12, No.1, January 23, 2007) by Emily Rubin, offer specific insights into learning styles and teaching strategies as they relate to students with Asperger's Syndrome (AS) and high-functioning autism (HFA).

> *"...[S]everal contemporary neuropsychological studies have led to greater recognition of the potential differences in learning styles (Tsatsanis, 2004)...Individuals with AS often present with verbal IQ that is higher than performance of nonverbal IQ, while individuals with HFA often present with the opposite pattern."*

"...Individuals with AS may prefer verbally mediated strategies, while children with HFA may prefer visual support .... [S]tatic visual information is more appropriate in supporting individuals with HFA ...for example, facilitating an understanding of the internal states of others may be accomplished with Comic Strip Conversations, a type of support in which another's thoughts are captured through pictorial representations within a "thought bubble" (Gray, 1994)."

"...[S]trengths in word prediction and language can support written language skills...Individuals with HFA also may develop the ability to process the written word, as their relative strengths in visual-spatial skills and rote auditory memory contribute to phonetic decoding...[A] written cue card may convey information more effectively than raising one's eyebrows and gesturing toward a student's desk. Similarly, the use of a written map to illustrate information about one's conversational partner— such as what they like to talk about, what experiences they have had, and their favorite activities— could be provided (Winner, 2002)."

LANGUAGE! and Students with High-Functioning Autism and Asperger's Syndrome

LANGUAGE!, with its parts-to-whole strategies and scaffolded, cumulative, repetitive structure, is an effective curriculum for teaching students with Asperger's Syndrome (AS) and high-functioning autism (HFA).

The AS child will show strengths with verbal language and verbal memory while the HFA child is better with visual-spatial perception and visual memory. Both will move more quickly through Steps 1 and 2 in *LANGUAGE!*—phonemic awareness to phonics to spelling—due to their better rote memory skills. But they will experience more difficulty once presented with vocabulary connections in context, **Multiple Meaning Maps**, **Define It**, and using context clues. They quickly master reading the words, but struggle with their meanings in and out of context.

Both AS and HFA students excel on Fluency Builders once the routine and words are learned. The use of the technology tools, such as *Sortegories* and *eReader*, further assists the HFA students who benefit from visual-spatial input. These students also gain understanding through the comic strips used during **Mini-Dialogs**, drawing pictures to match literal and figurative meanings of Idioms and Expressions of the Day, as well as when completing the **Write Your Own Mini-Dialog** activity.

LANGUAGE! teachers will see the student with AS do better in reading **Mini-** and **Mega-Dialogs**, verbalizing definitions while completing **Define It**, putting words into sentences after completing **Multiple Meaning Maps**, as well as using a more verbose conversational style when discussing stories during the "activate prior knowledge" and "after" activities in Steps 5 and 6. The HFA student does better when completing the graphic organizers once the information is presented. However, it will be necessary to lengthen the discussions and expand the vocabulary when talking about stories in Steps 5 and 6. There is no flexibility of thought because the broader concepts are more difficult. The students must be drilled on what to do and what to ask when they don't understand an activity or exercise.

Using *LANGUAGE!* with AS and HFA students requires that the teacher activate prior knowledge for the student before reading by distinguishing active reading from passive reading. Providing visual cues, such as a reader with a light bulb in his brain versus a person sleeping, demonstrates for the student what is expected when the teacher is reading passages during *Interactive Text* activities, as well as when reading Instructional and Challenge Text pieces. One mantra that is effective when preparing students for Steps 5 and 6 is "Stop-Think-Recall-Summarize." This establishes and reinforces a routine that goes along with each step.

Overall, *LANGUAGE!* is most beneficial to these students because of the routine of the daily lesson using the Six Steps from Sound to Text, the repetitiveness of the activities used within the Interactive Text, and the integrated, sequential, and cumulative development of the skills within the lessons. Most of all, differentiated instruction and the use of multisensory techniques to recruit all senses to learning hit on the unique and various learning styles and strengths for these students.

Mandy Songe Poche', M.A., CCC-SLP
Susan Rampp-Niette, M.C.D., CCC-SLP
Speech-Language-Learning Center

ACCOMODATIONS FOR STUDENTS WITH SPECIAL INSTRUCTIONAL NEEDS

The table below outlines various ways *LANGUAGE!* teachers can adjust instruction and modify the mode of student response. These modifications make it possible for students to access the instructional material and to demonstrate their competence.

Special Instructional Need	Accomodations
English Learners	• *LANGUAGE! eReader* CD that reads aloud while students follow along in the text • picture cards and realia for multisensory cueing • **Simulate It** exercises that use role plays to demonstrate comprehension and mastery • previews of vocabulary and content through **K-W-L**, **Explore It**, and other activities • *LANGUAGE! Focus on English Learning* provides ongoing oral fluency practice as well as preliminary instruction for each lesson • *LANGUAGE! Everyday English*, a separate curriculum for students with essentially no English skills
Dyslexic Students	• *LANGUAGE! eReader* CD that reads Instructional Text aloud while students follow along in the text, and allows cut-and-paste note-taking • text-to-speech and speech-to-text software for reading and writing assignments • keyboarding of written fluency tasks and dictation exercises • extensive use of color-coding to reinforce lesson content at letter, word, and text levels • extensive use of sticky notes and other manipulatives for practice of word- and text-level skills • sand trays, carpet squares, sandpaper letters, Wikki sticks, etc., that add multisensory dimensions to letter formation, letter-sound correspondence, and phonemic awareness overall
Deaf/Hard-of-Hearing students	• microphone and speaker system • small mirrors to aid phonemic production and replication • preteaching of graphic organizers and related terminology and concepts • drawing of idioms, expressions, and **Mini-Dialogs**
Curriculum Casualties	• thematic content that builds content knowledge systematically and cumulatively • previews of vocabulary and content through **K-W-L**, **Explore It**, and other activities • extensive use of "Mirror Text" that reflects students' interests, world views, and background knowledge • acceleration options
Students with High-Functioning Autism or Asperger's Syndrome	• comic strips and **Mini-Dialogs** that pair visual and written cues • enlarged laminated templates for mounting on the board; with prewritten sticky notes to aid student response • lesson plans that emphasize regular routines • visual and picture cues to signal learning and behavioral expectations
Students with Dysgraphia and/or Motor Skill Difficulties	• prewritten words for **Word Bank** activities • keyboarding of written fluency tasks and dictation exercises • enlarged worksheets and answer sheets that offer more space for written answers • electronic communication boards • sheet protectors and dry-erase markers that allow tracing as a way to assist letter formation and handwriting skills
Attention Deficit Hyperactivity Disorder	• exercise balls for chairs that allow students to move while staying on task • lesson plans that incorporate student movement and physical activity

CLASSROOM MANAGEMENT

Table of Contents

RESEARCH BITE

"Never use a corrective consequence that involves humiliation or ridicule of the student, and avoid using academic tasks as corrective consequences."

Sprick, Garrison, and Howard in *CHAMPs*, 1998

THE IMPORTANCE OF CLASSROOM MANAGEMENT

What You Need to Know

Managing behavior effectively is one of the most critical factors for a successful implementation of any curriculum, especially one that targets the struggling learner. We know from Dr. Peter Leone's work at the University of Maryland that students learn early to disguise their lack of ability in a cloak of misbehavior. Dealing with behavior issues on a daily basis will not only exhaust any teacher, but it will also negatively impact any curriculum. Anticipating these behavioral hurdles and planning for them offers a huge payoff for you as well as for your students.

Research has shown us the path to literacy for our students. Now, we need to create the environment to put the research into practice. Your students need to understand the procedures and policies in your classroom, and they will respond if your rules are enforced fairly and consistently.

The beauty of establishing effective procedures and routines in any classroom is that they truly reduce the amount of energy it takes, every day, to make your class run smoothly. Procedures and routines take on a life of their own. When students can reliably predict what will happen in your classroom, they are more apt to do what is expected, especially when these routines lead to noticeable improvements in their ability to read.

Effective classroom management must take your entire classroom environment into account. Room arrangement can aid or hinder your management abilities, for example. Forethought about procedures and routines will add confidence and efficiency to your lessons. And a smoothly operating classroom will allow you to focus the majority of your energies on teaching.

ORGANIZING YOUR CLASSROOM

When considering how to organize your classroom, arrange the physical space so that it promotes positive student/teacher interactions and reduces the possibility of disruptions. While there is no standard way to organize a *LANGUAGE!* classroom, there are certain aspects of your room set-up that will impact the effectiveness of your instruction.

With regard to the common instructional tasks within *LANGUAGE!*, having the focus on the front of the room will be extremely important. The high frequency of modeling and monitored responses makes it important for students to easily see the board. Given the behavioral dimension of struggling readers, proximity control will be important for providing positive feedback and monitoring off-task behaviors.

You may want to choose an arrangement that facilitates a smooth start to the year and offers you the greatest degree of control. Working in small groups may be something you work into as the year progresses and your students learn the routines. All of these factors may be compromised by the size of your room or the fact that as a secondary teacher, you change rooms every class period! The essential point here is that adjusting your room arrangement is an easy way to address behavior issues.

Classroom Organization

The following material is excerpted from *CHAMPs: A Proactive Approach to Classroom Management* (Eugene, Oregon: Pacific Northwest Publishing, Inc., 1998), by Randy Sprick, Ph.D.; Mickey Garrison, Ph.D.; and Lisa M. Howard, M.S. Reprinted with permission.

Arrange student desks to optimize the most common types of instructional tasks that you will have students engage in.

What follows are descriptions of four common arrangements for individual students' desks (i.e., desks clustered in fours; desks in rows— front to back; desks in rows—side to side; desks in a U shape around the perimeter of the classroom) and information about their relative pros and cons. Remember, as you consider what arrangement you want for your classroom (one of these or any other), you need to think about the instructional tasks students will be participating in and the level of classroom structure your students require.

Desks in Rows, Front to Back

- Excellent if you schedule frequent whole class instruction or have students do tasks for which they must see the board.

- For occasional cooperative learning activities, students can be trained to move quickly from the rows into groups of four, and back to the rows when the cooperative activity is completed.

- Allows students to interact, but the space between desks helps to keep off-task conversation down.

- Implies student attention should be directed to the front of the room.

- Allows easy circulation among students.

- Useful for classes that need medium to high structure.

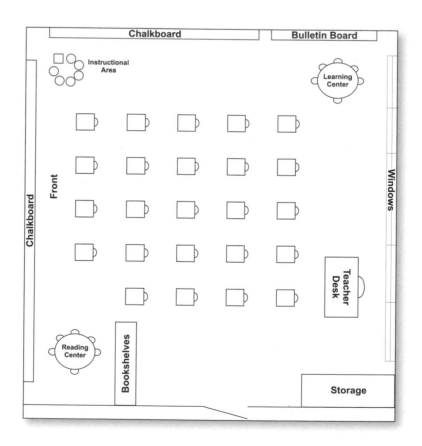

Desks in Rows, Side to Side

- Excellent if you use frequent whole class instruction where you have students do tasks for which they must see the board.

- For occasional cooperative learning activities, students can be trained to move quickly from the rows into groups of four, and back to the rows when the cooperative activity is completed.

- Allows for students to interact more easily than Desks in Rows, Front to Back, which may result in more off-task conversation than desired.

- Implies student attention should be directed to the front of the room.

- Maximizes available space in room to allow for centers, work areas, and small group instruction around the perimeter of the room.

- May hinder easy circulation among students—unless you arrange for one or two aisles running perpendicular to the rows so you do not have to go all the way to either side of the room to get from one row to another.

- Best for classes that would benefit from low to medium classroom structure.

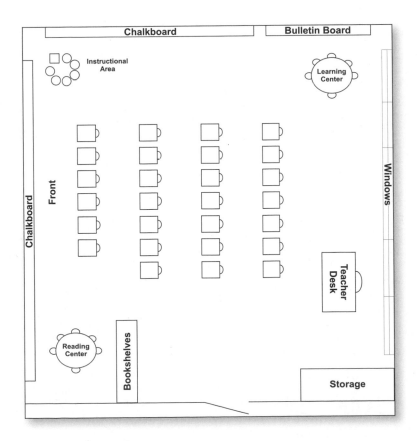

Desks in Clusters

- Allows easy access from any part of the room to any other part of the room, making it easy to circulate among students.

- Excellent if you schedule frequent cooperative learning tasks.

- Can be problematic if you have students who need less stimulation and distraction. Being part of a cluster may make it more difficult for them to behave responsibly, but separating them may make them feel excluded.

- Requires students to turn sideways or completely around to see the board or teacher-directed instruction.

- May result in frequent off-task conversation during independent work periods as well as during teacher-directed instruction.

- Usually best for classes of low to medium structure; clusters may prompt too much inappropriate student-to-student interaction for classes needing high structure.

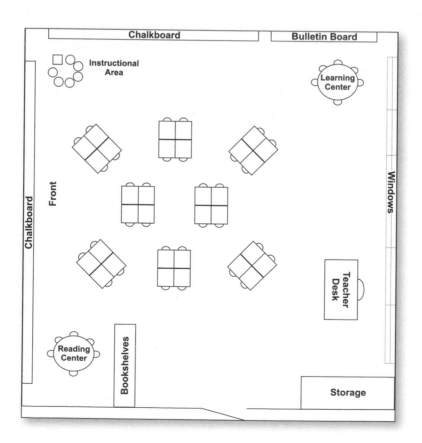

Desks in U-Shape

- Excellent for whole class discussions and teacher-directed instruction in which you want students to participate with verbal responses.

- Excellent for teacher proximity and circulation—you can get quickly to any student.

- Does not lend itself to cooperative group activities.

- Does not make good use of space (the area in the center of the U is largely unused). May not allow room for learning centers, small group instruction, and so on.

- Probably not feasible if you have a large number of students.

- If used with a large class, you may need to have two rows. You need to make sure the inside U has space so you can easily interact with the students in the outside U.

- You need to arrange for access from the inside of the U to the outside, so you/students are able to cross the room to turn something in, etc.

- Best for classes that need low to medium classroom structure. (Can work for classes needing high structure if you monitor students closely, use proximity management effectively, and provide for high rates of positive feedback.)

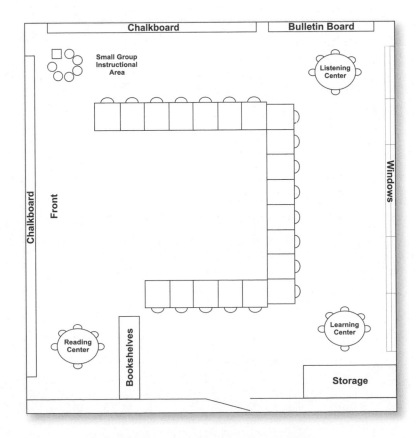

MANAGING BEHAVIORS PROACTIVELY

> ## What You Need to Know

Given the history of failure most of your students bring to your *LANGUAGE!* classroom, effective behavior management will be essential to successful implementation. Time spent developing a behavior management plan will be time well spent! First you need to consider possible reasons behind student misconduct. Research suggests most students misbehave in the classroom because they are:

- Unsure of what the teacher expects, or
- Unaware of when they exhibit inappropriate behavior, or
- Seeking attention and it is easier to get it through correction than praise, or
- Feeling powerless, so they embrace the power to make the teacher frustrated or angry, or
- Hoping to escape attempting a task that will make them appear stupid *(Sprick, R. CHAMPs, 1998).*

To better understand your students' behaviors, you need to realize that "behaviors which are supported and recognized are the ones which will increase." So the trick for you is to find ways to positively support and recognize appropriate behavior in ways that are meaningful to your students (Jensen, W., 2004).

Research also shows that putting the following elements into place in your classroom will assist you in managing behaviors proactively.

- Establish manageable, efficient classroom routines.
- Interact with students in upbeat, caring ways.
- Provide incentives, rewards, and recognition to encourage good conduct, class involvement, and learning.
- Set clear standards for classroom behavior and apply them fairly and consistently (Cotton, K. *Effective Schooling Practices: A Research Synthesis*, 1995 Update).

Establish manageable, efficient classroom routines.

When it comes to managing classroom behavior, an ounce of prevention is truly worth a pound of cure. Developing classroom routines will play a vital part in your overall behavior management plan. Make sure you articulate, model, and enforce orderly routines for the following everyday practices:

- At the beginning of class:
    - Getting materials for the class.
    - Taking part in a warm up routine, for example a daily "bell ringer" activity tied to *LANGUAGE!* content. (For examples see the Teacher's Tip.)
- During class:
    - Asking for help with an independent task.
    - Earning credit for class participation.
    - Performing routines during partner/small group work.
- At the end of class:
    - Putting materials away.
    - Paying attention while you clarify homework assignments or present other information.

If a procedure or routine is not working, change it!

Interact with students in upbeat, caring ways.

Your students may not be able to read books very well, but they are experts at reading people. It is critical that your room become a safe place for them to risk learning. It is critical that you are fair, firm, and consistent in how you treat your students. Positive reinforcement is a powerful tool for changing behavior and it can be as simple as a wink, a smile, or a pat on the shoulder (Sprague & Golly, 2004). Students must feel respected and liked.

What You Need to Know

Provide incentives, rewards, and recognition to encourage good conduct, class involvement, and learning.

As opposed to advocating bribery, this simply addresses the very human need to have incentives and receive recognition for good performance. Think about what makes you come to work each day. Our students need outside motivators as well. Relying primarily on punishment will not bring about the desired behaviors. Punishing behavior without a positive support system results in increased aggression, vandalism, truancy, and dropouts (Mayer & Sulzer-Azaroff, 1990; Peterson, & Williams, 1997 cited in Sprague, J. & Annemieke, G. *Best Behavior: Building Positive Behavior Support in Schools.* Sopris West: Longmont, CO. 2005).

Your plan should be easy to monitor and manage. Explore what your students are willing to work for and incorporate those things into your plan. You will likely find that time to talk with classmates, extra time at recess, and homework passes are high on most students' lists and relatively easy to provide within your classroom's structure and budget!

Set clear standards for classroom conduct and apply them fairly and consistently.

Enforcing consequences consistently will be as important as highly motivating rewards. Keep your rules realistic and straightforward. Make sure your room is set up for easy monitoring of the rules. This will help you with enforcement. Look for opportunities to recognize compliance as opposed to focusing on violations. Especially in the beginning, your reward system may not be strong enough to prevent misbehavior. Be prepared by developing a list of corrective consequences. Remain objective and calm when applying consequences, and be careful with your choice of consequences.

TEACHER'S TIP
Ideas for Bell Ringers

These activities helped get students "on task" for the lesson as soon as they walked into my room. I kept the following guidelines in mind as I created daily bell ringers.

- *Use the curriculum to formulate bell ringers.*

- *Focus on concepts that are giving students the most difficulty— which in my classroom was grammar!*

- *Keep the activity brief—3 to 5 minutes.*

- *Tell students how it will be "counted"—e.g., a part of their daily grade, checked on Fridays, and worth a certain number of points. (Make sure this procedure is very easy to monitor!)*

- *Give a few students the opportunity to share their responses with the group. This reinforces the value of the activity and helps you check for understanding.*

- *Have the activity waiting for the students every day, without fail.*

Here are some very simple ideas for bell ringers that accomplished all of my goals:

- *Sentence writing using unit words*

  - *Put a suitable multiple-meaning word on the board, such as* bat *or* fly. *Students use the word as a noun in a sentence and then as a verb in a sentence. As you move through your instructional sequence and add different parts of speech to your lessons, add them to this exercise as well. Have students share their responses, stopping once someone uses the word in each context correctly!*

  - *Ask for sentences that match where you are in the grammar strand—i.e., sentences with direct objects, sentences with present progressive tense verbs, etc.*

- *Put several blank sentence diagramming patterns on the board and have students fill in the lines.*

- *Put previously discussed idioms/expressions of the day on the board and have students use them in sentences.*

- *Write sentences on the board and have students diagram the sentences.*

- *Write kernel sentences on the board and have them add designated "painters."*

As you can see, the possibilities are endless. Just use the curriculum for inspiration. My students kept their responses in their notebooks and I checked them every Friday.

Jenny Hamilton, National *LANGUAGE!* Trainer
Daphne, Alabama

What You Need to Know

Motivating Reluctant Readers

When older students enter *LANGUAGE!*, they often have questions about why they are in the curriculum. As you prepare to teach it, think of how you might answer these common student questions.

- Shouldn't I already know how to read by now?
- Does being in this class mean that I'm stupid?
- Why do we do phonemic awareness drills?
- Why do some of the activities seem like they're for little kids?
- Why should I do it?

Your students might find some reassurance in knowing that they are not alone. According to National Assessment of Educational Progress, 25 percent of young people entering middle and high school experience difficulty reading and understanding grade-level texts and materials (NAEP, 2004). Be truthful with your students about why and how they were placed in the *LANGUAGE!* curriculum. But make sure to add that *LANGUAGE!* has a proven track record in helping kids learn how to read.

Creating an accepting and safe classroom environment will aid student willingness to take part. Students should treat their peers, themselves, and you with respect. Speaking to the students using correct yet accessible academic terminology will help dignify the curriculum. Explain the purpose of the activities to your students so they can see the value of participation. Seek opportunities to praise your students, even if you must cheer small successes at first. Create an engaging environment where students are eager to participate.

Rationale/research behind drills to motivate older students

Older struggling readers often need practice with the same phonological awareness tasks usually used with younger learners, though with different methods, timing, and explanations about phonology. Even though the approach may be different in older children, phonemic awareness is a critical building block for comprehension (Curtis, 2004). The phonemic awareness drills in the *LANGUAGE!* curriculum activate both hemispheres of the brain. This whole brain activation helps students to be better engaged in the rest of the lesson. Memory is also improved by using these multisensory techniques.

Teacher attitude towards these drills will greatly influence the attitude of students. Recognizing the fundamental importance of phonemic awareness and phonics-related skills, you need to communicate this information to your students. Sharing a brief explanation of brain research in regards to literacy and how multisensory techniques contribute to language and literacy development will help older students understand why they need to participate in phonemic awareness drills. Take the time to make sure your students understand the relationship between multisensory learning and retention.

How Charting Fluency Helps Motivate Students

Without goals, students do not have a clear idea of what they are trying to accomplish or why. For most students, reaching fluency goals is a first indicator that they are making progress. These goals might seem impossible to obtain when students begin the curriculum. It will help to set specific goals for each student depending on their initial level of fluency. (The fluency goals for each book are listed on page 34 in the *Assessment: Teacher Editions*.) As students chart their fluency, they will have a visual representation of the progress they are making.

TEACHER'S TIP
Creating Student Notebooks

With proper planning, students and teachers who use student notebooks will be rewarded with improved organizational skills, increased learning, and instructional efficiency. These tips will get your class started:

- *Use 1" binders with dividers.*

- *Store binders in the classroom, if space permits.*

- *Start with 3–5 sections labeled according to content or subject area.*

- *Model the organization and use of student notebooks, but have students build and manage their own notebooks.*

- *Use the notebooks regularly to document new learning and review concepts.*

- *Purge notebooks at the end of each unit, with the exception of the writing section; that way, you and your students can gauge their progress over time.*

For a more complete discussion of Student Notebooks, see page 436 in the Appendix.

EFFECTIVE HOMEWORK PRACTICES

What You Need to Know

Homework is a reality in classrooms, regardless of content or grade level. Fortunately for teachers and students, there is a growing body of research that addresses effective homework practices. Keeping this research in mind will ensure all students will benefit from time spent on a homework assignment. Homework options can be printed using the *Instructional Planning Tools* CDs for Books A–F.

Four research-based generalizations can guide teachers in the effective use of homework (Marzano, Pickering, & Pollock, 2001).

1. **Assign appropriate amounts of homework.** The amount of homework assigned to students should be different from elementary to middle school to high school. Students at lower grade levels should be given far less homework than students at higher grade levels (Marzano, Pickering, & Pollock, 2001).

2. **Minimize parent involvement in homework.** Many studies show minimal and even somewhat negative effects when parents are asked to help students with homework (Balli, 1998; Balli, Demo & Wedman, 1998; Balli, Wedman, & Demo, 1997; Perkins & Milgram, 1996). Parents or guardians should be informed about homework, but their involvement should focus on homework completion, not the reteaching of content.

3. **Identify and articulate the purpose of homework.** Two common purposes for homework are (1) practice and (2) preparation or elaboration (Foyle, Lyman, Tompkins, Perne, & Foyle, 1990). The best use of homework is to practice skills recently learned or previously mastered (Ruhl & Hughes, 2005). Homework should only be assigned for practice after direct instruction, guided practice, and independent practice of a skill have proven successful in the classroom. Homework assigned for practice could include timed fluency builders using word fluency, sentence fluency, or passage fluency. Independent reading with a reading log and/or a written response journal could also be part of the weekly homework routine.

An example of homework assigned for preparation or elaboration might occur at the beginning of and midway through a new unit. For example, students could generate a concept map or K-W-L chart using the

Unit 18 target word, *continent*, at the end of Unit 17. Several days later, students could be asked to revisit the same graphic organizer as homework and record new learning. This homework assignment would serve two purposes: First, the student would be practicing how to complete a graphic organizer that they are familiar with from class; second, the student would be preparing for, and later elaborating on, knowledge of unit content.

4. **Provide meaningful feedback.** Teacher feedback directly impacts the effectiveness of homework. Walberg (1999) found that homework assigned but not graded or commented on generates an 11 percentile gain. Homework that is graded jumps to a 28 percentile gain. Graded homework with written comments results in a 30 percentile gain.

Implementation Tips: Assigning Homework

Less is truly more when it comes to purposeful homework assignments. Frequent slivers of practice will help solidify skills and not overwhelm students. When homework mirrors class work, students feel more confident in tackling the task. Students need to understand the purpose of an assignment and how it will be graded. When homework is reviewed, students benefit from the corrective feedback.

Consider these practices when assigning homework (Marzano, Pickering,& Pollock, 2001):

1. Establish and communicate a homework policy including:

   a. Purpose of homework

   b. Amount of homework

   c. Consequences for not completing homework

   d. Description of the types of acceptable parental involvement (Marzano, Pickering, & Pollock, 2001).

2. Design homework assignments that clearly incorporate the purpose and outcome. Students should record the following three details about the assignment: the subject, due date, and purpose of the assignment.

3. Provide feedback

   a. Try to grade or comment on each assignment.

   b. Ask students to provide feedback, such as speed and accuracy on fluency.

   c. Provide verbal feedback during small group instruction.

CORRECTIVE FEEDBACK IN *LANGUAGE!*

What You Need to Know

The pedagogical approach of *LANGUAGE!* always starts with modeling. From the very introduction of a concept, we want to guide students in the correct practice of a skill—practice makes permanent. Improper reinforcement creates a challenge for the teacher and the student because it is very difficult to repair a skill once it has been learned and performed incorrectly (Sousa, D., 2001).

To promote mastery learning, approach all skill practice with the "I do" "We do" "You do" model. After modeling the expectations of any activity through "I do" demonstrations— what it is supposed to sound like or look like, for example— there needs to be ample opportunities for "We do." It is during this time that you can gauge how much more modeling and practice is necessary. Once students demonstrate their understanding or accuracy, you can release them for "You do" independent practice.

Skill mastery is developed through guided practice of that skill. These students have worked without confirmation for years and generally they have completed tasks incorrectly without constructive corrective feedback. Often they do not understand what makes their answers incorrect. When working through exercises in the *Interactive Text*, for example, teachers need to focus on ensuring understanding by monitoring, confirming, and correcting responses to help students truly master the concepts.

Effective feedback can help change skill development and student perceptions of their abilities. Students must expect success as well as value that success to be motivated to engage in any learning task.

When it comes to corrective feedback, you must always correct errors. This cannot be emphasized enough. It is critical that students learn a skill correctly and with accuracy—through differentiated instruction, if necessary.

Consider the following examples of corrective feedback:

Step 1: Phonemic Awareness and Phonics

Assignment: Practicing phonemic awareness drills.

Objective: Students must strengthen their phonemic awareness skills as a prerequisite for reading.

Modeling: Provide students with the prompt to be repeated and the task—phoneme segmentation, for example— "Say 'mash.'"Students respond and you repeat "Say the sounds in 'mash.'"

Monitoring: Listen carefully for proper pronunciation of the prompt as well as the correct response. In phoneme segmentation, listen for the correct segmenting and pronunciation of sounds. (By reviewing the Contrastive Analysis Charts, you can be prepared for certain predictable errors.)

Offering Corrective Feedback: "Let's do that one more time. Listen carefully. The word is 'mash.' Pay close attention to the ending sound. Let's say the sounds in 'mash.'"

Step 2: Word Recognition and Spelling

Assignment: Practicing a fluency builder.

Objective: Students practice reading lists of words with accuracy and ease.

Modeling: Demonstrate fluent reading of the fluency exercise.

Monitoring: Listen to student efforts; interrupt the exercise if students are mispronouncing or misreading words.

Offering Corrective Feedback: "Everyone, eyes on the first line. Listen to me and follow along... Roger, will you read line three?... Maria, line four?...Let's look at that line again. Listen to me and then you try again.

Note: With this approach, the most fragile learners as well as the most established readers practice the words. With each reading of a line, all students are given one more exposure to the proper pronunciation. If a mistake is made, it must be corrected.

Step 3: Vocabulary and Morphology

Assignment: Using idioms in sentences to demonstrate understanding.

Objective: To help students understand the figurative uses of language.

Modeling: Write the idiom on the board and tell the students what the idiom means. Create a scenario for the students and use the idiom. You may need to think of ways to visually help students understand what the idiom does and does not mean. Example: *to stop on a dime*. You may want to place a dime on the floor and stand on it, saying that this is not what this idiom means. Then pantomime driving a car and stopping quickly. Having an illustration ready to show students will help tremendously in their ability to understand.

Monitoring: Ask the students to think about what the idiom really means, and then say it in a sentence. Call on students to share their sentences. Make sure students use the idiom correctly from a meaning standpoint as well as a grammatical standpoint.

Offering Corrective Feedback: If students use the idiom incorrectly, help them repair their sentence and then have them repeat the sentence. Again focusing on what the students did correctly, say, "Let's see if we can make the meaning even clearer by adding…" If students' sentences all start sounding the same, interject that you want variety.

Step 4: Grammar and Usage

Assignment: *Interactive Text* activity involving grammar—focus on adverbs.

Objective: To demonstrate mastery of grammar concepts using **Masterpiece Sentences: Stage 3**.

Modeling: Read the directions, focusing on the key words. Think out loud about what those directions mean. Working always in the "I do" model first, complete the first task, thinking out loud about how you arrived at your answer. Read: "'The plant wilts on the hot sill.' What do I do first? That's right, underline the prepositional phrase, 'on the hot sill.' What question does 'on the hot sill' answer? It answers the 'where' question. I'm going to put that prepositional phrase at the beginning of my sentence, remembering to add a comma."

Monitoring: Read the next sentence, asking a student to identify the prepositional phrase. Ask "What question does it answer?" Always review the answers for an *Interactive Text* activity as soon as students have completed it. By calling on students to share their answers aloud, you are constantly monitoring understanding. Whenever possible, call students up to the board or overhead to share their responses. This raises the level of engagement and helps monitor comprehension.

Offering Corrective Feedback: If a student generates the wrong answer, stop and clarify. "'Past the still pond' answers the 'where' question. Let's think about how we answer 'where' questions...." Distinguish location answers from answers to the other question words, *how* and *when*. "Who can add 'how' to this sentence? Who can add 'when' to this sentence?" By reviewing all of the answers, you provide students with the opportunity to "repair" incorrect responses rather than continue to misunderstand the task. For students who are struggling with the content, consider providing a visual model for all of the answers in the form of a transparency. Students can then truly "repair" their incorrect responses and keep up with the answers being given by their peers.

Step 5: Listening and Reading Comprehension

Assignment: Working on passage fluency.

Objective: To build automaticity, accuracy, and prosody when reading.

Modeling: Read the passage for your students, paying special attention to your own rate and prosody. Reinforce the idea of "scooping" meaningful chunks within sentences. If your students are decoding poorly, put the passage on a transparency and help them see how you are "chunking" by physically scooping the phrases within the sentences.

Monitoring: Call on students to read sentences aloud, using their "scoops" for phrasing. Discuss how there are multiple ways to group phrases for meaning but that there are words that should not be separated. Call on students whose skills are intact as well as those who are struggling.

Offering Corrective Feedback: If students make mistakes while reading to the whole class, model a correct way to group or pronounce words and have them repeat it. You could also call on another student to see how they "scooped" the sentence. Move around the room once students are reading with their partners. Listen carefully for mispronunciations as well as choppy reading. Gently ask students to reread a sentence to correct any errors and then continue. If a timed reading is called for, make sure students practice for accuracy and prosody before timing begins.

Step 6: Speaking and Writing

Assignment:	Generating oral responses for **Answer It**.
Objective:	To respond to questions correctly and accurately.
Modeling:	Before beginning the exercise or activity, pose a question and demonstrate the correct way of answering. If helpful, you might model out loud where you found the answer in the text, or your thought processes for how you reached your answer.
Monitoring:	Listen to student efforts. If students use words incorrectly or fail to use proper grammar, they need to hear what the answer should sound like.
Offering Corrective Feedback:	For a question such as "What stories do ballads tell?": If the student provides the right information but in an incorrect form (e.g., "about heroes and bravery"), reinforce the correct answer while offering corrective feedback by saying "You have given me the correct information, but not in the correct format. Remember to use parts of the question and to answer in a complete sentence. The question was 'What stories do ballads tell?' Listen—'Ballads tell stories about heroes and their brave acts.' Repeat."

Content Mastery Tasks

Assignment:	Reviewing **Content Mastery** tasks.
Objective:	To clarify the intent of a **Content Mastery** task by reviewing the directions and the correct responses.
Modeling:	Read the directions, stopping to interpret and think "out loud" to give the directions real meaning. Go through each possible choice, thinking "out loud" to demonstrate why it is or is not the proper response. If many students missed these questions, have them answer a similar question on their wipe-off boards.

Monitoring	Have students understand the value of paying attention during this activity, and give participation points lavishly in the beginning. If students are asked to respond to another practice question on their wipe-off boards, have them hold up their boards showing their answers.
Offering Corrective Feedback:	If someone writes an incorrect response, clarify the proper response and continue to ask practice questions until everyone gets it right or you determine that it will require one-on-one instruction to help a student

It is essential that you keep corrections positive so students stay engaged and feel emotionally safe while participating. Keep in mind that within the body of the largest, toughest student in your class is a child who has continued to fail at reading. Many of them honestly believe this is a skill that they will never master. Sarcastic remarks from a teacher may not only wreck a teaching moment, but trigger embarrassment, shame, and distrust in the student.

Behavior Management Resources

If you would like more specific information on setting up research-based behavior management plans for your classrooms, you might consider the following resources:

CHAMPs by Randy Sprick, Ph.D.; Mickey Garrison, Ph.D.; and Lisa M. Howard, M.S. (Pacific Northwest Publishing, 1998). This video series and text offer solutions ranging from classroom organization to effective reward systems for grades K–12.

The Tough Kid Tool Box by William R. Jenson, Ph.D.; Ginger Rhode Ph.D.; and H. Kenton Reavis, Ed.D. (Sopris West, 1994). For grades 1–8, this text with reproducibles offers troubleshooting tips and step-by-step guidance to accomplish specific interventions.

Best Behavior: Building Positive Behavior Support in Schools by Jeffrey Sprague, Ph.D.; and Annemieke Golly, Ph.D. (Sopris West, 2004). This comprehensive, adaptable program provides an evidence-based system of scalable interventions.

SCHOOL-TO-FAMILY CONNECTIONS

Table of Contents

RESEARCH BITE

"The informal education that takes place in the family is not merely a pleasant prelude, but rather a powerful prerequisite for success in formal education from the primary grades onward"

Bronfenbrenner, 1991

OVERVIEW: SCHOOL-TO-FAMILY CONNECTIONS

What You Need to Know

The Value of School-Family Collaboration

The following is excerpted from *Working with Families for Student Success* by Sandra Christenson; originally drawn from previously published material, specifically *Schools and Families: Creating Essential Connections for Learning*, by Sandra Christenson and Susan Sheridan (2001) and a resource guide entitled *Enhancing School-Family Partnerships: A Teacher's Guide* (n.d.) by Michelle Rubenstein, Evanthia Patrikakou, Roger Weissberg, and Mashana Armstrong. Reprinted with permission.

Children's learning and development are influenced by the reciprocal relationships among the student, family, and school—or what Pianta and Walsh (1996) have referred to as the "three-legged stool." Consider the fact that students can spend only 9% of their time "breathing school air." From birth to age 18, students spend 91% of their time outside of school (Walberg, 1984). Once students start kindergarten, they spend 70% of their waking hours outside of school (Clark, 1990). These statistics underscore the critical nature of out-of-school time for students' levels of school performance, time for which parents are responsible and control. They also illustrate that optimal indicators of school performance are best achieved by accounting for learning experiences and fostering opportunities to learn during school and outside of school hours. We know that children perform most optimally in school when instructional, home, and home-school support for learning exists (Ysseldyke & Christenson, 2002).

Support and involvement of your students' families can be a great asset in the implementation of *LANGUAGE!* in your classroom. The best way to establish effective school-home interactions, research suggests, is for teachers and schools to offer early, positive, and constructive messages to students' families. The majority of parents and caregivers is willing to team with you to advance their children's education, but many do not know how best to contribute (Christenson, 2001).

Positive, proactive messages at the beginning of the semester will go far in establishing open lines of communication between you and your students' families. By taking the initiative and offering a clear outline of roles, policies, and responsibilities, you can guide the development of successful student-teacher-family partnerships. As the year progresses, such an approach has the added benefit of allaying potential parental defensiveness if and when discipline or academic troubles need to be addressed.

Establishing the Lines of Communication

From the initial entry into *LANGUAGE!* to the last unit, multiple opportunities exist to inform parents and guardians of their child's progress in the curriculum. Frequent and informative communication provides valuable reinforcement.

Samples of letters are included here to guide the types of information you should share. These include:

- A letter that introduces the *LANGUAGE!* program to families
- A letter outlining specific ways families can help their child succeed
- An end-of-unit progress report
- And end-of-book progress report
- A *LANGUAGE! Online Assessment* progress report.

These letters are available on the *LANGUAGE!* Web site for you to personalize and print on school letterhead. You can download these materials at *http://teachlanguage.com*.

Ideas for Family Support of *LANGUAGE!* Instruction

Family members should be encouraged to support their children at home and offered specific ideas on how to do so. As you determine the level of family support that may be available, you can suggest appropriate in-home activities.

Family support for student performance can take two main forms—academic and motivational, according to the University of Minnesota's Sandra Christenson in her report "Working with Families for Student Success" (2001):

- *Academic Support refers very broadly to the ways in which parents foster their children's intellectual and cognitive development. It is what parents do that is directly related to their children's experience in school.*

- *Motivational Support refers to the ways in which parents foster the development of attitudes and approaches to learning that are essential for school success.*

What You Need to Know

The effectiveness of family members' academic support depends largely on their own skills and comfort with reading. In addition, some research suggests that family assistance with homework can actually prove detrimental to student performance (Balli, 1998; Balli, Demo, & Wedman, 1998; Balli, Wedman, & Demo, 1997; Perkins & Milgram, 1996).

In contrast, motivational support can be provided by families whatever their circumstance. This positive reinforcement can take many forms, including the monitoring of homework completion, establishing study and reading routines, attendance at teacher-parent conferences and school events, and especially by offering encouragement and praise for effort and performance.

As the teacher and education professional, you are in a position to offer specific guidance to families in how best to promote their child's education. For *LANGUAGE!* in particular, the following family support can reinforce their children's learning and skill development:

- Monitor homework completion.
- Talk about the content of daily *LANGUAGE!* lessons.
- Practice **Essential Word Cards**.
- Practice fluency activities.
- Drill spelling words from the **Unit Words**.

Parents can also assist literacy development in other ways. They can:

- Encourage their children to read every day.
- Help their child choose books at an appropriate level. (You or your school's reading specialist can offer recommendations.)
- Be good role models by letting their children see them reading.
- Maintain a reading log to show support for independent reading, and make a point of celebrating their child's accomplishments.

SCHOOL-TO-FAMILY LETTERS

On the following pages, you will find letters in English and Spanish to aid effective communication with your students' families. These letters, described below, can be downloaded at http://teachlanguage.com and customized, or directly photocopied onto your school's letterhead.

Sample Letter—Introducing *LANGUAGE!*: Use this letter to inform families of students who are entering the *LANGUAGE!* curriculum.

Sample Letter—How Parents Can Help: Use this letter to suggest ways families of *LANGUAGE!* students can support their child's learning.

Sample Letter—End-of-Unit Progress Report: Upon completing a unit, use this letter to inform families of their child's progress.

Sample Letter—End-of-Book Progress Report: Upon completing a book, use this letter to inform families of their child's progress.

Sample Letter—*Online Assessment Report*: Upon completing a book, send this letter along with a copy of the *Online Assessment Report* to inform families of their child's progress.

Dear _____,

Your child _____ will be participating in a *LANGUAGE!* class. An upcoming workshop about the *LANGUAGE!* program will introduce the curriculum to you. We will share ideas about additional support you can give at home. The date and time of the workshop will be announced soon.

LANGUAGE! instruction helps students make rapid gains in reading and writing. To ensure that no students are left behind, we are placing students who need help in reading and writing into *LANGUAGE!* classes. Your child's teacher is _____.

LANGUAGE! is based on proven literacy research. It is comprehensive, providing direct instruction in six important areas of language arts: phonemic awareness and phonics; word recognition and spelling; vocabulary and morphology; grammar and usage; listening and reading comprehension; and speaking and writing. Upon successful completion of *LANGUAGE!*, students will be caught up to their grade level and return to the regular curriculum.

To achieve grade-level standards, all students need reading and writing skills. They need these skills to succeed in social studies, science, and math. Without grade-level literacy, they struggle to read their textbooks and tests. *LANGUAGE!*, with your help, will accelerate your child's progress and achievement in reading and writing.

Please contact our school at _____ if you have questions.

Sincerely,

Estimado(a) _____ ,

Su hijo/a _____ va a participar en una clase de *LANGUAGE!* Pronto se ofrecerá una sesión de información sobre el programa de *LANGUAGE!* En esta sesión se les presentará el plan de estudios del programa. Vamos a compartir ideas sobre el apoyo adicional que usted puede dar en casa. Se anunciarán pronto la fecha y la hora de la sesión.

La enseñanza del programa *LANGUAGE!* ayuda a los estudiantes a adelantar rápidamente en la lectura y la escritura. Para asegurar que no se deja atrás a ningún estudiante, estamos poniendo a los estudiantes del grado _____ que necesitan ayuda a leer y escribir en las clases de *LANGUAGE!* La clase se reúne _____. El/La maestro/a de su hijo/a es _____ .

El programa de *LANGUAGE!* se basa en las investigaciones probadas de la alfabetización. Es comprensivo y ofrece la instrucción directa de seis áreas importantes de los artes lingüísticos: la sensibilización fonémica y la fónica; el reconocimiento de palabras y la ortografía; el vocabulario y la morfología; la gramática y el uso; la comprensión auditiva y de lectura; hablar y escribir. Al terminar el programa de *LANGUAGE!* con éxito, los estudiantes se pondrán al nivel del grado y regresarán a su plan de estudio regular.

Para alcanzar los estándares del nivel del grado, todos los estudiantes necesitan las habilidades de leer y escribir. Necesitan estas habilidades para tener éxito en los estudios sociales, las ciencias y las matemáticas. Sin la alfabetización del nivel del grado, tienen dificultades en leer sus libros de texto y exámenes. Con su ayuda, *LANGUAGE!* va a acelerar el progreso de su hijo/a y su éxito en la lectura y la esacritura.

Si usted tiene preguntas, póngase en contacto con nuestra escuela al

_____ .

Atentamente,

Dear _____,

We know it's hard to find enough time in our busy world. But as part of the *LANGUAGE!* program, we hope you will to take an active role in your child's efforts to learn. As adults, our examples and encouragement are so important in helping our students and children develop the good learning habits and skills they need to succeed.

Here are some suggestions of ways—small, big, and even fun—that you can support the learning process.

- Set up regular routines and a quiet space for your child to read and do homework.
- Check that homework has been completed.
- Ask about what's being taught in *LANGUAGE!* and other classes at school.
- Help your child find books he or she likes at the right level.
- Encourage your child to read every day.
- Ask your child to read out loud to you, or share the reading of a book together.
- Be a good role model by letting your children see you reading, writing letters, and doing other literacy-related tasks.
- In a visible place, keep an updated list of books your child has read.

Most importantly, let them know that you're proud of them as they read, study, and learn!

Please call our school at _____ if you have questions or would like other ideas on how you can help.

Sincerely,

Estimado(a) _____,

Nosotros sabemos que es difícil encontrar suficiente tiempo en nuestro mundo ajetreado. Pero como parte del programa de *LANGUAGE!* nosotros esperamos que usted vaya a participar activamente en los esfuerzos de su hijo/a para aprender. Como adultos, nuestros ejemplos y estímulos son tan importantes para ayudar a nuestros estudiantes e hijos a desarrollar las habilidades y los hábitos buenos de aprender que necesitan para tener éxito.

A continuación ofrecemos algunas sugerencias de maneras —pequeñas, grandes e incluso divertidas—en las que usted puede apoyar el proceso del aprendizaje.

- Establezca rutinas habituales y un lugar tranquilo donde tu hijo/a pueda leer y hacer los deberes.

- Compruebe que se han terminado los deberes.

- Pregunte por lo que se enseña en las clases de LANGUAGE! y las otras asignaturas.

- Ayude a su hijo/a a encontrar libros al nivel apropiado que le gustarían.

- Anime a su hijo/a a leer cada día.

- Pídele a su hijo/a que lea en voz alta o comparta la lectura de un libro juntos.

- Sea un buen modelo de conducta enseñándoles a sus hijos que usted lee, escribe cartas y hace otras actividades relacionadas con la alfabetización.

- En un lugar visible, mantenga una lista actualizada de los libros que su hijo/a ha leído.

Más importante, dígales a sus hijos que ¡usted está orgulloso de ellos mientras ellos leen, estudian y aprenden!

Por favor, llame nuestra escuela al _____ si usted tiene preguntas o le gustaría aprender otras maneras de ayudar.

Atentamente,

Dear _____,

Your child _____ has completed *LANGUAGE!* Unit

_____.

The purpose of this letter is to inform you of your child's progress. The scores below reflect current performance in each target area. Skills are assessed at different points in the program, so you may not see a score reported for every step for every unit.

The Content Mastery tasks measure mastery of different skills in reading and writing.

Content Mastery Tasks for Unit ____

Step 1	Step 2	Step 3	Step 4	Fluency
Phonemic Awareness and Phonics	**Word Recognition and Spelling**	**Vocabulary and Morphology**	**Grammar and Usage**	☐ Sound ☐ Letter ☐ Word ☐ Phrase ☐ Sentence ☐ Passage
_____% (Mastery = 80% or higher)	Posttest 1: _____% Spelling Postest 2: _____% (Mastery = 80% or higher)	_____% (Mastery = 80% or higher)	_____% (Mastery = 80% or higher)	_____ correct words per minute Student's goal: _____

Additional comments:

_____

_____

_____

Please call our school at _____ if you have any questions or concerns.

Sincerely,

Estimado(a) _____,

Su hijo/a _____ ha terminado *LANGUAGE!* Unidad _____ .

El propósito de esta carta es informarle del progreso de su hijo/a. La puntuación abajo refleja el rendimiento actual para cada objetivo. Se evalúan las habilidades en distintos momentos del programa, así que puede que no vea una puntuación para cada paso de cada unidad.

Las tareas de maestría del contenido miden la maestría de diferentes habilidades de leer y escribir.

Tareas de maestría del contenido para la unidad _____

Paso 1	Paso 2	Paso 3	Paso 4	Fluidez
Sensibilización fonémica y fónica	**Reconocimiento de palabras y ortografía**	**Vocabulario y morfología**	**Gramática y uso**	☐ Sonido ☐ Letra ☐ Palabra ☐ Frase ☐ Oración ☐ Texto
_____% (Maestría = 80% or más)	Post test de ortografía 1: _____% Post test de ortografía 2: _____% (Maestría = 80% o más)	_____% (Maestría = 80% o más)	_____% (Maestría = 80% o más)	_____palabras correctas por minuto Objetivo de estuidante:_____

Comentarios adicionales:

_____

_____

_____

Por favor, pónganse en contacto con nuestra escuela al _____ si usted tiene alguna pregunta o duda.

Atentamente,

Dear _____ ,

Your child _____ has completed Book____ in *LANGUAGE!*
As part of the assessment process, we administer **Summative Tests and Progress Indicators** at the end of every book. Different skills are tested at different points in the curriculum; therefore, a score may not be reported in every area for every book.

End-of-Book Content Mastery tests measure cumulative content mastery.

Step 1		Step 3			Step 4	
Word Study	Vocabulary	Word Relationships	Morphology	Grammar	Sentence Structure	Usage
____% Mastery = 80% or higher	____% Mastery = 80% or higher	____% Mastery = 80% or higher	____% Mastery = 80% or higher	____% Mastery = 80% or higher	____% Mastery = 80% or higher	____% Mastery = 80% or higher

Progress Indicators measure progress toward proficient reading and writing.

Step 2	Step 5	Step 2	Step 6	
Test of Silent Contextual Reading Fluency (TOSCRF) Measures the speed of word recognition in a series of printed passages.	*LANGUAGE!* Reading Scale Measures reading comprehension.	TWS-4 Measures mastery of spelling patterns.	Writing Measures written expression.	
			Trait	
			Ideas and Content	____/4
			Organization	____/4
			Voice and Audience Awareness	____/4
Grade Equivalent: _____ Goal: _____	Unit Score: _____ Goal: _____ Lexile® Measure: _____ Goal: _____	Grade Equivalent: _____ Spelling patterns to work on: _____	Word Choice	____/4
			Sentence Fluency	____/4

			Conventions:
			  Capitalization and Punctuation
			  Grammar and Usage
			  Spelling
				____/4
				____/4
				____/4

			Area of writing to work on: _____	

Additional comments _____
_____
_____
_____
_____

Please contact our school at _____ if you have questions or concerns.

Sincerely,

Estimado(a) _____ ,

Su hijo/a _____ ha terminado el libro _____ de *LANGUAGE!*
Como parte del proceso de evaluación, administramos **Pruebas acumulativas
e indicadores del progreso** al final de cada libro. Diversas habilidades se
prueban en puntos diversos en el plan de estudios. Por lo tanto, es posible que
no haya ninguna puntuación anotada para cada parte de cada libro.

Los exámenes de la **maestría del contenido al final del libro** miden el
dominio acumulativo del contenido.

Paso 1		Paso 3			Paso 4	
Estudio de palabras	Vocabulario	Relaciones entre palabras	Morfología	Gramática	Estructura de las oraciones	Uso
_____% Maestría = 80% o más	_____% Maestría = 80% o más	_____% Maestría = 80% o más	_____% Maestría = 80% o más	_____% Maestría = 80% o más	_____% Maestría = 80% o más	_____% Maestría = 80% o más

Los **indicadores del progreso** miden el progreso hacia la competencia en la
lectura y escritura.

Paso 2	Paso 5	Paso 2	Paso 6	
Prueba de habilidad de la lectura contextual en silencio (TOSCRF) Mide la velocidad del reconocimiento de palabras en una serie de textos escritos.	*LANGUAGE!* Escala de lectura Mide la comprensión de lectura.	TWS-4 Mide la maestría de patrones de ortografía.	Escritura Mide la expresión escrita.	
			Rasgo	
			Ideas y contenido	____/4
			Organización	____/4
			Voz	____/4
			Uso de vocabulario	____/4
Nota equivalente: _____ Objetivo: _____	Puntuación de unidad: _____ Objetivo: _____ Medida Lexile®: Objetivo: _____	Nota equivalente: _____ Patrones de ortografía que se necesitan mejoramiento: _____	Fluidez de oraciones	____/4
			Convenciones: Capitalización y puntuación	____/4
			Gramática	____/4
			Ortografía	____/4

Comentarios adicionales: _____

Puntos para mejorar: _____

_____

_____

_____

Por favor póngase en contacto con nuestra escuela al _____
si tiene alguna pregunta o duda.

Atentamente,

Dear _____,

Your child _____ has completed Book _____, Unit
____in *LANGUAGE!*

This letter is to keep you up to date with your child's progress. The attached scores reflect your child's performance on the type of assessment checked below.

☐ **Content Mastery Tasks**

The **Content Mastery** tasks measure mastery of material in each unit.

☐ **End-of-Book Content Mastery Tests**

End-of-Book Content Mastery tests measure cumulative mastery after each book (every six units).

☐ **Progress Indicators**

Progress Indicators measure critical literacy skills and progress in reading and writing at the end of each book (every six units). The results show your child's progress toward proficient reading and writing.

Additional comments:

_____

_____

_____

_____

_____

_____

If you have any questions, please call our school at _____.

Sincerely,

Estimado(a) _____,

Su hijo/a _____ ha terminado el libro _____, Unidad
_____ de *LANGUAGE!*

Esta carta sirve para mantenerle/la informado/a sobre el progreso de su
hijo/a. Las puntuaciones adjuntas reflejan el rendimiento de su hijo/a en
el tipo de evaluación marcado abajo.

☐ **Tareas de maestría del contenido**

Las tareas de maestría del contenido miden el dominio de la información
de cada unidad.

☐ **Los exámenes de la maestría del contenido al final del libro**

Los exámenes de la maestría del contenido al final del libro miden el
dominio acumulativo después de cada libro (cada seis unidades).

☐ **Indicadores del progreso**

Los indicadores del progreso miden las habilidades críticas para leer y
escribir y el progreso en la lectura y escritura al final de cada libro (cada
seis unidades). Los resultados muestran el progreso de su hijo/a hacia la
competencia en leer y escribir.

Comentarios adicionales:

_____

_____

_____

_____

_____

Si tienes alguna pregunta, por favor póngase en contacto con nuestra
escuela al _____.

Atentamente,

You know you're a *LANGUAGE!* teacher when...

You find your keys and wallet stuffed in your pocket chart.

Your teenage daughter uses a **Define It** to explain her new boyfriend's "attributes."

You appreciate multiple meaning humor, such as "Two antennae met, fell in love, and got married. The ceremony wasn't much, but the reception was excellent!"

Someone tells a long-winded story, and you stop her and ask "What step are you on?"

You break into the conversation at dinner or at a party and start talking about the various syllable types.

You start correcting your principal's grammar in his memos.

You tell your teenager that "Whatever!" is not an **Essential Word**.

You forget someone's name but remember that it had a schwa!

You catch yourself saying to your spouse or significant other, "Honey, listen, repeat, listen, repeat...."

Then you know you are a *LANGUAGE!* teacher!

Ron Klemp, Secondary Literacy Coordinator
Los Angeles, California

GLOSSARY OF TERMS

For more complete explorations of these and other terms used in *LANGUAGE!,* see the Glossary of Terms in the Appendix of the *Teacher Edition.*

Note: Words that appear in **bold** within a definition are also defined in this glossary.

1-1-1 pattern. Spelling rule in English that says to double a final consonant before adding a suffix beginning with a vowel when (1) you have a one-syllable word, (2) this word contains one vowel, and (3) it also ends in one consonant (e.g., *hopping, robbed*). *(*Also called the **Doubling Rule**.*)*

Academic English. A formal standard of written language used in textbooks, newspapers, and other informational writing.

Adjective. A word class used to describe nouns and pronouns.

Adverb. A word class used to describe verbs, adjectives, another adverb, or a clause.

Affix. A morpheme added to the front or the back of a word to change its function or meaning. There are two types of affix: (1) **prefix** and (2) **suffix**.

Affricative. A consonant phoneme that begins with a stop and releases with a fricative (e.g., / ch / = / t + sh /).

Alphabet. A set of symbols or letters used to encode words. English spelling is based on an alphabet of 26 letters.

Alphabetic principle. The idea that letters are used to represent individual phonemes in spoken words.

Analogy. Explores word relationships by means of comparisons.

Antonym. A word that means the opposite of another word (e.g., *above/ below, dead/alive*).

Article. A type of adjective that limits nouns. There are three articles: (1) *a*, (2) *an*, and (3) *the.*

Assessment. An instrument, such as a test, for measuring student performance.

Attribute. A characteristic or quality, such as size, shape, color, function, or texture.

Automaticity. The ability to recall or perform a task quickly and effortlessly.

Background knowledge. Previously learned content information that readers can use to interpret new text.

Be **verb.** A **linking verb** that has the following forms: *am, is, are, was, were, be, being, been.*

Blend. A consonant sound pair in the same syllable. The consonants are not separated by vowels.

Bloom's Taxonomy. System of classifying levels of educational objectives; named for psychologist Benjamin S. Bloom (1913–1999).

Breve. A curved mark (˘) used to indicate a short vowel sound.

Circumflex. A diacritical mark placed over a vowel to indicate a specific pronunciation (e.g., *château*).

Cluster deletion. A **phonemic awareness** task in which a consonant cluster is deleted from a word (e.g., When the cluster / *str* / is deleted from *street*, it becomes / *ēt* /).

Cognitive. Relating to thought or learning.

Compare and contrast essay. A type of paragraph or composition that tells how two or more things are alike and/or how they are different.

Compound words. Words consisting of two individual words combined to form a new term (e.g. *backpack, laptop*).

Comprehension. Understanding spoken (listening comprehension) or written (reading comprehension) language.

Concept. Idea that connects words, facts, and other ideas into a logical thought or principle.

Conjunction. A part of speech that joins words, phrases, clauses, or sentences (e.g., *and, but, or*).

Connotation. An implied meaning or association related to a word or phrase.

Consonant. A closed speech sound (phoneme) in which the airflow is restricted or closed using the lips, teeth, or tongue (e.g., / *t* /, / *d* /, / *r* /, / *g* /).

Consonant cluster. A group of three or more consecutive consonants (e.g., / *str* /, / *scr* /, / *spr* /, and / *spl* /) appearing together in a syllable without a vowel to separate them. Each **consonant phoneme** is pronounced.

Context. The parts of a conversation or a piece of text that surround a word, phrase, or line that might help to explain or clarify its meaning.

Contraction. Two words combined, or contracted, into a single word; omitted letters are represented by an apostrophe (e.g., *don't = do not; she'd = she would*).

Control group. In research, an experimental set that for comparison purposes is left unaffected by a process.

Curriculum. A planned, integrated course of study.

Curriculum Casualty. A student who does not respond to traditional instruction or who for other reasons has been unsuccessful in school.

Decodable text. Written material that can be read using sound-symbol relationships that have already been taught.

Decoding. The initial stage of reading when written language is translated into spoken language. **Graphemes** (letters) are associated with the corresponding **phonemes** (sounds). Decoding does not imply comprehension. (See **Grapheme, Phoneme**.)

Denotation. Literal meaning of a word or phrase.

Derivational endings. Suffixes that can change the class of a word (e.g., *depart* [verb], *departure* [noun]).

Diacritical mark. A mark near or through an orthographic or phonetic character indicating a phonetic value. Three marks used extensively in English are: (1) the breve (˘) to indicate a short vowel sound, (2) the macron (ˉ) to indicate a long vowel sound, and (3) the circumflex (^) to indicate a specific pronunciation (e.g., *château*).

Dictation. Instructional exercise in which students write down words, phrases, or sentences that are read to them.

Differentiated instruction. Teaching strategies—including review, reteaching, and acceleration—that are customized to a student's individual needs.

Digraph. Two successive letters that represent one sound (e.g., **sh** as in *ship* and **ea** as in *eat*).

Diphthong. A gliding single-syllable vowel sound that begins with the sound of the first vowel and moves toward the sound of the second vowel (e.g., *oil, boy*).

Dysgraphia. A learning disability that can affect motor skills and processing related to writing skills.

Dyslexia. An impairment of neurobiological origin, associated with phonological difficulties that affect reading accuracy and fluency.

Encoding. The process of converting sounds (phonemes) into orthographic symbols (e.g., writing or spelling).

English learners. Students for whom English is not their first language.

Essential Words. Words that are used often and is not content-specific. Also called *high-frequency* or *general-utility words*.

Etymology. The study of the origins and development of words, including any changes over time in form, meaning, and use.

Explicit instruction. Teaching that progresses from defining, modeling, and/or demonstration to student-guided practice with corrective feedback. (Also called *direct instruction*.)

Expression. A common way of saying something. It is similar to an **idiom**, but an expression does not usually have the grammatical structure of an idiom (e.g., *at any rate, don't get it, odds and ends, you bet*).

Fiction. A literary **genre** that includes imaginary stories. Fiction is sometimes based on real people, places, or events.

Figurative language. Language that is not literal; it means something other than what it says. Includes literary devices such as **hyperbole, idiom, irony, metaphor, metonymy, personification, simile,** and **symbolism**.

Fluencies. Exercises that measure student rate of decoding writing at word, sentence, and passage levels.

Fluent. Effortless and automatic, especially in regard to language abilities.

Formal language. A formal standard of written language used in textbooks, newspapers, and other informational writing. (Also called ***Academic English, Standard English***.)

Form vs. function. Form refers to the word itself. **Function** refers to the job the word performs in a sentence or a context.

Fricative. A consonant phoneme that is produced by the frictional passing of expired breath through a narrow distance between the articulators, creating a hissing sound (e.g., / s /, / z /, / f /).

Genre. A literary category, including autobiography, biography, fantasy, **fiction,** folktale, historical fiction, mystery, nonfiction, novel, science fiction, and short story.

Grammar. A system of rules for a language that includes word formation, sentence formation, speaking and writing, and standards of correctness.

Grapheme. An orthographic symbol used to represent a **phoneme** (e.g., **t** in *top* represents / t /; **sh** in *wish* represents / sh /; **ck** in *luck* represents / k /).

Greek-combining forms. Greek morphemes that act like the small words in a compound word (e.g., *phon(o)* + *graph* = *phonograph*; *tele* + *phon(e)* = *telephone*).

Helping verb. An auxiliary verb that precedes the main verb in a sentence. Helping verbs include forms of *be*, forms of *do*, forms of *have*, and modals.

High-frequency words. A word that appears more often than other words in a language (e.g., *a, the*). (Also called **Essential Words** in *LANGUAGE!* or *general-utility words*.)

Homograph. One of two or more words spelled alike but different in meaning, derivation, or pronunciation (e.g., *bow of a ship; bow and arrow*).

Homophone. A word that sounds the same as another word but is spelled differently and has a different meaning (e.g., *there/their/they're; would/wood*).

Idiom. A common phrase that cannot be understood by the meanings of its separate words—only by the entire phrase. The words in the phrase cannot be changed, or the idiom loses its meaning (e.g., *hit the sack = go to bed; pat on the back = encourage*).

Inflectional suffix. A suffix that changes number, possession, comparison, and tense but not its part of speech.

Informal language. The language most often used when people speak to each other.

Intervention. Additional or revised instruction provided to help a struggling student.

Kinesthetic learning. Style of learning that emphasizes physical action and engagement.

LANGUAGE! Online Assessment System (LOLA). A Web-based program for recording and analyzing student performance.

Lexile. A method for measuring the readability of text.

Linguistics. The study of language and the structures and properties that govern language, including **morphology, phonology,** and **syntax.**

Literacy. The ability to read and write.

Literary analysis essay. An essay that analyzes and evaluates a work of literature.

Loan words. Words that come from other languages.

Macron. A straight diacritical mark (ˉ) used to indicate a long vowel sound.

Manipulatives. Instructional tools, such as letter cards, that lend themselves to physical handling.

Metacognitive. Relating to self-awareness or self-monitoring.

Metaphor. A figure of speech that compares people, places, things, or feelings without using the words *like* or *as* (e.g., *Our dog is an alarm clock*).

Metonymy. A figure of speech in which an attribute stands for the thing itself (e.g., *sweat* for *hard work; press* for *news media*.)

Morpheme. A single unit of meaning in a word (e.g., *pre, scrip*, and *tion*—the three meaningful units of the word *prescription*). Morphemes include prefixes, suffixes, roots, and whole words.

Morphology. The branch of **linguistics** that examines the smallest meaningful parts of words—morphemes. A study of word formation as it relates to inflection, derivation, and compounding.

Multiple meaning words. Words that have more than one meaning (e.g., *fire* means *heat and flames, to end employment,* or *to shoot a gun*).

Multisensory learning. Teaching strategies that engage more than one sense.

Multisyllable word. A word that has more than one syllable (e.g., *taxi, computer, television*).

Nasal. A consonant phoneme produced when air flows through the nasal cavity (e.g., / m /, / n /).

Nonphonetic word. A word that is not spelled the way it sounds (e.g., *the, sure, through*).

Noun. A word that names a person, place, thing, or idea.

Orthography. The means by which a spoken language is coded, or written down.

Parts of speech. Word classifications that indicate contextual usage. Parts of speech include **noun, verb, adjective, adverb, pronoun, preposition, conjunction**, and **interjection**.

Phoneme. A single unit of sound in a spoken word (e.g., / t / at the end of *bat*; / m / at the end of *am*, / ă / In the middle of *cat*).

Phoneme-grapheme correspondence. The relationship between a speech sound and the letter used to represent it.

Phonemic analysis. An examination of the individual sounds that make up a word.

Phonemic awareness. The ability to distinguish and manipulate individual phonemes in words.

Phonics. The study of the relationships between letters and the sounds they represent.

Phonogram. A combination of letters that represents a specific sound or sound set (e.g., **kn-** represents the sound / n /; -*sion*, -*tion*, -*cian*, and -*xion* all represent the sound set / *shun* /).

Phonological awareness. An understanding that words are made of individual speech sounds that can be manipulated.

Phonology. The scientific study of speech sounds and their features as well as the rules that govern how these sounds interact with one another.

Phrasing. The manner in which words are chosen or put together in oral and written language.

Predicate. One of two main parts of a sentence. It contains a verb with or without objects and other modifiers and usually follows the subject.

Prefix. A morpheme added to the beginning of a word to modify its meaning (e.g., **re-** changes the meaning of *build* in *rebuild*).

Preposition. A part of speech that links **nouns**, **pronouns**, and phrases to other words in a sentence. It usually indicates the placement of the object with respect to the rest of the sentence.

Prewriting. The initial stage of writing that occurs prior to the first draft and involves organization of thought, planning, and outlining.

Pronoun. A function word used in place of a noun.

Prosody. The use of rhythm and intonation in language.

Punctuation. A set of symbols in text that provides a signal to a reader, increases the ease of reading, and clarifies a writer's thoughts.

Question. Seeks information and often begins with question words (e.g., *who, what, when, where, how, why*). It ends with a question mark (e.g., *Where did she go?*).

Report. A type of **nonfiction** writing that is based on a writer's research into a topic.

Response to Intervention (RTI). Alternative method of instruction or student expression in response to learning delays.

Revision. Process of rethinking and rewriting text to correct, clarify, and improve it.

Root. The basic meaning part of a word.

Scaffolded instruction. Teaching strategy that gradually evolves from explicit instruction to student-guided practice with corrective feedback.

Schwa. A vowel phoneme in an unstressed syllable that has reduced value or emphasis. The symbol for schwa is ∂. The schwa sound is similar to / ŭ / in *cut*.

Scope and sequence. An educational plan that lists what is to be taught and in what order.

Semantic category. A grouping of words that are connected in some way and define each other as a group (e.g., the word *cat* is in the semantic category *animals*).

Semantics. The study of meaning in words and phrases.

Sentence. A group of words that has at least one subject and one predicate and conveys a complete thought.

Sight word. A word that is identified instantly without sounding out.

Silent letters. Letters that occur in a printed word but are not pronounced (e.g., **e** in *cape*; **n** in *hymn*; **k** in *know*).

Simile. A figure of speech that makes a comparison. A simile always uses the words *like* or *as* (e.g., *as smart as Einstein, He runs like the wind*).

Sound. The vocalizations made in speech.

Sound-letter correspondence. The relationship between **phonemes** and **graphemes**.

Sound-symbol correspondence. The relationship between a speech sound and the letter used to represent it.

Standard English. A formal standard of written language used in textbooks, newspapers, and other informational writing.

Stop. A consonant **phoneme** characterized by closure of the airflow with the lips, teeth, or tongue (e.g., / p /, / b /, / t /).

Stress. The emphasis that syllables have in words (e.g., *transmit´, mu´sic*).

Subject. The noun or pronoun that names the person, place, thing, or idea in a sentence.

Suffix. A word ending that modifies a word's meaning (e.g., *-able, -ed, -ing, -tion*). A suffix can change the meaning or function of a word (e.g., *sad + ly = sadly* = noun + suffix = adverb).

Syllabication. The process of dividing words according to their syllable components.

Syllable. A word or word part that has one vowel sound.

Syllable analysis. The breakdown of words into individual syllables and syllable types (e.g., *basket* is made of two closed syllables: *bas • ket*).

Syllable counting. The division of words into syllables and then counting the syllables.

Syllable division. The dividing of words into separate syllables using rule-governed principles.

Synonym. A word that has the same or similar meaning as another word (e.g., *big/huge, quick/fast, fix/repair*).

Syntax. The set of rules for forming grammatical sentences.

Tense. A grammatical category for verbs that is used to express distinctions between periods of time.

Trigraph. A three-letter **grapheme** that represents one sound (e.g., *-tch* as in *match*).

Venn diagram. An illustration using closed circles to demonstrate the relationship between elements or groups of elements that share properties in common.

Verb. A part of speech that describes an action or a state of being.

Vowel. A speech sound in which the airflow is open. Vowels are **a**, **e**, **i**, **o**, **u**, and sometimes **y**.

Word pair. Two words that are somehow associated or related. They can be **antonyms**, **synonyms**, or **attributes**. The symbol : joins the two words (e.g., *first : last*).

Writing. The act of using symbols to encode spoken language.

PHONOLOGY SCOPE AND SEQUENCE

Book A

Unit	Phonology Concepts	
1	short /a/:	(bat)
	m	(mat, bam)
	s	(sat, cats)
	t	(tam, mat)
	c	(cat)
	f	(fat)
	b	(bat, tab)
2	n	(nap, tan)
	l	(lab, pal)
	h	(hat)
	r	(rat)
	j	(jam)
	p	(pat, tap)
	s for /z/	(has)
3	short /i/:	(dim)
	g	(gab, dig)
	d	(dip, bad)
	v	(vat)
4	k	(kid)
	-ck	(back)
	w	(wig)
	y	(yap)
	z	(zip)
5	short /o/:	(hop)
	o for /aw/	(off, toss)
	-ss	(pass)
	-ll	(doll)
	-ff	(miff)
	-zz	(jazz)
6	qu for /kw/	(quit)
	x for /ks/	(tax)

Book B

Unit	Phonology Concepts	
7	short /e/:	(bed)
	x for /gz/	(exam)
8	ng	(sing)
	nk	(bank)
	ch	(chin, such)
	th	(thin, math)
	th	(this)
	sh	(ship, gosh)
	wh	(when)
	-tch	(hatch)
	-ch	(chin, rich)
9	short /u/:	(sun)
	o for short /u/	(come)
	u for /ʌ/	(put)
10	**Spelling** final silent -e:	
	a_e	(make)
	e_e	(Pete)
	i_e	(side)
	o_e	(rode)
	u_e	(cube)
11	**Initial blends:**	
	w blends:	(twin, swam)
	l blends:	(black, flat, clam, glad, plan, slim)
	r blends:	(brim, crab, drop, fret, grid, prim)
	s blends:	(skill, smash, snap, spot, stand)
	Final blends:	
	-ft:	(drift, soft)
	-mp:	(clumps, pump)
	-sk:	(ask, dusk, whisk)
	-st:	(best, frost, trust)
	-nd:	(blond, grand, sand)
	others:	(act, grasp, kilt, silk)
	Clusters:	
	scar:	(scram, script)
	str:	(strap, string)
	spl:	(splash, split)
	spr:	(sprang, sprint)
12	**Review of Units 7-12**	

Book C

Unit	Phonology Concepts

13	**Syllabication:** words may have one, two, or several syllables
	
	English Syllable Type #1:
	Closed Syllables:
	Introduction of **schwa** phoneme:
	Listening for the unstressed syllable
	
	  a) within words and
	
	  b) within running speech
	
	Shifting the syllable stress = shifting the schwa position (con' vict; con vict')

14	**English syllable type #2:** *-r Controlled Syllables:* (part, form, number, first, fur) o for short /u/ + -er (mother)
15	**English Syllable Type #3:** *Open Syllables:* (over, me, October)
16	**English Syllable Type #4:** *Final Silent -e Syllables:* (inside)
17	**Y in the English Spelling System:** y for long /e/ (body) y for long /i/ (my) y with silent -e (type) y in open syllables (hydrant) short /i/ mid position (system)
18	**Review:** First 4 of the 7 Syllable Types of English **Review:** 8 Inflectional Suffixes of English

Book D

Unit	Phonology Concepts
19	**Phonology Review** **Introduction to Vowel Digraph Syllables:** **ai** for /ā/ (*rain*) **oa** for /ō/ (*boat*) **ee** for /ē/ (*feet*)

20	**Vowel Digraphs:**
	ay for /ā/ (*hay*)
	ea for /ē/ (*bead*)
	    /ā/ (*break*)
	ie for /ē/ (*grieve*)
	    /ī/ (*tie*)
	ey for /ē/ (*key*)
	ow for /ō/ (*low*)
	oe for /ō/ (*hoe*)

21	**Schwa Conditions** 1. When a begins or ends a word of more than one syllable (*amaze*) 2. In the second syllable of a two-syllable word (*pilot*) 3. In an unaccented syllable of a multi-syllable word (*enemy*)
22	**c + -le** **Vowel Digraphs:** **ui** for /ĭ/ (*build*) **ou** for /ŭ/ (*touch*) **ea** for /ĕ/ (*bread*)
23	**Diphthongs oi, oy, ow, ou**
24	**Syllable Type Review**

Book E

Unit	Phonology Concepts	
25	soft **c**	(*city*)
	and **g**	(*germ*)
	-dge for / j /	(*judge*)
26	**o͝o** for / ͻ /	(*book*)
	o͞o for / ͻ /	(*boot*)
	ou for / ͻ /	(*route*)
	ui for / ͻ /	(*fruit*)
	ue for / ͻ /	(*blue*)
27	**Long Vowel Digraphs:**	
	ui for / ī /	(*guide*)
	ou for / ō /	(*soul*)
	ey for / ā /	(*obey*)
	ei for / ē /	(*either*)
	/ ā /	(*rein*)
	ti, ci, xi for / sh /	(*spatial, social, anxious*)
	si, for / zh /	(*vision*)
	English Loan Words (*Romance*)	
	i for / ē /	(*radio*)
	a for / ŏ /	(*father*)
	e for / ā /	(*allegro*)
28	**Phonograms: au, aw, eu, ew**	
	tu for / ch /	(*factual*)
	du for / j /	(*gradual*)
29	**Phonograms wa, al, all, alk, war, wor, qua**	
30	**Summary and Review Unit**	
	ph for / f /	(*phone*)
	gh for / f /	(*tough*)
	sc for / s /	(*science*)
	ch for / k /	(*chord*)
	que for / k /	(*opaque*)
	English Loan Words (*African/Middle Eastern*)	
	Syriac	(*abbey, muslin, etc.*)
	Arabic	(*jar, lute, etc.*)
	Egyptian	(*gum, bark, etc.*)

Book F

Unit	Phonology Concepts	
31	**Review Schwa/focus on -r controlled Phonogram ear**	
	ear/air/ar for /âr/	(*bear, air, care*)
	ar/arr for /ăr/	(*paragraph, arrow*)
	ear for /är/	(*heart*)
	ár/er/err for /ĕr/	(*library, very, berry*)
	oar for /ôr/	(*oar*)
	ear for /ûr/	(*earth*)
	ear/eir/ier/er/eer for /îr/	(*appear, fierce, weird, cereal, cheer*)
	ss/s for / sh /	(*tissue, sugar*)
	s/g for / zh /	(*usual, garage*)
32	**Phonograms -old/olt, -oll/ol, -ost, -ind, -ild**	
	Breaking the rule of short vowels in closed syllables	
	English Loan Words (*Asian*)	
	Cantonese	(*chow, wok, etc*)
	Japanese	(*futon, sushi, etc.*)
	Hindi	(*cot, cushy, etc.*)
33	**Phonograms igh, eigh, ough**	
	eigh for /ā/	(*sleigh*)
	igh for /ī/	(*high*)
	ough for /ō/	(*dough*)
34	**English Loan Words** (*Native American*)	
	Algonquin	(*skunk, woodchuck, etc.*)
	Nahuati	(*chili, tomato, etc.*)
	Tupi	(*cashew, cougar, etc.*)
	wr for /r/	(*wrong*)
	-gn for /n/	(*sign*)
	kn for /n/	(*knock*)
	-mb for /m/	(*comb*)
	rh for /r/	(*rhyme*)
	-mn for /m/	(*hymn*)
	ps for /s/	(*psychology*)
	-lm for /m/	(*calm*)
35	**Polysyllabic Words:**	
	Shifting the syllable stress: watching the schwa move	
36	**Summary and Review Unit**	

Word	Unit	Word	Unit	Word	Unit
a	1	cough	31	how	6
about	8	could	9	I	1
abroad	19	courage	23	into	7
again	16	course	20	iron	22
against	19	curtain	19	is	1
all	7	daughter	33	island	34
almost	10	day	14	journal	22
alone	10	debt	23	journey	22
already	10	dinosaur	33	know	11
also	10	do	2	language	19
although	10	does	4	laugh	17
always	10	door	26	leopard	21
answer	17	down	6	limousine	24
any	8	Dr.	12	listen	24
are	1	each	11	little	14
bargain	34	engine	17	look	13
be	4	every	11	lose	32
beautiful	21	extraordinary	22	machine	25
beauty	21	find	12	many	8
been	9	flood	26	marriage	25
behalf	30	floor	26	may	14
billion	27	for	6	me	6
blood	26	four	26	million	27
body	11	friend	20	mortgage	33
both	32	from	3	most	13
bought	28	gone	13	mountain	30
bouquet	30	good	15	move	32
broad	30	great	15	movement	26
brought	28	guarantee	20	movie	32
bury	31	guard	20	Mr.	12
business	21	guess	20	Mrs.	12
busy	21	guest	20	Ms.	12
buy	31	half	24	naughty	28
call	7	he	4	new	14
captain	19	her	6	ninth	34
carriage	25	herb	23	none	18
caught	28	here	5	now	6
certain	17	honest	23	nuisance	19
clothes	34	honor	23	ocean	33
colleague	22	hour	23	of	3

Word	Unit
often	34
oh	29
oil	17
only	12
opinion	27
our	7
out	8
peculiar	22
penguin	31
people	13
pigeon	25
pint	32
plough	33
poor	17
pour	24
prove	32
region	27
religion	27
right	15
said	2
say	14
see	13
sew	30
she	4
shepherd	30
shoe	25
should	9

Word	Unit
small	7
soldier	31
sound	16
source	28
straight	29
surgeon	25
sword	34
tambourine	24
that	1
the	1
their	7
there	5
these	5
they	3
this	1
those	5
though	15
thought	11
through	15
to	2
today	16
tomorrow	16
tongue	33
too	9
toward	31
two	9
union	27

Word	Unit
very	11
view	28
villain	24
want	16
was	3
water	13
way	14
we	4
were	3
what	3
when	4
where	5
who	2
whole	29
whom	29
whose	29
why	5
wolf	29
women	21
word	8
work	16
would	9
write	8
year	15
you	2
your	2

GUIDE TO ENGLISH ORTHOGRAPHY*
by Louisa C. Moats, *Ed.D.*

Sound-Symbol Correspondence

The English alphabet contains only 26 letters, six of which are used for vowel spellings (a, e, i, o, u, y). However, it has at least 40 speech sounds that must be represented. These are spelled in more than 250 ways. There are more than 1,000 ways depending on the system used for counting correspondences. Letter combinations, of necessity, are used for most of these spellings. A grapheme is a letter or letter combination that corresponds to a speech sound or phoneme; most graphemes are letter combinations. Phonemes are classified as either consonants or vowels; there are 25 consonant phonemes and 15 vowel phonemes (see vowel and consonant phoneme charts, following). There is no one universally accepted delineation of the phonemic or orthographic systems of English, so the one presented here represents a synthesis of several authoritative sources.

Common Spellings for Consonant Phonemes

Phonetic Symbol	Phonic Symbol	Word Examples	Graphemes Used for Spelling
/p/	p	pit	p
/b/	b	bit	b
/m/	m	mitt, comb, hymn	m, mb, mn
/t/	t	tickle, mitt, sipped	t, tt, ed
/d/	d	die, loved	d, ed
/n/	n	nice, knight, gnat	n, kn, gn
/k/	k	cup, kite, duck, chorus, folk, quiet	c, k, ck, ch, lk, q(u)
/g/	g	girl, ghost, fatigue	g, gh, gue
/ŋ/	ng	sing, bank	ng, nk
/f/	f	fluff, sphere, tough, calf	f, ff, ph, gh, lf
/v/	v	van, dove	v, ve
/s/	s	sit, pass, science, psychic	s, ss, sc, ps
/d/	z	zoo, jazz, nose, as, xenon	z, zz, se, s, x
/θ/	th	thin	th
/ə/	th	this	th
/ʃ/	sh	shoe, sure, Chicago, precious, mission, nation	sh, s, ch, ci, si, ti
/ʒ/	zh	measure, azure	s, z
/tʃ/	ch	cheap, etch	ch, tch
/dʒ/	j	judge, giant, wage	j, g, ge, dge
/l/	l	lamb, call, single	l, ll, le
/r/	r	reach, wrap, herd, turn, bird	r, wr, er/ur/ir
/y/	y	you, use, feud, onion	y, u, eu, io
/w/	w	witch, queen, one	w, (q)u, (w)o
/ʰw/ or /ʍ/	wh	where	wh
/h/	h	house, whole	h, wh

* The information in this guide can be found in elaborated form in L.C. Moats (2000), Speech to Print: Language Essentials for Teachers. Baltimore, MD: Paul Brookes. Sections of this summary are used by permission of the publisher.

GUIDE TO ENGLISH ORTHOGRAPHY

Invariant Consonant Correspondences

A few speech sounds are spelled consistently with one letter or letter combination, as follows:

Consonants	Vowels
/b/ = b	/a/ = a
/p/ = p	
/t/ = t	
/d/ = d	
/v/ = v	
/th/ = th	

Variant, Conditional Consonant Correspondences

Most consonant and vowel spellings vary according to the position of the sound in the word or syllable, the phonemes that precede or follow the sound in the syllable, the language from which the word came, and/or the syllable stress. Some consonant spelling generalizations follow:

Phonetic Symbol	Graphemes Used for Spelling	Notes
/m/	mb, mn	These "silent letter" spellings only occur at the ends of words. The **mn** combination is used in words of Greek origin.
/t/	t, tt	The double **tt** is used only at the ends of a few words (**putt**, **butt**, **mutt**).
/n/	kn, gn	These silent letter spellings occur only at the beginnings of words of Anglo-Saxon origin (**knight**, **gnat**).
/ŋ/	n, ng	The **n** spelling for /ng/ is used before the velar consonants /k/ and /g/, as in **lanky** and **language**.
/g/	gh, gue	A family of ghoulish words from Anglo-Saxon uses **gh** initially; a family of French words uses **-gue** in final position (**fatigue**, **intrigue**).
/k/	k, c, ch, ck	/k/ is spelled with a **k** before the vowels **i** and **e**; with a **c** before **a**, **o**, and **u**; with a **ch** in Greek-derived words; and with a **ck** after accented short vowels. The suffix syllable **-ic** ends with a **c** because it is unaccented.
/kw/	qu	This sound combination in the beginnings of words or syllables is spelled **qu**. **Qu** is the only two-letter spelling unit that works together to spell two unique sounds. The letter **u** stands for the consonant /w/ here, as it does in **assuage**.
/f /	ff, ph, gh	A double **ff** is used after short, accented vowels (**puff**, **stiff**); a **ph** is used in Greek-derived words (**chlorophyll**); and a **gh** is used at the ends of a few Anglo-Saxon words (**laugh**, **tough**).
/tʃ/	ch, tch	The **-tch** is used after stressed, short vowels (**batch**, **ketch**, **ditch**, **blotch**, **butcher**) but the **-ch** is used after long vowels or after consonants (**pouch**, **pooch**, **punch**, **purchase**).
/dʒ/	dge, ge	At the ends of words, /dʒ/ is spelled **-dge** after stressed, short vowels but is spelled **-ge** after long vowels or schwa (**badge**, **edge**, **ridge**, **lodge**, **budge**; **wage**, **village**, **stooge**).

The Letter y

The letter **y** has four jobs in English orthography: It represents three vowels and one consonant. The consonant is the glide /y/, as in **yellow** and **yes**. The vowels are /e/ as in baby and **lady**; /I/ as in gym and chlorophyll; and /ai/ as in **cry, by, sly, try**.

The Letter w

The letter **w** represents a consonant in the category of glides. The position is a rounding of the lips with the tongue retracted to the back of the mouth. It is difficult to segment a glide from the vowel that always follows it. The letter **w** is also used as part of some vowel graphemes (**ow, ew, aw**), but it is never classified as a vowel letter by itself. Children often confuse it with **y**, because the letter name **y** starts with the same sound as the sound represented by **w**.

The Letter x

The letter **x** most often represents the /**k** + **s**/ combination when it is used after a vowel. It is the only single letter used to represent two speech sounds. If it begins a word, it represents /z/ in English.

Vowel Spelling Generalizations

Vowel spellings are much less predictable than consonant spellings. Although the short vowels are much more predictable for spelling purposes than the long vowels, many long vowel spellings are pattern-based, as follows:

Vowel Phoneme	Spellings				Examples
	Open syllable, ending with a long vowel	Middle of a syllable, vowel team, or vowel + consonant + **e**	End of a word	Other, less common spellings	
/i/ (long **e**)	e	ee, ea	y	ei, ie, ey, e-e	fever, see, sea, baby, piece, deceive, key, Pete
/e/ (long a)	a	a-e, ai	ay	ei, eigh, ey, ea	savor, date, bail, pay, vein, eight, they, great
/ai/ (long i)	I	i-e, igh	y	ie, y-e, ind, ild	bicycle, rice, fight, cry, pie, find, wild
/o/ (long **o**)	o	o-e, oa	ow	oe old, ost, ough	potion, stoke, boat, flow, toe, bold, most, though
/u/ (long **u** and **yu**)	u	u-e	ew	ue, ui, eu	ruby, music; flute, cute; chew, few; blue; suit; euphonic
/ɔ/ (aw)	—	au (**aw** before **n** and **l**)	aw	a, alk, all, augh	applaud, paw, pawn, crawl, water, talk, tall, caught
/ɔi/ (diphthong)	—	oi	oy		boisterous, boil, coy, toy
/æw/	—	ou (**ow** before **n**, **l**, and sometimes **d**)	ow		shout, ground, crown, crowd, owl

Seven Types of Syllables in English Orthography

The seven types of English syllables are:

Syllable Type	Examples	Definition
Closed	**dap**ple **hos**tel **bev**erage	A syllable with a short vowel sound, ending in one or more consonants.
r- controlled	**spur**ious con**sort** **char**ter	Any syllable in which the vowel is followed by an /r/. Vowel pronunciation often changes before /r/.
Open	**pro**gram **ta**ble **re**cent	A syllable that ends with a long vowel sound that is spelled with a single vowel letter.
Vowel + Consonant + **e** (**vc** + **e**)	com**pete** des**pite** con**flate**	A syllable that has a long vowel sound and is spelled with a vowel, a consonant, and silent **-e**.
*Vowel Digraph (Team)	**awe**some **train**er con**geal**	Syllables with long or short vowel spellings that use a vowel team or digraph.
Consonant + **le**	bi**ble** bea**gle** lit**tle**	An unaccented final syllable containing a consonant before /l/, followed by a silent **e**.
*Diphthong	**spoil**age **lou**d	Diphthongs /ɔi/ and /æw/ are included in this category. Diphthong is a term that is used to refer to a vowel sound that glides in the middle.

Some unstressed and odd syllables, such as **-age** in verbiage, **-ture** in sculpture, and **-tion** in adoration, do not fit into these six main categories. Following are some exceptions in which initial sounds change to /sh/ and /ch/:

Add this beginning ...	... to this ending, and see the sound pattern change.					
	-al	**-on**	**-an**	**-ence**	**-ent**	**-ous**
ci-	special	suspicion	magician	conscience	prescient	spacious
ti-	spatial	nation	Martian	patience	patient	pretentious
si-		mission				
su-	usual					sensuous
tu-	mutual		gargantuan			impetuous

Orthographic Rules and Spelling Conventions

Some general conventions of English:

- Some letters in English can never be doubled within a syllable or between syllables, such as **j, y, i** (exception: **skiing**), and **k** (exception: **bookkeeper**).

- Consonant digraphs (**sh, th, wh, ch, sh, ng, ph, gh**) act as relational units and spell single speech sounds; they also cannot be doubled.

- A doubled consonant or its substitute must intervene between a stressed short vowel syllable and an inflected ending beginning with a vowel (grabbing; **drugged**). The complex spellings **ck, dge, tch,** and **x** replace or act as doubled consonants after short vowels, in words such as **picnicking, dodger, pitching,** and **boxer,** and they signal that the vowel is short. (Exceptions to the **tch** generalization: **much, rich, which, such, bachelor**).

- Long vowel sounds can never be spelled with single vowel letters before the complex consonant units **ck, dge, tch,** and **x**.

- Some letters in English are never used in the final position in a word, particularly **j** and **v**. Thus, the permissible spellings for word-final /dʒ/ are **dge** and **ge**. In words ending with /v/ such as **love, have, sieve, live, dove, leave,** and **salve,** the marker **e** is placed at the end of the word so that it does not violate the **v** rule, regardless of the pronunciation of the vowel. In this way, then, all the v words are predictable—not according to sound-symbol correspondence necessarily, but according to orthographic convention.

- The letter **e** has several uses in orthography. Sometimes it acts a relational unit; that is, it represents phonemes directly (**wet; be**), and sometimes it acts as a marker within a larger orthographic pattern (**spade, enrage**). The letter **e** indicates when a vowel is long, as in **drape** and **probe**. It also indicates when a **c** or a **g** should have its "soft" sound, as in **stooge, receive,** and **nice**. It is also placed at the ends of words with final /s/ to keep them from looking like plurals, not to mark the vowel (**please,** not **pleas; horse,** not **hors; mouse,** not **mous**).

- The letter **u** is a marker in words such as guest and guide. If it did not intervene between the **g** and the **e** or **i** to follow, the **g** would have its soft sound /dʒ/.

The Ending Rules

There are three major orthographic rules that govern addition of endings onto words of certain syllable types. They are applicable for both reading and spelling. These rules are much easier to learn and teach if syllable constructions are already understood. The rules are:

1a. Consonant Doubling: When a one-syllable word with one vowel ends in one consonant, double the final consonant before adding a suffix beginning with a vowel (**wettest, sinner, crabbing**). Do not double the word's final consonant if the suffix begins with a consonant. (See Unit 9 Map.)

1b. Advanced Consonant Doubling: When a word has more than one syllable, and if the final syllable is accented and has one vowel followed by one consonant, double the final consonant when adding an ending beginning with a vowel (**labored** vs. **remitted; signaling** vs. **imbedded**).

2. Drop Silent -e: When a root word ends in a silent e, drop the e when adding a suffix beginning with a vowel. Keep the e before a suffix beginning with a consonant (**blaming, confinement, extremely, pasted**). (See Unit 23 Map.)

3. Change y to i: When a root ends in a **y** preceded by a consonant, change **y** to i before a suffix, except **-ing**. If the root word ends in a y preceded by a vowel (**ay, ey, uy, oy**), just add the suffix without changing any letters. Note that **y** changes to i even if the suffix begins with a consonant. (See Unit 23 Map.)

---

*Vowel teams and diphthong syllables are sometimes combined into a single category of syllable called double vowel. When this occurs, there are six syllable types.

The Layers of English Orthography

Beyond the sound-symbol system that characterizes our base vocabulary, syllable structures and the meaningful units of words (morphemes) are represented in the English spelling system. The content words of expository text at the middle grade levels and beyond are derived primarily from the Latin and Greek layers of English, each of which has a characteristic structure. Latin-based words are usually composed of a root (e.g., tract, fer), a suffix, and/or a prefix. Derivational morphemes include suffixes that, when added to the base word or root, change the part of speech of the word (tractor, traction, attract, detractable).

Language of Origin	Letter-Sound Correspondences	Syllable Patterns	Morpheme Patterns
Anglo-Saxon	Consonants: • Single • Blends • Digraphs (examples: mad, step, that) Vowels: • Short • Long (**vce**) • Teams • Diphthong • **r-** controlled (examples:, pin/pine, part, coin, peach)	• Closed • Open • vce • **r-** controlled • c + le • Vowel team • Syllables with schwa phoneme (examples: rabbit, silver, hobo, cabin, turtle, poem)	Compounds (examples: highlight, scatterbrain, railroad) Inflections: **-ed**, **-s**, **-ing**, **-er**, **-est** (examples: get, forget, forgetting)
Romance (Latin)		Syllables with a schwa phoneme are common in derivational words (example: define—definition)	• Prefixes (**mis-**, **in-**) • Suffixes (**-ment**, **-ary**) • Roots (**-fer**, **-tract**) (examples: erupting, conductor, infer) • Plurals (examples: curricula, alumnae)
Greek	• /l/ = y (gym, symphony) • /k/= ch (chorus) • /f/= ph (photo)		Combining forms (examples: biography, micrometer) • Plurals (examples: crises, metamorphoses)

PROGRESSION OF DIAGRAMMING

Sentence Pattern #1

Form: Noun / Verb

Function: Subject / Predicate

(red) **Doctors**	*(purple)* **heal**

Sentence Pattern #2

Form: Noun / Verb / Noun

Function: Subject / Predicate / Direct object

(red) **Doctors**	*(purple)* **heal**	*(blue)* **patients**

Sentence Pattern #3

Form: Noun + Noun / Verb

Function: Subject + Subject / Predicate

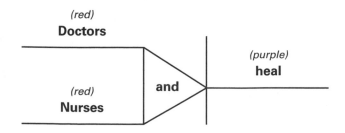

Color-coding Diagrams:

Simple subject	red
Simple predicate	purple
Direct object	blue
Indirect object	green
Adjective	orange
Adverb	teal
Prepositional Phrases:	
Acting as adjectives	orange
Acting as adverbs	teal
Function words (conjunctions, interjections, etc.):	black

Note: *Diagramming is an instructional means to teach word function in sentences. Color-coding is by function, rather than by form. For example, there is no color for noun, since a noun can have several different functions in a sentence.*

Sentence Pattern #4

Form: Noun / Verb + Verb

Function: Subject / Predicate + Predicate

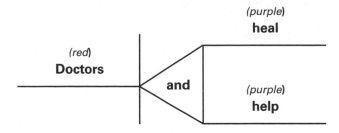

Sentence Pattern #5

Form: Noun / Verb / Noun + Noun

Function: Subject / Predicate / Direct object + Direct Object

Sentence Pattern #6

Form: Noun + Verb + Noun + Verb

Function: Subject + Predicate + Subject + Predicate

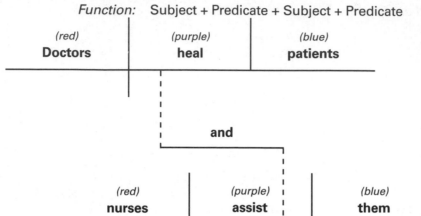

Sentence Pattern #7

Form: Noun / Linking Verb / Noun

Function: Subject / Predicate / Predicate Nominative

Sentence Pattern #8

Form: Noun/Verb/Noun/Noun

Function: Subject/Predicate/Indirect Object/Direct Object

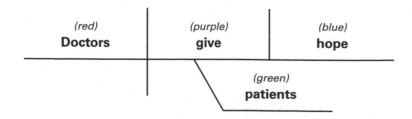

SIGNAL WORDS BASED ON BLOOM'S TAXONOMY

Category	Meaning	Location
Remember	Retrieve relevant knowledge from long-term memory.	**Units 7–8**
state	say or write specific information	**Unit 7**
recognize	use information you have learned	
name	label specific information	
locate	find specific information or show the position of something	
list	state a series of names, ideas, or events	
choose	make choices from specific information	
describe	state detailed information about an idea or concept	**Unit 8**
Understand	Construct meaning from instructional messages, including oral, written, and graphic communication.	**Units 9–12**
tell	say or write specific information	**Unit 9**
define	tell the meaning put together to reach our understanding about something	
predict	use known information to say what might happen in the future	
conclude	put information together to reach an understanding about something	
illustrate	present an example or explanation in pictures or words	
identify	give the name of something or select information from the text	**Unit 10**
explain	express understanding of an idea or concept	**Unit 10**
tell when	state a specific time or a period of time	**Unit 10**
discuss	present detailed information or examine a subject	**Unit 10**
paraphrase	restate information in different words to clarify meaning	**Unit 10**
contrast	state the differences between two or more ideas or concepts	**Unit 11**
categorize	create groups and place information into those gorups based on certain shared characteristics	**Unit 11**
compare	state the similarities between two or more ideas or concepts	**Unit 11**
sort	place or separate into groups	**Unit 11**
match	put together or connect things that are alike or similar	**Unit 12**
classify	arrange or organize information into groups with similar characteristics	**Unit 12**

Category	Meaning	Location
Apply	Carry out or use a procedure in a given situation.	**Units 13–15**
generalize	draw a conclusion based on presented information	Unit 13
infer	provide a logical conclusion using information or evidence	
show	demonstrate an understanding of information	Unit 14
use	apply a procedure	
Analyze	Break material into its constituent parts and determine how the parts relate to one another and to an overall structure or purpose.	**Units 16–18**
select	choose from among alternatives	Unit 16
distinguish	find differences which set one thing apart from another	
organize	arrange in a systematic pattern	Unit 17
outline	arrange information into a systematic pattern of main ideas and supporting details	
Evaluate	Require judgments based on criteria and standards.	**Units 19–21**
assess	determine value or significance	Unit 19
justify	prove or give reasons that something is right or valid	
critique	examine positive and negative features to form a judgment	Unit 20
judge	form an opinion or estimation after careful consideration	
Create	Assemble elements to form a whole or product; reorganize elements into a new pattern or structure.	**Units 22–24**
compose	make or create by putting parts or elements together	Unit 22
design	devise a procedure to do a task	
plan	make or create by putting parts or elements together	
hypothesize	formulate a possible explanation; speculate	Unit 23
revise	modify or change a plan or product	

Ackerman, P.T., & Dykman, R.A. (1996). The speed factor and learning disabilities: The toll of slowness in adolescents. *Dyslexia, 2,* 1–21.

Adams, M.J. (1997) About the NICHD program of research on reading development and disorders. *The International Dyslexia Association.* Baltimore, MD: Perspectives.

Anderson, L.W., & Krathwohl, D.R. (Eds.) (2001). *A taxonomy for learning, teaching, and assessing: A revision of Bloom's Taxonomy of Educational Objectives.* Addison Wesley Longman, Inc.

Bear, D., Invernizzi, M, Templeton, S., & Johnson, F. (2003). *Words their way.* (3rd Ed.) Upper Saddle River, NJ: Prentice Hall.

Beck, I.L., & McKeown, M.G. (1991). Conditions of vocabulary acquisition. In R. Barr, M. Kamil, P. Mosenthal, & P.D. Pearson (Eds.). *Handbook of reading research, Vol. II* (pp. 789–814). White Plains, NY: Longman.

Ben Ari, R., & Shafir, D. (1988). *Social integration in elementary school.* Ramat-Gan, Israel: Institute for the Advancement of Social Integration in the Schools, Bar Han University.

Berninger, V. (1999). Coordinating transcription and text generation in working memory during composing: Automatized and constructive processes. *Learning Disability Quarterly, 22,* 99–112.

Berninger, V.W., & Richards, T.L. (2002). *Brain literacy for educators and psychologists.* Amsterdam: Academic Press.

Biancarosa, G., & Snow, C.E. (2004.). *Reading next: a vision for action and research in middle and high school literacy: A report from Carnegie Corporation of New York.* Washington, DC: Alliance for Excellent Education.

Biemiller, A. (1999). *Language and reading success.* Cambridge, MA: Brookline Books.

Blevins, W. (2001). *Teaching phonics and word study in the intermediate grades.* New York: Scholastic.

California Department of Education (1999). *Reading/language arts framework for California Public Schools.* (Eds.). E.J. Kame'enui & D.C. Simmons Sacramento: California Department of Education.

Catts, H.W., Fey, M.E., Zhang, X. & Tomblin, J.B. (1999). Language basis of reading and reading disabilities: evidence from a longitudinal investigation. *Scientific Studies of Reading, 3,* 331–361.

Celce-Murcia, M., Brinton, D.M., & Goodwin, J.M. (1996/2002). *Teaching pronunciation: A reference for teachers of English to speakers of other languages.* Cambridge, UK: Cambridge University Press.

Chun, D.M. (1988). The neglected role of intonation and communicative competence and proficiency. *The Modern Language Journal, 72,* (3): 295-303.

Cunningham, A.E., & Stanovich, K.E. (1997). Early reading acquisition and its relation to reading experience and ability ten years later. *Developmental Psychology, 33,* 934–945.

Curtis, M. (2004.) Adolescents who struggle with word identification: Research and practice. In T. Jetton and J. Dole (Eds.). *Adolescent literacy research and practice.* New York: Guilford.

Curtis, M.E., & Longo, A.M. (1999). *When adolescents can't read: methods and materials that work.* Cambridge, MA: Brookline Books.

Dahloff, M. (1971). *Ability grouping, content validity, and curriculum process analysis.* New York. Teachers College Press.

Dole, J.A., Sloan, C., & Trathen, W. (1995). Teaching vocabulary within the context of literature. *Journal of Reading, 38* (6).

Ehri, L.C., & Soffer, A.G. (1999). Graphophonemic awareness: development in elementary students. *Scientific Studies of Reading, 3,* 1–30.

Fletcher, J., & Lyon., G.R. (1998). Reading: a research-based approach. In W. Evers' (Ed.). *What's gone wrong in America's classrooms? (pp. 49–90).* Stanford, CA: Hoover Institution Press.

Fletcher, J.M., Shaywitz, S.E., Shankweiler, D.P., Katz, L., Liberman, I.Y., Stuebing, K.K., Francis, D.J., Fowler, A.E., & Shaywitz., B.A. (1994). Cognitive profiles of reading disability: Comparisons of discrepancy and low achievement definitions. *Journal of Educational Psychology, 86,* 6–23.

Fry, E.B., Kress, J.E., & Fountoukidis, D.L. (2000). *The reading teacher's book of lists.* Paramus, NJ: Prentice Hall.

Fuchs, L.S., Deno, S.L., & Mirkin, P.K. (1984) The effects of frequent curriculum-based measurement and evaluation on pedagogy, student achievement, and student awareness of learning. *American Educational Research Journal, 21,* 440-60.

Gillon, G., & Dodd, B. (1995). The effects of training phonological, semantic, and syntactic processing skills in spoken language on reading ability. *Language, Speech, and Hearing Services in the Schools, 26,* 58–68.

Goldman, S.R., & Rakestraw, J.A. (2000). Structural aspects of constructing meaning from text. In M. Kamil, P.B. Mosenthal, P.D. Pearson, & R. Barr (Eds.). *Handbook of Reading Research, Volume 3* (pp. 311–335). Mahwah, NJ: Erlbaum.

Good, R.H., Simmons, D.C., & Kame'enui, E.J. (2001). The importance and decision-making utility of a continuum of fluency-based indicators of foundational reading skills for third-grade high-stakes outcomes. *Scientific Studies of Reading, 5,* 257–288.

Graham, S., Harris, K.R., and Loynachan, C. (1993). The basic spelling vocabulary list. *Journal of Educational Research. 86,* 363–368.

Henry, M. (1997). The decoding/spelling continuum: Integrated decoding and spelling instruction from pre-school to early secondary school. *Dyslexia, 3,* 178–189.

Jones, J., & Stone, C.A. (1989). Metaphor comprehension by language learning disabled and normally achieving adolescent boys. *Learning Disability Quarterly, 12,* 251–260.

Kamil, M. (2004). *Adolescents and Literacy: Reading for the 21st century.* Washington, DC: Alliance for Excellent Education.

Kulik, J. & Kulik, C. (1991). *Research on ability grouping: Historical and contemporary perspectives.* Storrs, CT: University of Connecticut, National Research Center for the Gifted and Talented. (ERIC Document Reproduction Service No. ED350777)

Longo, A.M. (2001). Perspectives: Improving comprehension and comprehension instruction. *The International Dyslexia Association Quarterly, 27,* 29–31.

Lou ,Y., Abrami, P., Spence, J, Poulsen, C., Chambers, B., & d'Apollonia, S. (1996). Within-class grouping: A meta-analysis. *Review of Educational Research. 66,* 423–458.

Lyon, G.R. (1995). Toward a definition of dyslexia. *Annals of Dyslexia, 45,* 3–27.

Mastropieri, M., & Scruggs, T. (1997). Best practices in promoting reading comprehension in students with learning disabilities: 1976 to 1996. *Remedial and Special Education, 18* (4), 197–213.

Mather, N., Hammill, D., Allen, E., & Roberts, R. (2004). *Test of silent word reading fluency (TOSWRF).* Austin, TX: PRO-ED.

McCardle, P., & Chhabra, V. (Eds.) (2004). *The voice of evidence in reading research.* Baltimore, MD: Brookes.

Moats, L.C. (1996). Phonological spelling errors in the writing of dyslexic adolescents. *Reading and Writing: An Interdisciplinary Journal, 8,* 105–119.

Moats, L.C. (2000). *Speech to print: Language essentials for teachers.* Baltimore, MD: Paul H. Brookes.

Moats, L.C., & Smith, C. (1992). Derivational morphology: why it should be included in assessment and instruction. *Language, Speech, and Hearing in the Schools, 23,* 312–319.

Nation, Paul. 1990. *Teaching and learning vocabulary.* New York: New York. Newbury House.

National Center for Education Statistics. (NCES, 2003). *National assessment of educational progress: The nation's report card* (NCESS Publication No. 2003-524). Jessup, MD: Institute for Education Sciences, U.S. Department of Education.

National Reading Panel. (2000). Teaching children to read: An evidence-based assessment of the scientific research literature on reading and its implications for reading instruction. Washington, DC: National Institute of Child Health and Human Development.

Nippold, M.A. (1998). *Later language development: The school-age and adolescent years.* Austin, TX: PRO-ED.

Oakes, J. (1985). *Keeping track: How schools structure inequality.* New Haven, CT: Yale University Press.

Pike, M. (1945). *The intonation of American English.* Ann Arbor: The University of Michigan Press.

Pressley, M., & Wharton-McDonald, R. (1997). Skilled comprehension and its development through instruction. *School Psychology Review, 26,* 448–467.

Rose, K. R., & Kasper, G. (Eds.). (2001). *Pragmatics in language teaching.* Cambridge, UK: Cambridge University Press.

Shankweiler, D., Crane, S., Katz, L., Fowler, A.E., Liberman, A.M., Brady, S.A., Thornton, R., Lindquist, E., Dreyer, L.G., Fletcher, J.M., Stuebing, K.K., Shaywitz, S.E., & Shaywitz, B.A. (1995). Cognitive profiles of reading-disabled children: comparison of language skills in phonology, morphology, and syntax. *Psychological Science, 6,* 149–56.

Shankweiler, D., Lundquist, E., Dreyer, L.G., & Dickinson, C.C. (1996). Reading and spelling difficulties in high school students: Causes and consequences. *Reading and Writing: An Interdisciplinary Journal, 8,* 267–294.

Shankweiler, D., Lundquist, E., Katz, L., Stuebing, K.K., Fletcher, J.M., Brady, S., Fowler, A., Dreyer, L.G., Marchione, K.E., Shaywitz, S.E., & Shaywitz, B.A. (1999). Comprehension and decoding: patterns of association in children with reading difficulties. *Scientific Studies of Reading, 31,* 24–53, 69–94.

Shaywitz, S.E. (2003). *Overcoming dyslexia: A new and complete science-based program for reading problems at any level.* NY: Knopf.

Shaywitz, S.E., Fletcher, J. M., Holahan, J.M., Shneider, A. E., Marchione, K. E., Stuebing, K. K., et al. (1999). Persistence of dyslexia: the Connecticut longitudinal study at adolescence. *Pediatrics, 104,* 1351-59.

Stahl, S.A. (1998). Teaching children with reading problems to decode: phonics and "non-phonics" instruction. *Reading and Writing Quarterly: Overcoming Learning Difficulties, 14* (2), 165–188.

Stanovich, K.E. and Siegel, L.S. (1994). Phenotypic performance of children with reading disability: A regression-based model test of phonological-core variable-difference model. *Journal of Educational Psychology, 86* (1), 24–54.

Stone, B. & Brady, S. (1995). Evidence of phonological processing deficits in less-skilled readers. *Annals of Dyslexia, 45,* 51–78.

Swan, M., & Smith, B. (Eds.). (2001). *Learner English* (2nd ed.). Cambridge, UK: Cambridge University Press

Swanson, H.L. (1999). Reading research intervention for students with LD: A meta-analysis of intervention outcomes. *Journal of Learning Disabilities, 32,* 504–532.

Taylor, B.M. & Beach, R.W. (1984). The effects of text structure instruction on middle-grade students' comprehension and production of expository text. *Reading Research Quarterly, 19,* 135–146

Templeton, S., & Morris., D. (2000). Spelling. In M. Kamil, P.B. Mosenthal, P.D. Pearson, & R. Barr (Eds.). *Handbook of Reading Research, Volume III* (pp. 525–543), White Plains, NY: Longman.

Torgesen, J.K., Alexander, A.W., Wagner, R.K., Rashotte, C.A., Voeller, K., Conway, T., & Rose, E. (2001). Intensive remedial instruction for children with severe reading disabilities: Immediate and long-term outcomes from two instructional approaches. *Journal of Learning Disabilities, 34,* 33–58.

Torgesen, J.K., Wagner, R.K., Rashotte, C.A., Alexander, AW, & Conway, T. (1997). Preventive and remedial interventions for children with severe reading disabilities. *Learning Disabilities: A Multidisciplinary Journal, 8,* 5–61.

Touchstone Applied Science Associates, Inc. (2000). Degrees of reading power (*DRP) handbook: J & K test forms.* Brewster, NY: Author.

Wagner, R., & Barker, T. (1994). The development of orthographic processing ability. In V. Berninger (ed.). *The Varieties of Orthographic Knowledge I: Theoretical and Developmental Issues* (pp. 243–276). Dordrecht, The Netherlands: Kluwer.

West, A. 1953. *A general service list of English words.* London: Longman.

Westby, C. (2004). Assessing and facilitating text comprehension problems. In H.W. Catts & AG Kamhi (Eds.). *Language and Reading Disabilities* (2nd Ed.) Boston: Allyn and Bacon.

Williams, J. (1998). Improving the comprehension of disabled readers. *Annals of Dyslexia, 48,* 213–238.

GLOSSARY OF
WHY DO/HOW TO ACTIVITIES

New instructional activities in *LANGUAGE!* are introduced with a Why Do/How To explanation.

- The rationale for the activity is provided in the Why Do.

- The How To explains the steps to do the activity.

This glossary presents all *LANGUAGE!* instructional activities listed in alphabetical order and accompanied by their Why Do/How To explanations. This list also indicates the Unit, Lesson, and Step in which each activity first appears in the curriculum with the Why Do/How To explanation. Subsequent uses of an activity do not repeat the Why Do/How To explanation; the rationale and method for doing any particular activity remain the same for subsequent uses even though the content of the activity changes according to the content focus of the unit.

Table of Contents

Table of Contents *(continued)*

Table of Contents (continued)

Add It

Book B, Unit 7, Lesson 3

Why Do: Students need to develop word analysis skills so that when they add an ending to a word, they spell the new word correctly.

How To: A variety of activities guide students to analyze words to determine the correct spelling when adding endings. These activities range from discoveries structured by questions or steps, which guide students to see when a rule needs to be applied, to activities structured by a template. Each type of activity helps students analyze both the base word and the suffix to determine if letters need to be doubled, dropped, or changed before adding the ending.

From *Transparencies and Templates*, page 1

Add It

Write the Base + Suffix										
No Rule										
Words ending in "y"										
vce Words — Don't Drop the e										
vce Words — Drop the e										
1-1-1 — Don't Double										
1-1-1 — Double										
Write the Suffix										

Anchor the Word

Book A, Unit 1, Lesson 1

Why Do: Students benefit from the use of kinesthetic procedures, which anchor each phoneme or word being studied into their memories and which establish a rhythm to the drill.

How To: Most phonemic awareness drills use this arm motion and related procedure:

- Hold your left arm out to the side, elbow bent, and hand in a fist with the palm side facing students. Have students mirror your arm position.

- Say the target phoneme or word while students listen and watch.

- Lower your bent elbow a few inches to signal students to respond. Have students make the same motion with their right arms as they repeat the phoneme or word.

- Repeat the phoneme or word two times.

Answer It

Book A, Unit 1, Lesson 3

Why Do: Students become more successful at answering questions after they have received direct instruction in how to formulate a response that specifically addresses a particular question.

How To: This activity uses the following process to help students formulate appropriate oral and written responses to questions:

- Explain the meaning of each of the signal words in the unit.

- Model the process of using a signal word to formulate a response to an **Answer It** question.

    1. Write the question on the board or on an overhead transparency.

    2. Identify and underline the signal word.

    3. Review the type of information required to respond to the question.

    4. Demonstrate using the text headings or other text features to identify the content for the answer.

    5. Reread the section to retrieve information, if needed.

    6. Use the signal word and the question to formulate a response.

    7. Have students answer the question orally and then write the response in the *Interactive Text* exercise or on a piece of paper.

Bank It

Book A, Unit 1, Lesson 2

Why Do: Having students compile and add to a list of words studied provides cumulative evidence of learning progress.

How To: This activity asks students to record new vocabulary in a **Word Bank**. Formats for word banks depend on students' ages and the pace of their learning. Word bank formats include individual index cards on a ring, the **Bank It** section of the *Interactive Text*, chart paper, or a word wall.

Blueprint for Reading

Book A, Unit 1, Lesson 5

Why Do: Examining text structure helps students improve comprehension and prepare for writing tasks. Students become better writers if they are given the opportunity to examine the work of other writers.

How To: In the **Blueprint for Reading** process, students mark up text using a coding system (colors and icons) to identify the underlying structure of the text. (The coding system is the same one used for the **Blueprint for Writing** to reinforce the reciprocal relationship of the reading-writing process.) The **Blueprint for Reading** process is taught gradually, using a variety of text structures and their respective transition words.

- Ask students to refer to the **Blueprint for Reading** in the *Interactive Text*. (The Instructional Text is reprinted in the *Interactive Text* for this activity.)

- Introduce the concept of the **Blueprint for Reading** as follows: Identifying the text structure in a reading selection is like looking at the blueprint for a completed house. The reading selection was written with a particular structure, or "blueprint," in mind. Finding that structure helps the reader understand the selection. It also helps organize information from which to write.

- Have students:

  1. Read through the entire paragraph or paragraphs.

  2. Identify the **main points** or **categories** of information in the paragraph(s). Use a blue highlighter or pencil to mark these points in the text.

  3. Find and circle the transition words in blue. These signal the structure of the text.

  4. Identify the **examples**, **explanations**, and **supporting evidence** for the main points. Use a pink highlighter or pencil to mark this information.

Blueprint for Writing

Book A, Unit 1, Lesson 5

Why Do: Graphic organizers help students gather information from listening or reading, organize the information or ideas, and make a plan for writing.

How To: Students record information from the selection on the graphic organizer, and then use the completed graphic organizer to write paragraphs or longer compositions.

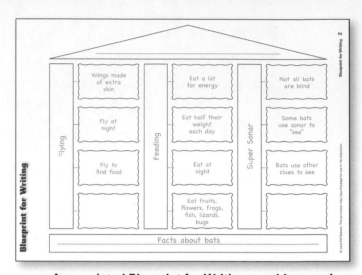

A completed Blueprint for Writing graphic organizer from Book A. A blank graphic organizer can be found in ***Transparencies and Templates*, page 2**

- Display the **Blueprint for Writing** transparency using the overhead projector. The specific steps are mapped out in each unit.

- Introduce the graphic organizer to students as follows:

  1. A paragraph is like a house. It has a **topic sentence**, which is like the **floor** or base of a house. The topic sentence supports the contents of the whole paragraph in the same way that a floor supports the whole house. You can use a brown marker to write the topic sentence on the floor of the house.

  2. Next, there are **key points** or **main ideas** that attach to or build from the floor. These are like the building's **walls**. All walls must be connected to the floor, as all attached points must logically attach to the idea in the topic sentence. Use a blue marker to write the key points or main ideas on the walls of the house.

  3. Just as a blank wall is boring, a paragraph that gives only the topic and key points lacks interest and information. **Examples**, **explanations**, and **supporting evidence** in a paragraph are like **pictures** on the walls. They add interest. Use a pink marker to write examples, explanations, and supporting evidence in the picture frames.

  4. Finally, a paragraph has a **conclusion.** This is the **roof** on the house. The conclusion must cover the contents of the paragraph in the same way as the topic sentence, though it would not be worded exactly the same. Use a green marker to write the conclusion on the roof of the house.

  5. Each of these components of a paragraph are present in well-written text that we read. They must also be present in what we write.

Blueprint for Writing: Outline with Icons

Why Do: Graphic organizers help students gather information from listening or reading, organize the information or ideas, and make a plan for writing.

How To: The **Blueprint for Writing** outline with icons serves as a bridge from the **Blueprint for Writing** graphic organizer to an outline format. The icons on the outline correspond to the elements of the graphic organizer. Students use the outline to record information from reading material (e.g., information highlighted in the **Blueprint for Reading** activity) in the same way that they use the graphic organizer. Students then use the information they have recorded to write paragraphs, essays, or reports. The specific steps are mapped out in each unit.

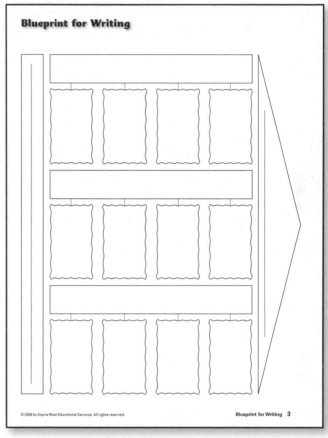

Blueprint for Writing

Blueprint for Writing **3**

From *Transparencies and Templates*, page 3

Blueprint for Writing: Outline

Book C, Unit 13, Lesson 4

Why Do: Graphic organizers help students gather information from listening or reading, organize the information or ideas, and make a plan for writing.

How To: The **Blueprint for Writing** outline without icons functions as a more conventional organizing device. The outline provides a plan for writing, much like a blueprint is a plan for building a house. The outline organizes information into a hierarchy. With an understanding of the outline structure based on the previous formats of the **Blueprint for Writing**, students use it to record information from reading material. Students then use the information they have recorded to write paragraphs, essays, or reports. The specific steps are mapped out in each unit.

1. **Topic:** The topic becomes the basis for the topic sentence or thesis paragraph. All contents of the paragraph or essay relate to the topic.

2. **Main Ideas:** The main ideas, or key points, expand the topic. Each main idea must be connected to the topic. The main ideas are written next to Roman numerals on the outline. (Main ideas are highlighted in blue on the Blueprint for Reading.)

3. **Details:** Details elaborate on the main ideas. The details can be in the form of examples, explanations, and supporting evidence. They are written next to capital letters on the outline. (Details are highlighted in pink on the Blueprint for Reading.)

4. **Conclusion:** Finally, a paragraph or essay has a conclusion. The conclusion must cover the contents of the paragraph in the same way as the topic sentence, though it should be worded differently.

Transition Words: While not part of a traditional outline, transition words are part of the **Blueprint for Writing**. These words or phrases, which show the relationship of ideas from one main idea to another, are recorded in circles next to the Roman numerals on the outline. (Transition words are circled on the **Blueprint for Reading**.)

Blueprint for Writing: Outline (Book C)

Topic _____

Main Idea I. _____
  A. _____
  B. _____
  C. _____
  D. _____

Main Idea II. _____
  A. _____
  B. _____
  C. _____
  D. _____

Main Idea III. _____
  A. _____
  B. _____
  C. _____
  D. _____

Conclusion _____

Blueprint for Writing: Outline 5

Build It

Book A, Unit 1, Lesson 1

Why Do: Students benefit from working on multisensory tasks that reveal and reinforce the parts-to-whole structure of the English language.

How To: These activities direct students to build words using a limited set of sound-spelling correspondences, syllable types, or morpheme elements that they have studied.

The following procedure is used to build students' familiarity with sound-spelling correspondences:

- Display the cumulative letter cards or other manipulative forms (e.g., tiles, magnetic letters) of the sound-spelling correspondences.

- Demonstrate how to move the cards or items to build a word composed of the sound-spelling correspondences.

- Model how to sound out and blend the component phoneme-grapheme correspondences to produce the word.

- Have students use their own manipulatives, such as self-stick notes, to build additional words and record them in the **Bank It** section of the *Interactive Text.*

The same process is used with cards or self-stick notes to build words from syllable units or morpheme elements (i.e., prefixes, roots, and suffixes).

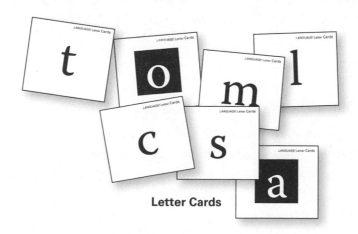

Letter Cards

Chain It

Book A, Unit 1, Lesson 4

Why Do: Forming new words by changing single letters in the given words builds students' familiarity with sound-spelling correspondences. This type of practice also improves fluency in spelling and reading.

How To: Chain It is a way of building words using either the **Chain It** template, self-stick notes, or letter cards.

When using the template, the steps are as follows:

- Have students write the phonemes for a word in the first row of boxes.

- Identify a sound-spelling correspondence at the beginning (B), middle (M), or end (E) for students to change. Have students circle the position.

- Have students write a new word by changing the phoneme in the designated position.

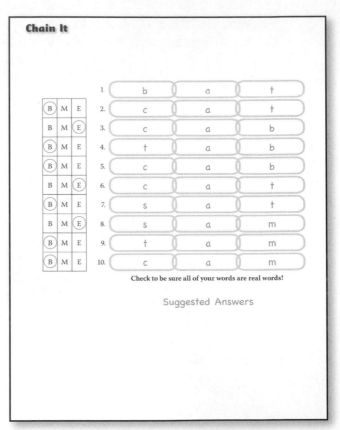

A completed Chain It template from Book A. A blank template can be found in *Transparencies and Templates*, page 11

- Continue this procedure with each remaining row.

- Have students read the compiled list of chained words to you or a peer.

When using self-stick notes or letter cards, students manipulate the notes or cards to build the new words.

Change It

Book C, Unit 17, Lesson 2

Why Do: Students need structured practice to learn when to apply the spelling rule that says to change the letter **y** to an **i** before adding a suffix.

How To: There are two questions to ask in considering the **Change y Rule**:

- Does the base word end in **y** preceded by a consonant?

- Is the suffix **-ing**?

Change It uses a template to structure the analysis of the word and suffix for these conditions of this rule. Students learn to ask and address these questions through the following procedure:

1. Analyze the base word to determine if it fits the change **y** pattern.

2. Decide whether to change the **y**:

- If the word ends in **y** preceded by a consonant, change the **y** to an **i** before adding a suffix.

- If the suffix is **-ing**, do not change the **y** to an **i**.

	Is There a . . .			Is the suffix **-ing**		
Write the Base Word	Consonant Before the y?	Vowel Before the y?	Write the Ending	Yes	No?	Put the Base + Ending Together
1. happy	✓		est		✓	happiest
2. happy	✓		ness		✓	happiness
3. funny	✓		er		✓	funnier
4. study	✓		ing	✓		studying
5. play		✓	ed		✓	played
6. try	✓		ed		✓	tried
7. lazy	✓		er		✓	lazier
8. copy	✓		ing	✓		copying
9. copy	✓		ed		✓	copied
10. windy	✓		est		✓	windiest
11.						
12.						
13.						
14.						
15.						

Change It

Change It 20

A completed Change It template from Book C. A blank template can be found in *Transparencies and Templates*, page 12

Choose It and Use It

Book A, Unit 2, Lesson 7

Why Do: Students need multiple opportunities to apply concepts and skills in sentence context.

How To: Students use target concepts and skills to select appropriate word forms to complete the given sentences.

Classify It

Book A, Unit 4, Lesson 6

Why Do: Building concepts and associations between words aids students' understanding and recall of the spelling, pronunciation, and meaning of those words.

How To: This activity challenges students to determine how to classify words. Word lists, word cards, and phrases are used as sources for the classification activities.

For English learners, this version of the activity is recommended:

- Display category sets (*animals*, *fruit*, etc.) from the picture cards in the *Teacher Resource Kit*.

- Write the name of the category on the board, and pronounce it several times.

- Have students:

  - Take turns displaying pictures of items within a category (*banana, apple, orange*).

  - Work in pairs at developing recall for names of items within a category.

  - Switch roles, so the other partner shows the pictures.

  - Use the word written on one side of the card to further develop a list of known words.

  - Practice classifying each word with this type of query: *A banana is a _____ (fruit).*

- Encourage students to practice the words in each picture-word category to mastery.

Code It

Book A, Unit 3, Lesson 6

Why Do: Students need structured practice to learn how to analyze the grammar components of sentences.

How To: Students mark, or code, designated components of connected text material. They find target concepts in the text material and code those elements—nouns, verbs, and other parts of speech, for example. Letters or symbols are used for the code.

Combine It

Book B, Unit 7, Lesson 6

Why Do: Students can learn to write more syntactically complex sentences through the process of sentence combining.

How To: To demonstrate the sentence combining process concretely, **Combine It** uses strips of paper, transparency, or **Masterpiece Sentence Work Strips**, which can be manipulated. Once sentence parts or sentences are arranged to form a compound or complex sentence, students adjust punctuation and capitalization.

Example using Book B vocabulary: To combine subjects from two sentences (dark gray boxes) to create a sentence with a compound subject, join the two subjects with a conjunction (light gray box).

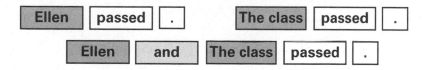

As students gain proficiency combining sentence elements manipulatively, they can apply the same process in a paper and pencil format.

Example using Book C vocabulary: To combine subjects from two sentences (dark gray boxes) to create a sentence with a compound subject, join the two subjects with a conjunction (light gray box).

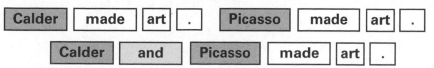

As students gain proficiency combining sentence elements manipulatively, they can apply the same process in a paper and pencil format.

Comprehend It

Book D, Unit 21, Lesson 4

Why Do: Students benefit from explicit instruction of metacognitive strategies that they can use to monitor their reading and improve their comprehension.

How To: Comprehend It guides students to learn and apply metacognitive strategies to determine the level of their understanding, to clarify meaning, and to adjust their understanding based on new information. Essential to all three of the following strategies is the frequent use of checkpoints during reading. Students stop after a paragraph or page of text to employ one or a combination of these strategies to remain actively engaged with the text and to check for understanding.

1. **Ask myself:** Students engage in active self-questioning about their level of understanding while reading. The strategy requires students to ask questions including:

   - Do I understand this?

   - Do I understand whom it is about?

   - Do I understand what happened?

   - Is there a word that I don't know?

2. **Re-read:** Students re-read a sentence or longer chunk of text to help them better understand the text. Re-reading portions of text can make things clearer and increase understanding.

3. **Make and confirm predictions:** By making and confirming predictions, students set a purpose for reading (to find out if their predictions are correct) and build a deeper understanding of the text. Making predictions helps students make connections between what they already know (prior knowledge) and the text. Questions to ask include:

   - What do I think is going to happen next?

   - What will the character do? How will that affect the other characters?

   - What might change in the next portion of the story?

All three strategies require that students learn to use strategies for word reading (e.g., **Divide It**), phrasing (e.g., **Phrase It**), and vocabulary acquisition (e.g., **Use the Clues**) to access the printed words accurately, fluently, and with expression. Beyond these strategies, students learn to use resources such as the dictionary, thesaurus, and teacher support to clarify meaning.

Consonant Chart

Book A, Unit 1, Lesson 2

Why Do: Effective sequential reading instruction requires keeping a cumulative record of consonant sounds that have been introduced.

How To: Consonant sounds close or restrict the airflow with lips, teeth, or tongue. The **Consonant Chart** organizes the consonant (closed) sounds by mouth position and type of sound. Teachers use the completed **Consonant Chart** transparency to provide an overview of consonant sounds. Students fill in the blank **Consonant Chart** in the *Interactive Text*, Book A, page R5, as they are introduced to new consonant sounds. A completed version of the chart is located in the *Handbook Section of the Student Text*, page H6. These charts are also included in the *Transparencies and Templates*.

Consonant Chart

Unit _____ Student _____ Date _____

		Mouth Position						
		Lips	Lips/Teeth	Tongue Between Teeth	Tongue Behind Teeth	Roof of Mouth	Back of Mouth	Throat
Type of Consonant Sound	Stops	/ p / / b /			/ t / / d /		/ k / / g /	
	Fricatives		/ f / / v /	/ th / / <u>th</u> /	/ s / / z /	/ sh / / zh /		/ h /
	Affricatives					/ ch / / j /		
	Nasals	/ m /			/ n /		/ ng /	
	Lateral				/ i /			
	Semivowels	/ hw / / w /			/ r /	/ y /		

Adapted with permission from Bolinger, D. (1975). *Aspects of Language* (2nd ed.) (p. 41). New York: Harcourt Brace Jovanovich.

Consonant Chart (completed) 19

Both blank and completed Consonant Charts can be found in *Transparencies and Templates*, pages 18 and 19

Contract It

Book B, Unit 7, Lesson 7

Why Do: Forming contractions is a challenging task. Students need structured practice to recognize and spell contractions correctly.

How To: Contract It has two components, each designed to bring attention to the structure of contractions. In the exercise, students will:

1. Match the contraction with the words that make up the contracted form.

   - Read the contraction.

   - Read the list of component words.

   - Draw a line to connect the contraction to the word combination that was compressed to form the contraction.

2. Form the contraction.

   - Read the contraction.

   - Read the component word combination.

   - Cross out the letters that are "squeezed out" and replaced with an apostrophe (').

   - Rewrite the contraction.

Define It

Book A, Unit 1, Lesson 3

Why Do: Students benefit from using an analytical approach to develop definitions for words. A visual format helps students organize verbal production and retrieval.

How To: There are three steps to **Define It**. First, students identify the category into which the word belongs. Second, they discuss attributes that differentiate it from other words in the same category. Finally, they combine the category and attribute information to create a definition.

The **Define It** template structures this process.

Example:

Word		Category		Attributes
atlas	=	book	+	contains maps

Definition: **An atlas is a book that contains maps.**

An alternative format is a definition starter:

An atlas is a **book** that **contains maps**.
                       category   attribute(s)

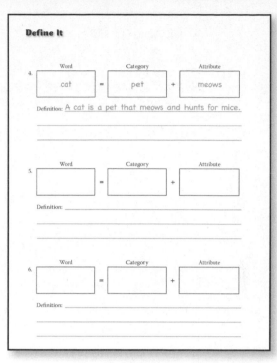

A completed Define It template from Book A. A blank template can be found in *Transparencies and Templates,* page 20

Diagram It

Book A, Unit 1, Lesson 6

Why Do: Students need the ability to recognize how the parts of a sentence are related.

How To: Sentence diagrams use a graphic format to differentiate the two parts of a base sentence, and to demonstrate how various modifiers relate to the base parts.

(See *Teacher Resource Guide*, page 436 for an explanation of the role of diagramming.)

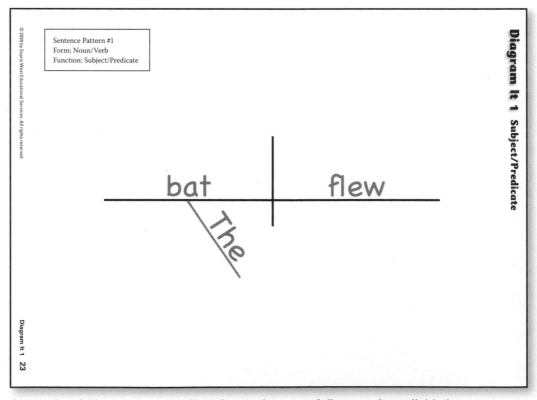

A completed Diagram It 1 template. A complete set of diagrams is available in *Transparencies and Templates*, **pages 23–30. For examples of all diagrams, see** *Teacher Resource Guide*, **Appendices, page 436**

Discover It

Book D, Unit 19, Lesson 1

Why Do: Identifying phonological, structural, and morphological patterns develops students' word recognition abilities.

How To: Discover It guides students to identify underlying sound-spelling patterns, syllable types, or morpheme units. The word study procedure directs students to:

- Listen to a list of words representing the target elements.

- Sort or analyze the words according to a designated element.

- Identify the pattern (e.g., sound-spelling pattern, syllable type, morpheme unit).

- Label the sorted words according to the pattern.

- State the "discovery."

Divide It

Book C, Unit 13, Lesson 8

Why Do: Students benefit from having a decoding strategy they can use to systematically identify patterns of syllables in multisyllable words.

How To: Words can be divided by syllable (sound-dependent) or by morpheme (meaning-dependent) units. The **Divide It** strategy employs both. Syllable identification helps unlock pronunciation; morpheme identification unlocks meaning. This strategy involves following a series of steps to divide words into smaller parts.

- First, check the word for prefixes and suffixes. Circle them. (Note: Do not start this activity by reading the word, since the word is the answer.)

- Next, look at the rest of the word:

  1. Underline the **first** vowel. Write **V** under it.

  2. Underline the **next** vowel. Write **V** under it.

  3. Look at the letters **between** the vowels. Mark them with a **C** for consonant.

  4. Look at the pattern at right and divide according to the pattern.

  5. Place a diacritical mark over each vowel.

- Finally, read the word.

Example: disconnected

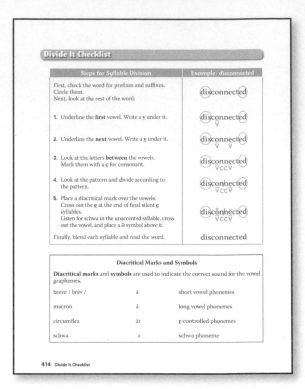

From Book C _Interactive Text_

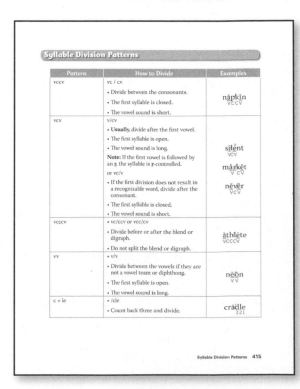

From Book C _Interactive Text_

Double It

Book A, Unit 6, Lesson 4

Why Do: Students need to develop word analysis skills so that when they add an ending to a word, they know to double the final consonant to spell the new word correctly.

How To: Double It provides a systematic format for practice in applying the spelling rule to double the final consonant before adding suffixes. **Double It** uses a template to structure the analysis of the word and suffix for these conditions of this rule. Students learn to ask and address these questions through the following procedure:

1. Spell the base word.

2. Analyze the structure of the word to determine if it fits the 1-1-1 pattern (i.e., one vowel, one consonant, one syllable after the vowel).

3. Identify the first letter of the ending to determine whether or not to double the final consonant on the base word.

4. Write the word with the ending.

Draw It: Idioms

Book A, Unit 4, Lesson 10

Why Do: Students' understanding of idioms is aided by nonverbal expression of meaning.

How To: Students illustrate the literal and figurative meanings of idioms. Students who experience difficulty drawing can cut pictures from magazines, catalogs, or other picture sources.

Write the Base Word	One Vowel?	One Consonant After the Vowel?	One Syllable?	1-1-1	Not 1-1-1	Suffix	Write the Base + Suffix
1. hop	1	1	1	✔		–ing	hopping
2. sit	1	1	1	✔		–ing	sitting
3. pass	1		1		✔	–ing	passing
4. tap	1	1	1	✔		–ing	tapping
5. kick	1		1		✔	–ing	kicking
6. stop	1	1	1	✔		–ing	stopping
7. win	1		1	✔		–ing	winning
8. cross	1		1		✔	–ing	crossing
9. swim	1	1	1	✔		–ing	swimming
10. lock	1		1		✔	–ing	locking
11.							
12.							
13.							
14.							
15.							

A completed Double It template. A blank template can be found in ***Transparencies and Templates*, page 31**

Drop It

Book B, Unit 10, Lesson 4

Why Do: Students need to develop word analysis skills so that when they add an ending to a word, they know whether or not to drop the final **e** on a word to spell the new word correctly.

How To: This activity provides a systematic format for students to practice the application of the spelling rule to drop the final silent **e** before adding suffixes. There are two conditions to check in the **Drop e Rule**:

1. Does the base word end in **e**?
2. Does the suffix begin with a vowel?

Drop It uses a template to structure the analysis of the word and suffix for these conditions of this rule. These steps analyze these conditions:

1. Analyze the structure of the word to determine if it fits the **Drop e Rule** pattern.

2. Identify the first letter of the suffix to see if it begins with a vowel or not.

3. Decide whether to drop the **e**: If the suffix begins with a **vowel**, drop the **e** from the base word. If the suffix begins with a **consonant**, do not drop the **e** from the base word.

Drop It

Unit _____   Student _____   Date _____

	Write the Base Word	Ends in e	Does Not End in e	Write the Ending	Ending Begins With Vowel?	Ending Begins With Consonant?	Put the Base + Ending Together
1.	hope	x		ing	x		hoping
2.	hope	x		ful		x	hopeful
3.	dive	x		ing	x		diving
4.	hope	x		less	.	x	hopeless
5.	fade	x		ed	x		faded
6.	wish		x	ing	x		wishing
7.	wave	x		ing	x		waving
8.	vote	x		ed	x		voted
9.	crack		x	ed	x		cracked
10.	hate	x		ful		x	hateful
11.							
12.							
13.							
14.							
15.							

Drop It 22

A completed Drop It template. A blank template can be found in *Transparencies and Templates*, page 32

Explore It

Book C, Unit 13, Lesson 1

Why Do: The acquisition of literacy involves gaining cumulative and comprehensive knowledge of vocabulary words.

How To: This activity uses a graphic organizer to structure word exploration. Each cell of the organizer explores a different dimension of the word.

> **Word:** This cell focuses on the structural and grammatical features of the word. Students indicate the number of syllables and grammar functions for the word.

> **Meaning:** This cell captures information about the meaning parts (i.e., roots, prefixes, suffixes) and word relationships.

> **Sentence:** Use of the word in the sentence moves word knowledge to the application level.

> **Reading:** Information from reading selections expands the connections to meaning. Reading material is the source of examples and other facts related to the word.

The graphic organizer can be used to direct whole-class discussion or small-group work. Students should be encouraged to use the dictionary, thesaurus, and other resources.

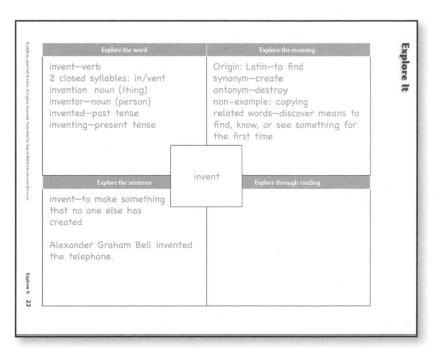

A completed Explore It graphic organizer. A blank graphic organizer can be found in *Transparencies and Templates*, page 34

Expression of the Day

Book B, Unit 7, Lesson 1

Why Do: All students, particularly those learning English, benefit from oral practice of common expressions.

How To: A common expression is taught in most unit lessons. The procedure is as follows:

- Display the common expression on a white board, bulletin board, or pocket chart.

- Discuss the meaning and model the expression in a sentence.

- Take turns having students use the expression in their own sentences.

- Bring attention to the expression of the day.

- Give points throughout the day to students who use the expression correctly in their spoken language.

- Or, throughout the day when you or a student use the key expression, have the class acknowledge it verbally by saying an agreed-upon word or phrase such as *Whoop! There it is!* or *Express It!*

Find It

Book A, Unit 1, Lesson 1

Why Do: Students need practice in reading carefully to identify elements and information in text.

How To: Students find target concepts in the text material and underline the words with pencils or pens.

Folder Activities

Book A, Unit 1, Lesson 1

Why Do: Appropriate use of manipulatives for concept and skill practice has been shown consistently to foster learning and aid retention.

How To: Use file folders and self-stick notes to create reusable activities. Make the self-stick notes for the activity for the students or dictate activity-specific content and have students write out the self-stick notes themselves. Label the folders according to unit and content type for easy storage and retrieval.

General principles for Folder Activities:

- Use decodable vocabulary. The emphasis of the activity is to practice specific concepts or skills. It is critical that the words used follow the scope and sequence.

- Include items in sorting activities that do not fit the sort. This encourages thinking about the concepts.

- Provide a "Think Space" area for sorts. Students use this space if they are uncertain about a word or phrase.

Student use of Folder Activities:

- **Individual use:** Manipulate the self-stick notes according to the targeted concept or skill.

- **Partner use:** Read the words while a partner determines the column into which the word fits. After completing the sort, both students check their work for accuracy.

Folder Activities *(continued)*

Book A, Unit 1, Lesson 1

The type of folder activity dictates the content. Possible folder activities:

- **Alphabetize**: Arrange decodable vocabulary from the current or previous units into alphabetical order.

- **Word Sorts**: Sort groups of words into the designated categories. Select vocabulary from the current or previous units for the elements targeted in the sort.

  - Phoneme Discrimination: Choose two or three phonological elements. This sort must be done in pairs.

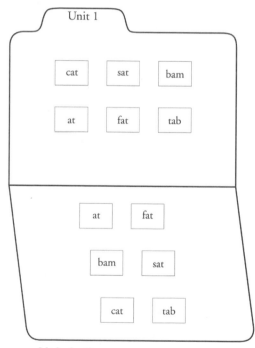

Alphabetize

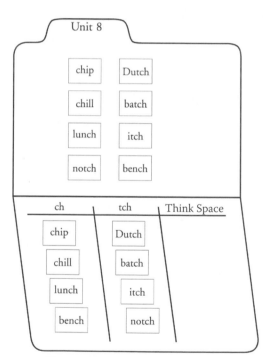

Phoneme Discrimination

Folder Activities *(continued)*

Book A, Unit 1, Lesson 1

- **Grammar Sort**: Choose two or three grammar concepts.

- **Semantic Sort**: Select words that can be grouped according to meaning. For a closed sort, provide the label for the categories. For an open sort, have students generate the category labels.

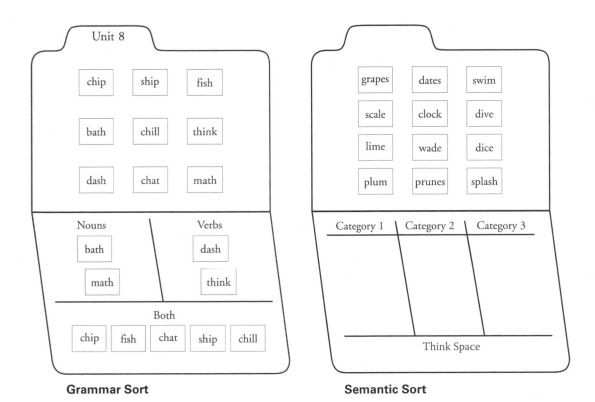

Grammar Sort   **Semantic Sort**

Folder Activities *(continued)*

Book A, Unit 1, Lesson 1

- **Syllable Sort:** Choose two or more syllable types to sort. Write or dictate the syllables for the sort. Use syllables from real multisyllable words (e.g., mar-ket, rab-bit, si-lo).

- **Word and Phrase Sort:** Use words and phrases from the current or previous units. Sort them according to the comprehension questions that they answer.

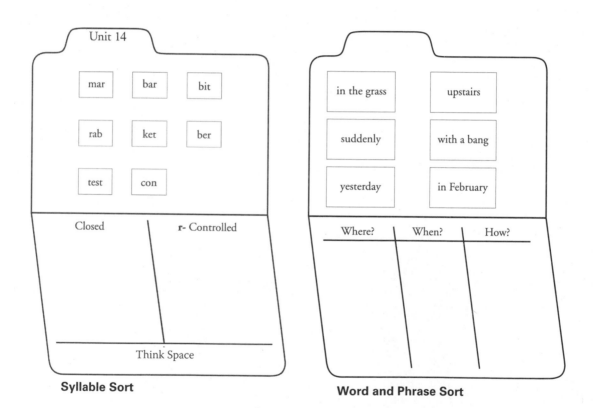

Syllable Sort

Word and Phrase Sort

Folder Activities *(continued)*

Book A, Unit 1, Lesson 1

- **Sentence Unscramble:** Use sentences from the decodable text or sentence dictation activities. Write one word from the sentences per self-stick note. Place the words in mixed-up order on the top half of the folder. Unscramble the sentence by placing the words in the correct sequence on the bottom half of the folder. Point out the use of Sentence Signals, capital letters, and punctuation to identify the correct word order.

- **Fill-in-the-Blanks:** Use this type of folder activity to practice multiple ways to spell the same sound (e.g., / k / = **c**, **k**, or -**ck**). Place multiple self-stick notes for the target elements on the top half of the folder (e.g., **k** or -**ck**). Write the word with a blank for the missing element on the **bottom half** of the folder (e.g., du**ck**).

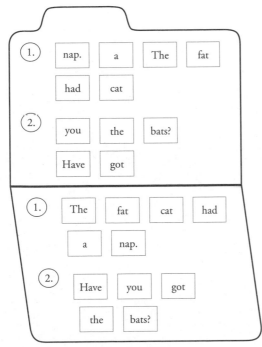

Sentence Unscramble

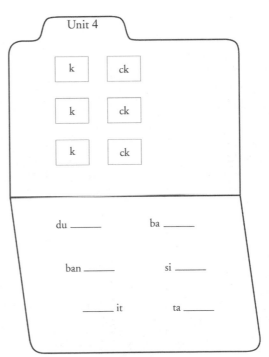

Fill-in-the-Blanks

Folder Activities *(continued)*

Book A, Unit 1, Lesson 1

- **Tic-Tac-Toe:** This variation of folder activities can be created in two ways: The words or syllables can be written directly on the folder or on self-stick notes. If written on the folder, play the game by covering the words to get three in a row. If written on self-stick notes, play the game by moving the self-stick notes onto the grid to get three in a row—vertically, horizontally, or diagonally.

    - **Essential Words:** Use **Essential Words** from the current or previous units to make this tic-tac-toe grid.

    - **Syllable Types:** Use two types of syllables (e.g., closed and r-controlled). Write examples of the two syllable types on individual self-stick notes. Place all of one type of syllable on the same color self-stick notes. Place the notes on the top half of the folder. Draw a blank tic-tac-toe grid on the bottom half of the folder. Rather than <u>x</u> and <u>o</u>, the type of syllable is used to designate the player's move.

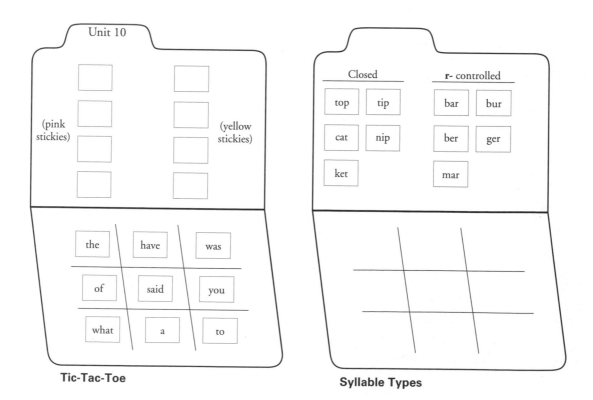

Tic-Tac-Toe   **Syllable Types**

Handwriting Fluency

Book A, Unit 1, Lesson 1

Why Do: Students benefit from learning how to quickly and correctly form the letters of the alphabet. Improving handwriting proficiency impacts the quantity as well as the quality of student composition (Berninger et al., 1999).

How To: Handwriting fluency tasks set time limits for students to practice writing the alphabet as well as copying tasks. Students generally write for 30 seconds and their sample is scored. While not all handwriting activities are timed, they all are aimed at improving handwriting fluency with a stress on proper letter formation in either print or cursive. If practice is to make perfect, the teacher needs to establish "perfect practice" by modeling proper letter formation before the students are asked to practice. Constant reinforcement of proper letter formation will help students achieve mastery.

Identify It

Book A, Unit 1, Lesson 4

Why Do: Students benefit from activities that reinforce their knowledge of terminology for concepts, particularly in the areas of morphology and grammar.

How To: Students identify the correct terminology (i.e., concept labels) for targeted word forms or functions.

IVF Sentences

Book A, Unit 1, Lesson 10

Why Do: Understanding the construction of an effective topic sentence helps students write well-developed paragraphs and multiparagraph essays. Providing a visual model for the construction of a topic sentence helps them better understand the components and how an effective topic sentence is built.

How To: **IVF Sentences** help students develop effective topic sentences that provide an overview of the paragraph without providing all of the details on the subject. (I = Identify the Item; V = select a verb; F = Finish the thought.) Example for a summary paragraph:

- Identify the Item: Students provide the book, the article, or other source of information

- Select a Verb: Verb choice tells what the item does—e.g. explains, compares, shows, etc.

- Finish the Thought: provides the main idea of the paragraph or summary

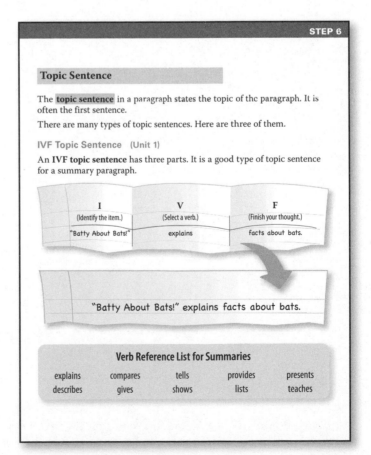

STEP 6

Topic Sentence

The **topic sentence** in a paragraph states the topic of the paragraph. It is often the first sentence.

There are many types of topic sentences. Here are three of them.

IVF Topic Sentence (Unit 1)

An **IVF topic sentence** has three parts. It is a good type of topic sentence for a summary paragraph.

I	V	F
(Identify the item.)	(Select a verb.)	(Finish your thought.)
"Batty About Bats!"	explains	facts about bats.

"Batty About Bats!" explains facts about bats.

Verb Reference List for Summaries

explains	compares	tells	provides	presents
describes	gives	shows	lists	teaches

From *Handbook Section of the Student Text*, page H59

K-W-L

Book C, Unit 14, Lesson 1

Why Do: Graphic information organizers help students progress as readers. The organizers promote active reading, critical thinking, and retention of information.

How To: The **K-W-L** process comprises three steps:

- **K** = What do you **K**now? This part of the process allows students to activate prior knowledge about a topic.

- **W** = What do you **W**ant to know? This step asks students to identify what they anticipate learning about the topic.

- **L** = What did you **L**earn? This part of the graphic organizer allows students to reflect and recall new information.

The first two parts of the graphic organizer are used before reading a selection. The third part is used after reading.

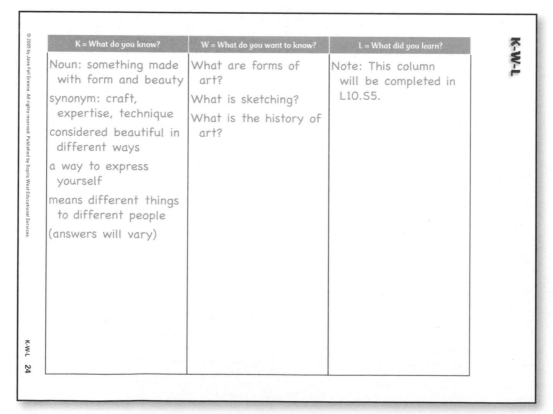

K = What do you know?	W = What do you want to know?	L = What did you learn?
Noun: something made with form and beauty synonym: craft, expertise, technique considered beautiful in different ways a way to express yourself means different things to different people (answers will vary)	What are forms of art? What is sketching? What is the history of art?	Note: This column will be completed in L10.S5.

A partially completed K-W-L graphic organizer that explores the question "What is Art?"
A blank K-W-L graphic organizer can be found in *Transparencies and Templates*, page 39

Letter-Name Fluency

Book A, Unit 1, Lesson 8

Why Do: Students must develop accurate and automatic retrieval of letter-name associations.

How To: Letter-Name Fluency activities direct students to work with peer partners to time, listen to, and record each other's performance in recognizing and saying the names of letters.

Note: Students use a timer for this activity. Goal setting is discussed in *Assessment: Teacher Edition.*

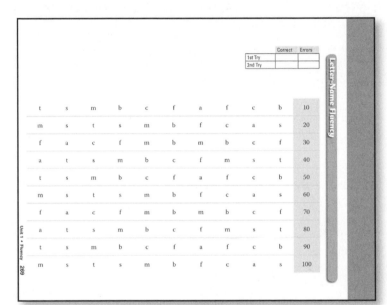

		Correct	Errors
1st Try			
2nd Try			

t	s	m	b	c	f	a	f	c	b	10
m	s	t	s	m	b	f	c	a	s	20
f	a	c	f	m	b	m	b	c	f	30
a	t	s	m	b	c	f	m	s	t	40
t	s	m	b	c	f	a	f	c	b	50
m	s	t	s	m	b	f	c	a	s	60
f	a	c	f	m	b	m	b	c	f	70
a	t	s	m	b	c	f	m	s	t	80
t	s	m	b	c	f	a	f	c	b	90
m	s	t	s	m	b	f	c	a	s	100

Letter-Name Fluency

Unit 1 • Fluency 269

Letter-Name Fluency page for Unit 10

A blank chart for recording fluency trials

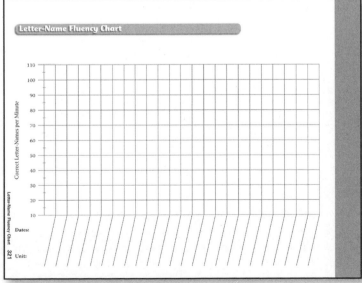

Letter-Name Fluency Chart

Correct Letter-Names per Minute

110
100
90
80
70
60
50
40
30
20
10

Dates:

Unit:

Letter-Name Fluency Chart 321

Letter-Sound Fluency

Book A, Unit 1, Lesson 3

Why Do: Students must develop accurate and automatic retrieval of sound-symbol associations.

How To: Letter-Sound Fluency activities direct students to work with peer partners to time, listen to, and record each other's performances in recognizing and saying the sounds made by individual letters. Partners time each other for one minute. They then repeat the process and record the times for both trials in the *Interactive Text*.

Note: Students use a timer for this activity. Goal setting is discussed in *Assessment: Teacher Edition*.

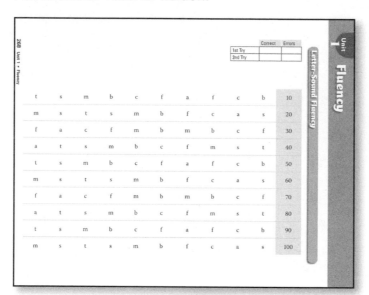

Letter-Sound Fluency page for Unit 1

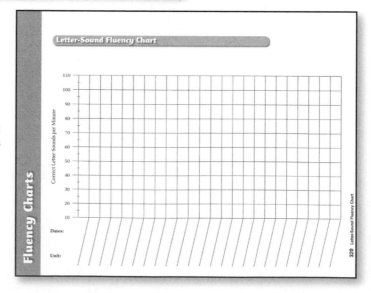

A blank chart for recording letter-sound fluency trials

Listening for Sounds in Words

Book A, Unit 1, Lesson 3

Why Do: Identifying where a phoneme is positioned in a word or syllable helps students develop both phonemic awareness and phonic knowledge. This activity is based on the Elkonin procedure, which is a visual and concrete way to represent phonemes in words.

How To: Students practice identifying where a phoneme is positioned in a word by marking the position of a sound or sounds in a word in a series of boxes.

- Students place an X in the box to represent the position of the target phoneme.

  Example: For the word *mat*, ask "Where do you hear the / m / in *mat*?" Students place an X in the first box.

- Students write the letter(s) in the beginning, middle, and end boxes for each phoneme in the word.

  Example: For the word *back*, students would write:

- Students identify a specified sound in a word.

  Example: For the word *tick*, students identify the vowel sound (/ ĭ /) and mark the letter representing the sound with a breve (˘).

a e ĭ o u

Note: Any phonetically predictable word from the **Unit Words** list can be used for this activity. After students learn sound-spelling associations, the activity can be done using letters.

Listening for Stressed Syllables

Book C, Unit 13, Lesson 6

Why Do: Students need to learn stress patterns in longer words to associate spoken words with their written forms, and to recognize and differentiate between noun and verb forms of words.

How To: This activity provides practice in listening for stress patterns in multisyllable words. The procedure involves the use of concrete objects and movements to introduce the concept of stress in words. For example, you might display a row of tiles representing each syllable in a multisyllable word.

Listening for Word Parts

Book A, Unit 1, Lesson 3

Why Do: Students need to be able to recognize syllables within multisyllable words they hear.

How To: Careful selection of multisyllable words is the key to this activity. Each multisyllable word used in the activity contains a syllable composed of sound-spelling associations focused on in the unit. For example, in Unit 1, Ala<u>bam</u>a contains *bam*, which consists of three sound-spelling associations taught in the unit, and which is a decodable component students can spell.

Say the underlined word part; say the entire word; repeat the underlined word part.

Example: <u>bam</u>, Ala<u>bam</u>a, <u>bam</u>

Map It

Book D, Unit 20, Lesson 4

Why Do: Students need to be able to organize information presented in the selections they read. The use of graphic organizers helps activate prior knowledge, shows the relationship of information to improve comprehension, and provides a concrete model for gathering and organizing information for writing.

How To: The graphic organizers used in **Map It** support the instructional process for concepts and content with a concrete structure. The graphic organizers include:

Reasons: Shows the relationship among the position, reasons, and supporting details.

Plot: Shows the relationship of the elements of a fiction piece: introduction, conflict, climax, resolution, and conclusion.

Compare and Contrast: Organizes comparative information—similarities and differences.

To use **Map It**:

1. Select the graphic organizer suited to the targeted concept or content.

2. Record information on the organizer based on reading, discussion, or prior knowledge. You use the template transparency; students use copies of the template.

3. Direct students to use the completed organizer to study or write.

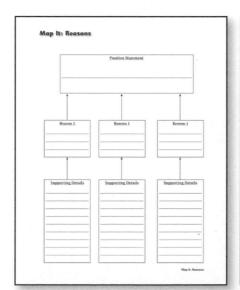 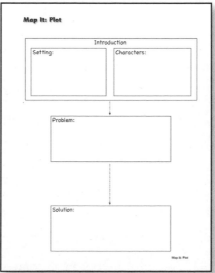

From *Transparencies and Templates*

Masterpiece Sentences: A Six-Stage Process

Book A, Unit 1, Lesson 1

Why Do: Guiding students to construct an excellent sentence, element by element, strengthens their understanding of grammar and syntax.

How To: Each **Masterpiece Sentence** stage is taught individually and cumulatively through oral and written exercises. Writing a sentence is compared to painting a masterpiece, but with words. Initially, picture prompts provide content for sentences. Later, reading material becomes the source.

The Masterpiece Sentence stages are:

Stage 1: Prepare Your Canvas: Build the base sentence. Choose (identify) a noun for the subject. The subject answers the question *Who (or what) did it?* Choose (identify) a past tense verb for the predicate. The verb answers the question *What did they (he, she, or it) do?*

Stage 2: Paint Your Predicate: Expand the predicate. Answer questions about the action: *Who or what did they do it to? When, where, or how?*

Stage 3: Move the Predicate Painters: Vary sentence structure by moving the predicate painters within the sentence.

Stage 4: Paint Your Subject: Expand the base subject. Answer questions about the subject (noun): *Which one, what kind, or how many?*

Stage 5: Paint Your Words: Strengthen the sentence through more precise, descriptive word choices.

Stage 6: Finishing Touches: Revise the sentence by moving sentence parts, refining word selections, and checking spelling and punctuation.

To write a **Masterpiece Sentence**, have students:

- Refer to the **Masterpiece Sentence: Six-Stage Process Cue Chart**. (See *Transparencies and Templates*, page 44.)

- View a picture or refer to a designated reading selection.

- Reply to questions or do the action specified in each stage.

- Write answers on individual strips of paper or the **Masterpiece Sentence Work Strips** template. (See *Transparencies and Templates*, page 44.)

- Manipulate the sentence parts to arrange them into a sentence.

- Say or write the complete sentence.

Match It

Book A, Unit 1, Lesson 8

Why Do: Activities that match word, meaning, or sentence elements help students identify the relationship between language elements.

How To: Students match related elements—such as words with their definitions, phrases with other phrases to create sentences, and words with other words—to build compound words.

Memorize It

Book A, Unit 1, Lesson 1

Why Do: Automatic recognition of frequently used English words enhances reading and writing fluency and comprehension.

How To: Essential Words are words that occur often in English. A number of these words are not phonologically predictable. Students memorize **Essential Words** as sight words, even though many become decodable in later units.

Using the **Essential Word** cards from the back of the *Interactive Text*, display and say the word. Students then say the word, trace and name the letters in the word, and repeat the word.

Essential Word Cards		
Unit 1		
are	I	is
that	the	this
Unit 2		
do	said	to
who	you	your

Essential Word Cards **327**

From Book A *Interactive Text*

Move It and Mark It

Book A, Unit 1, Lesson 7

Why Do: Visual and concrete representations of phonemes in words help students learn to manipulate phonemes in words.

How To: Use colored tiles from the *Teacher Resource Kit* to represent the sounds in a particular word. Say the word, moving one tile represented by the arrow as you say each sound. Blend the sounds represented by the tiles. Move your index finger under the tiles from left to right. Say the word. Have students follow your model.

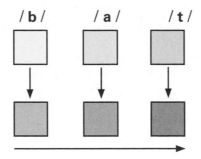

Multiple Meaning Map

Book A, Unit 1, Lesson 1

Why Do: Activities that build rich associations for words enhance retrieval and comprehension of those words.

How To: Using an overhead projector, display the **Multiple Meaning Map** transparency. Write the target word in the center space. Discuss meanings of the target word. Fill in other spaces of the map. Have students use the target word orally in sentences that convey each specific meaning of the word.

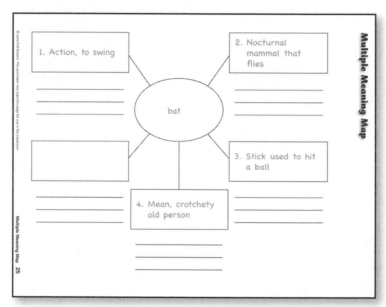

A completed Multiple Meaning Map template. A blank template can be found in *Transparencies and Templates,* **page 54**

Name and Write

Book A, Unit 1, Lesson 7

Why Do: Students need to develop automatic name-letter associations to gain proficiency in spelling and writing.

How To: Dictate letters by name. Have students write the letter corresponding to the name while saying the letter name.

Passage Fluency

Book B, Unit 7, Lesson 2

Why Do: Repeated oral readings of text help students build fluency by improving their reading speed, accuracy, and skills in phrasing.

How To: Model reading the **Passage Fluency** selection to students. Next, have students practice untimed readings with peer partners. Then students should read the **Passage Fluency** under timed conditions for one minute.

- Model how to read Passage Fluency 1 in the *Interactive Text*, while students follow along. Emphasize the importance of reading with accuracy and proper phrasing expression.

- Have students work in pairs to:

    1. Read Passage Fluency 1 in the *Interactive Text*.

    2. Read the passage to a partner, who then provides feedback on misread words.

    3. Switch roles and repeat.

    4. Read the Passage Fluency 1 page for one minute to a peer partner or as a whole class. Errors should be marked. Repeat the one-minute timing.

    5. Use the word count on the page to calculate the correct words read per minute for each try.

    6. Graph the better trial on the Passage Fluency Chart in the *Interactive Text*.

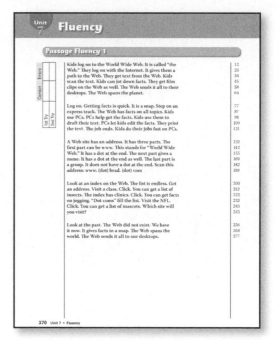

A Passage Fluency page for Unit 7

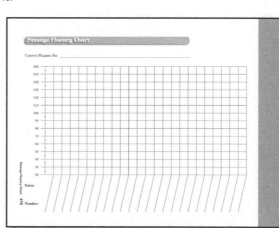

A blank chart for recording fluency trials

Phonemic Awareness: Blending

Book A, Unit 1, Lesson 3

Why Do: Blending constituent sounds to make words is a fundamental reading skill.

How To: This is the only word-level drill that does not begin with **Anchor the Word**. In this drill, the word is the answer.

- Begin this procedure by saying: *listen* (fingers to ear) *and repeat* (fingers to lips).

- Produce the word's phonemes three times. The first time, model the process; the second and third times, say the sounds together with students.

- Say the sounds in the word. Raise a finger for each phoneme as you say it.

- After the last "listen and repeat," have students blend the sounds together to form the word.

Phonemic Awareness: Deletion

Book A, Unit 1, Lesson 5

Why Do: Students need to be able to recognize and separate the individual sounds within words. This activity develops students' awareness of phonemes by having them delete, or omit, a specific sound from a word.

How To: Begin with your left arm and the students' right arms in position for the **Anchor the Word** motion.

- Say the target word two times.

- Have students repeat and anchor the word each time.

- Have students delete, or omit, a specific sound from the word and produce the remaining sounds, doing the **Anchor the Word** motion as they respond.

Example: Say *mat*. Response *mat*. Say *mat*. Response *mat*. Say *mat* without the / m /. Response *at*.

Phonemic Awareness: Isolation

Book A, Unit 1, Lesson 1

Why Do: Students need to be able to recognize and separate the individual sounds within words. This activity builds students' awareness of individual sounds in words.

How To: Begin with your left arm and the students' right arms in position for the **Anchor the Word** motion.

- Anchor the word two times.

- Designate a phoneme in the word—first, middle, or last— for isolation.

- Anchor the response of the isolated sound.

Example: Say *mat.* Response *mat.* Say *mat.* Response *mat.* What's the first sound in *mat*? Response / *m* /.

Phonemic Awareness: Production and Replication

Book A, Unit 1, Lesson 1

Why Do: Students need to be able to recognize and separate the individual sounds within words. This activity clarifies the correct production of specific speech sounds.

How To: Begin with your left arm and the students' right arms in position for the **Anchor the Word** motion.

- Say the target phoneme.

- Students repeat the sound as you all move your bent elbows down a few inches.

- Watch and listen for correct sound pronunciation.

- Repeat each phoneme two times.

Example: Teacher: Left arm is up. Teacher says: Say / *êr* / (as in *her*). Student: Right arm is up. Student and teacher pull down right arm and say / *êr* /. Repeat.

Phonemic Awareness: Reversal

Book A, Unit 1, Lesson 7

Why Do: Students need to be able to recognize and separate the individual sounds within words. This activity increases facility with phoneme manipulation by reversing the order of sounds in words.

How To: Begin with both arms bent at the elbows and extended upward like goal posts. Explain to students that their left arm will represent the beginning of the word and their right arm will represent the end.

- Say the target word two times.

- Have students repeat the word, moving each arm at the appropriate moment in the **Anchor the Word** motion.

- Have students change the first sound to the last, while moving the left hand down to horizontal position as they change the first sound to the last. (Mirror the students' movement.)

- Cue the students to respond by extending both arms in front of the body. (Have students mirror this movement.)

Example: Say *tab*. Response *tab*. Say *tab*. Response *tab*. Now, reverse the first and last sounds. Response *bat*.

Phonemic Awareness: Rhyming

Book A, Unit 1, Lesson 4

Why Do: Students need to be able to recognize and separate the individual sounds within words. This activity focuses on generating rhyming words. Rhyming requires the manipulation of phonemes in words (i.e., deletion followed by substitution of the first sound).

How To: Use the **Anchor the Word** arm motion and say the prompt word. Have students say the word while anchoring it. Repeat the word and **Anchor the Word** arm motion. Request a rhyming word. Do the **Anchor the Word** arm motion when students respond.

Example: Say a word that rhymes with *mat*. Students' responses can be any real or nonsense word that rhymes with *mat*, such as *hat, cat, flat, chat*, or *at*. Monitor the production of the rhyming words.

Phonemic Awareness: Segmentation

Book A, Unit 1, Lesson 2

Why Do: Students need to be able to recognize and separate the individual sounds within words. This activity involves segmenting words into their constituent sounds.

How To: Begin with your left arm and the students' right arms in position for the **Anchor the Word** motion.

- Reach to the opposite side of the body (cross the midline).
- Beginning with the thumb, raise one finger at a time to correspond to each sound in the word.
- Form a fist again and move the fist while saying the word.

Example:

- Say *mat*. Response *mat*. Say *mat*. Response *mat*.
- Raise the thumb while saying / *m* /.
- Raise the index finger while saying / *a* /.
- Raise the middle finger while saying / *t* /.
- Have students: move their fists left to right at shoulder level while saying *mat*.
- Simultaneously, move your fist from right to left.

Phonemic Awareness: Substitution

Book A, Unit 1, Lesson 6

Why Do: Students need to be able to recognize and separate the individual sounds within words. This activity increases facility with phoneme manipulation by omitting and replacing specific sounds in words.

How To: Begin with your left arm and the students' right arms in position for the **Anchor the Word** motion.

- Say the target word two times.
- Have students:

  Repeat and anchor the word each time.

  Substitute a specific sound in the word and produce the new word, doing the **Anchor the Word** motion to signal them to respond.

Example: Say *mat*. Response *mat*. Say *mat*. Response *mat*. Now change the first sound to / *s* /. Response *sat*.

Phrase Fluency

Book A, Unit 1, Lesson 1

Why Do: Students need to be able to read phrases with accuracy and appropriate intonation. The **Phrase Fluency** process enhances comprehension, increases automatic word recognition, and discourages word-by-word reading.

How To: The **Phrase Fluency** activity has two steps. First, students learn to read the words accurately. Second, they learn to say the phrases as if speaking them. **Phrase Fluency** sections for each unit are located in the back of the *Interactive Text*.

Note: Use a timer for this activity. Goal setting is discussed in the *Assessment: Teacher Edition*.

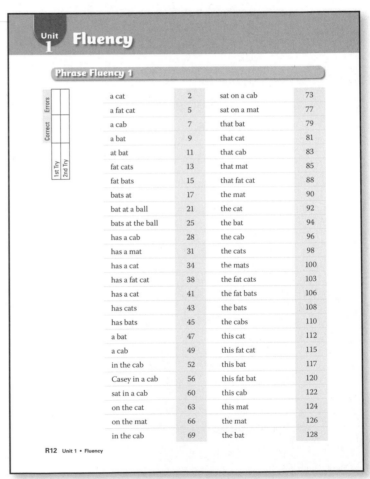

Unit 1 Fluency				
Phrase Fluency 1				
	a cat	2	sat on a cab	73
	a fat cat	5	sat on a mat	77
	a cab	7	that bat	79
	a bat	9	that cat	81
	at bat	11	that cab	83
	fat cats	13	that mat	85
	fat bats	15	that fat cat	88
	bats at	17	the mat	90
	bat at a ball	21	the cat	92
	bats at the ball	25	the bat	94
	has a cab	28	the cab	96
	has a mat	31	the cats	98
	has a cat	34	the mats	100
	has a fat cat	38	the fat cats	103
	has a cat	41	the fat bats	106
	has cats	43	the bats	108
	has bats	45	the cabs	110
	a bat	47	this cat	112
	a cab	49	this fat cat	115
	in the cab	52	this bat	117
	Casey in a cab	56	this fat bat	120
	sat in a cab	60	this cab	122
	on the cat	63	this mat	124
	on the mat	66	the mat	126
	in the cab	69	the bat	128

R12 Unit 1 • Fluency

A Phrase Fluency page for Unit 1

Phrase It

Book B, Unit 7, Lesson 1

Why Do: Students need to recognize meaningful word groups in connected text in order to read fluently and with comprehension.

How To: This program uses a three-phase procedure for improving phrase recognition. **Phrase It** focuses on phases 2 and 3.

> **Phase 1:** Model phrasing while reading to students.
>
> **Phase 2:** Model the use of cueing questions from grammar to identify meaningful groups of words as they read.
>
> > For example, in the sentence *"Some inventors create devices just for fun,"* the questioning process to identify the phrases would be:
> >
> > > *Who or what did it?* . . . . **Some inventors**
> > >
> > > *What do they do?* . . . . **create devices**
> > >
> > > *Why do they create them?* . . . . **just for fun.**
> >
> > Then, reread the sentence with the proper inflection at the ends of phrases.
>
> **Phase 3:** Students scoop with a pencil to mark the phrase units. After marking the phrases, they reread the sentence.

Example: Some inventors create devices just for fun.

Phrase It exercises appear in the *Interactive Text* so that students can mark the text. Students then do the same process with Decodable Text in the *Student Text* using their index finger or the eraser on a pencil.

Punctuate It

Book D, Unit 19, Lesson 6

Why Do: Students need to use appropriate punctuation marks in written English.

How To: Punctuate It activities target specific punctuation marks, including apostrophes, commas, and quotation marks. Each activity provides practice in identifying and applying these markers, which impact comprehension when reading and writing.

Replace It

Book C, Unit 11, Lesson 10

Why Do: The process of changing elements in sentences and reading the revised sentences aloud builds students' knowledge of word meanings and sentence structure.

How To: The following procedure is used for text-based application of concepts:

- Direct students to the text material.

- Identify a specific concept (e.g., type of word relationship, part of speech).

- Underline or code the words to replace in the text.

- Have students:

  Replace each target word.

  Read the new version of the text.

Note: Encourage the use of a thesaurus to locate precise word choices.

Revise It

Book C, Unit 14, Lesson 9

Why Do: One of the most effective methods for improving students' writing skills is guiding them to revise text passages, particularly ones they have written. Revision provides guided application of learned writing skills.

How To: The goal of **Revise It** is to guide students to use skills and content to improve sentences and paragraphs. **Revise It** activities cue students to apply strategies and procedures to improve text selections. The activities begin with structured text selections and progress to application to original writing. Several key activities include:

- **Masterpiece Sentences**: Focuses on improvement at the level of individual sentence development.

- **Rewrite It**: Focuses on strategic application of specific skills such as verb forms and pronoun referents.

- **Combine It**: Focuses on sentence combining to improve sentence structure variety.

- **Spelling Rules**: Focuses on accurate application of spelling generalizations such as **Double It**, **Drop It**, and **Change It**.

Rewrite It

Book A, Unit 1, Lesson 7

Why Do: Students benefit from being provided with preestablished contexts in which to apply concepts in writing.

How To: Use prepared text to model the skill. Read the text, identify the element to modify, and rewrite the sentence.

Say and Write

Book A, Unit 1, Lesson 1

Why Do: Success in reading and writing requires development of the auditory-to-visual memory link for letter-sound associations.

How To: Demonstrate how to simultaneously write and say the sound that corresponds to a particular letter. Have students repeat the sound as they write the letter.

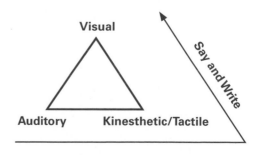

Scoop It

Book A, Unit 1, Lesson 1

Why Do: Students benefit from opportunities to practice reading with proper phrasing.

How To: Students use a pencil or eraser to "scoop" words from left to right while reading the phrases. Starting at the left dot, they drag the pencil point or eraser to the right dot while reading the group of words.

Example: •‿some inventions‿•

See and Name

Book A, Unit 1, Lesson 7

Why Do: Students need structured practice to develop automatic letter-name recognition.

How To: Insert each letter card into the pocket chart. Display one letter and demonstrate how to simultaneously see the letter and say the name that corresponds.

See and Say

Book A, Unit 1, Lesson 1

Why Do: Development of the visual-to-auditory memory link for letter-sound associations is fundamental to reading and writing success.

How To: Insert each letter card into the pocket chart. Display one letter and demonstrate how to simultaneously see the letter and say the corresponding sound while tracing the letter on the desktop or other surface.

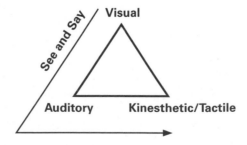

Sentence Dictation

Book A, Unit 2, Lesson 7

Why Do: Students need practice with target phonological, morphological, and syntactic content to build skills and grow as readers and writers.

How To: Say each sentence twice. Have students repeat the sentence, write it, and read it.

Sentence Fluency

Book A, Unit 4, Lesson 2

Why Do: Students benefit from repeated reading activities. Repeated reading of sentences helps students develop automatic and accurate word recognition.

How To: Direct students to read the **Sentence Fluency** while you time them for one minute. (You can time the entire class or have students work with a partner.) After one minute, you or the student (or the student's partner) should mark errors and tally the number of words read correctly. Repeat the process. Direct students to record their better score on the Sentence Fluency Chart in the *Interactive Text*.

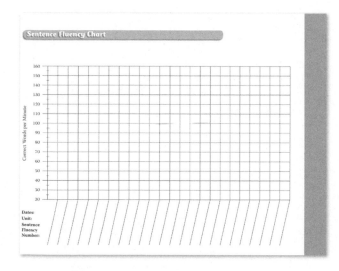

From Book A *Interactive Text*

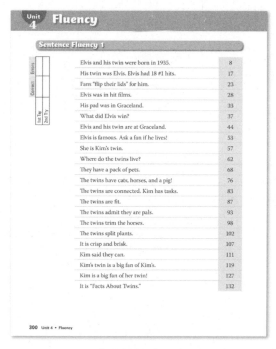

From Book A *Interactive Text*

Sentence Morphs

Book A, Unit 1, Lesson 1

Why Do: In order to develop fluency, students need opportunities to group words into phrases while reading.

How To: The **Sentence Morphs** activity has two steps. First, students read a sequence of phrases. Second, they read the same phrases as part of a sentence. The goal is for students to transfer reading the sentence with the same phrase groupings saying them as they would speak them. Encourage students to group words into phrases as they read, and avoid staccato, word-by-word reading.

A Sentence Morphs activity from Book A
Interactive Text

Sort It

Book A, Unit 1, Lesson 1

Why Do: The act of sorting builds concept knowledge, which aids understanding and recall.

How To: Use word lists, word cards, or phrases to give students opportunities to sort content. Sorts can be closed or open.

- Closed Sorts: Categories are identified for students.

- Open Sorts: Students determine categories, which then become labels for the sorted content.

For English learners, this version of the activity is recommended:

Use mastered picture cards (word side up), from two or more categories, to sort content.

- Select picture cards from each mastered category.

- Have students:

    - Select pictures to sort items into the appropriate categories.

    - In pairs, partners work at automatic recall of category name/item name.

    - Switch roles, so the other partner shows the pictures.

    - Use the word, written on one side of the card, to further develop a written list of known words.

- Encourage students to continue practicing the words in each picture-word category to mastery.

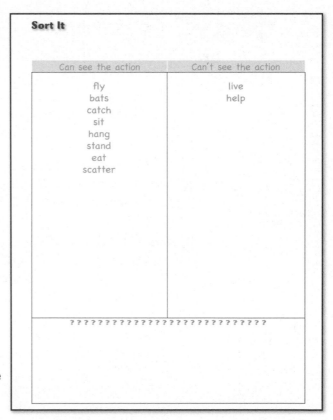

A completed Sort It template. A blank template can be found in *Transparencies and Templates*, pages 71 and 72

Spelling Pretest

Book A, Unit 1, Lesson 1

Why Do: Students need direct spelling instruction to develop as writers. Spelling lists comprising words with instructed patterns are provided with each unit. Italics designate **Essential Words**.

How To: Dictate each word on the list, say it in a sentence, and then repeat the word. Have students write the word. Check answers with students.

Spotlight on Characters

Why Do: Examining a story's structure, including character analysis, helps students improve their comprehension.

How To: The following activities can be used to help students analyze characters:

1. **Act It**: Allows students to role-play characters to understand their personalities, motives, and behaviors. Students assume the role of different characters and act out a scene from the reading selection. The goal is to assume the persona of the character.

2. **Character Interview**: Examines the motives of characters through an interview process. Students explore the mental and emotional aspects of a character. The activity includes these steps:

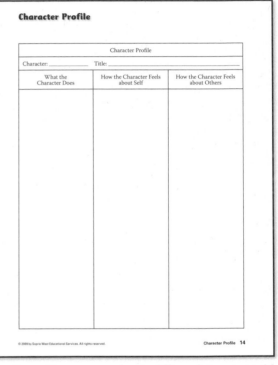

From *Transparencies and Templates*, page 14

- Students work in groups to write interview questions to ask a character. The question can be based on the text or general questions that are not related to the story. (For example, questions might pertain to the character's favorite color or hobbies.)

- You write five questions on paper strips and distribute them to five different students.

- You select students to portray the story characters. This requires them to take on the persona of the character.

- The remaining students interview the character using the prepared questions.

Syllable Awareness

Book A, Unit 3, Lesson 7

Why Do: Students benefit from activities that guide them to recognize syllable components of words.

How To: Syllable Awareness activities engage students in manipulating syllable-size parts of words. The activities include:

Segmentation:

- Say the word two times.

- Have students repeat the word.

- Beginning with the thumb and index finger, touch the thumb to one finger to correspond to each syllable in the word. Say the part as each finger touches the thumb.

- Repeat the word while holding up the fingers that were touched to the thumb. The number of fingers raised equals the number of syllables or vowel sounds in the word.

  Example:

  Say *napkin*. Response *napkin*. Say *napkin*. Response *napkin*.

  Touch the thumb to the index finger while saying *nap*.

  Touch the thumb to the middle finger while saying *kin*.

  Hold up the two fingers that were touched while saying *napkin*.

An extension of this activity includes segmenting the word as described above, counting the number of syllables, and identifying the vowel sound in each syllable. This process is structured by a worksheet in the *Interactive Text*.

Deletion:

- Say the word two times.

- Have students repeat.

- Ask students to delete, or omit, a syllable from the word and produce the remaining syllable.

  Example:

  Say *napkin*. Response *napkin*. Say *napkin*. Response *napkin*.

  Say *napkin* without *nap*. Response *kin*.

Take Note

Book A, Unit 3, Lesson 4

Why Do: Students need opportunities to closely examine text and select and record information from it.

How To: Take Note strategies are used in conjunction with the *Interactive Text* **Text Connection** activities and *Student Text* activities.

Strategies include:

- Noting key words or phrases.

- Paraphrasing information.

- Highlighting text using a color-coded system for the hierarchy of information.

- Coding text with different notations to represent levels or types of information.

- Using self-stick notes to mark text.

These note-taking strategies are often used along with the **Map It** graphic organizers to organize information for study or writing.

Tense Timeline

Book A, Unit 4, Lesson 9

Why Do: Working with a concrete representation of time conveyed by verbs can help students gain a better understanding of English tenses and tense forms of verbs.

How To: Display the **Tense Timeline** on the board or an overhead transparency.

Explain the terms used to convey points in time—past, present, and future.

Explain the position of these points in time on the timeline.

Model the process of using timeline cues that signal time, such as endings or helping verbs.

Yesterday	Today	Tomorrow
Past	**Present**	**Future**
-ed	-s or -es	will
was	am	will be
were	is	
	are	

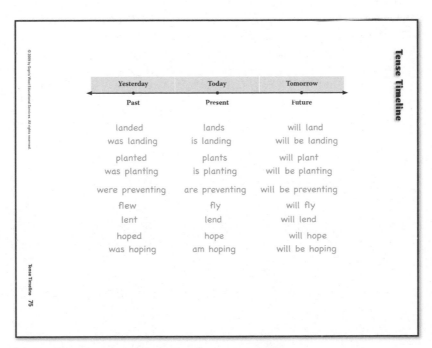

From *Transparencies and Templates*, page 75

Text Connection

Book D, Unit 19, Lesson 3

Why Do: Students need to apply strategies to learn vocabulary, understand grammatical concepts, and analyze different types of text to increase comprehension.

How To: Beginning in Book D, the **Text Connection** feature of the *Interactive Text* provides structured activities based on the Instructional Text reading selections from the *Student Text*. The activities make explicit connections between three steps in the curriculum and the reading selections for the unit. The activities in the three steps include:

- Step 3: Vocabulary and Morphology: Vocabulary strategies, including **Use the Clues**, are applied to the reading selection. These **Text Connection** activities are designed to preteach words and phrases to increase understanding of the selection.

- Step 4: Grammar and Usage: A variety of activities help students transfer knowledge of grammatical concepts to better understand the reading selection. These activities are often teacher-directed to help students identify and understand the grammatical concepts in less controlled text conditions.

- Step 5: Listening and Reading Comprehension: The **Text Connection** activities linked to Step 5 provide structured formats to guide analysis of the text. The format is matched to the type of text—informational or fiction. Students are directed to identify and mark specified information on the **Text Connection** pages. The identified information is often used as the basis for subsequent writing assignments.

Type It

Book A, Unit 1, Lesson 4

Why Do: Students need repetition of the letter sequences for sight words to increase retention.

How To: Have students keyboard the **Essential Words** in a unit using different fonts and colors. Have them say the word, say the letter names aloud as they keyboard, and then repeat the word.

Example: For the word *gone*, students say *gone*; type and say g-o-n-e; say gone.

Use the Clues

Book B, Unit 7, Lesson 3

Why Do: Context-based strategies help students develop vocabulary and comprehension.

How To: Use a context-based strategy to determine the meaning of unknown words. Select the strategy based on the available contextual information.

1. **Meaning Cues**: Look for meaning cue words. They provide cues to the definition of a word in context. Meaning cue words include *is/are, it means which stands for, can be defined as,* and more.

The <u>Internet</u> (is) a <u>network of computers.</u>

2. **Substitutions**: Look for words or phrases that rename nouns. Substitutions are often synonyms or distinctive features of the noun.

The internet <u>links</u>, or <u>connects</u>, computers around the world.

The word *connect* renames the word **links**.

3. **Pronoun Referents**: Use pronouns to identify meaning clues to define unknown vocabulary words in context.

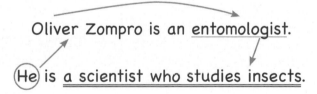

Oliver Zompro is an <u>entomologist.</u>

(He) is <u>a scientist who studies insects.</u>

4. **Context Cues**: Look for cues to the meaning of an unfamiliar word.

It is a movie <u>review</u>. The writer <u>gives an opinion</u> about a new movie.

5. **Visual Information**: Use pictures, charts, and other visual information that accompanies the text to understand the meaning of new vocabulary words.

Using a Dictionary

Book E, Unit 25, Lesson 10

Why Do: Students benefit from efficient use of reference tools such as a dictionary. They learn about all of the information provided in a dictionary, well beyond the definition. They also learn the organization of the dictionary and how to efficiently find a word in a dictionary or using an on-line version.

How To: Using a Dictionary guides students to search for information on certain words. Students may be asked to answer a variety of questions about a word:

- Number of syllables — with an emphasis on types of syllables and the resulting vowel sound

- Use the diacritical marks in the word to determine pronunciation.

- Morphological units — with an emphasis on how these build the meaning of the word

- Word origin — with an emphasis on understanding not only the meaning but the implications for spelling and word building. They learn a word's "etymology" is its origin.

- Synonyms/Antonyms — with an emphasis on building a useful oral and written vocabulary through word networking.

Vowel Chart

Book A, Unit 1, Lesson 3

Why Do: Effective sequential instruction requires maintaining a cumulative record of the vowel sounds that have been introduced. The **Vowel Chart** organizes the vowel (open) sounds by positions of production. The **Vowel Chart** records each new vowel sound and variant spellings of the sound, listed in order of frequency.

How To: Use the completed **Vowel Chart** transparency to provide an overview of the vowel sounds. Have students fill in the blank **Vowel Chart** in the *Interactive Text*, page R4, as vowel sounds are introduced. A completed version of the chart is located in the Handbook Section of the *Student Text*, page H7.

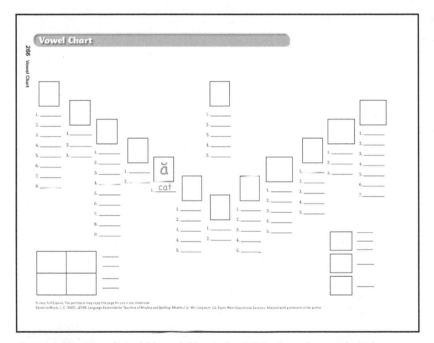

A partially completed Vowel Chart. Both blank and completed Vowel Charts can be found in *Transparencies and Templates*, pages 76 and 77

Word Fluency

Book A, Unit 1, Lesson 2

Why Do: Automatic, accurate word recognition of **Unit Words** and **Essential Words** is necessary for comprehension.

How To: Time students as they read as many words on the **Word Fluency** as they can in one minute. Mark errors, then repeat the procedure. Record the best time in the *Interactive Text*. Time the entire class or have students work with peer partners.

A Word Fluency page for Unit 1 from Book A *Interactive Text*

A blank Word Fluency chart for recording Word Fluency trials from Book A *Interactive Text*

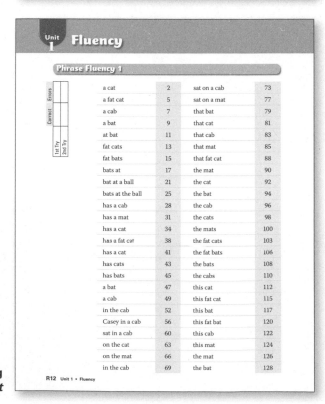

Word Line: Degrees of Meaning

Book D, Unit 19, Lesson 1

Why Do: Students need to recognize the degrees of meaning among words with related meanings.

How To: This semantic differentiation procedure provides practice in ranking words along a continuum (i.e., a semantic differential scale), selecting words from a thesaurus, and using words from the ranking in sentences according to their distinctions in meaning.

1. The simplest form of rank order places opposites on each end of the line, and a neutral or midrange term at the mid-point. More words are then added between these three positions on the line. For example, *chilly* might be added between *cold* and *room-temperature*; *warm* might be added between *room-temperature* and *hot*.

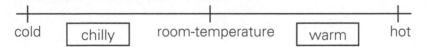

2. A more advanced form of rank order has a 7-point scale. In this form, the neutral term can be in the center or to the left. After a word has been established as an end-point, words of gradual differences in intensity are positioned along the line.

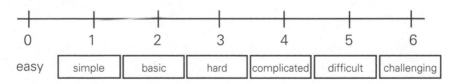

The **Word Line: Degrees of Meaning** activity provides practice in ranking words, selecting words from a thesaurus, and using words from a ranking in sentences according to their distinctions in meaning.

Word Wheel

Why Do: Students need knowledge of literal and figurative meanings to develop rich associations for words.

How To: Display the **Word Wheel** transparency on an overhead to organize literal and figurative information about a targeted word. There are three steps to **Word Wheel**. First, students write the target word in the center space and discuss the meanings of the word. Second, they fill in the inner ring with literal meanings and meaning relationships: multiple meanings of the target word, and synonyms and antonyms. Finally, they fill in the outer ring with figurative meanings and meaning relationships: analogies, common figurative uses, and idioms and expressions.

Note: It is not always possible to fill in all parts of the **Word Wheel** for a particular word. For example, words that are nouns will not have an antonym.

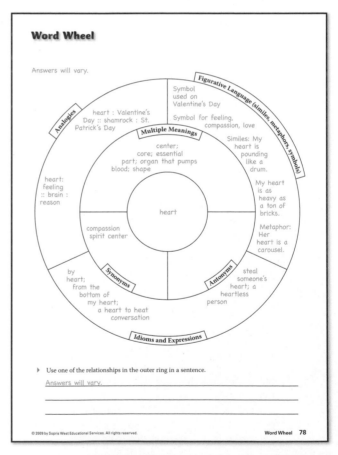

A Word Wheel template. A blank template can be found in *Transparencies and Templates*, page 78

Word Relationships

Book C, Unit 13, Lesson 5

Why Do: Students need to develop rich associations between words to speed retrieval and increase knowledge of meaning.

How To: Using a variety of activities, students learn four word relationships:

- Antonym: A word that means the opposite of another word.

- Synonym: A word that has the same or similar meaning as another.

- Attribute: A characteristic or quality, such as size, part, color, or function.

- Homophone: A word pronounced the same way as one or more other words with different meanings and spellings.

Word network activities progress from recognizing these four word relationships to producing them. Activities include selecting words from a Word Bank to fit a specified relationship, graphically organizing information such as an attribute matrix or Venn diagram, and building analogies. The activity selection is based on the particular vocabulary in the unit.

Write It

Book A, Unit 1, Lesson 4

Why Do: Students benefit from working with formats which guide them to develop particular types of written compositions, including paragraphs, essays, and reports.

How To: Specific **Write It** activities are explained in each unit. These activities:

- Model and scaffold writing increasingly complex forms of composition.

- Guide the application of concepts, content and skills from other steps including grammar, usage, vocabulary, and morphology.

- Demonstrate the use of graphic organizers and outlines for planning writing assignments.

- Provide practice revising written compositions.

Write It activities focus on different paragraph types, essays, and reports. Through these activities, explicit connections are made between the pre-writing, writing, and revision phases of the writing process.

Write Your Own Mini-Dialog

Why Do: Create opportunities for students to practice the language of interpersonal exchanges.

How To: Model for students the proper exchange for basic directions.

- Display the **Write Your Own Mini Dialog** on the overhead.

- Write the opening statement for an interpersonal exchange in the first dialog balloon.

- Have students:

    - Say the response as you write it on the second dialog balloon.

    - Continue the exchange for the third balloon.

    - Role-play the exchange using the **Mini-Dialog** template as a guide.

- Encourage students to use accurate information.

Note: **Mini-Dialogs** can also be used to practice the use of idioms.

Writer's Checklists

The Six Traits of Effective Writing serve as the foundation for the students' Writer's Checklists. (See *Teacher Resource Guide* page 246 and the *Assessment: Teacher Edition* pages 109–113 of any book level for more information.) The checklists are designed to help students edit and revise their written work using the same categories of content and skills that are used by the teacher when evaluating writing for Benchmark and Progress Indicator papers.

The Writer's Checklists are tailored to each book in the curriculum and are designed to capture the expanding content and skills that the students are learning in *LANGUAGE!* that impact writing. For example, as a spelling rule is introduced in Step 2, students are then expected to check for the application of the rule to their writing. Similarly, if a type of sentence is introduced in Step 4, then students are expected to incorporate that type of sentence into their writing. The items on the checklists are cumulative book-to-book.

In Books A through D, a single checklist is used for the writing assignments throughout the book. They are titled according to the book.

- Book A Writer's Checklist
- Book B Writer's Checklist
- Book C Writer's Checklist
- Book D Writer's Checklist

Book A Writer's Checklist

Trait	Did I...?	Unit
Ideas and Content	❏ Focus all sentences on the topic ❏ Provide supporting details for my topic sentence ❏ Include examples, evidence, and/or explanations to develop the supporting detail sentences	1 1 5
Organization	❏ Write a topic sentence ❏ Tell things in an order that makes sense ❏ Use transition words and/or phrases ❏ Write a concluding sentence	1 1 4 5
Voice and Audience Awareness	❏ Think about my audience and purpose for writing ❏ Write in a clear and engaging way that makes my audience want to read my work; can my reader "hear" me speaking	6 6
Word Choice	❏ Try to find my own way to say things ❏ Use words that are lively and specific to the content	2 2
Sentence Fluency	❏ Write complete sentences ❏ Expand some of my sentences by painting the subject and/or predicate	1 3, 6
Conventions	Capitalize words correctly: ❏ Capitalize the first word of each sentence ❏ Capitalize proper nouns, including people's names	1 3
	Punctuate correctly: ❏ Put a period or question mark at the end of each sentence ❏ Put an apostrophe before the s for a singular possessive noun ❏ Use a comma after a long adverb phrase at the beginning of a sentence	1 2 5
	Use grammar correctly: ❏ Use the correct verb tense ❏ Make sure the verb agrees with the subject in number	4 4
	Spell correctly: ❏ Spell all **Essential Words** correctly Apply spelling rules ❏ The doubling rule (1-1-1)	1 6

In Book E, the checklists become specific to the type of writing students are doing. The following checklists are used in Book E:

Literary Analysis Writer's Checklist

- Problem-Solution Essay
  Writer's Checklist

- Persuasive Essay
  Writer's Checklist

- Personal Narrative
  Writer's Checklist

In Book F, the following checklists are added:

Research Report Writer's Checklist

- Fictional Narrative
  Writer's Checklist

- Personal Essay
  Writer's Checklist

The common denominator between the Writer's Checklists and the Writer's Rubrics is the Six Traits of Effective Writing. The goal is for students' assessed writing to improve with ongoing attention to all of the aspects of writing included on the Writer's Rubrics.

Persuasive Essay Writer's Checklist

Trait	Did I...?	Unit
Ideas and Content	❑ Clearly state my position on an issue	29
	❑ Focus the content of each paragraph on the topic	7
	❑ Include examples, evidence, and/or explanations that are logically, emotionally, or ethically compelling	29
	❑ When necessary, include recent, relevant, reliable research to validate my position	29
	❑ Create a title	20
Organization	❑ Write an introductory paragraph that captures the reader's interest and contains a clear thesis statement that serves as a "map" for my essay	29
	❑ Sequence body paragraphs logically and use transition sentences that make clear the relationship between my ideas	7
	❑ Write a concluding paragraph that restates my position and issues a call to action	29
Voice and Audience Awareness	❑ Write in a voice that is confident and reasonable *	35
	❑ Write in a tone of voice that suits my audience and my purpose for writing	35
	❑ Demonstrate that I have considered the beliefs and opinions that others might have on the topic *	29
	❑ Acknowledge one or more objections that others may make to my own position *	29
Word Choice	❑ Use words that are lively, accurate, specific to the content, and convey authority	2
	❑ Vary the words so that my writing does not sound repetitive	13
Sentence Fluency	❑ Write complete sentences	1
	❑ Expand some of my sentences by painting the subject and predicate	3, 6
	❑ Write complex sentences	28
	❑ Avoid sentence fragments	29
	❑ Avoid run-on sentences	25

Conventions	❑ Edit my work for:
	  ❑ Capitalization
	  ❑ Punctuation
	  ❑ Grammar and usage
	  ❑ Spelling
	
	For specific rules governing any of these items, refer to the Handbook section of the *Student Text*.	

*Feature of persuasive writing

© 2009 by Sopris West Educational Services.   **Persuasive Essay Writer's Checklist** R11

Peer Writing Review

Gives students specific things to consider and evaluate when conducting peer-writing reviews

- Presents the main elements of good writing in three basic categories that align with the six-trait rubric: Ideas and Development, Organization and Flow, Strong Sentences

- Provides space to write some notes to guide feedback/discussion

- Focuses on strengths as well as areas that need work

Peer editing trains students to read their own work with a more critical eye. Before having students evaluate each other's writing, use the instructions for how to conduct a **Peer Writing Review.** These instructions will help them understand the spirit and intent of this kind of evaluation.

How to Conduct a Peer Writing Review

All writers benefit from receiving feedback on their writing. Giving feedback has benefits for writers, as well. It trains writers to read their own papers more carefully. So be sure to read your partner's paper carefully and give the best feedback you can. The following steps will help you.

Directions to the Reader

1. Read the entire draft once without making any marks.

2. Read the draft again. Make these marks in the margin:

    ! next to things you like or think are well done

    ? next to things that are unclear

    + next to places where you want more information or details

3. Tell your partner what you think. First, say what you like or think is working well. Next, give your partner some suggestions to make the writing better.

4. Remember that it is not your job to "fix" your partner's paper. Just give your honest reactions to the writing. Be respectful when making your comments. The goal is to provide feedback that will help your partner make the writing stronger.

Directions to the Writer

1. Listen carefully to the comments your partner makes.

2. Ask for clarification if you don't understand a comment.

3. Carefully consider your partner's feedback. Remember that your partner is giving one reader's opinion. You may not agree with everything your partner has to say. On the other hand, the comments may show that there are things you could do to make your writing stronger.

4. It is up to you to decide whether or not you will revise your paper based on your partner's comments. If you agree that something needs more work but are not sure how to improve your paper, check with your teacher.

CREATING A
STUDENT NOTEBOOK

A student notebook is one way students can learn to organize the many instructional components. The sections of the notebook can be tailored according to students' ages and needs. Possible sections include:

- Word banks

- Plastic sleeves for **Essential Words**, **Word Building Letter** cards, and **Morphemes for Meaning** cards

- References (e.g., **Syllable Division Patterns**, **Masterpiece Sentence Six Stage Process Cue Chart**, **Writing Checklists**)

- Fluency charts and checklists

- Illustrations (e.g., idioms, phrases, vocabulary words)

- Templates for activities (e.g., **Multiple Meaning Map**, **Define It**, **Double It**)

- Reading log

- Portfolio of writing (e.g., **Masterpiece Sentences**, compositions)

- Writing journal

- Work samples

- Homework

A three-ring binder is recommended for the student notebook. This format allows maximum flexibility to create a customized notebook to meet student needs. Pages can be added and deleted as instruction and mastery occur.

Major sections of the student notebook should be tabbed. Within a section, students can create additional tabs by attaching self-stick notes or by cutting up the right-hand margin of the page. This facilitates easy access to the information within a section.

NONFICTION BOOKBAG

These high-interest, nonfiction books focus on key topics in history, social studies, and science. Spanning Grades 3–8, these books cover important milestones and historical figures such as Susan B. Anthony and Elizabeth Cady Stanton's work in the Women's Suffrage Movement; Jo Ann Robinson and Martin Luther King, Jr.'s Montgomery Bus Boycott; and the accomplishments of migrant worker and organizer, Cesar Chavez. Also covered are compelling scientific topics such as the origins of hurricanes, volcanoes, and stars. This bookbag, containing 18 books, can be a valuable source for independent reading material and may be a good accompaniment to social studies or science themes covered in content area classes. Because of the sensitive nature of some of the titles that deal with historic social injustices, it is highly recommended that you or your school's reading specialist review each book for its appropriateness in your classroom.

Grade 3 and Above

All for the Better: A Story of El Barrio
Nicholasa Mohr

When Evelina Lopez's mother sends her from Puerto Rico to the United States at 11 years old, Evelina learns about the needs of her community. Living with her aunt and going to school, she learns English and eventually leads a movement to improve the quality of schools in the South Bronx, or El Barrio.

Building a Dream: Mary Bethune's School
Richard Kelso

In a time of school segregation, African-American children received a lesser education than white children. Mary Bethune dreamed of building a good school for black children, and despite the prejudice from others against her dreams, she founded a school, raised the money to support it, and fulfilled her dream. The school she built over 100 years ago still stands today.

Why They Marched: The Struggle for the Right to Vote
Donna Elam, Ed.D.

During the 1960s in the South, a courageous group of people began a movement that finally granted all adult Americans the right to vote. Thousands of people marched from Selma, Alabama, to Montgomery for their rights, and the bravery demonstrated by these people got the attention of those in power, eventually leading to the Voting Rights Act of 1965.

Grade 4 and Above

A Walk in the Desert
Rebecca L. Johnson

Discover the different biomes of North America and delve into the hot climate of the desert. Learn about a variety of fascinating creatures and plants that dwell in the desert from the kit fox to the cactus. Examine photographs of fascinating creatures with interesting names such as chuckwallas, skinks, and spiny horned lizards.

Tales from the Underground Railroad
Kate Connell

Through the story of William Minnis, learn how African Americans dared to escape to freedom on the Underground Railroad during the time of slavery. Adopting the name Mr. Young and lightening his skin with makeup, William Minnis embarks on a brave and dangerous journey to gain his freedom.

The Tenement Writer: An Immigrant's Story
Ben Sonder

When seven-year-old Anzia Yezierska and her family immigrate to America, she learns to persevere through discrimination and poverty. Though her father does not approve of her learning, she fights to get an education and to become a writer. The stories she writes eventually make her a famous American author.

Grade 5 and Above

Hurricanes! Fascinating Facts, Quizzes, and Photos!
Susan Hood

Learn about the origins of hurricanes through fun quizzes and photos of real hurricanes. Find out how big hurricanes get, what to do if a hurricane is coming toward you, and how hurricanes get their names. Also, discover the top five costliest hurricanes and the top five deadliest hurricanes in history.

Walking for Freedom: The Montgomery Bus Boycott
Richard Kelso

Famous civil rights leaders such as Rosa Parks and Martin Luther King, Jr., help one woman organize a successful boycott to change segregation laws. When Mrs. Jo Ann Robinson attempts to sit in a "whites only" section on the city bus, she is discriminated against and organizes a boycott of the bus system in Montgomery, Alabama.

These Lands Are Ours: Tecumseh's Fight for the Old Northwest
Kate Connell

Learn about the Shawnee chief, Tecumseh, and his unrelenting fight for the right to the land of his people. Tecumseh has a vision to unite the tribes to stand against those who attempt to take the land from the American Indians. Tecumseh never gives up his dream of tribal unity and dies protecting his rights.

Time Line for Freedom: Victories of the Civil Rights Movement
Jason Powe

During a turbulent time in American history, a number of courageous leaders demand basic civil rights for all people. Documenting such events as Brown v. Board of Education, the Nashville Sit-Ins, and the March on Washington, this timeline demonstrates how ordinary people can stand up for the rights of all people.

Grade 6 and Above

Ultimate Field Trip: Adventures in the Amazon Rain Forest
Susan E. Goodman

Take a field trip with a group of middle school students through the rain forest and learn about the Amazon River, trade with Amazonian Indians, and the different problems that threaten the rain forest today. See photographs of interesting Amazonian creatures and plants such as the toucan, the night monkey, and the gecko.

La Causa: The Migrant Farmworkers' Story
Dana Catherine de Ruiz and Richard Larios

Through many trials with his family as migrant farmworkers, young Cesar Chavez learns what injustice is and how to stick up for the rights of his community. As Cesar grows older, he and many other migrant farmworkers risk their lives to go on strike for their rights. Their nonviolent protests eventually gain the attention of those in power.

Grade 7 and Above

Earth's Fiery Fury
Sandra Downs

Learn what is inside a volcano, why they erupt, and what temperature lava is just by looking at its color. Also, see photographs of different volcanoes throughout history, and explore the different regions where volcanoes are still active today.

They Shall Be Heard: Susan B. Anthony and Elizabeth Cady Stanton
Kate Connell

Susan B. Anthony and Elizabeth Cady Stanton speak out for women's rights. Throughout their lives, these two women lay the groundwork in the movement that eventually grants women the right to vote. Through speaking to religious leaders and heads of state, these women challenge the authority of men and demand that their voices be heard.

Grade 8 and Above

Star Factories: The Birth of Stars and Planets
Ray Jayawardhana

Learn about the mysterious places in our galaxy, find out why scientists think that the dark places in the sky are simply covering up more stars, and explore how stars and planets are born. See close up photographs of the stars and planets that cover the night sky, and learn fascinating facts about the research being done today.

Osceola: Patriot and Warrior
Moses Jumper and Ben Sonder

The courageous Seminole war chief Osceola fights with his people to protect their freedom and land from the government that tries to take it by force. Through arrest, imprisonment, and battle, this warrior fights for what belongs to his tribe.

A Place Called Heartbreak: A Story of Vietnam
Walter Dean Myers

Major Fred V. Cherry serves as a soldier in Vietnam and observes the realities of war. Fred is captured and kept as a prisoner of war for seven and a half years. Though he is beaten almost to death, he does not cooperate with his captors or renounce the mission of the United States in Vietnam.

From Civil War to Civil Rights: America's Struggle
Jason Powe

From the Civil War to the Civil Rights Movement, African Americans went from enduring the forced and unjust system of slavery to becoming voting American citizens. Read about the brave men and women who fought injustice, and learn about the events that changed the unfair laws in the United States.

BOOK LIST FOR INDEPENDENT READING

This list features high-interest fiction and nonfiction books that reflect a diversity of cultures and subjects. Spanning grades 3–12 and arranged by readability level, these books can be a source of independent reading material for your students. Although these books were chosen for their quality and cultural awareness, it is highly recommended that you or your school's reading specialist review them for their appropriateness for your students.

Student Texts: A–B / Grade levels: 3–5 / Lexile range: 200–850

Amelia Earhart
Philip Abraham

Pilot Amelia Earhart loved to fly and set many records. She was the first woman to fly alone across the Atlantic, and went on to write books and teach people about flying. In 1937, Earhart disappeared while attempting to fly around the world.

Grades 3–5
Lexile: 220L
24 pages
ISBN: 978-0516236001
Children's Press
Other books in this series include: **Helen Keller**, **Harriet Tubman**, and **Christopher Reeve**.

Afternoon on the Amazon
Mary Pope Osborne

Brother and sister Jack and Annie travel to the rain forest and encounter piranhas, snakes, and jaguars. Lost along the Amazon, the siblings search for a secret and then must find their way back to the magic tree house.

Grades 3–5
Lexile: 290L
80 pages
ISBN: 978-0679863724
Random House
Other books in this series include: **Pirates Past Noon**, **Sunset of the Sabertooth**, and **Midnight on the Moon**.

The Bravest Cat!
The True Story of Scarlet
Laura Driscoll

The true story of a heroic cat who runs into a burning building to rescue her five kittens.

Grades 3–5
Lexile: 310L
48 pages
ISBN: 978-0448417035
Grosset and Dunlap

Stringbean's Trip to the Shining Sea
Vera B. and Jennifer Williams

Stringbean, his older brother Fred, and their dog, Potato, travel across the country in a pickup truck. The story is told through the postcards and sketches Stringbean sends home.

Grades 3–5
Lexile: 380L
48 pages
ISBN: 978-0688167011
Harper Trophy

An ALA Notable Book

Horrible Harry and the Dragon War
Suzy Kline

A fun school project turns vengeful when best friends Song Lee and Harry have different ideas about dragons. According to her Korean heritage, Song Lee sees dragons as lucky and wise. Harry, on the other hand, envisions a terrifying monster. Can the friends find something in common to stop the dragon war?

Grades 3–5
Lexile: 430L
64 pages
ISBN: 978-0142501665
Puffin

Aunt Clara Brown: Official Pioneer
Linda Lowery

After buying her freedom from slavery, Clara Brown heads west with a wagon train. While other pioneers are searching for gold, Clara Brown searches for her daughter, who was sold as a slave. After working as a laundress in Colorado, Ms. Brown earns enough money to bring two dozen freed slaves out West to start new lives, but she never stops searching for her daughter.

Grades 3–5
Lexile: 470L
46 pages
ISBN: 978-1575054162
Carolrhoda Books

The Gift Giver
Joyce Hansen

While struggling to keep her family together, Doris befriends Amir, the new boy in the neighborhood. Despite his differences, Amir soon finds his place among the children on the block and teaches Doris about the meaning of friendship and family.

Grades 3–5
Lexile: 490L
118 pages
ISBN: 978-089919-8521
Clarion Books
Other books in this series include: **Yellow Bird** and **Me and One True Friend**.

Cracking the Wall
Eileen Lucas

In 1957, Central High School in Little Rock, Arkansas, offers a stage for a famous scene in the struggle for desegregation. This book tells the story of "the Little Rock Nine," nine black students chosen to attend a high school that had traditionally educated only white students.

Grades 3–5
Lexile: 540L
48 pages
ISBN: 978-1575052274
Carolrhoda Books

Rosa Parks
Eloise Greenfield

Growing up in Montgomery, Alabama, in the early twentieth century, Rosa Parks was taught to respect herself and others. She bristled at the unfair rules for black people. In December of 1955, Ms. Parks refused to give up her seat on the bus to a white man. Many people took courage from Rosa Parks's decision and worked for equality.

Grades 3–5
Lexile: 600L
64 pages
ISBN: 978-0064420259
Harper Trophy

Talented Animals
Mary Packard

Meet several amazing animals—a water-skiing squirrel, an artistic dog, and a gorilla who knows sign language and recorded her first CD!

Grades 3–5
Lexile: 630L
48 pages
ISBN: 978-0516246093
Children's Press
Other books in this series include: **Animal Rescuers**, **Animal Masterminds**, and **Rare Animals**.

Yang the Youngest and His Terrible Ear
Lensey Namioka

Recently arrived in Seattle from Shanghai, nine-year-old Yingtao struggles to find his place in his family and his new country. Although he loves baseball, Yingtao's family are gifted musicians and expect the same of him, the youngest son. With a recital looming, Yingtao and his American friend Matthew come up with a plan to solve everyone's problems.

Grades 3–5
Lexile: 700L
144 pages
ISBN: 978-0440409175
Yearling

Multiple state awards

Beating the Odds
Mary Packard

Four athletes overcome physical disabilities to reach their goals. Olympic runner Wilma Rudolph fought through childhood polio to become one of the fastest women in the world. Diagnosed with cancer, cyclist Lance Armstrong battled the disease to continue winning top bicycle races. Although legally blind, Marla Runyan is an Olymic runner. Mountaineer Tom Whittaker climbed the highest mountain in the world despite being an amputee.

Grades 3–5
Lexile: 720L
48 pages
ISBN: 978-0516246826
Children's Press

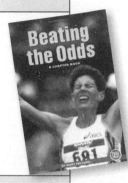

Secrets of the Mummies
Harriet Griffey

Explore the legends, secrets, and science of mummies around the world through pictures and historical accounts.

Grades 3–5
Lexile: 820L
48 pages
ISBN: 978-0789434425
Dorling Kindersley
Other books in this series include: **Extreme Machines, The Story of Muhammad Ali,** and **Creating the X-Men: How Comic Books Come to Life**.

Student Texts: A–B / Grade levels: 6–8 / Lexile range: 200–850

Shoeshine Girl
Clyde Robert Bulla

Stubborn and vulnerable, Sarah Ida arrives in Palmville to spend a forced summer vacation with her aunt. Forbidden an allowance, Sarah Ida finds a job shining shoes. She is enjoying her job and learning some valuable lessons when there is a terrible accident and Sarah Ida must make an important, grown-up decision.

Grades 6–8
Lexile: 330L
36 pages
ISBN: 978-0064402286
Harper Trophy

Young Champions: It's All About Attitude
Linda Barr

Meet eight amazing young athletes, each of whom has overcome challenges to succeed at his or her chosen sport. Embodying the qualities of courage, confidence, determination, and strength, these athletes refuse to let their physical disabilities stand in the way of their dreams.

Grades 6–8
Lexile: 400L
48 pages
ISBN: 978-0736857420
Capstone Press
Other books in this series include: **A History of Hip-Hop: The Roots of Rap** and **SpaceShipOne: Making Dreams Come True**.

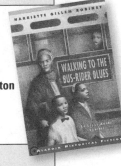

Milkweed
Jerry Spinelli

Without name, family, or home, Misha (also known as Stopthief and Stupid) is a boy of the streets. Naïve, tiny, and fast, he must rely on his small stature to squeeze through the holes and cracks in Nazi-occupied Warsaw to feed his friends and survive.

Grades 6–8
Lexile: 510L
212 pages
ISBN: 978-0375913747
Knopf

Booklist Editor's Choice, multiple state awards

Walking to the Bus-Rider Blues
Harriette Gillem Robinet

It is the summer of 1956 in Montgomery, Alabama, six months into the bus boycott. While earning enough to pay the bills, Alfa Merryfield, his sister, and their great-grandmother use the tactics of nonviolence to solve the mystery of the missing rent money and defend themselves against accusations of stealing.

Grades 6–8
Lexile: 550L
160 pages
ISBN: 978-0689838866
Aladdin
Other books by this author include: **Washington City is Burning**, **Mississippi Chariot**, and **Children of the Fire**.

Multiple state awards

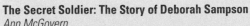

The Secret Soldier: The Story of Deborah Sampson
Ann McGovern

Late in the 1700s, unrest brews between England and the American colonies. After being passed from one family to another and treated as a servant, Deborah Sampson is finally 18 and free. Deborah disregards the traditional path for a young woman of marrying and raising a family, in favor of travel and adventure. In 1782, she seeks adventure in another form. Disguised as a man, Deborah joins the army and fights in the Revolutionary War!

Grades 6–8
Lexile: 590L
64 pages
ISBN: 978-0590430524
Scholastic Biography

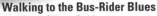

Any Small Goodness *Tony Johnston* Life in Arturo's L.A. community is filled with laughter, family, and hope. Each chapter is a touching story of growing up Hispanic in a chaotic American city.	Grades 6–8 Lexile: 600L 128 pages ISBN: 978-0439233842 Scholastic Smithsonian Notable Book, multiple state awards
Trapped Between the Lash and the Gun *Arvella Whitmore* Jordan embarks on a fast-paced adventure back through time, to the nineteenth-century lives of his ancestors on a cotton plantation. While he explores his heritage, Jordan finds parallels to his contemporary life where he struggles to stand against the local gang.	Grades 6–8 Lexile: 630L 186 pages ISBN: 978-0141303192 Puffin Multiple state awards
La Línea *Ann Jaramillo* When Miguel's parents send for him, he must make the dangerous journey north across the border to the United States. Miguel's younger sister sneaks away to join him, endangering both of their lives, but proving the importance of family and trust.	Grades 6–8 Lexile: 650L 136 pages ISBN: 978-1596431546 Square Fish ALA Best Book for Young Adults, Booklist Editors' Choice
The Buffalo Soldiers and the American West *Jason Glaser* This graphic novel-style history tells the story of the Buffalo Soldiers, African-American military units deployed to the Western frontier after the Civil War to maintain peace between settlers and Native Americans.	Grades 6–8 Lexile: 660L 32 pages ISBN: 978-0736862042 Capstone *Other books in this series include:* **The Sinking of the Titanic, The Adventures of Marco Polo,** and **The Salem Witch Trials.**
Snowboarding *Matt Doeden* Learn the gear and tricks that make up this exciting sport.	Grades 6–8 Lexile: 700L 32 pages ISBN: 978-0736852272 Capstone *Other books in this series include:* **Skateboarding, Mountain Biking,** and **BMX Freestyle.**
A Long Way From Chicago *Richard Peck* Joey and his sister, Mary Alice, spend a week each summer visiting their grandmother in rural Illinois. A great schemer and storyteller, Grandma involves the children in all sorts of adventures they never found with their parents in Chicago.	Grades 6–8 Lexile: 750L 150 pages ISBN: 978-0142401101 Puffin ALA Notable Book, multiple state awards

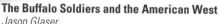

Stunt Double
Aileen Weintraub

Trained to perform dangerous feats, stunt doubles and stunt coordinators ensure that possibly injurious acts occur safely. This book traces the history of stunt doubles and the careful planning, dedication and skill involved in their work.

Grades 6–8
Lexile: 820L
48 pages
ISBN: 978-0516278674
Children's Press
Other books in this series include: **Bodyguard**, **Bomb Squad Specialist**, and **Bounty Hunter**.

Student Texts: A–B / Grade levels: 9–12 / Lexile range: 200–850

Coverup
Jay Bennett

What happened last night? Brad can't remember much about how he got home, but he has a sneaking suspicion that he and his best friend Alden have something to do with the fact that a man is dead.

Grades 9–12
Lexile: 340L
144 pages
ISBN: 978-0449704097
Fawcett

Define "Normal"
Julie Anne Peters

With her black lipstick, piercings, and tattoos, "Jazz" couldn't look more different from her peer counselor, honor-roll student Antonia. But as their sessions progress, the two find that they both feel like outsiders. Maybe feeling left out is more common than feeling normal.

Grades 9–12
Lexile: 350L
208 pages
ISBN: 978-0316734899
Little, Brown & Company Books for Young Readers

ALA Best Book for Young Adults

Dead-End Job
Vicki Grant

Frances spends her nights working at the local convenience store, saving money for art school and sketching when there is a lull between customers. A boy startles her one night and suddenly he seems to be everywhere Frances looks. Is Devin a harmless new kid in town, or does he have sinister motives?

Grades 9–12
Lexile: 440L
104 pages
ISBN: 978-1551433783
Orca
Part of the Orca Soundings series of teen novels for reluctant readers.

Skellig
David Almond

In the midst of moving, school, soccer, and an ailing baby sister, Michael finds a mystery in the garage. At first unsure if the man is alive, Michael soon questions whether the stranger is even human. Michael and his friend Mina carefully nurse the strange Skellig back to health and learn the power of poetry, love, and family.

Grades 9–12
Lexile: 490L
192 pages
ISBN: 978-0440416029
Yearling

Carnegie Medal

Good Night, Maman
Norma Fox Mazer

World War II has broken out in France and like other Jews, Karin, her brother, Marc, and their mother are on the run from the Nazis. As the situation grows more dangerous, and their mother more ill, the children must flee alone to America and wonder if they will ever see their mother again.

Grades 9–12
Lexile: 510L
192 pages
ISBN: 978-0064409230
Harper Trophy

The Hindenburg Disaster
Matt Doeden

This graphic novel tells the true story of the Hindenburg airship—its final flight and fiery crash.

Grades 9–12
Lexile: 530L
32 pages
ISBN: 978-0736868781
Capstone
Other books in this series include: **The Apollo 13 Mission**, **The Attack on Pearl Harbor**, and **The Donner Party**.

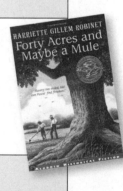

If You Come Softly
Jacqueline Woodson

The first day at his new high school, Jeremiah falls in love with Ellie, and she with him. But Miah is black and Ellie white and Jewish. Even while their love grows, few others are accepting of their relationship.

Grades 9–12
Lexile: 570L
192 pages
ISBN: 978-0142406014
Puffin

Forty Acres and Maybe a Mule
Harriette Gillem Robinet

In 1865, the Freedmen's Bureau allotted land to former slaves. Pascal and his brother Gideon leave the plantation to claim the promised property—forty acres on which to start their own farm. But not everyone accepts the idea of former slaves as landowners, and the night riders are determined to evict blacks from the land that they have worked hard to claim.

Grades 9–12
Lexile: 610L
144 pages
ISBN: 978-0689833175
Aladdin

Scott O'Dell Award

The Bully
Paul Langan

Darrell isn't happy when his mother moves the family from Philadelphia to California, and things get even worse when he gets on the wrong side of bully Tyray. Desperate to both fit in and stand up for himself, Darrell joins the wrestling team. Will his growing confidence be enough to stop a bully?

Grades 9–12
Lexile: 700L
208 pages
ISBN: 978-0439865463
Scholastic
Other books in the Bluford High series include: **Brothers in Arms**, **Until We Meet Again**, and **Blood is Thicker**.

The Jumping Tree
René Saldaña, Jr.

This collection of interwoven short stories follows Rey, a teenager growing up on the Texas/Mexico border. Rey is also on the border of adulthood, and struggles to fit in with his friends, respect his parents, and find his own identity.

Grades 9–12
Lexile: 770L
182 pages
ISBN: 978-0440228813
Dell Laurel Leaf

When The Emperor Was Divine
Julie Otsuka

The evacuation order appears in the spring of 1942, and soon the family finds itself imprisoned along with other Japanese families in a detention camp in the Utah desert. Three dusty, deprived years later, the family returns to their looted home and must readjust to a life still ruled by prejudice.

Grades 9–12
Lexile: 810L
160 pages
ISBN: 978-0385721813
Anchor

Voices From The Fields: Children of Migrant Farmworkers Tell Their Stories
Betty Smith

Through photographs, poems, and interviews, this book illuminates the lives of migrant farmworker families. In telling their stories, the children emphasize pride in their work and love for their families, as well as triumph and sacrifice.

Grades 9–12
Lexile : 850L
96 pages
ISBN: 978-0316056205
Little, Brown & Company Books for Young Readers

ALA Best Book for Young Adults

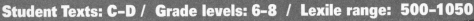

Student Texts: C–D / Grade levels: 6–8 / Lexile range: 500–1050

The Great Chicago Fire of 1871
Kay M. Olson
The history and drama of the Chicago Fire comes alive in this graphic novel. Poor communication, inadequate response, and a hot, dry summer result in a city engulfed in flames.

Grades 6–8
Lexile: 500L
32 pages
ISBN: 978-0736868754
Capstone Press
Other books in this series include: **The Apollo 13 Mission**, **The Hindenburg Disaster**, and **The Donner Party**.

Stand Tall
Joan Bauer
Six foot three-and-a-half inches and growing, Tree is the tallest twelve-year-old anyone has seen. As if life weren't difficult enough, his parents are in the middle of a divorce, his grandfather must learn to walk again after his leg is amputated, and his new friend is a social outcast. With their help, though, Tree learns to accept and take pride in himself.

Grades 6–8
Lexile: 520L
192 pages
ISBN: 978-0142404270
Putnam

ALA Notable Book, multiple state awards

Suitcase
Mildred Pitts Walter

Tall and gangly, Alexander is the brunt of every joke. He would rather draw than play basketball, but doesn't feel that his talents are appreciated by his family, especially his father. With dedication and persistence, Alexander shows that by being true to himself, he can achieve his dreams.

Grades 6–8
Lexile: 550L
112 pages
ISBN: 978-0380732104
Armistad

A Taste of Blackberries
Doris Buchanan Smith

A boy must face life without his energetic and fun-loving best friend. Suddenly, food no longer tastes good and games aren't worth playing. How does life go on after a tragedy?

Grades 6–8
Lexile: 640L
96 pages
ISBN: 978-0064402385
HarperTrophy

ALA Notable Book

The Great Quarterback Switch
Matt Christopher

Identical twins Michael and Tom share looks, a passion for football, and a mental connection. A serious accident has left Michael in a wheelchair, stranding him on the sidelines while Tom plays as a quarterback. Tom wants to give Michael a chance to play, and Michael would love to be back in the game, but how can they switch places?

Grades 6–8
Lexile: 690L
97 pages
ISBN: 978-0316140775
Little, Brown & Company Books for Young Readers
Other titles in this series include:
Shoot for the Hoop, **The Comeback Challenge**, and **Return of the Home Run Kid**.

Maizon at Blue Hill
Jacqueline Woodson

Persuaded by her grandmother to accept a scholarship to Blue Hill, a prestigious boarding school, Maizon finds herself caught between many worlds. The wealthy, mostly white, school is a far cry from the Brooklyn block where Maizon lived. Racially and economically separated from her classmates but unwilling to disappoint her grandmother, Maizon just wants to feel like she belongs.

Grades 6–8
Lexile: 700L
160 pages
ISBN: 978-0698119574
Putnam

Search for the Shadowman
Joan Lowery Nixon

Andy grows excited about his family history project when he uncovers a mysterious ancestor that no one wants to talk about. Against the wishes of his family, Andy continues to investigate the "mystery man." Is Andy in over his head?

Grades 6–8
Lexile: 780L
154 pages
ISBN: 978-0440411284
Yearling

Multiple state awards

Storm Warriors *Elisa Carbone* Along the coast of North Carolina a crew of African-American surfmen scans the ocean for ships in trouble. The time period is just after the Civil War, and racism lingers, deterring twelve-year-old Nathan from his dream of joining the surfmen. Will he follow in his father's footsteps instead?	Grades 6–8 Lexile: 890L 170 pages ISBN: 978-0440418795 Yearling ALA Notable Book, multiple state awards
Shelter Dogs: Amazing Stories of Adopted Strays *Peg Kehret* Blind, neglected, and missing his sister and companion, there isn't much hope for the border collie Tyler. Ann, a volunteer at the Humane Society, takes a special interest in Tyler and scrapes together the money for his eye surgery so the dog can see again. Read about Tyler and other dogs abandoned at shelters. What will become of the rambunctious Great Dane mix and the skittish and frightened terrier? Can an unwanted puppy become a movie star or a hero?	Grades 6–8 Lexile: 940L 136 pages ISBN: 978-0807573365 Whitman Children's Book Award, multiple state awards 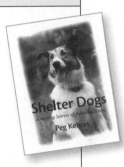
**Call Me María** *Judith Ortiz Cofer* Through poetry and prose, María tells the story of her transition from Puerto Rico to New York. Caught between her mother in Puerto Rico, where it is warm, sandy, and filled with the soft sounds of the language of her birth, and her father in the dark barrio in New York City, María must create her own world.	Grades 6–8 Lexile: 970L 130 pages ISBN: 978-0439385787 Scholastic
Amistad: A Long Road to Freedom *Walter Dean Myers* In August of 1839, a ship named Amistad anchors off the coast between Connecticut and New York. Those aboard are bound for slavery, but led by a young captive named Sengbe Pieh, the Africans fight for their freedom and take over the ship. Upon landing, they are charged with murder and their hope for freedom recedes. With woodcuts, newspaper clippings, and historic photographs, Myers presents a compassionate historical account of the rebellion and the fight for equality.	Grades 6–8 Lexile: 1050L 100 pages ISBN: 978-0141300047 Puffin 

Student Texts: C–D / Grade levels: 9–12 / Lexile range: 500–1050

Sports Cars
Matt Doeden

Learn fast facts about some of the world's sleekest, most powerful sports cars. The book features pictures and statistics on Corvettes, Porsches, Ferraris, and Lamborghinis.

Grades 9–12
Lexile: 500L
32 pages
ISBN: 978-0736827348
Capstone
Other books in this series include: **Dirt Bikes**, **Dragsters**, and **Lowriders**.

Kicked Out
Beth Goobie

Rebellious 15-year-old Dime moves from her parents' house to live with her handicapped older brother. With newfound independence, she begins to see her parents, friends, boys, and the trials of high school in a different light.

Grades 9–12
Lexile: 520L
92 pages
ISBN: 978-1551432441
Orca
Part of the Orca Soundings series of teen novels for reluctant readers.

Overdrive
Eric Walters

On his 16th birthday, Jake is thrilled to get his driver's license and take his older brother's prized car for a spin. But when he encounters the temptations of street racing, he learns the consequences can be disastrous.

Grades 9–12
Lexile: 610L
112 pages
ISBN: 978-1551433189
Orca
Part of the Orca Soundings series of teen novels for reluctant readers.

Taste of Salt
Frances Temple

The social and political turmoil of modern-day Haiti is examined through the eyes of Djo, a youth fighting to make sense of—and survive—the country's struggles.

Grades 9–12
Lexile: 650L
192 pages
ISBN: 978-0064471367
Harper Teen

The Folk Keeper
Franny Billingsley

Corrina uses her unique powers to keep the mysterious underground Folk from destroying crops and causing mayhem. When she brings her skills to a large seaside manor, she begins to uncover secrets about its residents—and herself.

Grades 9–12
Lexile: 690L
176 pages
ISBN: 978-0689844614
Aladdin

Seedfolks
Paul Fleischman

In an abandoned lot filled with trash, a young girl plants the lima bean seeds of a revolution. Her small act draws in curious neighbors who soon plant their own gardens in the lot. In the midst of growing eggplants, peppers, tomatoes, and lettuce, the diverse group of neighbors discovers that they share more than the soil.

Grades 9–12
Lexile: 710L
70 pages
ISBN: 978-0064472074
Harper Teen

Spiders in the Hairdo
David Holt

Have you heard the one about the dog in the microwave? How about the man who attached a jet engine to his car? An amusing collection of modern folk tales, or "urban legends"—some creepy, some funny, and some just plain gross.

Grades 9–12
Lexile: 720L
112 pages
ISBN: 978-0874835250
August House

Lost and Found
Anne Schraff

With her mom busy at work, her father gone, and her grandmother ill, Darcy is left to look after herself and her younger sister, Jamee. But life is piling up on Darcy—a suspicious stranger is following her, and Jamee disappears. Darcy feels it's up to her to save her family.

Grades 9–12
Lexile: 760L
133 pages
ISBN: 978-0944210024
Townsend Press
Other books in the Bluford Series include:
A Matter of Trust, **The Fallen**, and **Shattered**.

The Dark Side of Nowhere
Neal Shusterman

When 14-year-old Jason discovers that he, his friends, and his family are aliens left on Earth after a failed invasion, he finds himself in the midst of an identity crisis. With time running out, Jason has to decide whether he wants to be alien or human, and whether he wants to save the world from invasion.

Grades 9–12
Lexile: 850L
192 pages
ISBN: 978-0765342430
Starscape

Chinese Cinderella
Adeline Yen Mah

Unwanted and abused by her family, Adeline finds emotional escape through school and her academic achievements. Still, all she wants is love and support. This is the true story of a Chinese girl considered bad luck by her own family.

Grades 9–12
Lexile: 960L
224 pages
ISBN: 978-0440228653
Laurel Leaf

Thura's Diary: My Life in Wartime Iraq
Thura Al-Windawi

In March of 2003, U.S.-led troops invaded Iraq and 19-year-old Thura began keeping a diary. In the midst of bombings, chaos, and fear, Thura maintains her hope for the future.

Grades 9–12
Lexile: 990L
144 pages
ISBN: 978-0670058860
Viking

The Watsons Go To Birmingham—1963
Christopher Paul Curtis

The Watsons are close, but that doesn't mean life is easy for the Michigan family. As the middle child, Kenny is tormented by his older brother Byron and annoyed by his younger sister Joetta. Finally, their parents are at their wits' end with Byron's delinquent behavior and they pack up the whole family for a trip to Birmingham, Alabama, to visit Grandma. The Watson kids soon learn that life in the South in 1963 is far different, and far more tense, than life back home.

Grades 9–12
Lexile: 1000L
224 pages
ISBN: 978-0440228004
Laurel Leaf

Newbery Honor Book,
Coretta Scott King Award

Student Texts: E-F / Grade levels: 6-8 / Lexile range: 750-1150

Frozen Stiff
Sherry Shahan

Cousins Cody and Derek head into the Alaskan wilderness for a short camping trip, but a glacial surge sweeps away Cody's kayak and strands the teens. Without supplies, Cody and Derek must confront the dangers of the wild, including bears, snowblindness, and mysterious strangers.

Grades 6–8
Lexile: 750L
160 pages
ISBN: 978-0440413738
Yearling

Bounty Hunter
Holly Cefrey

Now called bail bond enforcers or fugitive recovery agents, bounty hunters perform the important job of tracking and capturing fugitives. This dangerous work involves clever planning, quick thinking, and a little detective work to make the streets safe.

Grades 6–8
Lexile: 760L
48 pages
ISBN: 978-0516278650
Children's Press
Other books in this series include:
Bodyguard, **Bomb Squad Specialist**, and **Stunt Double**.

Stuck in Neutral
Terry Trueman

Born with cerebral palsy, Shawn lives out his life in a wheelchair, unable to move a muscle. No one knows if Shawn is anything more than a vegetable, and Shawn's father can't bear the thought that his son may be suffering. Reading these pages offers a window into the rich and vibrant world of Shawn's mind—a world not open to his own father.

Grades 6–8
Lexile: 820L
128 pages
ISBN: 978-0064472135
HarperTeen

Booklist Editors' Choice, multiple state awards

The Cay
Theodore Taylor

World War II arrives in the Caribbean and Phillip couldn't be more excited. But while he and his mother are escaping to the U.S., their ship is struck by a torpedo, and Phillip finds himself stranded—and blind. He must rely on Timothy, an older West Indian man, to survive, but first he must overcome his prejudice.

Grades 6–8
860L
144 pages
ISBN: 978-0440416630
Yearling

A Single Shard
Linda Sue Park

A young orphan, Tree-Ear, lives under a bridge in the small Korean village of Ch'ulp'o with his friend Crane. While scavenging for scraps of food, Tree-Ear is distracted by the beauty of Min's pottery. Longing to work magic on the clay himself, Tree-Ear becomes Min's apprentice and must journey to the capital to win the potter a royal commission.

Grades 6–8
Lexile: 920L
160 pages
ISBN: 978-0395978276
Clarion

Newbery Medal, ALA Notable Book, Young Reader's Choice Award

To the Top of Everest
Laurie Skreslet with Elizabeth MacLeod

An avid hiker from a young age, Laurie continued to challenge himself physically and mentally, finally joining a team to reach the summit of Everest, the highest mountain on Earth. Color pictures help tell his story.

Grades 6–8
Lexile: 930L
56 pages
ISBN: 978-1550748147
Kids Can Press

And Nobody Got Hurt
Len Berman

Did you hear about the major league baseball player who ran the bases backwards? Or the blind golfer who hit a hole in one? Read about these and other amazing and humorous sports stories from all over the world.

Grades 6–8
Lexile: 930L
128 pages
ISBN: 978-0316010290
Little, Brown & Company Books for Young Readers

Emperor's Silent Army
Jane O'Connor

While digging for a well, two farmers in northern China discover an ancient clay warrior. Archeologists summoned to the site begin to uncover an elaborate army of terracotta soldiers—7,500 of them, buried over two thousand years ago. Discover the fascinating history behind these soldiers and the emperor who demanded the creation of this archeological wonder.

Grades 6–8
Lexile: 980L
48 pages
ISBN: 978-0670035120
Viking

Booklist Editors' Choice

Island of the Blue Dolphins
Scott O'Dell

Karana, a young American Indian girl, flees the ship evacuating her community from an island in the Pacific. Based on a true story, Karana finds the strength and creativity to live alone on the island for eighteen years, foraging for food and creating clothes and shelter from the animals that share this land.

Grades 6–8
Lexile: 1000L
192 pages
ISBN: 978 0440439882
Yearling

Newbery Medal,
ALA Notable/Best Books

Fire in Their Eyes
Karen Magnuson Beil

Dangerous and destructive, fire also creates and nourishes. When a fire burns out of control, brave and knowledgeable firefighters—hotshots, smokejumpers, and pilots—battle wilderness blazes across the country.

Grades 6–8
Lexile: 1010L
64 pages
ISBN: 978-0152010430
Harcourt

ALA Notable/Best Books

Woodsong
Gary Paulsen

The acclaimed wilderness adventure writer unleashes the story of his own connections to the outdoors. Paulsen recalls lessons learned from living among animals, particularly the close relationships forged with his sled dogs while training them for the Iditarod.

Grades 6–8
Lexile: 1090L
134 pages
ISBN: 978-1416939399
Aladdin

SLJ Best Book, ALA Notable/Best Books

Black Diamond: The Story of the Negro Baseball Leagues
Patricia and Fred McKissack

The all-American sport, baseball, barred African Americans from the major leagues until 1945, so talented athletes formed their own league. Though living and playing conditions were never equal, incredible men and women—including heroes Cool Pappa Bell, Satchel Paige, and Willie Mays—played in the Negro Leagues.

Grades 6–8
Lexile: 1100L
192 pages
ISBN: 978-0590682138
Scholastic

Coretta Scott King Award

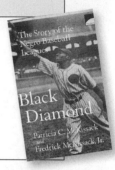

Student Texts: E–F / Grade levels: 9–12 / Lexile range: 750–1150

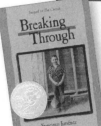

Breaking Through
Francisco Jiménez

In this memoir and sequel to *The Circuit*, Francisco struggles to navigate the boundaries within his life. Straddling the border between Mexico and the U.S. both literally and culturally, Francisco finds himself constantly on the move—between childhood and becoming an adult, between social classes, and between barriers of prejudice.

Grades 9–12
Lexile: 750L
200 pages
ISBN: 978-0618342488
Houghton Mifflin

ALA Notable Children's Book,
Booklist Editor's Choice,
America's Award Winner

Ask Me No Questions
Marina Budhos

Nadira always felt inferior to her older sister Aisha, the responsible one with perfect grades. But now with her father detained on suspicion of terrorism and the family facing deportation, it is up to Nadira to prove her father's innocence and reunite the family. This moving contemporary novel sheds light on the plight of Arab-Americans in the post-9/11 world.

Grades 9–12
Lexile: 790L
176 pages
ISBN: 978-1416949206
Simon Pulse

Homeless Bird
Gloria Whelan

Married at 13 then promptly widowed, Koly struggles to balance her own desires with the mandates of tradition. Abandoned by her mother-in-law and unable to return to her own family, Koly must find her own way in a world stacked against her.

Grades 9–12
Lexile: 800L
186 pages
ISBN: 978-0064408196
Harper Trophy

National Book Award Winner

We Beat the Street
Drs. Sampson Davis, George Jenkins, and Ramek Hunt with Sharon Draper

Three doctors, friends since childhood, trace their lives from the streets of Newark, New Jersey, to their current successes. As boys, they faced the challenges of poverty, peer pressure, gangs, and drugs. Through perseverance, hope, and a belief in themselves and each other, Sampson, George, and Ramek graduated from medical school.

Grades 9–12
Lexile: 860L
196 pages
ISBN: 978-0142406274
Puffin

Anthem
Ayn Rand

What does it mean to be an individual, to follow your dreams against the expectations laid out by society? Equality 7-2521 longs to pursue knowledge. But his desire is unacceptable in a world of forced conformity, and Equality 7-2521 is condemned to death. Will love and the pursuit of knowledge triumph over the will of the masses?

Grades 9–12
Lexile: 880L
66 pages
ISBN: 978-1434100351
Waking Lion Press

Code Orange
Caroline B. Cooney

Usually more interested in pursuing girls than schoolwork, Mitty finds himself drawn into the latest biology project on infectious diseases. After coming into contact with smallpox scabs, Mitty fears for himself and for his city. Could Mitty be used as a weapon of biological terrorism?

Grades 9–12
Lexile: 890L
224 pages
ISBN: 978-0385732604
Laurel Leaf

A Summer Life
Gary Soto

In this collection of essays and vignettes, the author recalls his 1950s childhood growing up Chicano in Fresno, California.

Grades 9–12
Lexile: 890L
160 pages
ISBN: 978-0440210245
Laurel Leaf

The Hitchhiker's Guide to the Galaxy
Douglas Adams

In this hilarious science-fiction spoof, Arthur Dent escapes Earth just before its demolition and sets off on a galactic journey filled with strange, brilliant, and loony characters.

Grades 9–12
Lexile: 1000L
216 pages (plus bonus material)
ISBN: 978-0345391803
Del Rey
Other books in this series include: **The Restaurant at the End of the Universe**, **Life, the Universe, and Everything**, and **So Long, and Thanks for All the Fish**.

Phineas Gage: A Gruesome but True Story About Brain Science
John Fleischman

A 13-pound iron rod enters the skull of a construction foreman—and he survives! This fascinating story about a traumatic accident in the 1800s offers insight into the history of brain science.

Grades 9–12
Lexile: 1030L
96 pages
ISBN: 978-0618494781
Houghton Mifflin

The Greatest: Muhammad Ali
Walter Dean Myers

A cultural heavyweight as well as a champion boxer, Muhammad Ali fought with courage against injustice and his opponents. In and out of the ring, Ali was—and continues to be—a commanding figure.

Grades 9–12
Lexile: 1030L
172 pages
ISBN: 978-0590543439
Scholastic

Farewell to Manzanar
Jeanne Wakatsuki Houston & James D. Houston

Life at Manzanar, a Japanese internment camp in California during World War II, means lines for food, for the bathroom, for work. The thin cabin walls do little to keep out the dust, heat, and cold. But there are also dances, picnics, and small elements of normal life. This is the true story of one family's experience behind barbed wire.

Grades 9 12
Lexile: 1040L
146 pages
ISBN: 978-0553272581
Bantam

Rascal
Sterling North

His mother dead, father absent much of the time, and his brother away at war, Sterling spent much of his youth on his own, exploring, working on projects, and raising his pet raccoon, Rascal. Eternally curious, Rascal leads Sterling on many adventures, invites trouble from the neighbors, and becomes a true friend and companion.

Grades 9–12
Lexile: 1140L
192 pages
ISBN: 978-0142402528
Puffin

Newbery Honor Book, Young Reader's Choice Award

Classroom Library Credits

References

Adams, M. J., Foorman, B. R., Lundberg, I., & Beeler, T. (1998). *Phonemic awareness in young children*: A classroom curriculum. Baltimore, MD: Brookes Publishing.

Adams, M.J. (1990). *Beginning to Read: Thinking and Learning about Print. Cambridge*, MA: Bolt, Beranek, and Newman, Inc.

Balli, S.J. (1998). When mom and dad help; Student reflections on parent involvement with homework. *Journal of Research and Development in Education*, 31(3), 142-148.

Balli, S.J., Demo, D. H., & Wedman, J.F. (1998), Family Involvement with children's homework: An intervention in the middle grades. *Family Relations: Interdisciplinary Journal of Applied Family Studies*, 47(2), 149-157.

Balli, S.J, Wedman, J.F. & Demo, D. H. (1997). Family involvement with middle-grades homework: Effects of differential prompting. *Journal of Experimental Education*, 66(1), 31-48.

Beck, I.L. and McKeown, M.G. (1991). Social studies texts are hard to understand: Mediating some of the difficulties. *Language Arts*, 68, 482-490.

Beimiller, A. (1999). *Language and reading success*. Cambridge, MA: Brookline Books.

Berninger, V.W. & Richards, T.L. (2002). *Brain literacy for educators and psychologists*. Amsterdam: Academic Press.

Biancarosa, G., & Snow, C.E. (2004). *Reading next: a vision for action and research in middle and high school literacy: A Report from Carnegie Corporation of New York*. Washington, DC: Alliance for Excellent Education.

Chall, J.S. (1996). *Stages of reading development (2nd ed)*. Fort Worth, TX: Harcourt Brace.

Connor, C. M., Morrison, F. J., & Underwood, P. (2007). A second chance in second grade? The cumulative impact of first and second grade reading instruction on students' letter-word reading skills. *Scientific Studies of Reading*, 11(3), 199-233.

Corticlla, C. (2005) No Child Left Behind: Determining Appropriate Assessment Accommodations for Students with Disabilities. National Center for Learning Disabilities.

Curtis, M. (2004). Adolescents who struggle with word identification: Research and practice. In T. Jetton and J. Dole (Eds.). *Adolescent literacy research and practice*. New York: Guilford.

Curtis, M.E., & Longo, A.M. (1999). *When adolescents can't read: methods and materials that work*. Cambridge, MA: Brookline Books.

Dole, J.A., Brown, K.J., & Trathen, W. (1996). The effects of strategy instruction on the comprehension performance of at-risk students. *Reading Research Quarterly, 31*, 62-88.

Dole, J.A., Sloan, C., & Trathen, W. (1995). Teaching vocabulary within the context of literature. *Journal of Reading, 38*(6).

Duffy, H. (2007). *Meeting the needs of significantly struggling learners in high school: A look at approaches to tiered intervention*. Washington, DC: National High School Center, American Institutes for Research.

Dutro, S. & Moran, C. (2003). Rethinking English language instruction: An architectural approach. In G.C. Garcia (Ed.). *English Learners Reaching the Highest Level of English Literacy*. Newark, DE: International Reading Association.

Eden, G. & Moats, L. (2002). The role of neuroscience in the remediation of students with dyslexia. *Nature Neuroscience*, 5, 1080-1084.

Ehri, L. and Snowling, M.J. (2004). Developmental variation in word recognition. In Stone, C.A., Silliman, E.R., Ehren, B.J., and Apel, K. (Eds.), *Handbook of language and literacy: Development and disorders*, pp. 433-460. New York: Guilford.

Ehri, L. C. (1996). Researching how children learn to read: Controversies in science are not like controversies in practice. In G. Brannigan (Ed.), *The Enlightened Educator: Research Adventures in the Schools*. Boston, MA: McGraw Hill.

Fletcher, J.M., & Lyon, G.R. (1998). Reading: A research-based approach. In W.M. Evers (Ed.), *What's gone wrong in America's classrooms*. Stanford, CA: Hoover Institute Press.

Floyle, H., Lyman, L., Tompkins, L., Perne, S., & Foyle, D. (1990). *Homework and cooperative learning: A classroom field experiment*. Emporia, KS: Emporia State University.

Foorman, B.R., Francis, D.J., Beeler, T., Winikates, D., & Fletcher, J.M. (1997). Early interventions for children with reading problems: Study designs and preliminary findings. *Learning Disabilities: A Multidisciplinary Journal*, 8, 63-71.

Gersten, R. Fuchs, L.S., Williams, J.P., Baker, S. (2001). Teaching reading comprehension strategies to students with learning disabilities: A review of the research. *Review of Educational Research, 71*, 279-320.

Guthrie, J.T., Wigfield, A, Metsala, J.L., & Cox, K.E. (1999). Motivational and cognitive predictors of text comprehension and reading amount. In R.B. Ruddell & N.J Unrau. (2004). *Theoretical models and processes of reading (5th edition)*, (pp. 929-953). Newark, DE: International Reading Association.

Henry, M.K. (2005). Spelling instruction in the upper grades: The etymology/ morphology connection. *Perspectives*, 31(3), 30-32.

Henry, M.K. (2003). *Unlocking literacy: Effective decoding and spelling instruction*. Baltimore, MD: Paul Brookes Publishing.

Hiebert, E.H. & Kamil, M.L. (2005). *Teaching and learning vocabulary: Bringing research to practice*. Mahwah, NJ: Lawrence Erlbaum Associates, Publishers.

Hill, J.D. & Flynn, K.M. (2006). *Classroom instruction that works with English language learners*. Alexandria, VA: Association for Supervision and Curriculum Development.

Kame'enui, E.J., & Simmons, D.C. (1998). Beyond effective practice to schools as host environments: Building and sustaining a school-wide intervention model in beginning reading. OSSC *Bulletin*, 41(3), 3-24.

Kamil, M. L. (2004). Vocabulary and Comprehension Instruction: Summary and Implications of the National Reading Panel. In P. McCardle & V. Chhabra, (Eds.). *The Voice of Evidence: Bringing Research to the Classroom* (pp.213-234). Baltimore, MD: Brookes Publishing.

Klingner, J.K., Vaughn, S., & Schumm, J.S. (1998). Collaborative strategic reading during social studies in heterogeneous fourth-grade classrooms. *The Elementary School Journal*, 99, 3-22.

Langer, J.A. (2001). Beating the odds: Teaching middle and high school students to read and write well. *American Educational Research Journal*, 38(4), 837-880

Lee, J., Grigg, W., and Donahue, P. (2007). *The Nation's Report Card: Reading 2007* (NCES 2007-496). National Center for Education Statistics, Institute of Education Sciences, U.S. Department of Education, Washington, D.C.

Lyon, G.R. & Chhabra, V. (2004). The science of reading research. *Educational Leadership*, 61:6, 12-17.

Marzano, R. J. (2007). *The Art and Science of Teaching.* Alexandria: ASCD.

Marzano, R., Pickering, D., & Pollock, J. (2001). *Classroom Instruction that Works* . Alexandria: ASCD.

McCardle, P. & Chhabra, V. (Eds.) (2004). *The voice of evidence in reading research*. Baltimore, MD: Brookes Publishing.

McLaughlin, B., August, D., Snow, C., Carlo, M., Dressler, C., White, C., et al. (2000). *Vocabulary improvement in English language learners: An intervention study*. A symposium conducted by the Office of Bilingual Education and Minority Languages Affairs, Washington, DC.

Meyer, B.J.F. & Poon, L.W. (2001). Effects of structure strategy training and signaling on recall of text. In R.B. Ruddell & N.J Unrau. (2004). *Theoretical models and processes of reading (5th edition)*, (pp. 810-843). Newark, DE: International Reading Association.

Moats, L.C. & Tolman, C. (2009). *Language essentials for teachers of reading and spelling (LETRS), Module 1: The challenge of learning to read, 2nd ed.* Longmont, CO: Sopris West.

Moats, L.C. (2000). *Speech to print: Language essentials for teachers*. Baltimore, MD: Paul H. Brookes.

Moats, L.C. (1996). Phonological errors in the spelling of dyslexic adolescents. *Reading and Writing: An Interdisciplinary Journal*, 8 (1), 105 119.

Nagy, W.E., & Scott, J.A. (2000). Vocabulary processes. In R.B. Ruddel & N. J. Unrau (Eds.), *Theoretical models and processes of reading* (pp. 574-593). Newark, DE: International Reading Association.

Nation, P. (2005). Teaching vocabulary. *Asian EFL Journal Press*, pp. 253-259.

National Reading Panel. (2000). *Teaching Children to Read: An evidence-based assessment of the scientific research literature on reading and its implications for reading instruction.* Washington, DC: National Institute of Child Health and Human Development.

O'Brien, N., Langhinrichsen-Rohling, J., Shelley-Tremblay, J. (2007). Reading problems, attentional deficits, and current mental health status in adjudicated adolescent males. *Journal of Correctional Education*, September, 2007.

Paribakht, T.S., & Wesche, M. (1997). Vocabulary enhancement activities and reading for meaning in second language vocabulary acquisition. In J. Coady & T. Huckin (Eds.), *Second language vocabulary acquisition* (pp.174-2000) Cambridge, UK: Cambridge University Press.

Perkins, P.G., & Milgram, R.B. (1996). Parental involvement in homework: A double-edge sword. *International Journal of Adolescence and Youth*, 6(3), 195-203.

Pressley, M. (2006). *Reading instruction that works: The case for balanced teaching, 3rd ed.* NY: Guilford Press.

Pressley, M. (2001). Comprehension instruction: What makes sense now, what might make sense soon. *Reading online*, 5(2). Retrieved on 11.15.07 from http://www.readingonline. org/articles/art_index.asp?HREF=/.

Pressley, M. (2000). What should comprehension instruction be the instruction of? In M. L. Kamil, P. B. Mosenthal, P. D. Pearson, & R. Barr (Eds.), *Handbook of reading research*, Vol. III (pp. 545-561). Mahwah NJ: Erlbaum & Associates.

Rayner, K., Foorman, B. F., Perfetti, C. A., Pesetsky, D., & Seidenberg, M. S. (2002). How should reading be taught? *Scientific American*, 286(3), 84-91.

Rayner, K., Foorman, B. F., Perfetti, C. A., Pesetsky, D., & Seidenberg, M. S. (2001). How psychological science informs the teaching of reading. *Psychological Science in the Public Interest*, 2: 31-74.

Rosenshine, B., & Meister, C. (1994). Reciprocal teaching: A review of the research. *Review of Educational Research*, 64,(4), 479-530.

Rosenshine, B., Meister, C., & Chapman, S. (1996). Teaching students to generate questions: A review of the intervention studies. *Review of Educational Research*, 66(2), 181 - 221.

Rubin, E. (2007). A unique mind: learning style differences in Asperger's Syndrome and high-functioning autism. *The ASHA Leader*, 12:1.

Ruhl, K., & Hughes, C. (2005). *Teaching LD*. Retrieved November 25, 2007, from Teaching LD: http://www.teachingld.org/default.cfm.

Scarborough, H. S. (2001). Connecting early language and literacy to later reading (dis)abilities: Evidence, theory, and practice. In S. Neuman & D. Dickinson (Eds.), *Handbook for research in early literacy* (pp. 97-110). New York: Guilford Press.

Seidenberg, S. & McClelland, J.L. (1989). A distributed, developmental model of word recognition and naming. *Psychological Review*, 96:523-568.

Shankweiler, D., Lundquist, E., Katz, L., Stuebing, K.K., Fletcher, J.M., Brady, S., Fowler, A., Dreyer, L.G., Marchione, K.E., Shaywtz, S.E. & Shaywitz, B.A. (1999). Comprehension and decoding: patterns of association in children with reading difficulties. *Scientific Studies of Reading*, 31, 24-53, 69-94.

Shaywitz, S.E. (2003). *Overcoming dyslexia: A new and complete science-based program for reading at any level*. New York: Knopf.

Shaywitz, S.E. & Shaywitz, B.A. (2004). Reading disability and the brain. *Educational Leadership*, 61:6.

Snow, C.E., Burns, S. & Griffin, P. (Eds.). (1998). *Preventing reading difficulties in young children. Committee on the Prevention of Reading Difficulties*. National Research Council.

Sousa, D. (2001). *How the Brain Learns, Second Edition*. Thousand Oaks, CA: Corwin Press.

Stahl, S. (1999). *Vocabulary development* (Volume 2 in the series from reading research to practice). Cambridge, MA: Brookline Books.

Stanovich, K. E. (2001). *How to think straight about psychology (Sixth Edition)*. Boston: Allyn & Bacon.

Surber, J.R., & Schroeder, M. (2007). Effect of *prior* domain *knowledge* and headings on processing of informative text. *Contemporary Educational Psychology*, 32(3), 485-498.

Tannenbaum, Kendra R.; Torgesen, Joseph K.; Wagner, Richard K. (2006). Relationships between word knowledge and reading comprehension in third-grade children. *Scientific Studies of Reading*, 10:4:381-398.

Taylor, B.M., Pearson, P.D., Garcia, G.E., Stahl, K.A., & Bauer, E.B. (2006). Improving students' reading comprehension. In D.A. Dougherty Stahl & M.C. McKenna (Eds.), *Reading research at work* (pp. 303-315). New York: The Guilford Press.

Torgesen, J. K., Houston, D. D., Rissman, L. M., Decker, S. M., Roberts, G., Vaughn, S., Wexler, J. Francis, D. J., Rivera, M. O., Lesaux, N. (2007). Academic literacy instruction for adolescents: *A guidance document from the Center on Instruction*. Portsmouth, NH: RMC Research Corporation, Center on Instruction.

Torgesen, J.K. (2005). Recent discoveries from research on remedial interventions for children with dyslexia. In M. Snowling and C. Hulme (Eds.). *Presentations and Publications*, pp. 521-537. Oxford: Blackwell Publishers.

Torgeson, J.K., Alexander, A.W., Wagner, R.K., Rashotte, C.A., Voeller, K., Conway, T. & Rose, E. (2001). Intensive remedial instruction for children with severe reading disabilities: Immediate and long-term outcomes from two instructional approaches. *Journal of Reading Disabilities, 34*, 33-58.

Torgeson, J.K., Wagner, R.K., Rashotte, C.A., Alexander, A.W. & Conway, T. (1997). Preventive and remedial interventions for children with severe reading disabilities. *Learning Disabilities: A Multidisciplinary Journal, 8,* 5-61.

Treiman, R., & Bourassa, D. (2000). Children's written and oral spelling. *Applied Psycholinguistics, 21*, 183–204.

Treiman, R., & Bourassa, D. (2000). The development of spelling skill. *Topics in Language Disorders*, 20, 1–18.

Tuley, A. C. (1998). *Never Too Late to Read*. Baltimore, MD: York Press.

Vellutino, F.R., Tunmer, W.E., Jaccard, J.J., & Chen, R. (2007). Components of reading ability: Multivariate evidence for a convergent skill model of reading development. *Scientific Studies of Reading*, 3-32.

Walberg, H.J. (1999). Productive teaching. In H. C. Waxman & H.J. Walberg (Eds.) *New directions for teaching practice and research*, 75-104. Berkeley, CA: McCutchen Publishing Corporation.

Woodcock, R. W., & Johnson, M. B. (1989). *WJ-R tests of cognitive ability*. Itasca, IL: Riverside Publishing.

ADDITIONAL RESOURCES AND REFERENCES

Web Sites

International Dyslexia Association
www.interdys.org

Northwest Regional Educational Laboratory—for more information on 6+1 Traits of Writing
www.nwrel.org

Council for Exceptional Children—for information regarding special needs students
www.cec.sped.org

American Speech-Language-Hearing Association (ASHA)
www.asha.org

International Reading Association (IRA)
www.reading.org

Alliance for Excellent Education—for recent publications on reading research
www.all4ed.org

Florida Center for Reading Research (NIH research site)
www.fcrr.org

Children of the Code – Public Television Documentary and Social Education Project
www.childrenofthecode.org

U.S. Department of Education
www.ed.gov

- Each state's department of education's Web site uses a different format. A quick internet search will pull up your state's department of education with state-specific information and resources.

Sopris West—instructional materials as well as professional development tools
http://sopriswest.com

Reading Rockets—a national multi-media project offering information and resources on how young kids learn to read, why so many struggle and how caring adults can help.
www.readingrockets.org

Colorin Colorado—a bilingual site for families and educators of English Language learners. Sponsored by Reading Rockets.
http://colorincolorado.org

LD OnLine—a national education service sponsored by WETA, the flagship PBS station in Washington, D.C.
www.ldonline.org

All About Adolescent Literacy—a national multi-media project offering information and resources to parents and educators of struggling adolescent readers and writers
http://adlit.org

REFERENCES

Books

This list is not intended to be an exhaustive listing but a starting point. Searching for other works by these authors would be well worth your time!

Adams, M. J. (1990) Beginning to Read: Thinking and Learning about Print. Cambridge, MA: MIT Press.

Jenson, W. R., Rhode, G., Reavis, H. K. (1994) The Tough Kid Tool Box. Longmont, CO: Sopris West.

Sprick, R., Garrison, M., Howard, L.M. (1998) CHAMPs: A Proactice and Positive Approach to Classroom Management. Longmont, CO: Sopris West.

Sousa, D.A. (2001) How The Brain Learns: Second Edition. Thousand Oaks, CA: Corwin Press

Stone, C.A., Silliman, E.R., Ehren, B.J., Apel, K. (Eds) (2004) Handbook of Language & Literacy: Development and Disorders. New York, NY: The Guilford Press.

Pinker, S. (2007) The Stuff of Thought: Language as a window into human nature. New York, NY: Viking Penguin.

Shaywitz, S. (2003) Overcoming Dyslexia. New York, NY: Alfred A. Knopf

Beck, I.L., McKeown, M.G., Kucan, L. (2002) Bringing Words to Life: Robust Vocabulary Instruction. New York, NY: The Guilford Press.

Moats, L.C. (2000) Speech to Print: Language Essentials for Teachers. Baltimore, MD: Paul H. Brookes

Jensen, E. (2005) Teaching with the Brain in Mind: 2nd Edition. Alexandria, VA. Association for Supervision and Curriculum Development.

Payne, R.K. (2001) A Framework for Understanding Poverty. Highlands, TX: aha! Process.

Moats, L.C. (2003) LETRs: Language Essentials for Teachers of Reading and Spelling. Longmont, CO: Sopris West.

Marzano, R.J, Pickering, D.J., Pollock, J.E. (2004) Classroom Instructional that Works: Research-based Strategies for Increasing Student Achievement. Alexandria, VA: Association for Supervision and Curriculum Development.

Stanovich, K.E. (2000) Progress in Understanding Reading: Scientific Foundations and New Frontiers. New York, NY: The Guilford Press

Henry, M.K. (2003) Unlocking Literacy: Effective Decoding and Spelling Instruction. Baltimore, MD: Paul H. Brookes.

McCardle P., Chhabra, V. (2004) The Voice of Evidence in Reading Research. Baltimore, MD: Paul H. Brookes.

Lyon, G.R., Rumsey, J.M. (1996) Neuroimaging: A Window to the Neurological Foundations of Learning and Behavior in Children. Baltimore, MD: Paul H. Brookes.